Measuring the Flow of Time

Classics in Southeastern Archaeology
Stephen Williams, Series Editor

Publication of this work has been supported in part
by the Dan Josselyn Memorial Fund.

Measuring the Flow of Time

The Works of James A. Ford, 1935–1941

Edited and with an Introduction by
Michael J. O'Brien and R. Lee Lyman

Foreword by
Gordon R. Willey

THE UNIVERSITY OF ALABAMA PRESS
Tuscaloosa and London

1 2 3 4 5 6 7 8 9 • 07 06 05 04 03 02 01 00 99

∞

The paper on which this book is printed meets the minimum requirements of
American National Standard for Information Science-Permanence of Paper for
Printed Library Materials, ANSI Z39.48-1984.

Library of Congress Cataloging-in-Publication Data

O'Brien, Michael J. (Michael John), 1950–
    Measuring the flow of time : the works of James A. Ford,
1935–1941 / Michael J. O'Brien and R. Lee Lyman ; foreword by
Gordon R. Willey.
    p. cm. — (Classics in southeastern archaeology)
    ISBN 0-8173-0991-8 (pbk. : alk. paper)
    1. Ford, James Alfred, 1911–1968. 2. Anthropologists—United
States—Biography. 3. Archaeologists—United States—Biography. 4.
Indians of North America—Louisiana—Antiquities. 5. Indians of
North America—Mississippi—Antiquities. 6. Louisiana—Antiquities.
7. Mississippi—Antiquities. I. Lyman, R. Lee. II. Title. III.
Series.
    E76.45.F67 O39 1999
    973'.07'202—dc21

                                    99-6142

British Library Cataloguing-in-Publication data available

Contents

Foreword

Gordon R. Willey

In previous statements (Willey 1969, 1988) I have noted that the late James Alfred Ford (1911–1968) was a powerfully innovative force in the development of Americanist archaeology in the mid-twentieth century. I still hold this opinion. Ford had high intelligence, amazing insight into complex matters, and a most forceful personality. Not surprisingly, he was both a highly stimulating and a difficult colleague. I was closely associated with him in Lower Mississippi Valley archaeological research in 1938 and 1939, and we again collaborated on the subject of eastern United States archaeology in late 1940. As these were years in which Ford was doing some of his most original and important work, the compilers of this volume, who are also Ford's biographers (O'Brien and Lyman 1998), have extended me the honor of writing a foreword to this reprinting of some of Ford's more important publications. I have accepted with pleasure but also with some trepidation, for what I have to say is necessarily both biographical and autobiographical, and autobiography, as we all know, involves the uncertain dangers of selective remembrance.

I first met Ford in the summer of 1937 when he came to Georgia to direct the reconstruction of the prehistoric ceremonial earthlodge at the Ocmulgee National Monument, a large prehistoric village-and-mound site on the outskirts of Macon. At the time I was an assistant to Arthur R. Kelly, the director of archaeological excavations at Ocmulgee, a position he had held since the early federal relief days of 1933 and which he had continued with the National Park Service. The ceremonial "earthlodge" had been a low, circular mound that, upon excavation in the early 1930s, had proved to be some sort of a council chamber. At some time in the prehistoric past, the wood-and-thatch roof of the structure had burned, collapsed, and been mounded over with earth. The park-service architects wanted to recreate such a roof and to make the chamber an important tourist attraction.

Kelly must have realized he was not up to taking hands-on charge of such a restoration job, and he knew that I wasn't either. Who then could take it over? Kelly and others in Macon who had followed the archaeological work at Ocmulgee from its beginnings immediately thought of Jim Ford, who, I should explain, had been Kelly's first assistant at Macon, back in 1933, and had worked there for several months. He had become something of a legend, almost a John Bunyanesque figure there in Macon for his organizing of the federal relief archaeological work. Ford came over to Macon that June of 1937. He immediately hit it off with the park-service architects, who wanted someone who not only knew about the archaeological aspects of the job but who could also collaborate effectively with them and their labor foreman. I remember Jim, his six-foot-four frame stripped to the waist in the oppressive heat inside the reconstructed dome, directing workmen and consulting with the architects, doing both in no uncertain terms.

I was engaged in other, more routine archaeology at Ocmulgee that summer, and I got to know Jim right from the start. We would often dine together, talking about little but archaeology. In such conversations Jim had a way of quizzing you, a kind of argumentative style to draw you out. He had only recently published his "Analysis of Indian Village Site Collections from Louisiana and Mississippi" (Ford 1936a)— a substantial monograph brought out by the Louisiana Department of Conservation that dealt with pottery types and their relative chronological ordering—and he seemed disappointed that it had attracted so little attention among archaeological colleagues.

I remember our discussing pottery-type definitions and nomenclature, and I showed him what I had been doing with pottery classification. I had a number of working types that I referred to as Lamar Complicated Stamped, Swift Creek Complicated Stamped, Ocmulgee Incised, and the like. Although we had not formally described these types, Kelly and I, as well as A. J. Waring Jr. and Preston Holder, both of whom were working on the Georgia coast at the time, so referred to them. I should add that all this came naturally to me. Before going to Georgia I had been brought up in southwestern archaeology at the University of Arizona, and out there "Tularosa Black-on-white," "Gila Polychrome," and so forth were the familiar units of a ceramic typology under which pottery was classified, described, and counted. In his Louisiana and Mississippi site-collections publication, Jim had designated his pottery units using a complex kind of numerical coding. These code definitions were an attempt to gather together such qualities as surface decoration, vessel and rim shapes, and even temper and qualities of manufacture. Whereas it was analytically sound, as a system of nomenclature and as a way to bring pottery types to one's visual memory it was too cumbersome. Jim realized he needed something simpler, and he was attracted to the sort of type names used in the Southwest and that we had been using informally in Georgia.

When the job with Kelly drew to a close, Jim went out to Chaco Canyon for the rest of the summer to have a firsthand look at southwestern archaeology. I saw him after he returned from New Mexico. Although he and his wife, Ethel, had enjoyed their stay there, Jim didn't seem especially impressed with southwestern archaeology or his experiences at Chaco. I never could quite figure out why. Maybe, for him anyway, he talked with the wrong people. In any event I think it likely that even before he went to New Mexico, he already had his mind made up on naming pottery types and how to use those types in chronology building, as well as on how he was going to go about it back home in Louisiana.

On his last trip to Macon that summer of 1937, shortly after his return from the Southwest, Jim invited me to return to Baton Rouge with him for a short visit and to have a look at Louisiana pottery. I did, and when I was there we went over his collections—many lab drawers of sherds and some whole pots on the shelves. We began to set up Louisiana pottery types in the southwestern binomial fashion—Coles Creek Incised, Marksville Stamped, and so forth. We spent two or three days at this. Jim was planning then to go to Ann Arbor and study at the University of Michigan with James B. Griffin. He told me that when he returned to Louisiana the next year he was going to set up a big Works Progress Administration–funded archaeological project under the sponsorship of the Louisiana Department of Conservation. It would have at least two excavation units and a laboratory for pottery and other artifact analyses in New Orleans, and he wanted me to be in charge of the lab. I accepted his offer, a year away though it was.

I joined Jim in New Orleans in September of 1938, not long after his return from Michigan. He had learned a lot there about eastern United States archaeology, and much of the credit for this goes to Griffin. Among other things, they organized and ran a conference on pottery typology (Ford and Griffin 1937, 1938) that formally brought the binomial system to the Southeast. They also launched into their relationship of amicable disagreement, which continued to the day of Jim's death. Both were strong-minded scholars, committed in their opinions and always willing to argue endlessly. One of the things they argued about was the then recently developed midwestern Taxonomic Method that W. C. McKern (1937, 1939) had popularized. Jim was uneasy with the way many eastern archaeologists used the various categories of cultural affiliation, and I was too. As an example, should the Louisiana Troyville period and complex be grouped under the same classificatory category as the obviously Hopewellian-related Marksville period and complex? Troyville pottery had clear antecedents in Marksville; in other ways, however, as in the presence of what appeared to be temple mounds, Troyville's relationships appeared to go in other taxonomic directions. In our opinion the Midwestern taxonomy ran too fast toward conclusions, building up, which Griffin had done by 1941, the big picture of cultural relationships for the whole of the East before we had local situations, especially local chronologies and sequences of development, worked out.

In those early days in the New Orleans lab I familiarized myself with Jim's shorter writings, two dating from 1935 (Ford 1935a, 1935b), one from 1936 (Ford 1936b), and one from 1938 (Ford 1938b). These were all devoted to the chronological procedures that Jim had developed in his longer monograph (Ford 1936a). Jim must have picked up some of the basic ideas on chronological ordering from the geographer Fred Kniffen, who had been his primary mentor in undergraduate courses he had taken at Louisiana State University in Baton Rouge. Kniffen had studied with A. L. Kroeber at the University of California, Berkeley, and it is likely that Kroeber's work on Zuñi potsherds (Kroeber 1916; see also Spier 1917) must have been known to Kniffen. Jim also had some stimulation in these directions from Henry B. Collins, an old friend and colleague from Mississippi and a Smithsonian Institution archaeologist who had taken Jim with him on archaeological expeditions to Alaska. Jim and I had frequent talks about such procedures during that year in New Orleans. It was my impression then that Jim didn't have a very close-up knowledge of the Kroeber or Spier papers. This is not to say that he was hesitant to give credit to others where credit was due; on the contrary, Jim was always very generous this way. Rather, he was fixated on the basic idea of chronological ordering, and he wanted to put it into practice and to encourage others to do the same. This was what Jim was saying in his articles and monograph. It is fair to state that at this time—the late 1930s—chronological procedures had not been used to any degree in southeastern archaeology except by Ford.

In those days Jim lived in Baton Rouge, where Ethel had a secretarial position at the university. He was on the move constantly between our field operations and the lab in New Orleans, with stopovers in Baton Rouge in between. He would pick up collections from the Crooks site in La Salle Parish, where Bill Mulloy and Arden King were digging, and from the Greenhouse site in Avoyelles Parish, where Stu Neitzel was working, and bring these down to the lab. Needless to say, running the lab kept me pretty busy. Jim, I think, would have to be classified as a stern taskmaster, certainly much more so than my previous boss, the easygoing Arthur Kelly. Ford would come loping into the fourth floor of the old French Quarter building that belonged to the Louisiana Department of Conservation, and where our lab was located, and get right down to business with no preliminary greetings.

"Say," he would address me, "get some of these fellows downstairs. There's a big load of stuff from Av-2 (Neitzel's Greenhouse site) that needs to be brought up in the elevator." I would no sooner comply with this directive than Jim would come up to me, serious-faced, telling me, "Look, those chaps over there at the pottery-restoration table should be moving along faster. They're still fooling around with some of the same pots they were doing last Friday. Tell them to get a move on."

Jim was all over the place intellectually as well. It would usually take me a minute or two to catch up to where he was and what it was all about. He would jump from what he considered to be a needed revision of one of the Greenhouse pottery types to a critique of the artist-draftsman's rendition of one of the profiles from the Crooks burial mounds. He was definitely the boss and was calling the shots on the preparation and writing of the Crooks report (Ford and Willey 1940). In the course of this preparation and writing I learned an enormous amount, on both intellectual and practical levels, from Jim's direction and coaching: how best to describe pottery and artifact types; how and when to move from specifics to generalizations; how to direct the artists, draftsmen, and photographer on illustrations; and even how to scissor-out objects from photographs and mount them on white cardboard layouts. Looking back on it, I can see that his direction and leadership were all to the good, although sometimes it was a little hard to take. Jim was exceedingly sparing of praise, but I suppose he had been brought up that way. At the same time, Jim was always generous in sharing credit. After all, he took me on as coauthor of the Crooks report, although given his position and my very definitely subordinate one, he needn't have done so.

Other things were going on with the project along with the Crooks and Greenhouse analyses. Reports came in to us that led to the discovery of the Tchefuncte site in St. Tammany Parish and subsequently to the culture of the same name, which Jim placed as pre-Marksville in the Lower Mississippi Valley culture sequence. Preston Holder, who joined the project for that summer, took charge of excavations at the Tchefuncte site, and later, George Quimby, my successor as Jim's righthand man in Louisiana, collaborated with Ford on that publication (Ford and Quimby 1945).

I was anxious to get back to graduate school in 1939 and was fortunate enough to have been given a scholarship to Columbia University for that fall. Early in September my wife, Katharine, and I left New Orleans for New York. One of my professors that fall was the distinguished Mesoamericanist George C. Vaillant of the American Museum of Natural History, who did part-time teaching at Columbia. He was kind enough to invite me to give a paper in a symposium on New World archaeological chronologies that he was organizing for the annual meeting of the American Anthropological Association to be held in Chicago. I was asked to speak on the southeastern United States. I was, naturally, quite excited and flattered by his invitation, but I also knew that I was not really up to it all on my own. I accepted with the provision that Jim be my coauthor, indeed, my senior coauthor. I notified Ford, and he was as pleased as I. He prepared the first draft of the paper we gave, and I would estimate that the final version was four-fifths his.

That summer of 1940 I and another Columbia graduate student, Dick Woodbury, carried out an archaeological survey along the Florida Gulf Coast, with chronology building as our primary objective. This work certainly followed in the Ford tradition, but I was beginning to branch out more on my own. I saw Jim briefly toward the end of that summer, and he told me then that he was planning to attend Columbia the next year and work toward a doctoral degree. This move led to our final collaboration on eastern archaeology, an article entitled "An Interpretation of the Prehistory of the Eastern United States," published in *American Anthropologist* in 1941 (Ford and Willey 1941).

The idea for preparing such an article was mine. I felt that what we had said at Chicago should be consolidated by a publication. Jim needed no coaxing. We expanded our earlier paper and its scope of coverage to take in essentially all of the East with an extension out into the Plains. Jim, again, led the way in its organizing and writing. Following our preliminary discussions about general chronology and terminology, and with a strong diffusionist emphasis, he set about preparing five "sloping horizon" charts that carried the main structure of our argument. Our first chronological profile extended from Louisiana up the Mississippi River and northward to Michigan; the second ran from St. Louis out into the Plains; the third began at the mouth of the Ohio River and went northeastward to upstate New York; the fourth also began at the mouth of the Ohio but went southeastward through the Tennessee basins and into Georgia; and the fifth related the chronologies of Arkansas to those of Louisiana and the Florida Gulf Coast. It was our basic thesis that most of the ideas about mound and earthwork construction, pottery, and general cultural elaboration originated in the south, essentially in the Lower Mississippi Valley. We felt that even earlier beginnings for these ideas might be traced farther southward to Mesoamerica, though we made no attempt to elaborate that point. And we originated a basic general chronology of Archaic, Burial Mound I, Burial Mound II, Temple Mound I, and Temple Mound II, scorning the terminology of the Midwestern Taxonomic Method.

I have said that our Chicago paper was four-fifths Ford's and only a fifth mine, and I would estimate the *American Anthropologist* article to be about three-fourths Ford's and a quarter mine. After all, I did control the Florida data and probably knew Georgia as well as, if not better than, Jim. The very heavy emphasis on diffusion and the south-to-north trajectory of ideas were heavily Jim's contributions, although I must admit that I went along with them quite contentedly. Today, of course, the paper is considered outdated and, in its south-to-north diffusionist emphasis, wrong; however, many of the major questions raised still have not been satisfactorily answered. Did burial-mound building and major earthwork construction begin in Illinois and Ohio?

If so, how about the very early dates—going back into the preceramic millennia—of the lower Mississippi Valley Poverty Point and even earlier cultures? I can remember that at that time Jim was more definite in his opinions than I. He originally entitled the paper "A Key to the Prehistory of the Eastern United States." I changed it at the last moment, I think without his clearance, using the more equivocal word "interpretation" in place of "key." This word choice might well sum up the difference between Jim and me in our basic attitudes toward archaeology.

Jim, like all of us, had his limitations. I think that the severest of these was that he always seemed embarrassed when confronted with questions of "why" in culture creativity or culture change. He would turn away from these concerns to diffusionism or to the rather sterile mechanics of material cultural evolution when asked to explain why peoples and societies behaved the way they did. It was almost as though he didn't want to ask such questions because of what he might find out. Still, I will close by saying what I have said more than once before, that I consider James A. Ford one of the great lights of Americanist archaeology. He was a sort of Sir Flinders Petrie or V. Gordon Childe in the way that he broke new ground and brought others along with him in doing so.

Preface and Acknowledgments

By any measure, James A. Ford is still recognized as one of the leading figures in the development of Americanist archaeology, especially the archaeology of the southeastern United States. When Ford entered the profession in the late 1920s as a field worker for the Mississippi Department of Archives and History, the revolutionary chronological work of A. V. Kidder, Nels Nelson, Leslie Spier, and A. L. Kroeber in the Southwest was barely a decade old. Archaeologists were becoming increasingly aware that the bits of pottery left by prehistoric peoples across the landscape could be used to measure the passage of time, but it was unclear how much time was really being measured. How long had the North American continent been occupied? Kidder and his colleagues working in New Mexico were convinced that there was considerable antiquity to the prehistoric occupation of the Southwest, but it wasn't until Jesse Figgins of the Colorado Museum of Natural History reported the discovery of spear points amidst the remains of extinct bison near Folsom, New Mexico, that it became clear that humans had been in North America since at least the tail end of the Pleistocene.

The publication of Figgins's report in 1927 coincided with Ford's first field season in Mississippi.

By the time Ford began working in the Lower Mississippi River Valley—first in Mississippi and then in Louisiana—the Southeast was years behind the Southwest in terms of what was known of the archaeological record. Because of the high visibility of the record in the Southwest, especially architectural remains, the region had long been favored by archaeologists and ethnographers from northeastern institutions. The Southeast had received sporadic attention by prehistorians in the late nineteenth century—most notably Cyrus Thomas and his Division of Mound Exploration personnel—but these were forays as opposed to sustained efforts. Things were not much different in the opening decades of the twentieth century, with the exception of Clarence B. Moore's concentrated efforts along major southeastern waterways and smaller projects undertaken by a few archaeologists, ethnographers, and ethnohistorians associated with the Bureau of American Ethnology. One predictable result of the disparity in attention focused on the Southeast relative to that on the Southwest was that the former lagged well behind the latter in matters of chronology. When Ford began working in Mississippi in 1927, there was no chronological framework other than a simple scheme that divided the archaeological record into two parts—one for the historical period and another for the prehistoric period. Today when archaeologists have at their disposal any number of means to impart chronological control, it seems almost unbelievable that such an elementary system was all that was available, but we need to keep in mind that when Ford began his career, it was barely three decades after Cyrus Thomas had had to publish a 730-page treatise in an attempt to dispel once and for all the notion that there had been an early race of mound builders in the eastern United States.

Despite the lesser amount of professional interest paid to it, the Southeast was known to have a rich and varied history of occupation by Native American groups. John Swanton and other members of the Bureau of American Ethnology had long been involved in attempting to document various southeastern languages and to understand the connections among them, and bureau ethnographers and archaeologists such as Henry B. Collins had been searching for traits in the material record that could be used to push the dates of occupation back beyond the historical period. This was the intellectual tradition that Ford inherited from Collins, for whom he worked both in Mississippi and Alaska: Use the ethnographic present as an anchor point for one end of the chronological sequence and then work backward in time, overlapping various cultural traits. What Ford learned from Collins served as the basis of all his subsequent chronological work.

Our interest in Ford began as an intellectual exercise to determine what the roots of his chronological methods were (O'Brien and Lyman 1998). Most Americanist archaeologists, when they think of Ford, immediately equate his name with seriation, the method of arranging objects or events in a sequence based on similarities in the appearance of those objects or events or in frequencies of their occurrence. We soon discovered, however, that Ford never used seriation in any of the work he did in the Southeast and South America. He and his colleagues often referred to his chronological orderings as seriation, but this was a complete misnomer. Rather, Ford relied on superposition as determined through excavation for his orderings, in the process formulating marker types—index "fossils"—that could be used for cross-dating purposes. Toward the end of his life he learned what seriation entailed, as the famous thumbs-and-paper clips drawing (Ford 1962) that graces many textbooks makes clear, but seriation played little or no role in how Ford eventually brought chronological order to the archaeological record of the Lower Mississippi Valley.

As we delved deeper into Ford's methods and especially his thinking on matters of chronology, we began to see that Ford's view of time was decidedly at odds with the way most of his colleagues viewed it. Thus it was natural that the way in which Ford went about carving time up into manageable units flew in the face of convention and led to some protracted arguments with his peers, including those with whom he had worked on occasion. Ford viewed time as a continuum, often referring to it metaphorically as a flowing stream. Because it was a continuum it didn't really matter where you broke it into segments. In other words, because the divisions are arbitrary anyway, one place was as good as another to end one temporal unit, usually referred to as a period, and to start another one. Some of Ford's colleagues—Philip Phillips, for example—viewed this as heretical. Surely, they argued, there are natural junctures in cultural development—junctures that can be recognized by an archaeologist clever enough to look in the right places. *Those* are the points at which time should be divided. Not to search for natural breaking points and simply to chop up time arbitrarily was simply shirking one's responsibilities toward writing intelligible, meaningful culture history.

Neither were most of his colleagues pleased with the way Ford viewed the pottery types he used to measure the passage of time. To Ford, types were simply tools. Although the types created by archaeologists might in some respects approximate some ideal that the original artisans carried in their heads about the way a finished product should look, the archaeologist was in no way obligated to try and get inside the artisans' heads and to translate those ideas into archaeological types. Ford's preferred method was simple: Use whatever works in creating archaeological types. You could tell they worked by the way they measured time. If it turned out that they *didn't* measure time, this meant that they were bad types. Simply throw them out and start over. Such a view was typical of Ford's commonsensical approach to archaeology.

One might think that it would take years of sustained effort to work out a chronology of any region, let alone one with such a complex history as the Lower Mississippi Valley. Ford, however, did it within approximately six years, from about 1935 to 1940. Throughout the next 15 years or so, Ford and his colleagues would add to the framework, but by the end of 1940 the basic chronology had been established. Ford was able to construct it in such a short period of time in part because it was in his nature to work quickly once he set his mind to a problem and in part because of the influx of federal money into archaeology that accompanied federal relief efforts in the face of the Great Depression. Through happenstance Ford became field director of the Works Progress Administration's archaeological effort in Louisiana and hired a corps of highly competent people to assist him in both the field and the laboratory. Ford's vision of that work focused on chronological ordering. He picked the locations of excavations carefully, tending to concentrate on archaeological sites that had the potential to fill in holes in the chronological ordering that he had tentatively laid out in 1935 and 1936 based on surface collections made in western Mississippi and eastern Louisiana and on three excavations in which he had participated between 1929 and 1933.

Using archival materials, we describe elsewhere (O'Brien and Lyman 1998) both the thought processes that guided Ford during the period in which he sketched out the chronology of prehistoric occupation of the Lower Mississippi Valley and the intellectual arena in which his work took place, but we found it impossible to do full justice to the work. We built what we believe to be a legitimate case for why Ford came to the conclusions he did, using excerpts from his publications where necessary to bolster our claims, but there is nothing like having the original texts speak for themselves. We decided that it would be helpful to archaeologists interested in the archaeology of the Lower Mississippi Valley to have Ford's critical publications available, and hence the idea for this volume was born. We also decided that to be most effective, the readings should be introduced by a brief essay that not only placed the articles and monographs in historical context but also discussed the progression in Ford's thinking during the period under consideration. Based on our experience, Ford's thinking is often difficult to track for several reasons. First, he often contradicted himself within even the same article or monograph. This is especially true in the works reproduced here, where it is clear that his ideas are in the formative stage. Second, he made little or no use of citations in his early work, which we finally realized was a product of his unfamiliarity with much of the literature in Americanist archaeology. Third, Ford tended to telegraph some of his thoughts, which makes understanding difficult for those who have only passing familiarity with the topics under consideration.

The bottom line is that to make sense of Ford and his thinking, one needs to read literally everything he wrote on a particular topic. Thus we include almost everything that he wrote on chronology between 1935 and 1941, beginning with what we consider to be his first real publication—a short piece that appeared in the journal *Louisiana Conservation Review*—and ending with a landmark summary article in the journal *American Anthropologist* that he coauthored with Gordon Willey. In between we add three other articles that appeared in various places, one short piece that was unpublished, and two monographs and excerpts of a third that appeared in the Louisiana Department of Conservation Anthropological Study series. Because of their importance to Ford's thinking, we also include two articles that were written by his early mentors, the first by Henry B. Collins on the excavation of the Deasonville site in western Mississippi and the second by Fred B. Kniffen on surface collections from southern Louisiana.

To enhance the volume both as a reference and as a research tool, we have retained the original pagination, with original page numbers appearing in brackets. Eight of the papers are reprinted in full, including illustrations and references. The exceptions are Collins's (1932) report on Deasonville, from which we excised the discussion of the excavations and the presentation of nonceramic artifacts; Ford's (1936a) report on surface-collected sites in Louisiana and Mississippi, from which we excised a few pages on the physical environment; and Ford and Willey's (1940) monograph on the Crooks site, from which we excised some of the discussion of the excavations and all of the presentation of nonceramic artifacts. To keep the number of reprinted pages as low as possible, cover pages, title pages, indices, and other relatively superfluous material are not reprinted.

As with the production of any book, a number of people need to be thanked for their contributions to the process. We greatly appreciate the help and encouragement we received from the University of Alabama Press, specifically from Judith Knight, and our editor, Joe Abbott. We also thank Stephen Williams for his support, his critical reading of the introduction, and his advice on what to include in the manuscript, especially regarding extracts from Ford's thesis. Steve at one time had the only known copy of the thesis, which he copied and placed in the hands of several southeastern archaeologists. Ian Brown kindly supplied us with a copy. We also greatly appreciate the help of Lewis Larson, who read the introduction and made numerous helpful suggestions for improvement.

We thank Keith Baca of the Mississippi Department of Archives and History for researching the department's files for correspondence, field records, and photographs related to Ford's work in Mississippi; Rebecca Saunders for allowing us unlimited access to the files at the Museum of Natural Science archives at Louisiana State University; William Haag and Carl Kuttruff for ensuring that we had access to some of Ford's important personal papers; and the late James Griffin for personal insights on Ford's work. We gratefully acknowledge the interest that Gordon Willey has shown in the project, over the years answering numerous queries about his and Ford's key roles in WPA archaeology in Louisiana. Willey worked closely with Ford in the Southeast during the late 1930s and early 1940s and graciously agreed to write a foreword that touches on their professional involvement, as well as their friendship. Finally, we thank Dan Glover for helping us with various aspects of manuscript production, including the drafting of figures, and E. J. O'Brien, who read the introduction, checked references, and made numerous suggestions for changes.

Measuring the Flow of Time

Introduction

Michael J. O'Brien and R. Lee Lyman

James Alfred Ford (Figure 1) was born in Water Valley, Mississippi, in 1911. At his death in 1968 he was widely acknowledged as one of the leading figures in American archaeology and one of the preeminent archaeologists of the southeastern United States. During his career Ford worked in other regions—Mexico, Colombia, Peru, and Alaska—but he was and is still best known for his contributions to southeastern archaeology, particularly that of the Lower Mississippi River Valley. Ford made numerous substantive contributions, but he is most remembered for his methodological accomplishments, especially methods related to chronological ordering. From the beginning of his career in 1927, when he joined fellow high school classmate Moreau B. Chambers in a site survey around Jackson for the Mississippi Department of Archives and History, through roughly 1955, Ford's major concern was establishing a chronological framework for the Lower Mississippi Valley. The basic chronology was completed by 1941, and over the next decade and a half, when he found the time from his doctoral course work at Columbia and his duties at the American Museum of Natural History, Ford worked on revisions to it. Despite his lack of graduate education at the time and his not having much of a grasp of the growing literature (O'Brien and Lyman 1998), Ford constructed a logical and defensible chronology for the Lower Mississippi Valley that exists today in its essentials. The approach that he used to bring temporal control to the archaeological record of eastern Louisiana and western Mississippi was simple enough in outline, at least from a modern perspective, but at the time its sophistication was unparalleled in the Southeast.

Various details of Ford's life have been examined in short biographical sketches (Brown 1978; Willey 1988), obituaries (Evans 1968; Webb 1968; Willey 1969), and a full-length intellectual history and biography (O'Brien and Lyman 1998). Our focus in this volume is solely on Ford's chronological methods and assumptions as reflected in his writings from the period 1935 to 1941. This introductory chapter is intended to serve as a guide to the 11 papers reprinted here. Nine of the selections were authored by Ford—with Gordon R. Willey or James B. Griffin serving as coauthors on three—and two were written by two of Ford's mentors, Henry B. Collins and Fred B. Kniffen. Both of those papers were remarkable in terms of methodological sophistication and serve as important milestones in the development of a workable chronology for the Lower Mississippi Valley.

Henry B. Collins and Deasonville

When Jim Ford and Moreau Chambers began working for the state of Mississippi in 1927, neither had had any training, formal or otherwise, in archaeological fieldwork. They were hired to locate sites through informant interviews and, where possible, to collect artifacts from site surfaces. In a few instances they conducted exploratory tests at select sites. Their lack of training is evident in their field notes,[1] although the records make clear that Ford and Chambers were highly dedicated employees, often working under less-than-ideal circumstances. They continued their work for the department in 1928 and 1929, during which time Ford met Henry B. Collins, assistant curator of ethnology in the U.S. National Museum, Smithsonian Institution, who had been conducting archaeological work in the Choctaw region of western Mississippi.

Collins, himself a Mississippian, had conducted extensive fieldwork in the Arctic, later employing Ford and Chambers on one trip north (Figure 2) and Ford alone on several others (O'Brien and Lyman 1998).

Figure 1. Photograph of James A. Ford in Louisiana, ca. 1933 (photograph courtesy W. G. Haag).

Collins began his work in the Lower Mississippi Valley in 1925, when he conducted a site survey in east-central Mississippi, expanding his search into southern Louisiana a short time later. It is clear from his brief reports (Collins 1926, 1927a, 1927b) that Collins not only was interested in temporal differences among artifacts from various sites in the Lower Mississippi Valley but also was very familiar with a practice that by the mid-1920s had become commonplace in the Southwest—anchoring chronological sequences in the near past and then working backward in time: "It is very desirable . . . to seize upon every available source of tribal identification of the cultures represented, and to accomplish this end there is probably no safer beginning than to locate the historic Indian village sites and to study their type of cultural remains for comparison with other sites of unknown age" (Collins 1927a:259–260). This method later became known as the "Direct Historical Approach."

In Mississippi Collins relied on pottery from known Choctaw villages for his analysis. He found similarly decorated pottery at several Choctaw sites in various Mississippi counties, leading him to note that the pottery "may safely be regarded as historic, in the sense that it is found thus far only at Choctaw sites known to have been occupied as late as the 19th century, but further than this its age cannot at present be determined" (Collins 1927a:263). Collins was interested in the origin of the pottery: Had it "developed locally" (Collins 1927a:263), or did it have its origins to the west? Was there even an earlier occupancy of Choctaw territory by some other tribe? To answer these questions, Collins (1927a:263) noted that it "would be very desirable . . . to have additional collections of pottery from other known Choctaw village sites and from the little known mounds and unidentified sites of central and western Mississippi." One site that provided additional collections was Deasonville, which Ford and Chambers had found during their survey of portions of Yazoo County (Figure 3). Collins, Ford, and Chambers spent a week in December 1929 and three days the following December excavating a small part of the site.

In beginning the section of his Deasonville report entitled "Distribution of the Pottery Types," Collins (1932a[1])[2] noted that the "most important immediate problem of Southeastern archaeology is to establish a basis for a chronology of prehistoric sites. From the fragmentary nature of the evidence this will have to be for the most part a disjointed and patchwork chronology, far less perfect and comprehensive than that which has been worked out in other areas. . . . The most valuable material for this purpose is pottery." Collins (1932b) echoed this statement in a paper he delivered at the Conference on Southern Pre-History in Birmingham, Alabama, the same year in which the Deasonville report was published. The way that Collins went about using the pottery from Deasonville to create a chronological ordering was innovative. He had already identified what he considered to be

Figure 2. Photograph of Moreau B. Chambers (left) and James A. Ford (right) on their return voyage from working with Henry B. Collins in the Bering Sea region of Alaska, October 1931 (photograph courtesy Mississippi Department of Archives and History).

Choctaw pottery (Collins 1927a), and by the time he was writing the Deasonville report, Ford and Chambers had succeeded in locating what appeared to be Natchez and Tunica sites in western Mississippi.

Collins turned his attention to sherds from Deasonville that contained overhanging incised lines (known later as Coles Creek Incised): "This is a style of decoration which Ford and Chambers have found to be characteristic of certain prehistoric sites in western Mississippi as distinguished from near-by historic sites of the Natchez and Tunica" (Collins 1932a:19). Ford and Chambers's data were important because they demonstrated that sherds containing the overhanging incised lines did not occur on sites known from ethnographic sources to have been inhabited by the Tunica or Natchez, the latter group's pottery exhibiting a "usually polished surface and scroll or meander design" (Collins 1932a:19). Nor were there at Deasonville any sherds of Choctaw ware, "which is characterized by straight or curving bands of very fine lines applied with a comblike implement [Collins 1927a], or of Tunica ware, in which the decoration consists of somewhat enlarged rims bearing indentations or scallops together with a single encircling line along the top" (Collins 1932a:19).

Given (a) the absence of pottery that had been found associated with

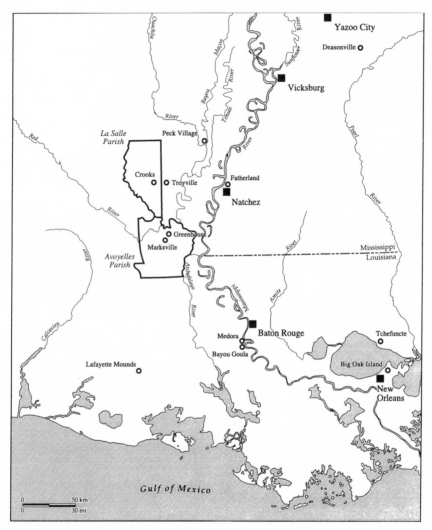

Figure 3. Location of archaeological sites mentioned in the text. La Salle and Avoyelles parishes were the two Works Project Administration units designated for archaeological work.

known groups, (b) the absence of European items, and (c) "the presence of another type [the one with horizontal, overhanging incised lines] which at other Mississippi sites appears just as definitely prehistoric," Collins (1932a:19) made the obvious conclusion: Deasonville was a prehistoric site. But he wasn't sure how old the site was: "Study of the

O'Brien and Lyman

potsherds from Deasonville fails to reveal any clues which might be of value as showing the chronological position of the site beyond the mere fact that it is prehistoric" (Collins 1932a:19). He commented further: "We must know . . . much more about the geographical range of the various types of Southeastern pottery and the relative position occupied by each, and especially we must know which types are found associated with European material and which types are never found in such association" (Collins 1932a:20).

James A. Ford and Louisiana Chronology

Ford was determined to answer these questions, and in 1933, after an 18-month stint of archaeological fieldwork in Alaska, he applied for and received a grant-in-aid from the National Research Council to continue the survey that he and Chambers had started six years earlier, this time concentrating on sites in Louisiana. His research design was short and to the point: "The determination of an archaeological chronology in this area would outline the prehistory of the Lower Mississippi Valley area and doubtless, through intrusive culture elements, would throw some light on neighboring Southeastern areas."[3] Ford completed the survey in 1934, during which time he conducted test excavations at one site, Peck Village, in Catahoula Parish (Figure 3). Ford enrolled at Louisiana State University in the fall of 1934 and began working on several papers in addition to writing up the results of his survey and excavation projects. In January 1935 he produced what we consider to be his first real publication on archaeology—an article entitled "An Introduction to Louisiana Archeology" (Ford 1935a[2]) that was published in the *Louisiana Conservation Review*. In it Ford summarized what was known of the archaeological record of the state, paying particular attention to remains from the historical period as well as to the pottery from Marksville, a site in Avoyelles Parish (Figure 3) that Ford and Frank M. Setzler of the U.S. National Museum had excavated in the fall of 1933 (Setzler 1933a, 1933b).[4] In the article, Ford laid out not only his basic ideas on culture but, more important, his ideas on how culture changes and how archaeologists read that change:

> [B]y "culture" is meant the component of the customs and styles of languages, handicrafts, arts and ceremonials practiced by any particular group of people at any one time. . . . It is in a continuous state

of evolutionary change since it is constantly influenced both by inventions from within and the introduction of new ideas from without the group. . . .

This principle of the gradual change of culture with the passage of time applies quite directly to the lives of the ancient Indians of Louisiana, and clear indications of it may be noted by a study of the articles they have left behind them. . . .

It is apparent that if the different forms of the various implements, houses, mounds, etc., used during time covered by one of these ancient cultures can be arranged in the sequence in which they occurred, it is possible to determine the relative ages of the various old towns. . . . The simplest means of arranging such a chronology is to select some one element of culture which appears commonly on the ancient sites and which was subject to rapid change in form. After the chronology of this one element is discovered, it serves as a "yardstick" for the remaining elements of the culture history. (Ford 1935a:9)

The obvious artifacts to use in uncovering the past were the millions of pottery sherds that littered the Louisiana landscape, and the obvious place to look for change was in designs on the pottery: "As the chronology of this key culture element is easier to discover by working from the known back into the unknown past, the first task becomes that of discovering the types of pottery and pottery decorations used by the tribes that came in contact with the whites" (Ford 1935a:10). By the early 1930s archaeologists working in Louisiana and Mississippi had tied specific kinds of pottery decoration to four major ethnic groups of the historical period: the Caddo, located primarily in northern Louisiana; the Choctaw, located in central Mississippi along and east of the Pearl River; the Natchez, located in western Mississippi from Vicksburg on the north to Natchez on the south; and the Tunica, located in extreme northeastern Louisiana and in western Mississippi from Vicksburg north to Yazoo City. Each had been preceded in various areas by prehistoric peoples, but it was unclear how far back in time individual pottery types or sets of types could be pushed (Collins 1932b).

In his article in the *Louisiana Conservation Review,* Ford focused only on Caddo and Natchez pottery, noting that "Comparative studies show . . . that although the Caddo had occupied the territory where they were first described longer than had the Natchez, both cultures at comparatively recent times had displaced others which had entirely different pottery designs and which very likely represented an entirely different people" (Ford 1935a:10). Here Ford equated what he later variously termed a "ceramic complex" or "decoration complex" with a culture; he would, in a few years, abandon this equivalency.

Ford's 1935 Chronological Ordering

A few months later Ford presented his notion of chronological ordering in another article in the *Louisiana Conservation Review* entitled "Outline of Louisiana and Mississippi Pottery Horizons" (Ford 1935b[3]), this time in graphical fashion. He was beginning to finalize his report on Peck Village and was analyzing the surface-collected sherds from sites in Louisiana and Mississippi. In a change from the way he had arranged the chronological ordering in the earlier article, Ford split the chronology into two geographically distinct pieces, one representing what he called the Yazoo City, Mississippi, area and the other representing what he called the Natchez, Mississippi, area (Ford 1935b:Figure 2). He stated that the "sites within the areas, as shown on the map . . . divide themselves according to the pottery decorations found on them into seven broad groups called 'complexes.' Some of these complexes were contemporaneous in different areas, hence they all fall into three main time divisions" (Ford 1935b:33), or what he labeled "horizons." The youngest of the three divisions (labeled "III"), which began sometime in the prehistoric past and continued up past A.D. 1700, contained pottery manufactured by the four historical tribes: the Caddo, Tunica, Natchez, and Choctaw. Ford's "intermediate" period ("II") consisted of pottery he placed in the Deasonville and Coles Creek complexes, and his oldest division ("I") contained pottery he placed in the Marksville complex.

Ford (1935b:34) defined a "ceramic complex" as "a small group of often unrelated [formally dissimilar?] pottery design types which were fashionable in the same region at the same time." Marksville was viewed as what might be termed the "basement" complex of pottery designs— a complex that at some unknown point in the past was replaced by the Coles Creek complex in the Natchez area and by the Deasonville complex in the Yazoo City area. Then, at some unknown point in the prehistoric past, the Coles Creek pottery-design complex was replaced by the Natchez and Choctaw complexes in the Natchez area, and the

Deasonville complex was replaced by the Caddo and Tunica complexes in the Yazoo City area. Ford illustrated various pottery decorations that allowed time and space to be carved up into the neat units, and he subdivided the sherds carrying various designs into types based on similarity in design. Descriptions of the various types appeared in the Peck Village report (see below) but were not reproduced in the popular article.

Ford did, however, address one very important issue in the article, and we examine it here briefly as background to his later discussions. In his Deasonville report, Collins (1932a:19) had lamented that analysis "of the potsherds from Deasonville fails to reveal any clues which might be of value as showing the chronological position of the site beyond the mere fact that it is prehistoric." Subsequent work at Marksville and other sites (especially Peck Village) was beginning to demonstrate there was some time depth to the prehistoric period, which Ford was already conceiving of as comprising two units—Marksville and either Deasonville or Coles Creek, depending on where in the Mississippi Valley a site was located. For a general audience Ford could have left things at that, but he didn't. Despite the neatness of the scenario, it oversimplified matters because it did not take into account sites that might contain sherds of more than one contemporaneous complex. Ford knew that the Deasonville site contained sherds of both the Deasonville and Coles Creek complexes, as did Peck Village. Similarly for the historical period, the Fatherland site in Adams County, Mississippi (Figure 3), contained sherds of the Natchez, Tunica, and Caddo complexes.

Ford must have realized his map was too clean, meaning that it misrepresented the true areal extent of individual pottery complexes, and thus he inserted two columns of letters in his Table I. The letters in the left two columns refer to the time periods shown in his Figure 2, ranging from time X in the prehistoric past up through time E. He would continue to use this system of capital letters to denote the boundaries of temporal periods in later work. What Ford was showing were the major and minor ceramic complexes that theoretically could (and in reality did) appear on a site depending on its location in the valley. For example, a village in northern Louisiana or west-central Mississippi—Ford's Yazoo City area—that was settled at time B and not abandoned until time D might contain large percentages of sherds of both the prehistoric Deasonville complex and the historical-period Tunica complex, and it might also contain a lesser percentage of Coles Creek–complex sherds. He subsequently used this discussion as a springboard for an extended treatment of the temporal span and areal extent of decoration complexes that appeared in his monograph on the surface collections.

Peck Village

Ford's monograph on Peck Village (Figure 3), entitled "Ceramic Decoration Sequence at an Old Indian Village Site near Sicily Island, Louisiana" (Ford 1935c[4]), initiated the newly established Anthropological Study series published by the Louisiana Department of Conservation through the Louisiana Geological Survey. In the 41-page monograph, Ford detailed the results of his excavations at the site in Catahoula Parish (Figure 4). In the first paragraph of the report Ford (1935c:1) stated his reason for excavating the site: "the possibility of vertical stratigraphy." Thus, Peck Village held the promise that no other site up to that time had: vertical—hence, implied chronological—separation of distinct "decoration complexes."

In a footnote Ford (1935c:1) defined a decoration complex as a "group of pottery decorations characteristic of an area at a definite period of time"—a definition that was a bit more open-ended than what he had presented a few months previously, in the second of his popular articles, for the term *ceramic complex*. Note the absence here of the qualifications "small group of unrelated pottery design types" found in the popular article and the presence of the perhaps more formal and explicit word *decorations* rather than the earlier *design*. Thus Ford's decoration complexes were analytical, or ideational, units (Lyman et al. 1997), the empirical manifestations of which—the actual sherds—indicated the distributions of the units in time and space. This critical fact is obscured in Ford's early writings because the historically anchored decoration complexes were established by extracting marker types from ethnographically documented tribal units.

In the Peck Village report Ford immediately presented his spatial-temporal ordering of decoration complexes and then demonstrated how he arrived at the ordering. Because of its location, Peck Village exhibited little pottery carrying the decorations evident on pottery from Deasonville and other sites in the Yazoo City area. It did, however, as had Deasonville, contain a large number of incised "Marksville complex" sherds. What made the presence of those sherds at Peck Village so important was their stratigraphic position. The separation was not perfect, but there was clear indication (Ford 1935c:Figures 5–9) that

Figure 4. Photograph of James A. Ford and Ethel Ford at Peck Village, Catahoula Parish, Louisiana, 1933 (photograph courtesy W. G. Haag).

coming up through the levels of the site, "marker type" sherds of the Marksville complex were being replaced in terms of relative abundance by sherds of what Ford was calling the Coles Creek complex.

The scenario was obvious to Ford: the Marksville complex was the basement of the Louisiana-Mississippi pottery sequence. At Peck Village sherds of that complex were replaced by sherds of the Coles Creek complex, whereas at Deasonville the Deasonville complex had replaced the Marksville complex—the scenario he had presented graphically in the second article in the *Louisiana Conservation Review*. The pottery complexes of the four historical-period groups had in turn replaced the Deasonville and Coles Creek complexes in each of the two regions (Yazoo City and Natchez), although at different times.

Ford's discussion of decoration complexes was derived from his view that culture constantly changes—that is, it is constantly in a state of becoming something else. But he stumbled because his complexes measured that change as discontinuous chunks, and those chunks—manifest as decoration complexes—were thought to represent, potentially at least, distinct cultures or peoples. Correlating pottery with ethnic groups provided a commonsensical warrant for the chunks. In his three 1935 publications Ford failed to explicitly acknowledge something for which he later would be famous (e.g., Ford 1951)—that the chunks were merely *arbitrary,* ideational (as opposed to "real," or empirical) units of measurement in the same way inches or grams are. Thus the kind of culture change he studied at Peck Village was one tied to the mechanisms of replacement or absorption—ethnologically documented mechanisms of culture change thought to be visible archaeologically. *Replacement* denoted the gradual cessation of one complex and the initiation of another, and *absorption* denoted the continuation of a type across sequent complexes—a direct phyletic continuity of a decorative theme (see Kidder 1917)—but with modifications from outside.

To this point we have focused almost exclusively on Ford's development and use of decoration complexes, but this overlooks the important point that the complexes comprised individual pottery *types,* which subsequently were lumped under one complex or another based on a combination of two things: similarity in decoration and perceived or inferred contemporaneity. As Jon Gibson (1982:264) aptly put it, to Ford "the goal of pottery classification virtually became one with deriving cultural chronology; there is no really logical way to separate them." Ford's earliest published categorization of pottery centered around sherds from his 1933 excavation of Peck Village. He noted that all "pottery decorations found at the Peck site were classified according to an index" that had been developed to study the large collections of sherds from the surfaces of sites in Louisiana and Mississippi (Ford 1935c:8). He obviously did not anticipate at the time that he would soon scrap his index system and implement a new system for the surface collections.

Ford (1935c:8) referred to his index system—the one used in the Peck Village report—as "merely a list of decoration types," noting that as "distinct decorations were encountered in the collections in sufficient numerical quantity and areal distribution to permit their acceptance as a type, they were illustrated on an index card" (Ford 1935c:8). The actual types he used were decoration based, but Ford recognized types only if they were represented by enough sherds and if they occurred across enough space to preclude them from being idiosyncrasies. Evidence that Ford's types may have been somewhat schizophrenic units is apparent in other remarks:

> Typologically related decorations found together in the same collections, thus indicating the probability that they represented variations of one major idea of decoration, were filed as "a", "b", "c", etc., under a common numerical heading. If no such grouping already existed for a newly-encountered decoration type, it was filed as "a" of a new numerical heading. These groups were used only for the most apparent relations and were intended to have no cultural or absolute typological significance; they served mostly to facilitate filing and reference to the index. (Ford 1935c:8)

The lack of clarity in Ford's procedure for constructing units at the scale of an artifact type is not apparent in his construction of his larger-scale aggregates of types, the decoration complexes. Regarding the sherds from Peck Village, for example, he stated, "The sherds from this site fall into four divisions: 1. Decorations, because of their consistent occurrence on typical Marksville sites, can be recognized as belonging to the Marksville Complex. 2. Sherds typical of the Deasonville Complex. 3. Sherds belonging to the Coles Creek Complex. 4. Unusual decorations which cannot with certainty be assigned to any of the above complexes" (Ford 1935c:10–11). Ford assigned types to one of the three prehistoric complexes based on the occurrence of sherds of those types on sites that he had already placed into one of the three complexes. New types were thought to represent a particular complex because they were associated with already-established types that were thought to represent a complex. It is unclear how the original definitive types of a prehistoric complex were determined, though we suspect they were extracted from collections that came from sites that did not contain sherds associated with one or more historical tribes.

Important to Ford's analysis of chronological change at Peck Village was the vertical distribution of what he termed "complex markers," which were pottery types that could be employed as index fossils in the usual sense of the term. Thus a multicomplex site was identified as such only if it exhibited *marker* types representing more than one complex. Ford stated that before his work at Peck Village there were only a few marker types for the Lower Mississippi Valley—two for the Marksville complex, six for the Coles Creek complex, and three for the

Deasonville complex. By the time he reported his analysis of the surface-collected sherd assemblages in 1936, Ford had expanded the number of Marksville-complex types to three and had reduced the number of Coles Creek–complex marker types to five and the number of Deasonville-complex marker types to two. The extra Marksville-complex type apparently was derived from his excavations at Peck Village. Ford used the marker types—and *only* the marker types—to demonstrate the replacement of Marksville sherds by Coles Creek sherds at Peck Village.

Examination of Ford's graphs of proportions of pottery types (marker types as well as nonmarker types) in each of the four stratigraphic cuts—his Figures 5–9—demonstrates that Deasonville-complex sherds were present in varying amounts throughout the sequence. It also is apparent from comparing his graph of marker types in the four cuts to the graphs showing the proportion of all types (marker or otherwise) that sherds of other, unmentioned complexes were present. Ford ignored those in his discussion because he was interested in the overall waxing and waning of marker types, not small fluctuations between excavation sections. Here, then, was his "one element of culture [pottery] subject to rapid change in form" (Ford 1935a) that allowed him to build a chronology.

The Louisiana-Mississippi Surface Collections

Ford extended his chronology out from Peck Village when he published the results of his and Chambers's survey of sites in Louisiana and Mississippi (Ford 1936a[5]). The report, entitled "Analysis of Indian Village Site Collections from Louisiana and Mississippi" and published in the Louisiana Department of Conservation monograph series, carries the imprint date of November 1936, although it was not released until June 1937. In the report Ford summarized sherd collections from 103 sites. After he published the Peck Village study, Ford abandoned the index system of type construction, noting that it "is highly subjective; much is left to the judgment of the classifier" (Ford 1936a:18). Because it was so dependent on the "classifier's acquaintance with the material"—a strong reflection of the extracted nature of his type definitions— Ford (1936a:18) decided it was "not suitable for presentation," being "only semi-systematic . . . non-analytical . . . meaningless unless memorized in detail, and . . . not capable of logical expansion."

His replacement system, which Gibson (1982:265) referred to as

Ford's "analytical formula plan," was based strictly on decoration. Ford's units were ideational—that is, the necessary and sufficient conditions for membership were stated explicitly—and what is more, they were not extracted from the sherds but rather were used to *identify* the set of attributes displayed by the sherds (Lyman et al. 1997; O'Brien and Lyman 1998). Types were particular combinations of attributes that were immutable, atemporal, and aspatial as opposed to being time- and space-bound. Ford's system allowed him to sum the frequency of occurrence of any attribute—whether a particular motif, an element, or an application—as well as the frequency of any class. Ford's analytical-formula system was, as Gibson (1982:265) suggested, "the most sensitive and rigorous classification scheme to be used in the Lower Mississippi Valley." The system was based on objective criteria—in other words, "it was uncontaminated by notions, suspected or stratigraphically demonstrated, of chronological order or cultural relationships" (Gibson 1982:266).

Several of the sites, especially those that had been occupied during the historical period, contained sherds of only one decoration complex, but many of them west and south of Natchez contained sherds of both the Marksville and Coles Creek complexes, and many of those around Vicksburg contained sherds of both the Marksville and Deasonville complexes (Ford 1936a:Figure 2). A few sites that were known locations of the historical-period Caddo and Tunica contained scattered Coles Creek–complex sherds, but no Choctaw or Natchez sites contained Coles Creek sherds, nor did any historical-period sites contain Deasonville-complex sherds. This pattern led Ford to suspect that the Coles Creek complex might have been in part contemporaneous with the Caddo and Tunica complexes and that it certainly outlasted the Deasonville complex. Further, Ford reasoned that if it were true "that the Coles Creek–Deasonville time horizon interlocks in this way with the historic horizon, then the time horizon of Marksville complex must have been the earliest of all" (Ford 1936a:254). Ford (1936a:254) referred to this method of chronologically arranging sites as "'complex linking'—connecting time horizons by the overlapping of complexes occupying neighboring areas."

Ford's placing the 103 sites in chronological order has been characterized as a "seriation" (e.g., Dunnell 1990:19; Watson 1990:43). We find this an inaccurate characterization for two reasons. First, Ford knew the basic sequence of marker types based on historical data and the relative stratigraphic positions of the types based on Peck Village.

But seriation is generally defined as "the arrangement of archaeological materials in a presumed chronological order on the basis of some logical principle other than superposition. . . . The logical order on which the seriation is based is found in the combinations of features of style or inventory which characterize the units, rather than in the external relationships of the units themselves" (Rowe 1961:326). Second, Ford (1936a:10) stated, "In this study the desired results are not the ages of individual sites, but the relative ages of the different schools of ceramic art." Each "school of ceramic art" was denoted by one or more marker types, and he merely assigned each site to a period based on its included marker types. Ford thus used stratigraphy to inform his ordering, and although he sorted the sites into a set of spatiotemporal units, he did not sort the sites within each period. In our view Ford's effort constitutes cross-dating rather than seriation.

Ford realized that "mixing" of sherds of different decoration complexes could result from several factors. In his "Outline of Louisiana and Mississippi Pottery Horizons," he had commented that there is a "system to this mixing of complexes. It can usually be attributed to one or two causes. Mixture often results from trade or borrowing of ideas having occurred between neighboring, contemporaneous complex areas [e.g., the presence of Deasonville sherds on sites containing primarily Coles Creek sherds], so that foreign designs become incorporated in the village refuse dumps" (Ford 1935b:34, 37). Ford assumed both conditions—trade and diffusion—had created the mixture of complexes seen in the 103 sherd assemblages he analyzed. He also was well aware that reoccupation of a site could result in the mixing of decoration complexes, but he discounted such a possibility as largely improbable: "The village dump or midden deposit was accumulated during the years of occupancy, and if [it] had reached any appreciable depth would show by changes in types of artifacts from the bottom to the top the transitions in style which had occurred while the town was alive. However, the great majority of Louisiana sites never had any great accumulation so that younger and older types are hopelessly intermingled" (Ford 1935b:37).

A year later Ford clarified what he meant. Reoccupation—that is, occupation after a preceding abandonment—was possible, but "it would be unlikely that a succeeding people should select the exact [previously occupied] habitation spot for their use. If the old locality had been intentionally reoccupied, the odds are that the dumps of the succeeding group would be located near but not precisely on those of the original inhabitants" (Ford 1936a:255). In short, mixing of complexes resulting from reoccupation was unlikely. Ford believed that mixing of complexes was more likely the result of continuous occupation: "It seems more reasonable to suppose that sites on which apparently subsequent complexes are mixed were either settled in the time of the older and were occupied on into the time of the following complex; or that the villages were inhabited during a period of transition from one complex to the other" (Ford 1936a:255–256).

Apparently, to Ford long-term continuous occupation was rare because most sites did not contain thick accumulations of artifacts. The few that did have such accumulations contained "transitional-period" assemblages. To demonstrate that there indeed were such transitional periods, Ford (1936a:262–268) discussed "certain decoration types which suggest that they are the results of an evolutionary trend which runs through two or more of the subsequent complexes," being careful to point out that such continuation "does not imply that this evolutionary process occurred in the local geographical area. In most cases it is more likely that the evidence is a reflection of the process taking place in some nearby territory." Thus Ford was suggesting that particular attribute states of decoration types originated in and diffused from one area to another, where they were subsequently incorporated into the local decoration complex by taking the place of or resulting in the modification of an attribute state of a vessel.

Given Ford's "dominant axiom of culture: it is always changing," why, within his framework, couldn't evolution happen in situ—that is, at the site producing the sherds? To Ford culture was a flowing (evolving) stream of ideas, but because cultures interact, the appropriate model for culture change was a *braided* stream, each intersection of two trickles representing "cultural influences"—a point that Matthew Stirling (1932:22) had stressed at the Birmingham Conference in 1932, which Ford had attended (O'Brien and Lyman 1997). Such influences were the result of ethnographically visible processes such as diffusion, trade, or even immigration, but regardless of which mechanism operated in a particular time-space context, they all provided a new source of variation for the local pottery tradition, just as in situ invention did. But Ford's decoration types evolved as a result of influences from outside—an idea perfectly in concert with, and probably derived from, the then-prevalent notion that it was unlikely that a "complicated technique of decoration" could be independently invented in two distinct areas at approximately the same time—a point Frank Setzler

(1933a:153) had made in one of his papers on Hopewell-like pottery from Marksville. New decoration complexes—aggregates of types—evident in an area thus represented the replacement of one culture by another.

Fred B. Kniffen and Seriation

By the time Ford completed his "Analysis of Indian Village Site Collections from Louisiana and Mississippi" in fall 1936, he had graduated from the School of Geology at Louisiana State University and had begun graduate studies there. One of the people who had a significant influence on Ford during his years at LSU was Fred B. Kniffen. Some of Kniffen's work undertaken in the mid-1930s provides important keys to Ford's thinking relative to chronological ordering—keys that are missing or only vaguely detailed in Ford's own publications. Kniffen, technically a geographer, had received his doctorate at the University of California, Berkeley, where he studied with Carl Sauer and A. L. Kroeber, working on several projects that Kroeber directed. As we discuss elsewhere (O'Brien and Lyman 1998), Kniffen undoubtedly knew of the work of Kroeber and two of his students, William Duncan Strong and Anna Gayton, who were seriating Max Uhle's pottery collections from Peru. They used both phyletic seriation and frequency seriation, as well as whatever evidence of superposition was available to them in Uhle's notes, to create a ceramic-based chronology (O'Brien and Lyman 1998). It is reasonable to assume that Kniffen, more interested in human geography and ethnology, was at least aware of the methodological underpinnings of what Kroeber, Strong, and Gayton were doing, as well as *why* they were doing it. It also is reasonable to assume that when he saw Ford's surface collections from Louisiana and Mississippi, Kniffen realized that here was an opportunity to put his Berkeley experience to good use.

Kniffen was involved in two studies of interest here, both undertaken as part of Richard Russell's geomorphological examination of several coastal Louisiana parishes. The first involved Plaquemines and St. Bernard parishes east and south of New Orleans. Kniffen (1936) made surface collections at a number of archaeological sites, and his method of ordering the collections chronologically was based on the simple assumption that prehistoric peoples lived along waterways and that as those waterways changed course, the inhabitants moved their settlements accordingly. If the sites could be dated, then not only could terminal dates be established for the landforms on which they were located—for example, levees—but the latest period of occupation, as demonstrated by pottery types, should date to the abandonment of the nearby river course. The real beauty of what Kniffen proposed, however, was not in the proposition itself but in how he went about dating the sites.

Coastal geomorphologists had long been interested in the development of the Mississippi Delta and the submergence of land in southern Louisiana caused by the sheer weight of the sediment continuously deposited by the Mississippi River and its distributaries. What was missing was a way to date the various events connected with subsidence and the development of deltaic lobes. In addition to dumping an astronomical amount of sediment onto the Louisiana coastal plain, both the Mississippi and its distributaries had changed course any number of times in response to changes in such things as water volume and sediment load. Many of the physiographic features that marked the dynamic history of the Lower Mississippi Valley were evident, but could they be dated?

Kniffen worked out a method of relative dating using pottery. As William Haag (1994:28) put it, "Kniffen recognized that the assemblage of potsherds in some areas was quite different from that in other areas. Further, he noted that some kinds of pottery were totally absent from other middens and mounds occurring along the natural levees. From these data he and his colleagues developed working hypotheses that enabled mapping the courses of the river and chronologically relating the prehistoric remains." In a short paper entitled "Archaeological Methods Applicable to Louisiana," Ford (1936b[6]) also indicated that "sites may be related to changes in the natural features of the landscape in order to determine their relative ages"—changes such as coastal subsidence and "shifting stream meanders" (Ford 1936b:103–104). He undoubtedly learned both notions from Kniffen and/or Russell while at Louisiana State University.

Kniffen recognized four kinds of sites—man-made mounds of either earth or shell, shell middens, and redeposited accumulations of artifacts on beaches. He also recognized two distinctive pottery complexes—an earlier Bayou Cutler complex and a later Bayou Petre complex—and argued that they were intermediate in age between what he called the Earthen Mound period (earliest) and the Late Prehistoric period (latest). With regard to his two newly named ceramic complexes, Kniffen indicated there were notable differences between the two. What he called Bayou Cutler sherds were often check stamped and not tempered with shell (they were clay tempered, though he did not point this out). Rim lugs and nodes were plentiful, but handles were not. Bayou Petre sherds were shell tempered and noncheck stamped. Rim lugs and nodes were absent, but handles were abundant. Kniffen immediately recognized formal similarities between the Bayou Cutler complex and Ford's Coles Creek complex. Central Louisiana is a long way from southeastern Louisiana, but based on his observations of formal similarities, Kniffen felt comfortable drawing comparisons between what he saw as contemporary pottery complexes. But what about two complexes from roughly the same area? Could they be contemporary, or were they from two distinct time periods? Kniffen came down decidedly in favor of the latter:

> The definite distinction between the Bayou Cutler and Bayou Petre complexes seems certain. It also seems clear that they must differ in time. It is unlikely that two [human] groups could exist side by side without showing some mixture of pottery designs. Assuming that they are different in time, it is important to know which is the older. The evidence is not conclusive. What there is favors the greater age of the Bayou Cutler complex. The check-stamp ware of the Bayou Cutler complex occasionally appears in the Bayou Petre. On the other hand, no diagnostic trait of the Bayou Petre complex, such as handles, appears in the type Bayou Cutler collections. (Kniffen 1936:414)

Note Kniffen's use of the word *trait* here. He did not say that no diagnostic *type* of the Bayou Petre complex showed up in Bayou Cutler collections; rather, he said no diagnostic *trait* showed up. This kept his argument from being tautological, meaning he did not decide an assemblage was either Bayou Cutler or Bayou Petre on the basis of a Bayou Cutler or Bayou Petre pottery type. He used specific traits—empirical things—to make such assignments. The absence of *some* empirical things—here handles—on *some* sites and the occasional presence of *other* empirical things—here check-stamped sherds—on *other* sites allowed him to construct an ordering. This was simply occurrence seriation (O'Brien and Lyman 1999).

The second study Kniffen conducted focused on Iberville and Ascension parishes in south-central Louisiana. Whereas in the Plaquemines and St. Bernard report he had used pottery traits, in the Iberville Parish report, entitled "The Indian Mounds of Iberville Parish" (Kniffen

1938[7]), he used types—a result, no doubt, of Ford's influence: "Making particular use of [decoration], Ford [1936a] has found it possible to group the sites of northern Louisiana and adjacent sections of Mississippi into a number of pottery complexes expressive of differences of either time or space or of both" (Kniffen 1938:198). Kniffen created a table (his Figure 23) in which he listed the frequencies of sherds collected from 12 Iberville Parish sites, and then arranged the sites so that

> the youngest appear at the top, the oldest at the bottom. The analysis is based on Ford's criteria. Figure 23 is really a summary of the several analyses; instead of expressing the percentage representation of each design type, the individual site is summarized as to percentage of "marker" (M) and percentage of characteristic but "other than marker" (OT) types for each complex represented. The percentage representation of design types not peculiar to, or diagnostic of, any complex is shown in the column headed "unrelated." (Kniffen 1938:199)

By "Ford's criteria," Kniffen was referring to those that Ford (1936a) had established in his surface-collection monograph for placing sherds in one of the seven pottery complexes he identified. But what about sherds/collections that didn't fit nicely into one complex or the other? Kniffen dealt with this, noting that "Ford has come to the conclusion that relatively few sites are occupied for long periods of time. Few sites are 'pure,' in the sense that they contain pottery all belonging to a single complex. Based on the percentage dominance of design types the sites are assigned to a single complex or to an intermediate position between two complexes differing in time or in place" (Kniffen 1938:198–199). This method of carving up time is evident in the right-hand column of his Figure 23. Kniffen created four periods—Historic, Historic–Bayou Cutler, Bayou Cutler, and Bayou Cutler–Marksville—each of which was represented by from two to four ceramic assemblages. No site contained sherds from only one period; rather, Kniffen simply decided whether there were so few sherds of another period present that he could ignore them when making the assignment of an assemblage to one period or another.

There were no sites in the sample that Kniffen identified as "pure" Marksville, though a few contained Marksville-complex marker types.

Gibson (1982:270) pointed out that based on the marker types Kniffen used, the Marksville assemblages identified by Kniffen dated to the latest part of the Marksville period—what in a few years would be referred to as Troyville. Each of those sites also contained large amounts of Bayou Cutler–complex sherds, so Kniffen accommodated the sites under a period he termed Bayou Cutler–Marksville—a transitional unit reflecting Ford's axiom that culture is always changing. Four sites seemed "pure" enough to warrant placing them in the Bayou Cutler period. Based on the overwhelming percentages at two sites of pottery that Collins, Ford, and others labeled as Natchez, Tunica, or Caddo, Kniffen placed the two sites in the Historical period. Three others, because of the mixture of sherds from both the Bayou Cutler and historical-tribes complexes, were placed in the Historic–Bayou Cutler period—another transitional unit.

Gibson made a number of interesting observations about Kniffen's use of pottery types and drew a conclusion with which we agree completely:

> The inclusion of Coles Creek markers along with Bayou Cutler diagnostic types in both the Historic–Bayou Cutler and Bayou Cutler periods is a very interesting admission, as is the inclusion of a column . . . showing types common to both Coles Creek and Bayou Cutler complexes. This implies that Kniffen, or perhaps Kniffen and Ford, had established some definite ideas about which pottery types "belonged" with each culture period. Unfortunately, neither Kniffen nor Ford ever published a "trait list," or similar device, detailing these marker types. (Gibson 1982:269)

We believe the truth of the matter is that Ford *had* decided which types went with which periods, just as he had earlier decided which types were "marker" types for a particular complex and which were "related" types. How he decided this is not at all clear. As we note elsewhere (O'Brien and Lyman 1998), we suspect he variously constructed, dismantled, and reconstructed types and complexes on a trial-and-error basis until he derived some that allowed him to measure time and space. This obscure procedure would lead, early in the 1950s, to several heated debates with some of his contemporaries. As we will see a bit later, what replaced the analytical system was what had been gradually developing in the Southwest, namely the binomial-type system. When it sprang up in the Southeast in the late 1930s, largely at the hands of Ford and James B. Griffin, it did so full grown. Ford and several of his southeastern colleagues were in a sense preadapted for the simpler type designations because what they had been using for years was, as Gibson (1982) pointed out, unwieldy. The new system would slice through all the dizzying array of variation, pick out a few variants, and wrap the subsets into neat little packages. Those kinds of types, at least in the Southeast, had their origins in Ford's use of marker types, which by definition were diagnostic—type fossils—of specific decoration complexes, which Ford (1936a) began referring to as "periods." Kniffen (1938) followed Ford's lead when he added the right-hand column to his table. Because marker types for any one complex occurred on sites that contained marker types for other periods, Kniffen was faced with the problem of what to call the periods. Ford must have given him the answer: create intermediate periods to reflect the occurrence at sites of marker types for more than one complex. Thus Kniffen ended up with a period labeled Bayou Cutler–Marksville and another labeled Historic–Bayou Cutler.

Gibson must have been correct that Ford and Kniffen knew which types went with which time period. The nice, neat arrangement shown in the table—much cleaner than Ford's (1936a:Figure 1) tabular summary of pottery types plotted against the surface-collected sites—is beguiling in its simplicity, which obscures all of the details that had characterized Ford's earlier work. Many of those details were difficult to deal with—this is why Ford abandoned the analytical-formula system—and maybe by 1937 he was fed up with detail when he could already see the patterns he was looking for. The blueprint was simple: use the existing marker types, which had been developed in part from ethnohistorical research (the historical-period types) and in part from stratigraphic positioning, to position assemblages temporally by means of what Ford (1936a) referred to as "complex linking." Then, turn the decoration complexes into periods to emphasize the temporal component. Where the situation warranted, create a new period and slide it into the sequence. The product was the creation of "index fossils"— marker types—to measure the slow, inexorable march of time. The problem was that the marker types were idiosyncratic, meaning that although Ford knew what they were, it was difficult to explain them to other archaeologists. Ford needed a simplified system, and he found one in the Southwest.

The Binomial System Comes to the Southeast

The year 1937 was a busy one for Ford. After he graduated from LSU in the spring of 1936 and began graduate studies there, he decided that the following fall he would transfer to the University of Michigan to complete his master's degree. James B. Griffin, who was fast developing a reputation as the premier pottery analyst in the eastern United States, had urged Ford to come north to graduate school and work with him. The immediate productivity of the union of Griffin and Ford was in part predicated on what Ford learned during the summer of 1937—a pivotal time for him in terms of his emerging ideas on culture history and pottery classification.

Ford's first important move was a return trip to Georgia to work with A. R. Kelly in June 1937. There he met Gordon R. Willey, who was working as Kelly's assistant on several federally funded excavations around Macon. The second important move for Ford occurred later that summer, when he spent six weeks in Chaco Canyon, New Mexico, as part of the University of New Mexico field school. Up to that point Ford had never set foot in the Southwest. He must have heard or read of the work of Kroeber, A. V. Kidder, and their colleagues—we're assuming he did from Kniffen—but it wasn't until 1938 that he ever cited the work of any southwestern archaeologist. By the time Ford returned to Baton Rouge in September 1937 he was full of ideas about expanding the scope of archaeology in Louisiana, which, following the early project at Marksville directed by Setzler and Ford, had grown rather quiet. Willey's recollection about the drive he and Ford made from Macon to Baton Rouge indicates something about Ford's vision for the future of archaeological work in the South:

> Jim told me that after a year at Michigan he would return to Louisiana and set up a big WPA program of excavation in the state. In this connection, he planned a large, central laboratory, and he wanted me to take charge of it for him. . . . I was excited by the idea. Jim could outline and present a research program like a call to arms. No loyal archaeologist could refuse. Victory was just over the horizon. Together we would solve all kinds of problems as we envisaged them then: Hopewellian origins, the rise of Middle Mississippian, the role of the Caddoan cultures. That night . . . I fell asleep and dreamt of archaeological glories to come. (Willey 1988:57)

Before those plans could be put in operation, Ford would have to further his formal education, and that need brought him to Griffin's doorstep in the fall of 1937.

Our main interest here is how Griffin approached the categorization of pottery during the period 1933 to 1937 because this set the stage for what Griffin and Ford together did in 1938. The centerpieces of Griffin's early work were his analyses of pottery from two large programs funded by the Tennessee Valley Authority—Norris Basin in eastern Tennessee (Griffin 1938) and Wheeler Basin in northwestern Alabama (Griffin 1939)—and of Fort Ancient pottery from the Upper Ohio Valley (Griffin 1943). To Griffin "pottery is the most important single factor in the interpretation of archaeological cultural relationships" (Griffin 1943:3). In his Fort Ancient monograph Griffin (1943:3) indicated that his description and classification of pottery was based on the notion of "types, in accordance with a method of approach that has been used with marked success in the Southwest and in other areas the pottery of which has been intensively studied." The ability to communicate between and among archaeologists was important, and as Griffin (1976:25) later noted, "One of the best tools for communication between archaeologists in the eastern United States was the development of the system of pottery type descriptions that came into widespread use during the late 1930s to the present." To us the development of that "system of pottery type descriptions" was perhaps *the* critical turning point in southeastern archaeology because no longer was it necessary in a report to write paragraph after paragraph of description; one had simply to insert a type name (and perhaps a short description) into the report and everyone who saw the name knew automatically what a vessel or sherd looked like.

Griffin (1976:25–26) later recalled his first exposure to Ford:

> When James A. Ford arrived in Ann Arbor to work on a Masters degree in the fall of 1937 he had just returned from a summer in the Southwest and (if I recall correctly) felt he should do his pottery classification of village site collections in terms of the Southwestern model. . . . As the result of innumerable conversations it was agreed that we should try to have a meeting of working archaeologists to discuss a typology framework. Ford only wanted to have a small number, while I argued we should invite as many as we thought would be able to contribute pottery descriptions. It was finally agreed

to hold the meeting in Ann Arbor in the Ceramic Repository, which was then my office, May 16–17, 1938.

One could infer that Ford's trip to Chaco Canyon was the catalyst for the meeting that Griffin and Ford proposed as a means of bringing order to pottery analysis in the East. Southwesternists (e.g., Gladwin 1936; Gladwin and Gladwin 1930) were routinely using the binomial classification procedure, with color or surface treatment constituting the first part of the type name and geographic locale the second part. This system of integrating time, space, and form was proposed at the original Pecos Conference in 1927 (Kidder 1927) and grew out of a consensus reached at the first Gila Pueblo Conference in 1930 (Brew 1946; Gladwin 1936). By the mid-1930s procedures and rules for naming new types had become fairly standardized (e.g., Colton and Hargrave 1937).

As important as his 1937 trip to the Southwest was to Ford's intellectual development, we have long suspected that Ford learned much of what he knew about the Southwest, especially pottery classification, as a result of his early friendship with Gordon Willey when they both worked in Georgia (O'Brien and Lyman 1998). Willey had the requisite training at the University of Arizona, studying with Byron Cummings and taking courses with astronomer A. E. Douglass, the developer of dendrochronology. Willey takes no such credit in his biographical essay on Ford, noting only that Ford "came back to Macon in September [1937], full of ideas about pottery classification, in the wake of the Southwestern experience" (Willey 1988:56). However, a few years ago one of us asked him if perhaps it hadn't been he who initially suggested to Ford that he try the southwestern binomial system on southeastern pottery. After pausing for a few seconds, almost as if he had never thought about it before, he responded, "Yes, I believe I was."

This small, seemingly insignificant admission is important because it helps complete the bridge between late 1936, when Ford finished the surface-collection monograph, and late 1937, when he and Griffin began preparing to reorganize pottery classification in the Southeast. Given Ford's interests and where he was intellectually in 1937, there was no better person to be around for a summer than Gordon Willey. He was fresh out of the master's program at the University of Arizona when he went to Georgia to work with A. R. Kelly, and from the time he arrived in Macon his main interest was chronology—first attempting to derive a master dendrochronological chart for the region (Willey 1937,

1938) and then concentrating on "relative chronology as this would be carried by pottery stratigraphy and seriation" (Willey 1988:42).

Throughout late 1937 and early 1938 Ford and Willey schemed on how to get other archaeologists interested in the binomial system (Lyon 1996; O'Brien and Lyman 1998). The need for a useful system was obvious; the frustration that southeastern archaeologists were beginning to experience in the late 1930s with existing pottery-classification systems was exacerbated by the frenzy of federally sponsored archaeological work in the region. In the words of Ian Brown (1978:8), "the resulting collections were . . . getting out of control. Each archaeologist, unaware of the work of others, had his own typological system. Chaos was imminent. The need for a uniform nomological system was apparent." And as Brown (1978:8) pointed out, "Griffin and Ford were the two principal agents in bringing it about." Late in 1937 Griffin and Ford circulated a short proposal calling for a "Conference on Pottery Nomenclature for the Southeastern United States" (Ford and Griffin 1937).[5] The opening paragraph of the proposal is instructive for what it tells us about how Ford and Griffin viewed the then-existing confusion over pottery types:

> It is felt by several of the investigators working in the southeastern states that the time has arrived for the development of a standard method of designating and comparing the different varieties of pottery in Southeastern archaeological research. Through the efforts of former and present investigators, it is probable that the major types of pottery of the region have already been excavated. A most significant problem is the ordering of this material. (Ford and Griffin 1937:5)

What Ford and Griffin were calling for was a way to organize the descriptions of the "major" types that had been discovered. How to apply standard terms was treated in a section of the proposal that had the heading "Discussion of the Theoretical Basis of Classification," though what the authors had to say was more methodological than theoretical. Ford and Griffin discussed "style" and its role in the creation of pottery types in the following terms: "Each of these styles consisted of several characteristic elements that tended to cling together through a limited span of time and space. These styles are expressed concretely by characteristic associations of certain specific decorations, shapes, appendages, materials, firing processes, etc. It is the most clearly rec-

O'Brien and Lyman

ognized of these associations that we want to name at this time" (Ford and Griffin 1937:6). This passage suggests type descriptions were extracted from specimens on hand, thus making the types historical accidents.

Ford and Griffin echoed a point that Ford had emphasized earlier: if pottery types were going to help untangle southeastern prehistory, then they had to have more than local significance. "[T]here is no excuse for setting up types on the basis of a few vessels from one site only. The specific combination of features must be repeated at different sites in order to be certain that we are dealing with a pottery style that had a significant part in the ceramic history of the area. In other words, there can be no such thing as a 'type site.' One must have series of sites which present materials clustering about a norm which is to be designated as a type" (Ford and Griffin 1937:7).

This passage makes it fairly clear that by late 1937 Ford was much less interested in documenting the kinds of subtle variation in decoration than he had been when he devised his intricate classification systems. Within a short time he had gone from teasing out minute variation to focusing on a central tendency, or norm. Variation was important only if it was informative about time or space: "Some of the types will doubtless prove to be rather variable. As demonstrated by experience in the Southwest, there is really no profit in labelling variations which can be readily recognized as related to types already set up, unless the variations can be demonstrated to have significance of either an areal or chronological nature. To do so will result only in pointless and confusing 'splitting'" (Ford and Griffin 1937:7). Splitting was acceptable if and only if the new type had time-space significance and could thus do analytical work. Griffin (1938) had begun to emphasize this in his report on the pottery from Norris Basin.

Thus after casting about for several years, trying one method after another to categorize his sherds and worrying about the meaning of types in a cultural sense, Ford found a way out of his predicament: create finite (bounded) units based on variation in decoration that were useful analytical tools and slap names on them, as was done in the Southwest.

It has been suggested by [Preston] Holder, Willey and Ford that names be applied to specific ceramic types in a manner similar to that used in the Southwest. It is felt by these men, however, that an improvement over the Southwestern system of nomenclature could be introduced by the use of a middle term in the name which would usually be a descriptive adjective modifying the last term. Then the first part of the name would be the name of the site from which the type was first adequately described or recognized. The second term would be a modifying or suggestive adjective; the last term would be a "constant" which would designate the broad class to which the type belongs. (Ford and Griffin 1937:7)

A two-day meeting was held in Griffin's office at the Ceramic Repository at the University of Michigan on May 16–17, 1938. Fifteen archaeologists attended the conference—subsequently recognized as the first Southeastern Archaeological Conference (Williams 1960:2). Willey did not attend, but the members thought enough of him that he was appointed, along with Griffin and Ford, to a board of review, the purpose of which was "to control and unify the processes of type selection, naming, and description" (Ford and Griffin 1938:17). The idea of a review board was dropped later that year at the second Southeastern Archaeological Conference (Griffin 1976:26).

Ford and Griffin summarized the meeting in their "Report of the Conference on Southeastern Pottery Typology" (Ford and Griffin 1938[8]),[6] which laid down agreed-on standards for creating pottery types. The authors began the report by noting, "For the purposes of discovering culture history, pottery must be viewed primarily as a reflector of cultural influence" (Ford and Griffin 1938:12), but from that point to the end of the paper, the term *culture* never appeared again except as a modifier to the word *history*. Once culture had been paid its perfunctory due, it was time to get on with the creation of pottery types that would organize the large amount of pottery coming out of the Southeast and help bring chronological and spatial order to it: "[Pottery's] immediate value to the field and laboratory archaeologist lies in its use as a tool for demonstrating temporal and areal differences and similarities" (Ford and Griffin 1938:12). The authors were equally clear on the role of types: "Types should be classes of material which promise to be useful as tools of interpreting culture history. . . . A type is nothing more than a tool" (Ford and Griffin 1938:12).

There was, in Ford and Griffin's eyes, "no predetermined system for arriving at useful type divisions. Types must be selected after careful study of the material and of the problems which they are designed to solve. . . . If divisions in an established type will serve that purpose more accurately, they should be made; otherwise there is little purpose

O'Brien and Lyman

in crowding the literature with types" (Ford and Griffin 1938:12). Perhaps the most important passages in the report are the following remarks about how to actually create a type:

> A type must be defined as the combination of all the discoverable vessel features: paste, temper, method of manufacture, firing, hardness, thickness, size, shape, surface finish, decoration, and appendages. The range of all these features, which is to be considered representative of the type, must be described. By this criteria two sets of material which are similar in nearly all features, but which are divided by peculiar forms of one feature (shell contrasted with grit tempering, for example) may be separated into two types if there promises to be some historical justification for the procedure. Otherwise they should be described as variants of one type.
>
> A type should be so clearly definable that an example can be recognized entirely apart from its associated materials. Recognition must be possible by others who will use the material, as well as by the individual proposing the type. (Ford and Griffin 1938:12)

If we take Ford and Griffin literally, what they proposed as the necessary ingredients of a type created an unworkable system, mired down as it would be in an endless list of types created to encompass the enormous variation in the "discoverable [read *observable*] vessel features" they listed. Griffin (personal communication 1996) stated that the recommendations in the 1938 report derived from a combination of typological procedures (a) used in the Southwest, (b) outlined in two of Carl Guthe's publications (Guthe 1928, 1934), and (c) used by Griffin in his Fort Ancient analysis (Griffin 1943). The heaviest borrowing was from Guthe's suggestions because, Griffin indicated, they were "more flexible." Ford, in both his index system and his analytical-formula system, had already shown the unworkability of such a scheme, meaning that no one wanted to take the time to understand it, let alone memorize it. Such a tool might have its place, but certainly not when one was faced with a tableful of potsherds to sort. Paradoxically, although Ford and Griffin listed a lengthy series of vessel features, the range of which should be considered in developing types, their take-home message was clear: keep the process short and simple; don't create new types unless they are useful for writing culture history.

It is difficult to overemphasize the importance of the Ann Arbor meeting in terms of what it meant for southeastern archaeology. Before we began this project and related ones (Lyman et al. 1997; Lyman et al., eds. 1997; O'Brien and Lyman 1997, 1998), we were under the erroneous impression that the Southeast was a recipient of a pottery-typing system that had been completely worked out in the Southwest to everyone's satisfaction. Nothing could be further from the truth. Although it is true that the binomial system began in the Southwest and was imported by Ford to the Southeast via the Ann Arbor meeting, little was settled in the Southwest by 1938. In fact, the unanimity among southeastern archaeologists reached after the Ann Arbor meeting was unduplicated in the Southwest. Ford must have felt some pride during his attendance at the 1938 Pecos Conference (Woodbury 1993:134), again held at Chaco Canyon, New Mexico, where one of the main topics of discussion was "debating the merits of Kidder's Pecos Classification versus the Gladwin scheme" (Woodbury 1993:134–135). Here is what Donald Brand (1938:14) had to say about that meeting:

> The Chaco conference opened Saturday evening, August 27, with a discussion of the proposed central shard laboratory for Southwestern pottery types. The plan in mind included a committee . . . for the purpose of standardizing terminology of these pottery types. Consensus of opinion on this subject pointed to the fact that such a laboratory or clearing house would be difficult to set up, because of the difficulty of getting cooperation among the various workers in the Southwest. The obvious stumbling block would be in setting up such a standard terminology to which everyone would agree.

That stumbling block might well have been overcome if Jim Ford had worked in the Southwest instead of the Southeast.

Types as Units of Evolution

In the same year that Ford and Griffin published the ceramics-conference report, Ford submitted his master's thesis, *An Examination of Some Theories and Methods of Ceramic Analysis* (Ford 1938a), which was "conducted under the close tutelage of James B. Griffin and Carl E. Guthe" (Griffin, personal communication, cited in Brown 1978:9). The thesis repeated many points Ford had raised in the reports on pottery from Louisiana and Mississippi (Ford 1935c, 1936a) and that Griffin had similarly raised in various reports (e.g., Griffin 1938). For example, Ford argued that the analyst (a) had to be familiar with all the pottery from a region, not solely that from a single locality (to avoid the problem of idiosyncratic types discussed earlier); (b) had to group the specimens into types on the basis of *significant* features; and (c) had to begin forming types at the start of analysis, not at the end. Too often, Ford realized, archaeologists had gone through laborious exercises, dividing and subdividing pottery assemblages based on subtle variations, to the point that there were almost as many "types" as there were sherds. This had happened to Ford when he attempted to categorize the Louisiana-Mississippi sherds, and he wanted to avoid such confusion at all costs, just as he and Griffin had advocated in their proposal and report. If, alternatively, one immediately began sorting sherds into *types* based on historically significant—usually decorative— attributes, one could avoid becoming bogged down in minutiae.

Ford, like Griffin, was interested in types from the standpoint of chronology, but there was another current that ran through his thesis—one that had run through his earlier reports. Ford (1936a) had explored the notion that pottery decoration evolved through time and that slow, gradual change in, say, a design motif could guide the chronological ordering of materials carrying that design. The obvious extension of this notion is to treat pottery types as "genetically linked" (e.g., Wissler 1916b), which Ford did in his thesis. He attempted to demonstrate that if types were created properly, it should be possible to show on the basis of homologous similarity that certain types could be grouped together into what he referred to as "significant idea groups"—the commonsensical, anthropologically based warrant that characterized much of culture history (Lyman et al. 1997). At that point one could conclude that the types within the group were derived from a common ancestor (Ford 1938a:30; see also Ford 1936a). Groups of types then could be linked together at successively higher levels of inclusiveness such as series and wares. These successively higher levels of grouping had but one purpose: "the translation of ceramic history into the history of cultural spread and development" (Ford 1938a:86). Ford (1940), in his review of Harold Colton and Lyndon Hargrave's (1937) "Handbook of Northern Arizona Pottery Wares," noted with approval their use of a hierarchical system of nomenclature for pottery categorization, but he took them to task for their failure to consider "that the division of the material must be controlled by the utility of types for discovering cultural history" (Ford 1940:264).

Brown (1978:11–12) pointed out the obvious flaws in Ford's scheme, not the least of which was how the analyst knows whether he or she has discovered "significant idea groups." This was, of course, an inference founded in common sense and the empirical generalization that different (historically documented) cultures—sets of shared ideas—produced different types of pottery, so different types of pottery must represent different sets of ideas. Ford clearly believed it was possible, through a mix of inductive and deductive reasoning, to discover "general principles which may be expected to underlie the phenomena" (Ford 1938a:5). The basis for the general principles Ford desired had been outlined by Kroeber (1931) a few years earlier, but no one noticed—as Kroeber (1943) later lamented—probably because the model of cultural evolution then being proposed (e.g., White 1943) and soon to be adopted by Americanist archaeologists and anthropologists was of a rather different sort than that originally in Ford's and Kroeber's minds.

One other point raised in Ford's thesis warrants mention. Ford (1938a:11, 68, 69) used the term *serration* to characterize what is more properly termed percentage stratigraphy (Lyman et al. 1998). That is, he used the term as a label for plotting the relative frequencies of artifact types against their stratigraphic provenience, which, as we indicated earlier, is not what seriation comprises. Gordon Willey (personal communication 1998) told us that he and others of Ford's collaborators had to convince Ford that *seriation* was the proper spelling; Ford used *serration* not only in his thesis but also in a letter to Willey written two years later.[7] In his thesis Ford (1938a:11) cited Leslie Spier's (1917) work but apparently did not read it closely because Spier (1917:281) did use the correct spelling. Such errors may seem trivial, but we believe they contributed to Ford's (1962) later misrepresentation of the history of the development of techniques for measuring time by Americanist archaeologists (O'Brien and Lyman 1998).

Decoration Complexes as Analytical Tools

The year Ford submitted his thesis he also submitted an article to the fledgling journal *American Antiquity* entitled "A Chronological Method Applicable to the Southeast" (Ford 1938b[9]). It was an important paper because it established in clear and concise language the methodological assumptions that underlay Ford's subsequent use of pottery to establish chronological control. The paper contains many of the same elements found in his earlier monographs and thesis, but they are presented in clear fashion. Part of the reason for this might have resided in the fact that by the time he wrote the paper he was aware of the attempts of others (e.g., A. V. Kidder, A. L. Kroeber, Nels Nelson, and Leslie Spier) in the Southwest to measure time from variation in artifacts. The paper made clear, like no other he had written previously, that he was interested almost exclusively in time. Ford's pottery types were based solely on decoration; whether a type was "real and significant" was determined by the "repeated occurrence of a certain decoration at separate sites [to ensure the type was not] merely a local variation" (Ford 1938b:262). To be a useful analytical tool, a type must have a distribution across *large* chunks of time and/or space. As he had noted earlier, Ford (1938b:262) indicated that "It probably will develop that not only one but several distinct decorations will be found associated at a number of sites. These associated decorations will be a group of styles that occur together, and form what has been termed a 'decoration complex.'"

For Ford (1938b:262), regularly associated decoration types represented not only a decoration complex but "probably a distinct time horizon. [Once decoration complexes are determined, such] stylistic time horizons that have existed in [an] area may now be logically separated." Although a horizon style might loosely be construed as a synchronic slice of time, this clearly is not true in practice. Ford's decoration complexes, shown as boxes in his Figure 18, were meant to represent "time periods" (Ford 1938b:262). Within the blocks are lines representing the spans of time covered by "definite style types." The particular combinations of these style types denote the position on the continuous time scale where boundaries should be drawn between periods. This criterion for defining period boundaries might seem to differ from that used by southwestern archaeologists, some of whom used the peaks in frequency of occurrence of types to denote "ceramic periods" (e.g., Kidder 1936), but it really doesn't because as Ford (1935c:21) had noted earlier, his decoration complex marker types "statistically dominate to a marked degree" an assemblage of pottery deposited during the span of one complex or "stylistic time period" (Ford 1935c:8). Ford, then, was mimicking Kidder.

The major difference from the Ford of 1936 was that he carefully pointed out that ceramic complexes were temporal units as opposed to cultural units: "it cannot be accepted that these ceramic complexes will represent different cultures or cultural phases. It is entirely possible that two cultures may have used the same pottery, or at different times a culture may have changed its pottery types. What the method attempts to do is to use ceramic decoration, probably the most flexible of the remaining cultural features, as 'type fossils' to distinguish the passage of time" (Ford 1938b:263). Thus, some style types might extend through only a single time period, indicated by the italicized "1's" in his Figure 18, whereas others might extend through two or more periods. Earlier, Ford (1935c, 1936a) had referred to the short-lived types as "marker types"; here he referred to them as "type fossils," the sole purpose of which was to "distinguish the passage of time." Ford ended his paper with the comment that "it is impossible to see, without chronology, how we can ever hope to discover the cultural history of the Indians of the Southeast" (Ford 1938b:263–264).

The Works Progress Administration Excavations

As he had promised Gordon Willey in 1937, Ford returned to Louisiana the following year to initiate a large federally sponsored project, and he hired Willey as part of his research team. Although Ford is rightfully recognized as the director of the WPA-sponsored program that began in Louisiana, he was not the person ultimately responsible for initiating it. Rather, as William Haag (1994:29–30) points out, it was Fred Kniffen who launched the program, although certainly at Ford's urging. Although there were only two officially defined work units within the project—one assigned to Avoyelles Parish and the other to La Salle Parish (Figure 3)—crews eventually branched out to work on sites in at least six other parishes. Excavation procedures usually consisted of trenching and, in the case of mounds, the subsequent peeling back of individual layers to expose horizontal surfaces. At several sites, including Greenhouse in Avoyelles Parish and Big Oak Island in Orleans Parish (Figure 3), hand augers were used to determine not only the depths of deposits but also the relations of the deposits to underlying physiographic features.

It is difficult to write a coherent summary of the WPA period in Louisiana—worse yet to attempt to follow individual lines of discussion—because only a single major excavation report was published during the course of the project. Ford's report on the Greenhouse site, which was excavated in 1938–1939, was not published for a dozen years (Ford 1951), although a short article written during excavation summarized the 1938 work (Ford 1939). Likewise, almost a dozen years passed between the time work was completed in 1940 at the Medora site in West Baton Rouge Parish (Figure 3) and the time of publication (Quimby

1951). Publication of investigations at the Tchefuncte site in St. Tammany Parish (Figure 3), together with those undertaken at other early ceramic-period sites in Vermillion, St. Martin, and Orleans parishes (Ford and Quimby 1945), although not as delayed as Ford's Greenhouse report, did not appear until four to six years after the excavations were completed. The greatest time lag involved the report on the Bayou Goula site (Quimby 1957) in Iberville Parish (Figure 3), which was excavated in 1940–1941. Regardless, Ford and his WPA colleagues *immediately* knew the chronological position not only of the Greenhouse site but of all the sites they worked on in Louisiana (O'Brien and Lyman 1998; contra Lyon 1996), and they knew it as soon as the laboratory crew had washed and labeled the sherds that came in from the field.

We base this statement on what is contained in various letters between Ford and Willey and later between Ford and Quimby (O'Brien and Lyman 1998) and also on what is contained in the one report we didn't mention above, that covering excavations made at the Crooks site in La Salle Parish (Figure 3) in 1938–1939. The report, entitled "Crooks Site, A Marksville Period Burial Mound in La Salle Parish, Louisiana" (Ford and Willey 1940[10]), was the third and final monograph in the Louisiana Department of Conservation's Anthropological Study series and was the only site report published during the course of the WPA program. It is invaluable from a historical perspective because it documents that by June 1940—not quite two years after the WPA excavation program started—Ford had added, not only in casual correspondence but also in print, two new periods—Troyville and Tchefuncte—to the master chronological chart for the Lower Mississippi Valley (Ford and Willey 1940:Figure 2). Primarily on the basis of the new material from Greenhouse and previously excavated material from Troyville (Figure 3), Marksville, and Peck Village, Ford squeezed apart the Marksville and Coles Creek periods and slipped Troyville in between. On the basis of a series of excavations primarily at sites along Lake Pontchartrain in St. Tammany and Orleans parishes, project personnel recognized a series of material—much of it undecorated—stratigraphically below Marksville marker types. This series, which was subdivided into several types (Ford and Quimby 1945), became the basis for creating the Tchefuncte period. Based on the wording in Ford and Willey's (1940) Figure 2, Ford knew that some of the material from Greenhouse, along with some from Peck Village and Troyville, resembled pottery from the Weeden Island complex in northwest Florida, as well as pottery still being referred to as the Deasonville complex. Given who his coauthor was, why *wouldn't* he have made the immediate correlation between the Greenhouse material and the Weeden Island complex? Willey, along with Richard B. Woodbury, had recently completed a manuscript on several sites on the northwest coast of Florida, and although it was not yet published (Willey and Woodbury 1942), Willey knew the chronology.

Ford and Willey suspected that Crooks, the most northerly of all the sites excavated during the WPA project, contained a Marksville-period component. This suspicion was based on the nature of the mounds at the site—one fairly high, conical structure, similar in shape and height to Mound 4 at Marksville, and one much lower mound, again similar to several of the low mounds at Marksville. The resemblance was difficult to miss—a point understated by Ford and Willey (1940:9) when they noted that the excavations at Crooks site were "undertaken because its superficial aspects indicated an occupation during the Marksville period." One didn't need sherds to tell the difference between a flat-topped "temple" mound, which indicated a later, Coles Creek–period, occupation, and a conical Marksville-period burial mound.

Stratigraphic evidence from the two mounds excavated at Crooks produced a pottery sequence that overlapped the one from Marksville, as well as the chronologically earlier sequence from the Tchefuncte sites. Comparisons of type percentages from excavated levels at Marksville and Crooks (their Figure 59) led Ford and Willey to suspect that Crooks was slightly earlier than Marksville. In their comparison of pottery assemblages from Marksville and Crooks, Ford and Willey did not use the material from Setzler's 1933 excavations, which was unavailable (O'Brien and Lyman 1998), but rather sherd samples that were excavated in the spring of 1939 when high water forced the field crew out of the Greenhouse site and up on the bluffs to Marksville.

Several statements made in the Crooks report underscored Ford's reliance on ceramic similarity as a way of inferring phyletic connection and hence temporal closeness. For example, he and Willey noted that in Louisiana "*Marksville Stamped* is ancestral to *Troyville Stamped,* a type of the Troyville period" (Ford and Willey 1940:74)—an evolutionary sequence based on similarities in design between sherds assigned to one type or the other. On the opposite (early) end of the time scale, they linked Tchefuncte-period sherds to those of the succeeding Marksville period:

> Certain features of the Crooks site suggest typological relation to the sites of the Tchefuncte period, which from recent evidences appears immediately to precede the culture of the Marksville stage in southern Louisiana. Five sherds of the Tchefuncte type *Tchefuncte Incised* were found in the fill of the burial platform and in the primary mantle of Mound A. Also some of the material listed as *Marksville Plain* shows very close typological relationship to *Tchefuncte Plain*. This is seen particularly in the fragments with tetrapodal supports, flanged bases, and notched rims. . . . The tendency for the Marksville type *Crooks Stamped* to increase in popularity early in Marksville time, as indicated by stratigraphic studies [their Figure 59], is also of significance in light of the fact that where Marksville period types have been found in Tchefuncte sites, this type is relatively abundant. (Ford and Willey 1940:137–138)

One could quibble with Ford and Willey that the Marksville-period type Crooks Stamped was relatively abundant in Tchefuncte sites (Ford and Quimby [1945] later listed a total of 12 sherds of that type from four of the Tchefuncte sites excavated during the WPA program: Tchefuncte middens A and B, Big Oak Island, and Lafayette Mounds [Figure 3]). However, there is no denying that stratigraphic evidence consistently demonstrated that sherds of Crooks Stamped and of other types they assigned to the Marksville period were superposed over sherds of types assigned to the Tchefuncte period. Of more importance here is the equivalence in Ford and Willey's scheme of periods, cultures, and stages: "Certain features of the Crooks site suggest typological relation to the sites of the Tchefuncte period, which from recent evidences appears immediately to precede the culture of the Marksville stage" (Ford and Willey 1940:137–138). It is clear that by 1940 Ford had completely turned to pottery types—not attributes or features of pottery but pottery types—to define not only periods but also cultures and stages.

Also of interest here is that it was in the Crooks report that Ford issued his first formal statement on diffusion—the topic that so consumed him at the time of his death in 1968 (Ford 1966, 1969). Throughout the 1930s archaeologists debated the direction of movement of

Hopewellian traits: Had Hopewell been a southern phenomenon that moved north—the position favored by Setzler (1933b)—or was it a northern phenomenon that moved south? Ford and Willey (1940:138–143) came down decidedly in favor of the south-to-north position, and the deciding factor was pottery:

> The pottery which is commonly referred to as the Hopewellian ceremonial ware [in the north] is very similar to the utility ware found at Marksville period village sites in Louisiana. The predominating pottery of Hopewellian sites in the various northern centers is a grit-tempered cord-marked ware, commonly referred to as Woodland. So far not a single cord-marked sherd has been found in a Marksville period burial mound, and only a few have been discovered in the top levels of the Marksville village site. However, a cord-marked type, *Deasonville Cordmarked,* is very common in the Troyville horizon, which immediately succeeds the Marksville in Louisiana. (Ford and Willey 1940:139–140)

To set the stage for their scenario, Ford and Willey (1940:141) stated that the "very fact that a Hopewellian complex of features is firmly planted in such widely separated areas as Louisiana, Illinois, Ohio, New York, Michigan, Wisconsin, Iowa, and Missouri, indicates that all of these occupations are not of the same age. The basic resemblances of the culture are so great that it must have been distributed from a common center which consequently would be older." And where was that common center? The presence of large numbers of fancy stamped and incised sherds throughout the Crooks deposit and the absence of cordmarked "utility-vessel" sherds—meaning that Marksville peoples were using fancy pottery for everyday use as well as for grave inclusions—argued strongly for the interpretation "that the cultural influence which all the Hopewellian manifestations had in common, appeared first in the lower Mississippi Valley" (Ford and Willey 1940:141). As it spread north, somewhere "in the comparatively unexplored region between Louisiana and southern Illinois, this stream of cultural influence became thoroughly mixed with Woodlandlike culture, a fact demonstrated principally by the addition of cord-marked pottery" (Ford and Willey 1940:142).

Ford and Willey were not content to view the spread of Hopewellian traits by mere diffusion; rather, they concocted an elaborate scheme based on their reading not only of artifactual evidence but of skeletal evidence as well:

> The scanty physical evidence at hand suggests that the Marksville period saw the introduction into the Lower Valley of a broadheaded people who practiced cranial deformation. The population of the preceding Tchefuncte period was cranially undeformed and dolichocephalic. . . . In several . . . Upper Valley areas, the period of Hopewellian culture saw the introduction of brachycephals into regions formerly held by longheaded peoples.

> Thus it is indicated that the northward drift of Hopewellian was not merely a movement of culture up the valley of the Mississippi; it rather was an actual movement of people. . . . Some mixing of peoples through absorption of the weaker groups may have taken place, and this may be what is indicated by the addition to the cultural complex of Woodland traits. However, since the simple hunting peoples who were being displaced probably had little to offer in the way of complex ceramic art, metal ornaments, smoking pipes, burial practices, or mound construction, it is not surprising that there is as much similarity in certain artifact forms as exists between the widespread manifestations. (Ford and Willey 1940:142–143)

The scenario painted by Ford and Willey (mainly Ford) for the development of Hopewell out of a Marksville base, which itself was seen as a "transplanted" culture—note their statement that the people responsible for Marksville were different from those responsible for the antecedent Tchefuncte—was interesting in how it appeared to accommodate available data. More important, it demonstrates that, in contrast to his earlier explanations of the Peck Village materials as involving diffusion but also at least some in situ evolution, by 1940 Ford was committed heavily to a diffusionist position, complete with population movements when he deemed it necessary. This apparent shift in thinking seems to have two proximate sources—the attempt to account for somatological as well as pottery data and Ford's earlier discarding of his index system of classification that had allowed close monitoring of attributes and their varied combinations and frequencies as types. The system of naming pottery types that grew out of the 1938 Conference on Southeastern Pottery Typology resulted in a focus on types as discrete objects having particular attribute combinations and less attention on particular attributes. These two factors played a major role in Ford's first attempt at synthesis and significantly influenced how he later interpreted the archaeological record.

The 1941 Synthesis

Ford and Willey (1940:143) concluded their report on Crooks by stating, "The accumulated data on eastern archaeology is beginning to yield to synthesis and to outline a story of the distribution of cultures over a large part of the Mississippi Basin. . . . [A]fter a few more years . . . it should be possible to narrate in detail how primitive agriculturalists built a complex and thriving culture in the Eastern United States." By the time the Crooks report was published, they had presented a paper on eastern prehistory at the American Anthropological Association annual meeting (see Willey's foreword to this volume) and were putting the finishing touches on the published version. Although the article, eventually entitled "An Interpretation of the Prehistory of the Eastern United States" (Ford and Willey 1941[11]), was coauthored, Willey (1969:67) later noted that the "vision and the bold conceptions were Ford's; my own role was a very junior one of formal organization and the injection of occasional cautionary and qualifying statements." The article stood as the only real archaeological synthesis of the region until Griffin (1946) published "Cultural Change and Continuity in Eastern United States Archaeology" a few years later.

Ford and Willey's major objective in the paper was to arrange archaeological cultures in spatial and chronological order to show the direction of diffusion of various cultural "features." A series of cross sections, or "chronological profiles, analogous to geological profiles" (Ford and Willey 1941:327), along major river courses illustrated the positions of cultural units—each designated by a "cultural name in common use" (Ford and Willey 1941:331), such as Hopewell—and key archaeological sites. Lines of different slope, bounding what Ford and Willey referred to as "stages," crosscut the profiles, demonstrating the temporal distributions across space of the cultural features under investigation, as well as the differences in rates of trait diffusion and/or population movement, given their view of absolute chronology, which comprised "frankly guesses" (Ford and Willey 1941:331). Their Figure 2—a cross section that runs northward along the Mississippi River from Baton Rouge to southeastern Iowa, then turns eastward to northern Indiana and then north to Grand Rapids, Michigan—shows most cultural features as occurring first in the Lower Mississippi Valley and then spreading northward. The Archaic stage was viewed as ending in the Baton Rouge area between A.D. 700–800 but not in the Grand Rapids area until roughly A.D. 1100. It was succeeded by the Burial Mound I and II stages, the latter lasting much longer in areas north of Vicksburg, Mississippi, than in the region to the south, where the Temple Mound I stage, characterized by rectangular "temple" mounds, began around A.D. 1150.

The Mississippi Valley chronological profile in some respects was the key to understanding eastern prehistory: "The Mississippi River and its tributaries form a great dendritic system of rich agricultural land through the central part of this region, providing an ideal artery for the dissemination of cultures based on an agricultural economy. . . . The heart of the eastern cultural area is the immediate valley of the Mississippi River and the lower portions of the valleys of its tributaries" (Ford and Willey 1941:326). The similarity between Ford and Willey's notion and Clark Wissler's (1916a) culture-area and age-area notions is striking, although Ford and Willey did not acknowledge the similarity or cite Wissler. They referred to Kroeber's (1939) rendition of the culture-area concept, but they did not acknowledge it as the source of their ideas regarding the relations among culture areas, culture centers, and the distribution of culture traits.

Publication of Ford and Willey's synthesis set in concrete the notion Ford had introduced a few years earlier in his *American Antiquity* article and Ford and Willey (1940) had reinforced in the Crooks report: Local diagnostic pottery types were to be used to create periods. Thus, "Cordmarking as a pottery surface treatment [an attribute] arrived in the Lower Mississippi Valley at the close of the Marksville period and achieved the peak of its popularity in the succeeding Troyville period" (Ford and Willey 1941:341), just as certain new decorative elements had originated somewhere other than the locations of his surface collections (Ford 1936a). Similarly, "The Troyville period in the Lower Valley gradually develops into that designated as Coles Creek" (Ford and Willey 1941:345), just as Coles Creek gradually replaced Marksville at Peck Village (Ford 1935c).

Because by this time Ford viewed cultural change as the result not only of diffusion but also of migration, gone were the detailed studies of the phyletic evolution of various attributes of pottery types prominent in his earlier work (e.g., Ford 1936a:262–268). Similarly, diagnostic pottery types might still be analytical units of the ideational sort that were useful for measuring time and space, but reverting to his 1935–1936 mode of thinking, he dropped his earlier disclaimer (Ford 1938b) that pottery complexes did not necessarily represent distinct cultures. As a result his periods took on nontemporal properties and were referred to as "cultures"—a practice begun in the Crooks report.

Confusion has always existed in the literature as a result of the myriad ways in which the term *period* has been used. Part of the confusion may have been fostered by Ford and Willey's (1941; see also Ford and Willey 1940) use of key terms such as *period* and *culture* without explicit definitions. Units such as Coles Creek, Hopewell, Adena, and the like were variously referred to as cultures, horizons, periods, cultural periods, and cultural complexes by Ford and Willey. They referred to units such as Archaic and Burial Mound I variously as stages, cultural horizons, cultural complexes, complexes of traits, and varieties of culture. The potential for conflation of these units was enhanced by their speaking metaphorically of "stages of a culture," such as Coles Creek, when they merely meant later sections of the time span occupied by the cultural unit. Also confusing was their mixing cultural traits—typically types of artifacts, many labeled with an inferred function—that supposedly were diagnostic of a particular cultural unit with those that were not diagnostic of any unit.

The absence of a logical structure of units of various sorts and scales in the synthesis is perplexing in light of the schemes then in use in the Southwest (e.g., Colton 1939; Gladwin and Gladwin 1934), where Willey was educated, and in the Midwest (e.g., McKern 1937, 1939)—schemes that both Ford and Willey were well aware of. We suspect that Ford's braided-stream notion of cultural change and the attempt to explain the archaeological record in ethnological terms resulted in the conflation of observations and units of measurement (his types) with interpretations and explanations. On top of that, any scheme that avoided focusing on time was anathema to Ford's way of thinking.

The Aftermath of the Louisiana WPA Program

One by-product of the Louisiana WPA program—one that certainly is evident in the Ford-Willey paper of 1941—was the abundance of information generated regarding the archaeological record of eastern Louisiana. Ford's sample of sites covered the known range of time as far as the ceramic period was concerned. Tchefuncte, Big Oak Island, and the Lafayette Mounds were selected because they appeared to contain pottery older than the Marksville period. Crooks was selected because it appeared to date to the Marksville period, and Greenhouse because it appeared to be a large Coles Creek–period mound group. Medora and Bayou Goula were identified as candidates to fill the gap between Coles Creek and the historical period (Medora) and to provide material from the historical period (Bayou Goula). From those excavations had come hundreds of thousands of artifacts that provided not only chronological information but also a detailed inventory of elements of the material record other than pottery.

Not all archaeologists were happy with the chronological sequence put forward first by Ford and Willey in the Crooks report and then later refined in other WPA reports. Part of the irritation arose as a result of how most archaeologists of the time chose to view cultural periods—that is, as real things. Not all archaeologists succumbed to this temptation, but enough of them did so that when Ford and Willey (1940) proposed their new sequence of periods in the Crooks report, archaeologists used to the old sequence—the one without Troyville and Tchefuncte that Ford had used in the Peck Village (Ford 1935c) and surface-collection reports (Ford 1936a)—were angered. Maybe they could understand adding a sub-basement (Tchefuncte) beneath the older basement (Marksville), but why in the world would Ford slide a new floor—Troyville—between Marksville and Coles Creek or, later, make matters worse by adding another floor—Plaquemine—between Coles Creek and the historical period (Natchez)? As Gibson (1982:271) put it, both Troyville and Plaquemine were "transitional units . . . carved out of ceramic complexes that had formerly been classified as something else. This confounded opponents who simply could not see how some cultural types could be Marksville or Coles Creek one day and Troyville or Plaquemine the next. These individuals apparently did not share Ford's view of culture as a gradually changing flow of ideas, with any one archaeological site encapsulating those elements which comprised a limited span of an unbroken continuum."

In his report on the Greenhouse excavations, which were completed in the 1930s but not published until 1951, Ford finally answered his critics:

The [WPA] excavation program has made possible the expected subdivision of the rough time scale that I presented in 1936 [Ford 1936a]. New classificatory terms have been interposed between each of the time-period names previously set up, thus giving a more accurate measure of the chronology in verbal terms. Of considerably more importance, however, is the fact that the stratigraphic data have produced a picture of quantitative change of ceramic styles. The sequence of period names "Marksville," "Coles Creek," and "Natchez" presented in 1936 was actually the limit of our control over ceramic chronology in this region at that time. While we were aware that these were probably gross divisions of a changing cultural continuum, this could not be demonstrated and had no more validity than a reasonable assumption deduced from experience with culture history in other areas where details were better known. Some of the ignorance that makes such a neat and "air-tight" classification possible has now been dispelled, and the expanded list of period names can be presented as nothing more than convenient labels for short segments of a continually changing culture history. . . .

This readjustment of the named divisions for the time scale in this area seems to have puzzled a few of the archaeologists working in the Mississippi Valley, even some of those who have been best informed as to the field-work which led to this rearrangement. Complaints have been made that pottery types that were formerly classified as Coles Creek in age are now assigned to the Troyville Period. Discussion develops the opinion that if this latest chronological arrangement is correct then the former must have been in error. The adoption of new names for all the periods in the more recent arrangement may have avoided some, but not all, of this confusion. These serious and earnest seekers after truth really believe that we have discovered these periods and that this is a more or less successful attempt to picture the natural divisions in this span of history. This is obviously an incorrect interpretation. This is an arbitrary set of culture chronology units, the limits of each of which are determined by historical accident, and which are named to facilitate reference to them. (Ford 1951:12–13)

One of those "seekers after truth" was Philip Phillips, who by 1970 was as wedded to cultural discontinuities marking the boundaries of periods as he was when he worked with Ford and Griffin two decades earlier on the Lower Mississippi Alluvial Valley Survey (Phillips et al. 1951). Here's what Phillips had to say about Ford's notion of a Troyville period:

The concept of a Troyville "period" in Lower Mississippi archaeology has been a target of criticism since it was first launched by Ford and Willey (1940). Many students have felt uneasy about it. Others have flatly stated that they could not use it in their particular area of interest. . . . The reasons for this almost universal discomfort lie, I believe, in the peculiar nature of Troyville as an archaeological formulation. . . .

Troyville [appears] to have been sliced out of Coles Creek [and] Marksville (Ford, 1951). But this could only work if there is a clear case of continuity between Marksville and Coles Creek. If there is discontinuity (and who can doubt it in this particular case?), that discontinuity would be automatically incorporated in the new Troyville phase. In my opinion it is, but the fact is not brought out in Ford's (1951) description of the Troyville complex. It seems to be nothing more than a mixture of two separate and distinct complexes. . . .

To conclude this digression into methodology, in setting up Marksville and Coles Creek in 1936, Ford was following the classic method of starting new periods with the appearance of new forms. Later it became necessary to subdivide these periods. If Troyville had continued to be simply a division corresponding to early Coles Creek (as Plaquemine to late Coles Creek), which is about what it was as originally defined by Ford and Willey in 1940, there would have been no difficulty. The "natural" (a word which Ford would not allow me to use) line of separation between the old Marksville and Coles Creek would have remained in place. But Ford's description of 1951, in failing to accent the new forms that belong specifically to Troyville, makes it appear to straddle this line. Actually, he is using a new criterion in marking off chronological divisions. Instead of coinciding with the appearance of new features and the disappearance of old, lines of separation are determined by their maximum occurrence. (Phillips 1970:908–909)

It is interesting that Phillips referred to Ford's break with "classic" archaeological method because in reality he hadn't broken with anything. In the Peck Village report (Ford 1935c) and in the surface-collection monograph (Ford 1936a) Ford did discuss "decoration complexes," and he also discussed the evolution of designs, using the latter to work out a sequence of pottery types. That the fancy Hopewell-like decorations dropped out and were replaced by overhanging lines and other things was certainly noticed by Ford, and he used that relative point in time as a period boundary—Marksville below the boundary,

Coles Creek above it. Given correlations made between decorations and historical tribes, Ford had a convenient late period with which to cap his sequence.

Phillips liked the Marksville–Coles Creek boundary as well as that between the Coles Creek and Plaquemine periods (the latter being presented for the first time in Ford and Willey [1941] on the basis of work at Medora [Quimby 1951] and Bayou Goula [Quimby 1957]). Even Ford's Tchefuncte period (Ford and Quimby 1945) was one of those "intelligible culture-historical units in the usual sense" (Phillips 1970:908). So when did Ford change his mind? The designations Tchefuncte and Plaquemine as periods—both "intelligible" units—appeared in print in 1940 and 1941, respectively, although the notion of a Plaquemine period—what Ford referred to as "a good transitional stage between Coles Creek and Caddoan"—was in the making a year earlier. Tchefuncte even made its initial appearance in the same publication in which Troyville made its appearance—the Crooks report (Ford and Willey 1940). So when did Ford have time to change his approach? Of course, he hadn't; the problem was that Phillips was fooled by, or didn't read closely enough, Ford and Willey's (1940:Figure 2) chronological chart.

If, Phillips later lamented, Ford hadn't toyed with the Marksville–Coles Creek boundary and had simply split the Coles Creek period into three pieces—Troyville (early Coles Creek), Coles Creek (middle Coles Creek), and Plaquemine (late Coles Creek)—everything would have been fine. But he had to go and ram the Troyville period between the two periods with which everyone was comfortable—Marksville and Coles Creek—in the process squashing them into shorter periods by squeezing them against either the solid basement period, Tchefuncte in the case of Marksville, or the equally solid ceiling period, Plaquemine in the case of Coles Creek. Neither of those two anchor periods was going to budge, so Marksville and Coles Creek took the brunt of the force. This apparent "rearrangement" threw everything out of whack because everyone but Ford was looking for discontinuities in the archaeological record. Certainly he might *use* an apparent discontinuity as a means of establishing a period boundary, as he did when he used the disappearance of fancy decoration to end the Marksville period, but he didn't *rely* on them. It just so happened that in almost every case he *had* used highly visible artifacts or designs to mark period boundaries, but this was simply coincidental to his real purpose—to cut up the continuum into a sufficient number of short-term periods so as to allow the measurement of the passage of time and the writing of culture history. That was the method Ford had *always* used.

Concluding Note

Several people in the annals of American archaeology might have had command of such a wide range of data as Jim Ford did, but few of them have been as single-minded as he was when it came to the proper goal of archaeology: Use whatever means are at your disposal to construct a chronology and don't worry too much about the reality of the units you're using or of the time periods you're creating. Ford had this singularity of purpose from the beginning, and although he became more sophisticated methodologically as time went on, his objective never changed. For Ford time was a continuum—a span over which culture changed—and the archaeologist's job was to track that change. The final product was the writing of culture history—literally, a chronicle of the changes that occurred as culture evolved over time.

Ford had demonstrated by 1936 that chronological order could be brought to the archaeological record of the Lower Mississippi Valley, as it earlier had been brought to the record of the Southwest. The archaeological literature since that time, although crediting Ford with being the primary author of that chronology, has completely missed the subtlety and cleverness of how he accomplished what he did. Received wisdom seems to be that Ford started in the historical period and worked his way through time, piggybacking one design complex on another until he had the complete sequence, at which point he used Peck Village as a check on his developmental sequence. In a manner of speaking he did, but this obscures the important point that Peck Village contained no pottery from the historical period. What Ford had was a prehistoric sequence that was represented stratigraphically—Marksville to Coles Creek, with a minor representation of Deasonville alongside Coles Creek—but it all apparently dated to the prehistoric period. This gave him stratigraphic control for one end of the sequence—he already had the other end anchored—but the two ends did not join. Rarely did a "late prehistoric" site—one containing an overwhelming preponderance of either Coles Creek or Deasonville pottery—contain any historical-period sherds, and even when one did, Ford could not be sure that there was not an occupational hiatus. He suspected, however, that geographically overlapping design complexes demonstrated contemporaneity, especially in the northeastern portion of the survey area, where sherds of the Coles Creek decoration complex occurred alongside a few sherds of the Caddo and Tunica complexes.

Ford's thinking grew naturally out of a perspective that culture was a peaceful, braided stream of ideas, each channel containing a more or less unique set of ideas that, upon intersection, exchanged varying amounts of what they were carrying. Cultures might occasionally "invent" new ideas, but this was a commonsensical process observable in the ethnographic record, just as were the more important mechanisms of change such as diffusion, migration, trade, and the like. There was no robust archaeological theory cast in terms of culture change and development, so Ford and his contemporaries borrowed heavily, and often uncritically, from anthropology, occasionally throwing in a term from biological evolution to help express the notion of cultural development. It was this uncritical borrowing that eventually weakened culture history as an enterprise (Lyman and O'Brien 1997; Lyman et al. 1997; O'Brien and Lyman 1998), though the resulting weakness was no reflection on the intellectual and methodological rigor that Ford brought to the construction of a usable chronology for the Lower Mississippi Valley. His articles and monographs on that subject are as important today as they were when they were written and deserve the careful attention of all southeastern archaeologists.

Notes

1. Ford's and Chamber's field notes are on file at the Mississippi Department of Archives and History.

2. References followed by brackets indicate that the work referred to is included in this volume; the number refers to the article number.

3. Application of Ford to the National Research Council (undated but written in early March 1933) (National Anthropological Archives).

4. When we started our research on Ford, we believed that a final report on Setzler and Ford's important excavations at Marksville did not exist; it was this report that Ford wanted to complete just before he died (Brown 1978). A meeting with William Haag revealed that Ethel Ford, after her husband's death in 1968, turned over his field notes and related correspondence to Haag. Based on inspection of the material, we suspected that Ford had at least started to write up the Marksville excavations. Carl Kuttruff found the unfinished manuscript in the archives of the LSU Museum of Natural Science (Kuttruff et al. 1997).

5. The original of this document is unpaginated, and here we use the pagination found in the version reprinted by Stephen Williams in the *Newsletter of the Southeastern Archaeological Conference* in 1960. The original copy had no author or editor listed; Williams (personal communication 1998) told us that when he was planning to reprint the document he had asked Griffin how to cite it in the reprint and that Griffin told him to cite it as Ford and Griffin.

6. Like the 1937 proposal by Ford and Griffin, the original of the report is unpaginated, and we again use the pagination found in the version reprinted in the *Newsletter of the Southeastern Archaeological Conference* in 1960. Willey and Sabloff (1993:149) indicate that "Ford is best described as the editor of this report, [and] there can be little doubt, in view of the phraseology and idea content, that [some statements in the report] are directly from him." Griffin (personal communication 1996) told us that "Ford was the correspondent" and implied that the report was coauthored.

7. Letter from Ford to Willey, May 5, 1940 (LSU Museum of Natural Science archives).

References

Brand, D. P.
  1938   The Chaco Conference, August 27, 28, 29, 1938. *Clearing House for Southwestern Museums, News-letter* 5:14–17.
Brew, J. O.
  1946   Archaeology of Alkali Ridge, Southeastern Utah. *Harvard University, Peabody Museum of Archaeology and Ethnology, Papers* 21.
Brown, I. W.
  1978   James Alfred Ford: The Man and His Works. *Southeastern Archaeological Conference, Special Publication* No. 4.
Collins, H. B., Jr.
  1926   Anthropological and Anthropometric Work in Mississippi. *Smithsonian Miscellaneous Collections* 78(1):89–95.
  1927a Potsherds from Choctaw Village Sites in Mississippi. *Washington Academy of Sciences, Journal* 17:259–263.
  1927b Archaeological Work in Louisiana and Mississippi. *Explorations and Field-Work of the Smithsonian Institution in 1931:* 200–207.
  1932a Excavations at a Prehistoric Indian Village Site in Mississippi. *United States National Museum, Proceedings* 79(32):1–22.
  1932b Archaeology of Mississippi. In *Conference on Southern Pre-History,* pp. 37–42. National Research Council, Washington, D.C.

Colton, H. S.

1939 Prehistoric Culture Units and Their Relationships in Northern Arizona. *Museum of Northern Arizona, Bulletin* 17.

Colton, H. S., and L. L. Hargrave

1937 Handbook of Northern Arizona Pottery Wares. *Museum of Northern Arizona, Bulletin* No. 11.

Dunnell, R. C.

1990 The Role of the Southeast in American Archaeology. *Southeastern Archaeology* 9:11–22.

Evans, C., Jr.

1968 James Alfred Ford 1911–1968. *American Anthropologist* 70:1161–1167.

Ford, J. A.

1935a An Introduction to Louisiana Archeology. *Louisiana Conservation Review* 4(5):8–11.

1935b Outline of Louisiana and Mississippi Pottery Horizons. *Louisiana Conservation Review* 4(6):33–38.

1935c Ceramic Decoration Sequence at an Old Indian Village Site near Sicily Island, Louisiana. *Louisiana Department of Conservation, Anthropological Study* No. 1.

1936a Analysis of Indian Village Site Collections from Louisiana and Mississippi. *Louisiana Department of Conservation, Anthropological Study* No. 2.

1936b Archaeological Methods Applicable to Louisiana. *Louisiana Academy of Sciences, Proceedings* 3:102–105.

1938a *An Examination of Some Theories and Methods of Ceramic Analysis.* Master's thesis, Department of Anthropology, University of Michigan.

1938b A Chronological Method Applicable to the Southeast. *American Antiquity* 3:260–264.

1939 Archaeological Exploration in Louisiana during 1938. *Louisiana Conservation Review* 7(4):15–17.

1940 Review of "Handbook of Northern Arizona Pottery Wares," by H. S. Colton and L. L. Hargrave. *American Antiquity* 5:263–266.

1951 Greenhouse: A Troyville–Coles Creek Period Site in Avoyelles Parish, Louisiana. *American Museum of Natural History, Anthropological Papers* 44(1).

1962 A Quantitative Method for Deriving Cultural Chronology. *Pan American Union, Technical Manual* No. 1.

1966 Early Formative Cultures in Georgia and Florida. *American Antiquity* 31:781–798.

1969 A Comparison of Formative Cultures in the Americas: Diffusion or the Psychic Unity of Man? *Smithsonian Contributions to Anthropology* 11.

Ford, J. A., and J. B. Griffin

1937 [A proposal for a] Conference on Pottery Nomenclature for the Southeastern United States. Mimeographed. [reprinted in *Newsletter of the Southeastern Archaeological Conference* 7(1):5–9]

1938 Report of the Conference on Southeastern Pottery Typology. Mimeographed. [reprinted in *Newsletter of the Southeastern Archaeological Conference* 7(1):10–22]

Ford, J. A., and G. I. Quimby Jr.

1945 The Tchefuncte Culture, an Early Occupation of the Lower Mississippi Valley. *Society for American Archaeology, Memoirs* No. 2.

Ford, J. A., and G. R. Willey

1940 Crooks Site, a Marksville Period Burial Mound in La Salle Parish, Louisiana. *Louisiana Department of Conservation, Anthropological Study* No. 3.

1941 An Interpretation of the Prehistory of the Eastern United States. *American Anthropologist* 43:325–363.

Gibson, J. L.

1982 *Archeology and Ethnology on the Edges of the Atchafalaya Basin, South Central Louisiana.* Report submitted to the U.S. Army Corps of Engineers, New Orleans.

Gladwin, H. S.

1936 Editorials: Methodology in the Southwest. *American Antiquity* 1:256–259.

Gladwin, W., and H. S. Gladwin

1930 A Method for the Designation of Southwestern Pottery Types. *Medallion Papers* No. 7.

1934 A Method for the Designation of Cultures and Their Variations. *Medallion Papers* No. 15.

Griffin, J. B.

1938 The Ceramic Remains from Norris Basin, Tennessee. In *An Archaeological Survey of the Norris Basin in Eastern Tennessee,* edited by W. S. Webb. *Bureau of American Ethnology, Bulletin* 118:253–259.

1939 Report on the Ceramics of Wheeler Basin. In *An Archaeological Survey of Wheeler Basin on the Tennessee River in Northern Alabama,* edited by W. S. Webb. *Bureau of American Ethnology, Bulletin* 122:127–165.

1943   *The Fort Ancient Aspect: Its Cultural and Chronological Position in Mississippi Valley Archaeology.* University of Michigan Press, Ann Arbor.

1946   Cultural Change and Continuity in Eastern United States Archaeology. In *Man in Northeastern North America,* edited by F. Johnson, pp. 37–95. *Robert S. Peabody Foundation for Archaeology, Papers* 3.

1976   A Commentary on Some Archaeological Activities in the Mid-Continent 1925–1975. *Midcontinental Journal of Archaeology* 1:5–38.

Guthe, C. E.

1928   A Method for Ceramic Description. *Michigan Academy of Science, Arts, and Letters, Papers* 8:23–29.

1934   A Method of Ceramic Description. In *Standards of Pottery Description,* by B. March, pp. 1–6. *University of Michigan, Museum of Anthropology, Occasional Contributions* No. 3.

Haag, W. G.

1994   Fred B. Kniffen: As Archaeologist. *Journal of Cultural Geography* 15:27–31.

Kidder, A. V.

1917   A Design-Sequence from New Mexico. *National Academy of Sciences, Proceedings* 3:369–370.

1927   Southwestern Archaeological Conference. *Science* 66:489–491.

1936   Introduction. In *The Pottery of Pecos,* vol. 2, by A. V. Kidder and A. O. Shepard, pp. xvii–xxxi. Yale University Press, New Haven, Conn.

Kniffen, F. B.

1936   A Preliminary Report on the Indian Mounds of Plaquemines and St. Bernard Parishes. In *Reports on the Geology of Plaquemines and St. Bernard Parishes,* by R. J. Russell, pp. 407–422. *Department of Conservation, Louisiana Geological Survey, Geological Bulletin* No. 8.

1938   The Indian Mounds of Iberville Parish. In *Reports on the Geology of Iberville and Ascension Parishes,* by R. J. Russell, pp. 189–207. *Department of Conservation, Louisiana Geological Survey, Geological Bulletin* No. 13.

Kroeber, A. L.

1916   Zuñi Potsherds. *American Museum of Natural History, Anthropological Papers* 18(1):1–37.

1931   Historical Reconstruction of Culture Growths and Organic Evolution. *American Anthropologist* 33:149–156.

1939   Cultural and Natural Areas of Native North America. *University of California, Publications in American Archaeology and Ethnology* 38:1–242.

1943   Structure, Function and Pattern in Biology and Anthropology. *Scientific Monthly* 56:105–113.

Kuttruff, L. C., M. J. O'Brien, and R. L. Lyman

1997   The 1933 Excavations at the Marksville Site by Frank M. Setzler and James A. Ford. Paper presented at the Southeastern Archaeological Conference, Baton Rouge, La.

Lyman, R. L., and M. J. O'Brien

1997   The Concept of Evolution in Early Twentieth-Century Americanist Archaeology. In *Rediscovering Darwin: Evolutionary Theory in Archaeological Explanation,* edited by C. M. Barton and G. A. Clark, pp. 21–48. *American Anthropological Association, Archeological Papers* No. 7.

Lyman, R. L., M. J. O'Brien, and R. C. Dunnell

1997   *The Rise and Fall of Culture History.* Plenum, New York.

Lyman, R. L., M. J. O'Brien, and R. C. Dunnell (editors)

1997   *Americanist Culture History: Fundamentals of Time, Space, and Form.* Plenum, New York.

Lyman, R. L., S. Wolverton, and M. J. O'Brien

1998   Seriation, Superposition, and Interdigitation: A History of Americanist Graphic Depictions of Culture Change. *American Antiquity* 63:239–261.

Lyon, E. A.

1996   *A New Deal for Southeastern Archaeology.* University of Alabama Press, Tuscaloosa.

McKern, W. C.

1937   Certain Culture Classification Problems in Middle Western Archaeology. In *The Indianapolis Archae. o . l Conference,* pp. 70–82. *National Research Council, Committee on State Archaeological Surveys, Circular* No. 17.

1939   The Midwestern Taxonomic Method as an Aid to Archaeological Culture Study. *American Antiquity* 4:301–313.

O'Brien, M. J., and R. L. Lyman

1997   The Bureau of American Archaeology and Its Legacy to Southeastern Archaeology. Paper presented at the 62d Annual Meeting of the Society for American Archaeology, Nashville, Tenn.

1998   *James A. Ford and the Growth of Americanist Archaeology.* University of Missouri Press, Columbia.

1999 *Seriation, Stratigraphy, and Index Fossils: The Backbone of Archaeological Dating.* Plenum, New York.

Phillips, P.
1970 Archaeological Survey in the Lower Yazoo Basin, 1949–1955. *Harvard University, Peabody Museum of Archaeology and Ethnology, Papers* 60.

Phillips, P., J. A. Ford, and J. B. Griffin
1951 Archaeological Survey in the Lower Mississippi Alluvial Valley, 1940–1947. *Harvard University, Peabody Museum of Archaeology and Ethnology, Papers* 25.

Quimby, G. I., Jr.
1951 The Medora Site, West Baton Rouge Parish, Louisiana. *Field Museum of Natural History, Anthropological Series* 24(2):81–135.
1957 The Bayou Goula Site, Iberville Parish, Louisiana. *Fieldiana: Anthropology* (47)2: 89–170.

Rowe, J. H.
1961 Stratigraphy and Seriation. *American Antiquity* 26:324–330.

Setzler, F. M.
1933a Hopewell Type Pottery from Louisiana. *Washington Academy of Sciences, Journal* 23:149–153.
1933b Pottery of the Hopewell Type from Louisiana. *United States National Museum, Proceedings* 82(22):1–21.

Spier, L.
1917 An Outline for a Chronology of Zuñi Ruins. *American Museum of Natural History, Anthropological Papers* 18(3):207–331.

Stirling, M. W.
1932 The Pre-Historic Southern Indians. In *Conference on Southern Pre-History,* pp. 20–31. National Research Council, Washington, D.C.

Watson, P. J.
1990 Trend and Tradition in Southeastern Archaeology. *Southeastern Archaeology* 9:43–54.

Webb, C. H.
1968 James A. Ford, 1911–1968. *Texas Archeological Society, Bulletin* 38:135–146.

White, L.
1943 Energy and the Evolution of Culture. *American Anthropologist* 45:335–356.

Willey, G. R.
1937 Notes on Central Georgia Dendrochronology. *University of Arizona, Tree Ring Bulletin* 4(2).

O'Brien and Lyman

1938   Time Studies: Pottery and Trees in Georgia. *Society for Georgia Archaeology, Proceedings* 1:15–22.

1969   James Alfred Ford, 1911–1968. *American Antiquity* 34:62–71.

1988   *Portraits in American Archaeology: Remembrances of Some Distinguished Americanists.* University of New Mexico Press, Albuquerque.

Willey, G. R., and J. A. Sabloff

1993   *A History of American Archaeology.* 3d ed. Freeman, New York.

Willey, G. R., and R. B. Woodbury

1942   A Chronological Outline for the Northwest Florida Coast. *American Antiquity* 7:232–254.

Williams, S.

1960   A Brief History of the Southeastern Archaeological Conference. *Newsletter of the Southeastern Archaeological Conference* 7(1):2–4.

Wissler, C.

1916a Correlations between Archeological and Culture Areas in the American Continents. In *Holmes Anniversary Volume: Anthropological Essays,* edited by F. W. Hodge pp. 481–490. Washington, D. C.

1916b The Genetic Relations of Certain Forms in American Aboriginal Art. *National Academy of Sciences, Proceedings* 2:224–226.

Woodbury, R. B.

1993   *60 years of Southwestern Archaeology: A History of the Pecos Conference.* University of New Mexico Press, Albuquerque.

1

[1] *From* Excavations at a Prehistoric Indian Village Site in Mississippi

By Henry B. Collins, Jr.
Assistant Curator, Division of Ethnology,
United States National Museum

Archeological work in the Southern States has in the past been confined almost exclusively to the excavation of Indian mounds. As these are the most imposing aboriginal remains of the region, it is natural that they should have received first attention. But there are other remains—Indian village sites—which promise to yield data that will be of considerable value when Southeastern archeology comes finally to be synthesized and interpreted. Due to the obliterating effects of white civilization there is little left to mark the site of the average prehistoric Indian village in the Southeast; usually only a scattering of pottery fragments and stone implements on the surface of the ground. It happens, however, that pottery is the most valuable single criterion for determining the relationships of tribal or regional groups; when, in addition, there is also the possibility of finding traces of ancient habitations, the importance of such village sites is apparent.

In December, 1929, at the request of Dr. Dunbar Rowland, director of the Mississippi Department of Archives and History, I was detailed by the Bureau of American Ethnology to cooperate with the department in the excavation of an old Indian village site in Yazoo County.

No. 2898.—Proceedings U.S. National Museum, Vol. 79, Art. 32. 67125-32-1

The site had been located by Dr. Rowland's representatives, Messrs. Moreau B. Chambers and James A. Ford, with whom I became associated in the work which is outlined below.

Owing to an unusual snowstorm, which left the ground in a soggy condition, we were unable to work longer than a week, but late in the following December we returned and spent three days in further excavation. The site is 1 mile west of Deasonville on the Yazoo City Highway and is located on the property of Mr. Claude H. Pepper in the SE. ¼, sec. 17, T. 11, R. 2 E. We are indebted to Mr. Pepper for granting us full permission to excavate and also to Mr. Homer Beall, of Deasonville, who rendered valuable assistance.

[2] Half a mile to the north of the village site is a small mound and half a mile beyond it five other mounds. Several of these had been dug into by treasure seekers and some were further tested by us. However, they proved to have been constructed of unstratified clay and no artifact of any kind, not even a potsherd, was found. The land on which the mounds are located is low and subject to overflow, so that if village-site material occurred about them it has long since been covered over by alluvial deposits. It is not known, therefore, what relation, if any, the mounds had to the village site in Mr. Pepper's field.

The site of the old village is now a cotton field, in which at intervals young pecan trees have been set out. Excavations were confined to the section of the field where potsherds and flint implements were most plentiful, about 150 feet south of the road and 100 to 200 feet west of a 6-foot bank which marks the dividing line between the slightly higher land on which the village was located and the lower land bordering a small near-by stream known as Ellison's Creek. At the first place we dug, the village refuse did not extend below the plowed ground, although a veritable maze of post holes was found sunk into the undisturbed yellow clay subsoil. Some of these postholes were arranged in lines but the ground was so honeycombed with others seemingly placed at random in every possible position that we were not able in the short time at our disposal to extend the excavation sufficiently to see what had been the outline of the structures represented.

[12] Pottery

Potsherds were found in abundance in the trenches and post holes and on the surface of the plowed ground. In order to determine the relative proportions of the various types of ware represented, a surface collection was made by picking up every sherd on and between three cotton rows for a distance of about 100 feet. This resulted in a collection of 398 sherds, as follows:

238 undecorated.
57 cordmarked.
50 painted.
47 incised.
4 punctate.
1 roulette or stamped.
1 small knob or rim.

These surface sherds were for the most part small, having been for many years plowed over or trampled upon. A larger collection, selected on the basis of decoration or shape, was made both from the trenches and the surface and has been utilized in the following description of the decoration, shape, paste, and color of the ware. There was no distinction between the sherds from different parts of the site; the same mixed type of pottery was found on the [13] surface, in the three house rings, in the post holes, and in the various sections of House Ring No. 1. The characteristics of the various types of ware will be described below in the order of their occurrence. They are also given in summarized form in Table 1.

Only two complete vessels (pl. 1, *a*, *b*) have been found at the site; *a* was found in trench C, House Ring No. 1, and *b* was presented to the Mississippi Department of Archives and History by Mr. Homer Beall, who had dug it up a few years previously.

Undecorated ware.—Vessels of undecorated ware were either rounded bowls, of which Plate 1, *a*, is an example, or steeper-sided jars.

[15] The paste is coarse and is tempered with pulverized potsherds; only an occasional sherd shows a shell tempering.

In color the paste is mainly of two shades, gray to black or reddish; firing has generally produced on the outside of the vessel a drab gray or light brown color. Both surfaces are polished to some extent. On those sherds in which the paste is of a dark color the polishing of the inner surface often produced a deep black, while the outer surface, subjected to more intense heat in firing, had been burned to a gray or brown color.

Cord-marked ware.—Vessels with cord-marked exteriors were mostly

[14] Table 1. Characteristic Features of Deasonville Pottery

Kinds of Wares	Shapes of Vessels	Paste			Surface			Rims	
		Texture	Color	Temper	Finish	Color	Decoration	Shape	Decoration
Undecorated	Bowls and jars	Coarse	Gray, black, or reddish	Pulverized potsherds	Usually smooth	Drab gray or light brown		Straight or slightly incurved	Occasionally a line on top
Cord marked	Jars	ditto	Buff, gray, or black	ditto	Cord marked	Light brown to dark gray	Cord impressions	Straight or slightly incurved (seldom everted)	
Painted	Conical and rounded bowls	Fine	Blue-gray	Pulverized mussel shells	Smooth	Red, white, and gray	Alternating red and white bands and scallops	Enlarged; slightly overhanging on both sides	Usually painted red
Incised (rim only)	Bowls and jars	Coarse	Gray, black, or reddish	Pulverized potsherds	Usually smooth	Gray or brown	Band of lines below rim	Straight or slightly incurving	Occasionally a line on top
Incised (body of vessel)		Usually fine; some porous	Light brown or gray	Pulverized mussel shells (some vegetable fiber)	Somewhat rough	Buff or cream	Straight and curved lines over body of vessel	Straight, incurved, and everted	Looped handles
Punctated		ditto	ditto	ditto	ditto	ditto	Punctations, usually in bands	Usually everted	ditto
Roulette or stamped		Fine	Gray	Pulverized mussel shells			Rouletted or finely stamped area enclosed by deep lines		

high, straight-sided jars, although a few lower vessels with rounded sides were also represented.

Most of the sherds are light brown in color, while others range from light gray to almost black. The inner surface is smooth and shows a black polish where the paste is of a dark color.

As in the case of the plain ware, the paste is coarse and contains ground potsherds as tempering material. In color the paste is buff, gray, or black.

The surface decoration, if it may be called such, was produced usually by means of a cord-wrapped paddle; a few sherds bear impressions of woven textiles. Typical sherds are shown in Plate 2.

Painted ware.—The outstanding type of decorated pottery bears bold patterns in bright red and white pigment applied to both surfaces of the vessel. (Pl. 3.)

The most common shape was a graceful jar or bowl with wide mouth and straight sides which tapered down to a small flat circular base. Shallow rounded bowls appear also to have been present, to judge from the shape of some of the sherds, although no rounded bottoms were actually found. The rim was usually formed of a more or less rounded coil of clay, overhanging on both sides. Almost invariably a line had been incised just below the overhanging rim, sometimes on one side, sometime on both sides. Other rims are merely somewhat enlarged, while a few are straight. All of the rounded rims are painted red.

In contrast to the plain and cord-marked ware the paste is of a smooth, fine texture, being tempered with finely pulverized mussel shells; its color is a light bluish or steel gray.

The decoration, as far as could be judged from the sherds, was mainly of two types. Most commonly there was a red center at the base of the vessel from which radiated red panels, narrow at the bottom and increasing in width toward the top. These were separated by fields of pure white or bluish gray. The white and red combination was the prevailing one, both colors having been applied as a heavy slip. The blue-gray color, which appears less [16] frequently, was not applied as a slip but was produced by polishing the fine-textured blue-gray paste. The other principal decoration consisted of broad white scallops along both sides of the rim, with the rest of the surface bearing a plain red slip. In some sherds the red slipped decoration was replaced by a light brown or chocolate.

Incised ware.—In the numerical distribution of the pottery types given on page 12, sherds bearing an incised decoration are for convenience all grouped together. There are, however, two clearly differentiated types into which this incised ware falls. First is a type of pottery, represented almost entirely by rim sherds, which in color, paste, and tempering material is identical with the undecorated ware previously described. It differs only in having one to four—usually two—parallel incised lines encircling the vessel immediately below the rim. Some of the sherds have also a line incised along the top of the rim. Most of the lines below the rim are somewhat deep and were made by trailing a sharp stick held straight against the side of the vessel. (Pl. 4, *d-f, k-m.*) In some cases, however, the implement had been held with the point toward the rim, resulting in a somewhat wider and beveled line, deeper at the top and having an "overhanging" appearance. (Pl. 4, *a-c, g-i.*) The possible significance of this type of decoration will be referred to later.

The body of the vessel below the rim bears no other ornamentation, so it may be regarded as certain that a number of the undecorated sherds, which are identical in color, surface finish, paste, and tempering, were from vessels having this simple incised decoration restricted to the region of the rim.

The shapes of the vessels were usually shallow rounded bowls, although a few steeper-sided jars were represented.

The second variety of incised ware (pl. 5) differs in paste, color, and tempering material, as well as surface finish and decoration. The incised lines, instead of being applied in parallel bands and only to the rims of vessels, are usually curvilinear and are applied over the surface of the vessel generally. Plate 1, *b*, one of the two whole vessels found, is an example of this type.

The color of the paste is usually a light brown or gray, to which firing has brought a more uniformly buff or cream color. The paste is of two kinds, most commonly smooth and fine textured with a shell tempering, and less frequently soft and somewhat porous, having had apparently a tempering material, probably vegetable, which had been mostly destroyed in firing.

The surface finish is somewhat rough, not having been polished like the incised ware first described. In that type the surface was [17] relatively smooth, because polished, even though the paste and tempering material was coarse. Here the reverse is true, for the surface appears rough through lack of polishing, even though the paste and tempering is mostly of fine texture.

The sherds of this type are small and few in number, so that nothing can be learned of the vessel shapes aside from the vase shown on Plate 1.

Punctate decoration.—In paste, tempering material, and color this ware is identical with that just described.

Most of the punctations are arranged in bands, outlined by deeply incised lines. (Pl. 6.) The indentations are round, conical, or elongate, depending on the shape of the point used.

Roulette or stamped decoration.—Only two sherds of this type were found in addition to the one small example from the numbered surface collection.

The paste is smooth, gray in color, and is shell tempered.

The decoration consists of very finely stamped or rouletted areas in bands, enclosed by deeply incised broad lines. (Pl. 5, *n*.)

Effigy head.—No effigy heads were found in addition to the one from the surface collection. This was a crudely modeled head of an animal which had been applied to the rim of a vessel.

Rim knobs and handles.—On Plate 7 are shown examples of the handles and lugs that were attached to some of the vessels. These appear to have been restricted to vessels in which the paste was either somewhat porous or coarse and shell tempered. The surface lacks a polish and the decoration consists of incised lines (of the second variety described above) or of punctations.

Distribution of the pottery types.—The most important immediate problem of Southeastern archeology is to establish a basis for a chronology of prehistoric sites. From the fragmentary nature of the evidence this will have to be for the most part a disjointed and patchwork chronology, far less perfect and comprehensive than that which has been worked out in other areas, notably in the Southwest, where ruins of all periods are well preserved and where at times even such perishable materials as basketry, textiles, and wood are found, and where in addition there still exist native tribes whose customs, social structure, and economic activities continue along much the same lines as those of their direct ancestors, the builders of the prehistoric remains in the same region. The task of working out a chronology for Southeastern archeology will be much more difficult and there is therefore all the more reason for painstaking examination and study of such aboriginal remains as are still available. The obvious beginning toward such a study is to determine wherever possible the nature of the remains left behind by the historic occupants of the area, most of whom have long since [18] disappeared or been removed to reservations. Practically, this means locating exactly from historical sources the sites of old Indian villages and collecting what may be available for comparison with similar material from earlier sites of unknown age. The most valuable material for this purpose is pottery; and broken fragments, if sufficiently numerous, are very nearly as useful as whole vessels, or even more so if the latter should not happen to include the entire range of types present. In 1925, by utilizing the pioneer work of Henry S. Halbert, I was able to locate and make collections from certain historic Choctaw village sites in eastern Mississippi.[7] The result was the determination of the historic Choctaw type of pottery, on the basis of which comparison with pottery from sites of unknown age is now possible. A few years later similar work was undertaken for the Mississippi Department of Archives and History by Messrs. Moreau B. Chambers and James A. Ford, who were able to locate certain historic Natchez and Tunica sites in western Mississippi. In a forthcoming paper by James A. Ford the potsherds from these historic sites as well as those from neighboring older sites are to be described. Having participated to some extent in locating the Natchez site and having had an opportunity to examine the other materials found by Ford and Chambers, as well as the manuscript referred to, I am able to make use of these additional data as comparative references in the following brief summary.

Red and white painted ware was the most characteristic single type of decorated pottery found at the Deasonville site. Its occurrence elsewhere in the State seems restricted to the Mississippi River section, where it has been reported by Moore from Warren, Bolivar, and Tunica Counties.[8] At these sites Moore also found vessels of the same shape as some of the red and white painted bowls from Deasonville—inverted truncated cones with small circular bases, low sloping sides and very wide mouths.[9] Vessels bearing bold designs in red and white have been found more frequently in Arkansas, in Phillips, Lee, Crittenden,

7. Collins, Henry B., jr., Potsherds from Choctaw Village Sites in Mississippi. Jour. Wash. Acad. Sciences, vol. 17, No. 10, pp. 259–263, May 19, 1927.

8. Moore, Clarence B., Some Aboriginal Sites on Mississippi River. Jour. Acad. Nat. Sciences, Philadelphia, Vol. XIV, pp. 383, 387, 393–395, 412.

9. Moore, Clarence B., op. cit., pp. 401, 409–410, 441, 458, 476.

and Mississippi Counties along the Mississippi River, and they are also found on the St. Francis, Arkansas, and Red Rivers.[10] European material was found by Moore at several of the sites from which came the red and white painted pottery.[11]

[19] In describing the incised ware from Deasonville, mention was made of the fact that some of the lines encircling the rims of vessels otherwise undecorated were applied in such a way as to have an "overhanging" appearance; that is, the lines were deeper at the top than at the bottom. (Pl. 4, *a-c, g-i.*) This is a style of decoration which Ford and Chambers have found to be characteristic of certain prehistoric sites in western Mississippi as distinguished from near-by historic sites of the Natchez and Tunica. The presence of this type at Deasonville is therefore of interest, although its full significance can not be understood until its entire range and the relative position it occupies elsewhere is known.

In this same connection it should also be noted that the Deasonville sherds contained no examples of historic Choctaw ware, which is characterized by straight or curving bands of very fine lines applied with a comblike implement;[12] or of Tunica ware in which the decoration consists of somewhat enlarged rims bearing indentations or scallops together with a single encircling line along the top. Typical Natchez pottery with its usually polished surface and scroll or meander decoration is also absent at Deasonville, although some of the incised ware of the second variety (rough surfaced, shell tempered, and sometimes soft and porous) bears a curved line ornamentation of this general type. (Pl. 5)

The Deasonville collection includes three sherds, which despite their small number are of especial interest. These bear a decoration consisting of finely stamped or rouletted bands outlined by deeply and broadly incised lines. (Pl. 5, *n.*) I have found this style of decoration at Pecan Island, in southwestern Louisiana, and Moore has found it in Sharkey

10. Moore, Clarence B., Antiquities of the St. Francis, White, and Black Rivers, Ark. Jour. Acad. Nat. Sciences, Philadelphia, Vol. XIV.

Idem, Some Aboriginal Sites on Red River, ibid., Vol. XIV.

Idem, Certain Mounds of Arkansas and Mississippi, ibid., Vol. XIII.

11. Idem, Certain Mounds of Arkansas and Mississippi, pp. 513, 525.

Idem, Some Aboriginal Sites on Mississippi River, p. 431.

12. Collins, Henry B., jr., op. cit.

County, Miss., on the Mississippi River.[13] It is also a design which occurs typically on the pottery of the highly developed Hopewell culture of Ohio.

Study of the potsherds from Deasonville fails to reveal any clues which might be of value as showing the chronological position of the site beyond the mere fact that it is prehistoric. Thus the absence of pottery types definitely attributable to the historic Choctaw, Tunica, or Natchez (as well as the absence of metal or other European material), and the presence of another type which at other Mississippi sites appears just as definitely prehistoric, places the Deasonville site in the latter category. This is a conclusion which might have been expected in view of the fact that Deasonville is in an area not known to have been inhabited by any historic tribe but lies between the territories formerly occupied by the Choctaw on the east and the Tunica and Yazoo on the west.

[20] As for the spatial distribution of the ceramic types represented, all that can be said is that the affinities of those which are sufficiently distinct to have a correlative value appear to be with the West—western Mississippi, Arkansas, Louisiana—rather than with Alabama or Florida. While it is to be regretted that the conclusions arrived at are so indefinite, the nature of the material available for comparison precludes for the present any more exact interpretations. We must know, for instance, much more about the geographic range of the various types of Southeastern pottery and the relative position occupied by each, and especially we must know which types are found associated with European material and which types are never found in such association. Eventually, no doubt, these things will be known and it will be a comparatively simple matter to assign newly found material to its proper position. Meanwhile, the Deasonville sherds are presented descriptively until such time as interpretations may be in order.

---

13. Moore, Clarence B., Certain Mounds of Arkansas and Mississippi, p. 587.

Plate 1

Vessels from the Deasonville site

Collins

Plate 2

Potsherds showing cord-marked exteriors

Plate 3

Potsherds with bold designs in red and white pigment

Plate 4

Potsherds with incised lines at rims

Plate 5

Potsherds showing incised decoration over body of vessel

Collins

Plate 6

Potsherds with punctuate ornamentation

Plate 7

Examples of handles and lugs on pottery

2

[8] An Introduction to Louisiana Archeology

By J. A. Ford
Louisiana State University

Contrary to popular belief, the history of the region included within the present bounds of the State of Louisiana begins not with the discovery of the Mississippi River, but long before that time, even before the dawn of the Christian Era. The pre-Columbian inhabitants of Louisiana and neighboring southern states were neither the "wild and woolly" Indians of ten-cent novel fame, nor the romantic people of the *Leatherstocking Tales*. They were farmers who lived in villages situated on favorable spots on the waterways and tilled their laboriously cleared fields of corn, beans and pumpkins. Wild game formed only a part of their diet, and they had no domestic animal except the dog. Slaves to their religion, they built vast earthworks for temple sites and monuments to the dead. Some of these rival the pyramids of Egypt in size. Protective fortifications encircling many of the villages indicate interludes of warfare, probably struggles between the different groups for the more favorable sections of territory. In many ways their culture might be compared with that of the European barbarians in the days when Julius Caesar was conquering Gaul.

Ruins of old Indian villages, fortifications and burial sites are scat-

House built on Indian mound which is located on the right bank of Lake La Rose. This stream lies in the eastern portion of St. Martin Parish. This photograph was taken during the flood season.

tered along the borders of the streams and lakes of Louisiana in almost unbelievable numbers. These indicate a fairly dense ancient population and occupation over a long period of time.

The paucity of present information concerning these dwellers in Louisiana is partially due to the meager records left by early white explorers and settlers, but lack of knowledge of their history is due more to the ignorance of the Indians themselves. This lack of knowledge resulted, of course, from absence of any form of writing. It is true that traditional tales of tribal origin and movements were passed from generation to generation, but little or no reliance may be placed on them. While some phases of these legends may have been founded on fact, in their entirety they have taken on such a mythological cast that the truth is very obscure.

Thus the student in beginning the labor of reconstructing the fascinating past hinted at by the great earthworks and extensive village sites must start with the authentic accounts of the early explorers. The first step in recovering this lost history is to locate by means of the

Another photograph of the Indian mound shown in preceding photograph. Photograph taken during the low water season.

early descriptions and [9] maps the sites inhabited at the time of first contact with Europeans. From this point the story may be followed back into the unknown past by the aid of one of the dominant axioms of culture: it is always changing. It should be understood that by "culture" is meant the component of the customs and styles of languages, handicrafts, arts and ceremonials practiced by any particular group of people at any one time. Culture is in reality a set of ideas as to how things should be done and made. It is in a continuous state of evolutionary change since it is constantly influenced both by inventions from within and the introduction of new ideas from without the group. Such change taking place in our modern culture is called "progress". It may not in the strict sense of the word always be progress, nevertheless, the changes in the different elements of our modern civilization are constantly occurring with varying speed. Perhaps the best present illustration of one of the more rapidly changing modern cultural elements is the way in which women's dresses, though all slavishly alike at any one time, change from season to season.

This principle of the gradual change of culture with the passage of

Small Indian mound along Bayou Garafier, a stream which flows out of Lake La Rose. Photograph taken during flood period in the Atchafalaya basin.

time applies quite directly to the lives of the ancient Indians of Louisiana, and clear indications of it may be noted by a study of the articles they have left behind them.

By examining the sites of their prehistoric towns are found mounds, erected as part of the religious ceremonialism and which often served as cemeteries for the dead; remains of houses in which the people lived; and the midden deposits—the village garbage dumps—where broken pottery and worn out flint knives, arrowheads, axes, etc., were deposited. All of these man-made things were subject to the principle of constant change, hence those on any one site are *more or less* peculiar to the time that produced them.

It is apparent that if the different forms of the various implements, houses, mounds, etc., used during time covered by one of these ancient cultures can be arranged in the sequence in which they occurred, it is possible to determine the relative ages of the various old towns, not in the accurate terms of years but in relation to one another. The origins, migrations, developments and final disposition of the different groups of people by this means are made apparent. Thus the prehistory of the area is outlined. Such an arrangement of cultural elements, called a

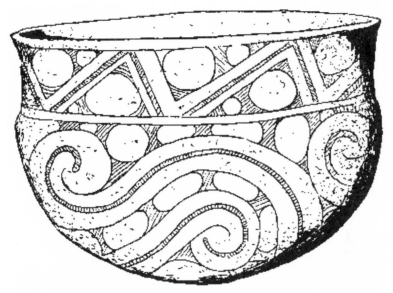

Fig. 1. A pottery vessel of the historic Caddo type from the "Fish Hatchery"
site near Natchitoches, La.

chronology, is one of the primary purposes of archaeological research.
The simplest means of arranging such a chronology is to select some
one element of culture which appears commonly on ancient sites and
which was subject to rapid change in form. After the chronology of this
one element is discovered, it serves as a "yardstick" for the remaining
elements of the culture history.

On prehistoric villages in Louisiana and neighboring southern states,
the most common of the remaining elements of the old cultures, and
fortunately one which appears to have been subject to fairly rapid
change, is the pottery found in graves and in the village garbage heaps.
As the chronology of this key culture element is easier to discover by
working from the known back into [10] the unknown past, the first
task becomes that of discovering the types of pottery and pottery decorations used by the tribes that came in contact with the whites.

Several of the historic tribal pottery types have already been discovered. That of the Caddo Indians occupying the northwestern part of
the state was definitely determined at the "Fish Hatchery" site near
Natchitoches by Mr. Winslow Walker, of the Bureau of American Ethnology, in 1931. (See *Journal of the Washington Academy of Sciences*,
Vol. XXIV, No. 2, Feb. 15, 1934, pps. 99-104.) This ware is characterized by incised lines which form elaborate scroll and meander designs

and by a profuse use of spurs and delicate cross-hatching (Figure 1). This pottery is identified as historic by implements found accompanying it which were traded to the Indians by the Europeans.

Pottery characteristic of the Natchez tribe was discovered at a village near Natchez, Mississippi, by Mr. M. B. Chambers, of the Mississippi Department of Archives and History, in 1929. This ware was similar to, but not identical with, the Caddo. It is ornamented with graceful scrolls and meanders formed by bands of three lines (Figure 2). A definite date of 1720 is indicated for this pottery not only by the early descriptions of the Natchez villages, but by the quantity of French trade objects accompanying the finds.

Thus by identification of the historic pottery a basis is established for a chronology. Comparative studies show, however, that although the Caddo had occupied the territory where they were first described longer than had the Natchez, both cultures at comparatively recent times had displaced others which had entirely different pottery designs and which very likely represented an entirely different people.

The people of this pre-Natchesan and Caddo pottery that disappeared before the historic period merely for convenience are called "Coles Creek" people. They appear to be descended, culturally at least, from a still older group of people known as "Hopewell".

Probably it is because of their relative antiquity that these "Hopewell" people are particularly interesting. At one time they occupied the entire valley of the Mississippi from Wisconsin to the mouth of the Mississippi River. All of this peculiar culture had disappeared, however, before the discovery of North America by Europeans. "Hopewell" was discovered and named in 1908 in southern Ohio. There it appeared to be so different from and superior to the surrounding rather sombre cultures that it was decided connection must lie, as certain indications pointed, down the Mississippi Valley. At Marksville, Louisiana, a village site of this culture was discovered and excavated during the summer of 1933 by Mr. Frank Setzler of the United States National Museum. This excavation showed that the people [11] living there during the time of the ancient "Hopewell" culture were agriculturists. They occupied square semi-subterranean houses in a village which was enclosed on three sides by earth embankments, probably surmounted by a wooden stockade, and on the fourth side by the steep bluffs bordering an old steam bed. Large rectangular earthworks strangely reminiscent of the stone pyramids of Central America were erected as sites for their ceremonial buildings. Some of the dead, probably officials of the

Fig. 2. Vessel used by Indians of the Natchez Tribe about 1720.

group, were deposited in a large log-roofed vault buried beneath a conical mound twenty feet high. Copper from the Lake Superior region, galena from the mountains of Arkansas, conch shells from the Gulf of Mexico—all were brought to serve the needs of the people living in the old town near Marksville. Pottery smoking pipes of a typical platform or monitor design were in common use. The pottery was tastefully decorated with conventionalized birds and geometric figures formed by line-enclosed bands of rouletting (Figure 3).

Surface indications have identified a number of other villages of "Hopewell" age in both Mississippi and Louisiana. Although their relative antiquity is indicated by studies of cultural history, the significance of the peculiar fact of their frequent occurrence on oxbow lakes, old abandoned stream channels, is not yet understood.

This brief outline of part of Louisiana's prehistory has been determined within the past few years. It is still only partially substantiated. There are numerous points which are yet uncertain, and many more gaps remain to be filled in. No answer can yet be made to the primary questions: From where did these people come? Why? What happened to them?

Fig. 3. A pottery vessel from the site at Marksville, La., typical of the "Hopewell" culture in the South.

Systematic archaeology in the southeastern states is yet in its infancy. The spectacular remains of southwestern America have occupied the attention of the competent investigators for the most part. Consequently the prehistory of that region is not only known in terms of culture periods, but through recent studies of the annual growth of tree rings, most of the sites can be given definite calendrical dates. However, during recent years, scientific research in archaeology of the southeast has taken great forward strides. Not only are the large national institutions becoming actively interested in the field, but several of the state universities have established museums and departments for systematic investigation and the teaching of prehistory.

Constructive field research is at present under way at a site on the south shore of Lake Ponchartrain. This project was initiated by the Louisiana Department of Conservation in January, 1934, and made possible through the Civil Works Administration of Louisiana. In September of 1934 the Department of Conservation transferred the supervision of the project to the School of Geology of Louisiana State University and such work is being made possible through the Emergency Relief Administration. It is hoped that a state-wide survey to locate and study the state's aboriginal remains in a systematic and thorough manner may be undertaken soon.

The conservation of Louisiana's prehistoric monuments is fast becoming a pressing question. Through cultivation, road-building, clearing with subsequent erosion and commercial "pot hunting", the Indian remains are fast disappearing. Although most of the civilized countries have regulations concerning the preservation of antiquities, there is none in America. However, many old town sites with their accompanying monuments have been set aside in most states by either the Federal or state governments for preservation as parks.

The research of the archaeologist is often compared with the reading of a book written in hieroglyphics. The scientific excavation of an old site is comparable to opening carefully and reading one of the musty pages. Careless or incompetent destruction of a mound or village site tears a page from the story that may never be replaced or read.

(Figures one and three sketched by permission of the United States National Museum.)

3

[33] Outline of Louisiana and Mississippi Pottery Horizons

By J. A. Ford
Louisiana State University

The most promising means to an understanding of the story of the lower Mississippi River Valley before 1700, the beginning of reliable documented history, lies, as explained in an article in the January issue of the *Conservation Review*,[1] in the studies of styles of pottery made, used, broken and cast aside as garbage on the sites of the old towns. By discovering the time sequence of the various modes of ceramic ornamentation, a scale or chronology is outlined by which old ruins may be dated, movements of people and of culture be detected, and eventually it is hoped, the origins of the American Indians and their peculiar cultures may be known. Like the geological chronology, this scale can be approximated only in terms of periods of years.

It is not the present purpose to detail the theories and the stages of the research which for the past few years has been directed toward this end in both Mississippi and Louisiana, but rather to present an outline of the indicated results in such a way that those who are suffi-

1. Ford, J. A., "An Introduction to Louisiana Archeology," Louisiana Conservation Review, *La. Dept. Consv.*, Vol. 4, Jan., 1935, pp. 8-11.

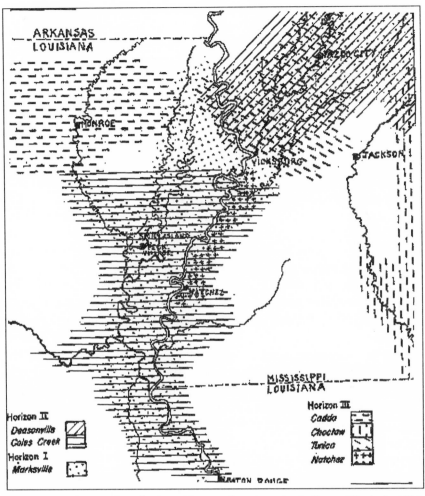

Fig. 1. Map Showing Distribution of Pottery Complexes in the Lower Mississippi Valley

ciently interested may by gathering a few dozen decorated potsherds determine for themselves with fair accuracy the relative antiquity of ancient towns. It frequently occurs that historians, attempting to find aboriginal towns mentioned in early documents go blithely forth and select the nearest impressive group of mounds, when an elementary knowledge of the archaeological chronology would show from the material occurring on the site that it had been abandoned long before the voyage of Columbus.

The sites within the areas, as shown on the map (Fig. 1), divide themselves according to the pottery decorations found on them into seven broad groups called "complexes". Some of these complexes were contemporaneous in different areas, hence they all fall into three main time divisions as follows:

III. Youngest. Used about 1700 and immediately before. Choctaw, Natchez, Tunica and Caddo. These complexes are named after the historic Indian tribes with which they have been identified.

II. Intermediate. Did not extend to historic times, and were mostly abandoned before the historic types came into vogue. Coles Creek and Deasonville. Named for type sites.

I. Oldest. Abandoned before the intermediate complexes became predominant. Marksville. Named for type site.

There are indications that several of these complexes extend far outside the regions indicated on the map, but the details of their [34] relations there must be the subject of future field work.

These "ceramic complexes" are so called from the fact that they consist of a small group of often unrelated pottery design types which were fashionable in the same region at the same time. In like manner our present clothing complex consists of certain types of clothing for men's business and evening wear, and peculiar costumes for boys, women and girls at different times of the day. These specific types make up the present clothing complex of the region; they were somewhat different last year, and next year's styles will incorporate more changes.

Excepting the Caddo and Choctaw complexes which extended up to the historic period, but for whose exact connections with the past there is yet insufficient data, the time sequence of the Lower Mississippi Valley design complexes are shown in the graph (Fig. 2). Time is represented vertically with the oldest complex, the Marksville, at the bottom, and the recent or historic Tunica, Caddo, Choctaw and Natchez cutting the horizontal line near the top. This line denotes the year 1700 A.D. These latest native pottery styles died not long after this date as the Indians adopted the white man's trade utensils and the making of pottery became a lost art.

How far into the past this scale extends is a question which is impossible to answer satisfactorily at present. Various estimates of from 800 to 2000 years have been made for the Hopewell Culture with which the Marksville pottery complex is identified. These are admittedly guesses.

At the earliest period considered in this chronology, the Marksville complex of pottery designs held sway throughout the entire area. The

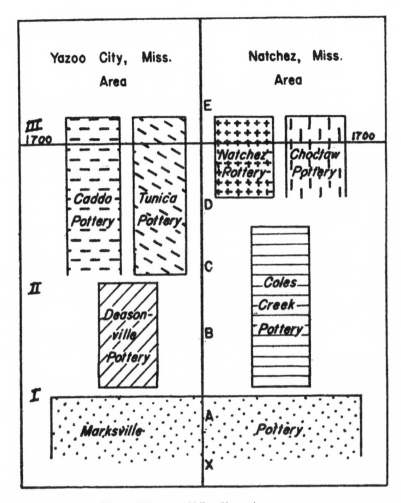

Fig. 2. Diagram of Lower Mississippi Valley Chronology

second or intermediate period was marked by a replacement of Marksville in the southern part of the area by Coles Creek and in the north by Deasonville. Then in the third and last period, sometime before the invasion of the Europeans, Coles Creek disappeared giving way to Natchez, Caddo and other unidentified historic types, while Tunica, and to some extent Choctaw, took over the region of the Deasonville pottery.

Drawings of potsherds and a few vessel shapes representative of each of seven complexes are shown in figures 3 to 12. Almost every sherd is marked with a type number which can be disregarded except in selecting the decorations that numerically predominate the various complexes as indicated in Table II. Other features listed in the same table will assist in identifying village site collections.

The features of bottle shapes, handles and shell tempering it will be noted appear in the period II in the Deasonville complex and extend up to the historic types. They are not found in the Marksville complex.

Ceramic complexes found on Louisiana Indian village sites very rarely, except in the case of the Marksville, occur unassociated with potsherds representative of some other complexes. There is, however, system to this mixing of complexes. It can usually be attributed to one or two causes. Mixture often results from trade or borrowing of ideas having occurred between neighboring, contemporaneous complex areas, so that foreign designs become incorporated in the village refuse [37] dumps. To explain the second cause of mixture, the average Indian village site must be conceived as having been settled, occupied for a longer or shorter period of time and then abandoned. In relation to the total time covered by the chronology under consideration the period of occupancy is very brief. Abandonment may have resulted from depletion of arable land or similar cause, while superstitious fear prevented the old sites from being reinhabited except in a few cases. The village dump or midden deposit was accumulated during the years of occupancy, and if [it] had reached any appreciable depth would show by changes in the types of artifacts from the bottom to the top the transitions in style which had occurred while the town was alive. However, the great majority of Louisiana sites never had any great accumulation so that younger and older types are hopelessly intermingled. For this reason it is fortunate that the brief tenure of the sites usually prevented the deposition of more than two subsequent design complexes.

The combinations of complexes on any one site which have been observed seem in average cases to be due to the above two conditions and are listed in the following table (Table I). It will be noted that there are four complex areas involved in time horizon III, three in horizon II and only one in horizon I. The letters in the time column at the left of the diagram refer to the chronological diagram (Fig. 2). As would be expected, the major proportions of any specific collection consist of the sherds representative of the styles in the region in which the village is located, while designs introduced from neighboring areas form minor proportions.

Of course a skeleton time scale such as this is only a means to the end of recovering all possible knowledge of the history and manner of

Table I

Village Settled at Time	Village Abandoned at Time	Area of N. La.– W. Central Miss.		Area of S. La.–S. W. Miss.	
		Major Proportion	Minor Proportion	Major Proportion	Minor Proportion
D	E	Tunica	Natchez Caddo Choctaw	Natchez	Tunica Caddo Choctaw
C	D	Tunica	Coles Creek	Coles Creek	Tunica
B	D	Tunica Deasonville	Coles Creek	Coles Creek	Tunica Deasonville
B	C	Deasonville	Coles Creek	Coles Creek	Deasonville
A	B	Deasonville Marksville	Coles Creek	Coles Creek Marksville	Deasonville
X	A	Marksville		Marksville	

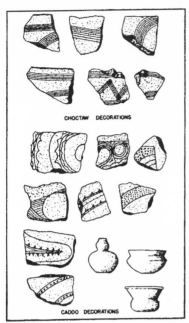

CHOCTAW DECORATIONS

CADDO DECORATIONS

Fig. 3

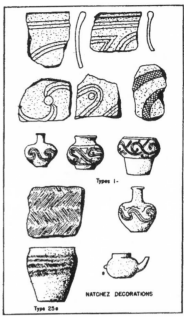

Types 1-

NATCHEZ DECORATIONS

Type 25a

Fig. 4

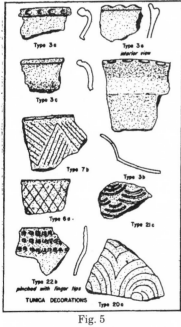

Type 3a

Type 3a
interior view

Type 3c

Type 7 b

Type 3b

Type 6 a .

Type 21 c

Type 22 b
pinched with finger tips

TUNICA DECORATIONS

Type 20 a

Fig. 5

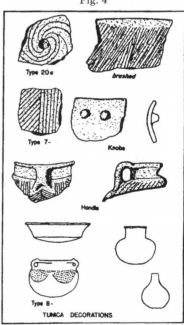

Type 20 a

brushed

Type 7-

Knobs

Handle

Type 8 -

TUNICA DECORATIONS

Fig. 6

Ford

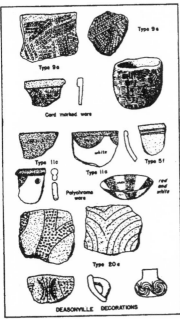

Fig. 7

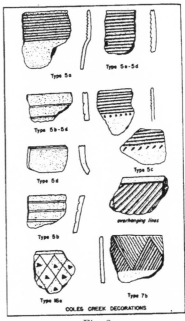

Fig. 8

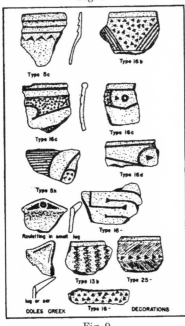

Fig. 9

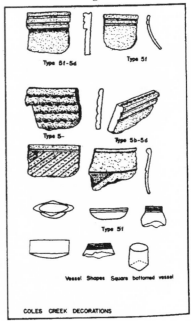

Fig. 10

Table II—List of Characteristics of Lower Mississippi Valley Pottery Complexes

Time Period	Complex	Predominant Designs	Vessel Shapes	Handles	Temper [1]
III	Caddo	Unclassified See figure 3	Pot Bowl Bottle	Present	Grit Crushed potsherds Shell
	Choctaw	Unclassified See figure 3	Pot Bowl Bottle	Present	Grit Crushed potsherds Shell
	Natchez	Type I See figure 4	Pot Bowl Bottle	Present	Grit Crushed potsherds Shell
	Tunica	Types 3a, 3b, 3c See figures 5, 6	Pot Bowl Bottle	Present	Grit Crushed potsherds Shell
II	Deasonville	Types 9a, 11a, b, c See figure 7	Pot Bowl Bottle	Present	Grit Crushed potsherds Shell
	Coles Creek	Types 5a, b, c, d, e, f See figures 8, 9, 10	Pot Bowl	Absent (Lugs or ears)	Grit Crushed potsherds
I	Marksville	Types 12a, 14a See figures 11, 12	Pot Bowl	Absent	Grit Crushed potsherds

[1] Temper is hard material worked into clay while plastic to prevent cracking when vessel is fired.

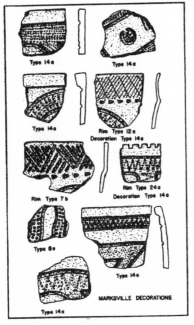

Fig. 11

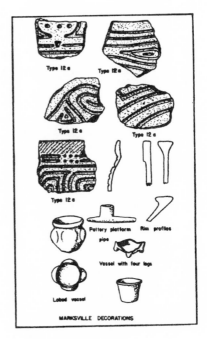

Fig. 12

living of the original Americans. Innumerable details must be discovered and fitted into their proper places in the story. In considering and applying this brief outline three points should be borne in mind: that collecting surveys on which this work is based have been confined to the areas indicated on the map (Fig. 1); that few of the historic pottery types of the area are known at present; that most definitely this outline at the present stage of knowledge cannot be considered as conclusive. It is merely a tool which may lead to a better understanding. Although this chronology is indicated by the present evidence, no follower of science worthy of the name would object to a complete reversal of opinion in the face of convincing evidence of error.

4

CERAMIC DECORATION SEQUENCE AT AN OLD INDIAN VILLAGE SITE NEAR SICILY ISLAND, LOUISIANA

by

J. A. FORD
School of Geology, Louisiana State University

INTRODUCTION

———■———

In the summer of 1933, while engaged in a survey of
the Indian village sites of northeastern Louisiana, an interesting situation was observed which promised the possibility of vertical stratigraphy.[1] This was at an old site
on the plantation of Mr. William Peck in Catahoula Parish,
two miles south of the town of Sicily Island, Louisiana.
The town of Sicily Island is located on the western side of
an elevated area, called Sicily Island, rising above the Mississippi valley floor. In the bottom of small washes, cutting
through a twenty-inch accumulation of midden debris, were
found potsherds characteristic of three decoration complexes[2] that theoretically had been used in the region in two
distinct prehistoric time periods. The uniqueness of the
situation did not lie in the particular combination of decoration complexes, since that has been observed at a number of
other sites, but rater in the unusual depth of midden deposit, which indicated a possibility of vertical division of
the two time periods.

In recognizing the elements involved in the Peck Village situation, it was necessary to take into consideration
work which had been done on collections from a number
of other sites in the lower Mississippi Valley; however,
to present this evidence in any detail would require too
lengthy a discussion. A comprehensive study of Louisiana
and Mississippi survey collections is now being undertaken
and may be completed in 1936. A preliminary outline of

---

[1] This season's survey was made possible through a Grant-in-Aid
from the National Research Council. The writer wishes to express
his appreciation to Mr. William Peck for permission to excavate the
village site on his plantation, and to Mr. L. L. Lovell, field assistant
for the summer of 1933, for his capable and cheerful efforts.

[2] By the term "decoration complex" is meant a group of pottery
decorations characteristic of an area at a definite period of time.

1

the seven known complexes of this area has been given in
the April, 1935 issue of the *Louisiana Conservation Review*.[2a]

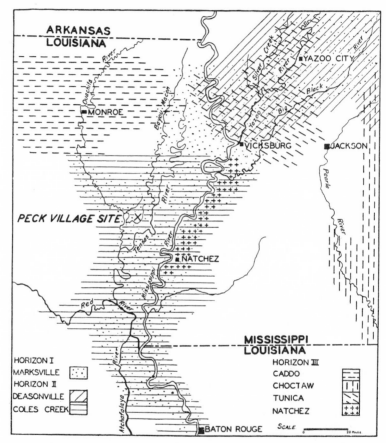

Fig. 1. Location of Peck Village site in relation to the Louisiana pottery decor
ation complexes of northeastern Louisiana and southwestern Mississippi.

This previous work indicated that the three complexes
involved in the Peck Village situation were in vogue through

[2a] Ford, J. A., "Outline of Louisiana and Mississippi Pottery
Horizons", Louisiana Conservation Review, *Louisiana Department of
Conservation*, Vol. 4, No. 6, April, 1935, pp. 38 ff.

Ford

two separate, though contiguous, time periods. The complex used during the earlier period has been named "Marksville".[3] It is characteristic of certain old village sites found scattered through the Mississippi Valley as far as the survey has been conducted.

The two later complexes, "Deasonville"[4] and "Coles Creek",[5] appear to be contemporaneous but spacially separated. Deasonville occurs on a number of sites in the lower Yazoo-Mississippi River Basin and the adjacent hills to the east; Coles Creek sites are found throughout the Mississippi Valley south of Vicksburg, Mississippi. The distribution of these three complexes and several others not considered in this paper is shown by the map, Figure 1. Time relations of these complexes as indicated by horizontal stratigraphy are given graphically in Figure 2. From its surface collections and geographic position, the Peck Village fits into this sequence in the "Natchez-Central Louisiana Area". It was inhabited through the period indicated on the vertical time scale as "A" to "B".

---

[3] The old village excavated by F. M. Setzler at Marksville, Louisiana serves as the type site for this pottery complex. Setzler considers this site to be closely related to the Hopewell Culture of Ohio. See Setzler, F.M., "A Phase of the Hopewell Mound Builders in Louisiana", *Exploration and Field-Work of the Smithsonian Institution in 1933*, pp. 38-40, and "Pottery of the Hopewell Type from Louisiana", *Proceedings of the United States National Museum*, Vol. 82, Art. 22, pp. 1-21, pls. 1-7. In applying the name "Marksville" to the pottery complex found there, the writer is merely "begging the question". Yet the presence of typical Hopewell pottery on these other southern sites cannot be accepted as guarantee for the presence of the remainder of that culture's characteristics.

[4] The type site is near Deasonville, Mississippi, and was excavated by H. B. Collins, Jr., in 1928-1929. See Collins, H. B., Jr., "A Prhistoric Indian Village Site near Deasonville in Mississippi", *Proceedings of the United States National Museum*, Vol. 79, Article 32, pp. 1-22, pls. 1-13.

[5] The "Coles Creek" pottery complex was first recognized at a small site twelve miles south of Fayette, Mississippi on the highway leading to Natchez. The village is on the east bank of Coles Creek.

Although excavation was not the primary purpose of the survey, it was thought advisable to make at least pre-

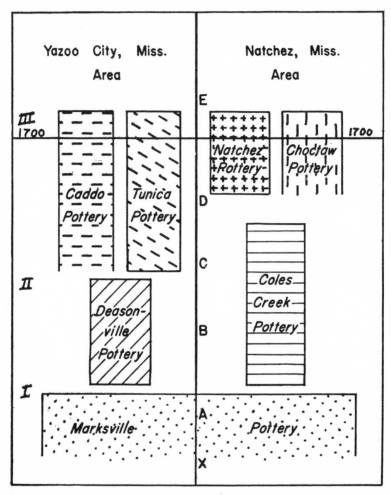

Fig. 2. Graphical representation of chronological relations of Louisiana-Mississippi ceramic complexes, as indicated by horizontal stratigraphy.

liminary investigations in the Peck Village midden to test the possibility of the indicated relationships.

TOPOGRAPHY

The area known as Sicily Island is near the western edge of the alluvial valley of the Mississippi River. It is the southern extension of Maçon Ridge, a slightly elevated remnant of an old Mississippi River terrace that divides the drainage of the Ouachita and Tensas Rivers. To the east and south it is bordered by the Mississippi flood plain, and on the west is separated from the main range of the Ouachita Hills by the Ouachita River. Lake Louie or Lovelace Lake and its southward and westward continuation, Bayou Louie, both of which appear to be parts of an abandoned meander of the Tensas River, form the eastern and southern bounds of the island. The highlands of the Catahoula Hills occupy the western part, while the central and eastern portions are slightly dissected prairie.

The refuse dump of the Peck Village site, covering about half an acre, is located along Lake Louie on the edge of the fifteen-foot bluff that marks the eastern extent of the elevated terrace." A house with accompanying outbuildings occupies most of the midden deposit. As this spot is pointed out as being the site of the first plantation home on the island, it probably has never been under cultivation. One hundred yards to the south is the mouth of Hooter Bayou, a small stream emptying into the lake from the island. A short distance further along the bank of the lake are two conical mounds; one is about four feet in height, the other about eight feet in height, and each is about fifty feet in diameter.

One mile north of this site, at the plantation home of Mr. Peck, is a group of five mounds, the largest a truncated pyramid about fifteen feet high. The smaller mounds are badly mutilated. Surface material was very meager, and no excavation was made there. The small amount of pottery found differs from that occurring at the Peck Village, indicating possibly that they were not contemporaneous.

" The Peck site is located in SW ¼ of SW ¼ of Section 28, Township 10 North, Range 8 East.

METHOD OF EXCAVATION

A method of "sectioned cuts" was decided upon as the best means of studying the possibility of stratification of pottery decorations with the limited funds and time available. This consisted of laying out four ten-foot square areas in different parts of the midden (Fig. 3). Each of these areas, referred to as a "cut", was carefully dug by trowelling. A level floor was maintained until an appreciable amount of material was found. The depth of the cut was then measured and designated as section "1" of that cut. The second lowering of the cut floor was known as section "2", etc. Material recovered was saved separately

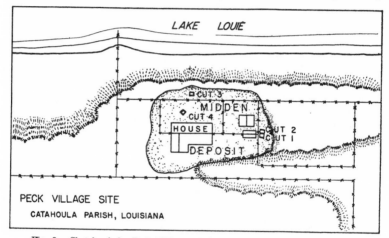

Fig. 3. Sketch of the Peck Village midden showing its relation to Lake Louie (Lovelace Lake) and the locations of stratified cuts into the midden.

in paper bags and marked with cut number, section number, depth, and date. Excavation notes served to check identification and depths of the various sections.

The deposit was fifteen inches deep where it was pierced by cut number 1, but a more general average seems to be about twenty inches, which was the depth at the points tested by cuts 2, 3 and 4. The quantity of material occurring decreased markedly as the excavations neared the bottom of the midden. Hard dun-colored clay was found underlying the midden base. Although leaching from the old surface beneath the deposit was apparent, no development of loam could be discerned. This was probably due to its inclusion in the characteristically black midden soil.

Scattered and irregularly spaced postholes at the bottom of cut 3 were the only evidence of aboriginal structures. An area twenty by thirty feet was excavated with shovels about cut 3 and although a few more postholes were found, no regularity of arrangement could be determined.

CLASSIFICATION OF SHERDS

The material recovered from the four cuts made into the Peck Village included animal bones and mussel shells, but consisted mostly of broken fragments of pottery. Approximately one-fifth of these potsherds bore parts of vessel decoration, showed the shape of vessel bottoms, were rims, or were otherwise distinctive. The plain unornamented sherds will be disregarded in this study since they can add little or nothing to a consideration of pottery design. Even a quantitative comparison of plain and decorated pieces would be questionable; there can be no certainty that each plain sherd represents an individual vessel.

Since decoration is the most prominent feature of design which is readily determined from potsherds, it must form the basis of the classification system. However, as in a general way, within certain geographic and chronological limits, it correlates with the other features of vessel shape, paste, use of handles, and rim shapes, these other features may be included broadly with decoration in designating a type.

At the present elementary stage of knowledge of southeastern ceramic art, a tentative dissection of decorations into their original or basic elements seems rather hopeless. Therefore, as far as possible each specific mode of ornamentation has been dealt with as a unit.

Theoretically, a pottery chronology comprises the various time changes in styles of pottery design of an area or group of people. Absolute quantitative evaluation of the products of these stylistic time periods is practically impossible; any method of minute classification must unavoidably consider design from a more or less subjective viewpoint. Questions of the degree of variation from the mean allowable within a type must in large degree depend upon the judgment and experience of the classifier. An attempt has been made to minimize the subjective element as much as possible by the employment of only one classifier.

All the pottery decorations found at the Peck site were classified according to an index which had been developed in studying surface sherd collections made in the course of archeological surveys of Mississippi and Louisiana. In effect this is merely a list of decoration types. As distinct decorations were encountered in the collections in sufficient numerical quantity and areal distribution to permit their acceptance as a type, they were illustrated on an index card and described as to vessel shape, temper, execution, and other pertinent information. Typologically related decorations found together in the same collections, thus indicating the probability that they represented variations of one major idea of decoration, were filed as "a", "b", "c", etc., under a common numerical heading. If no such grouping already existed for a newly-encountered decoration type, it was filed as "a" of a new numerical heading. These groups were used only for the most apparent relations and were intended to have no cultural or absolute typological significance; they served mostly to facilitate filing and reference to the index.

Due to the varying degree of complication of each decoration, the index card descriptions assume unequal diagnostic value. For example, the presence of typical cord-marking (type 9a, Plate V) can be determined from a very small sherd, while even a moderately large piece will often

←— MARKSVILLE —→←— DEASONVILLE —→←———————— COLES CREEK ————————→

TYPES		8f	12a	14a	14d	9a	11c	20-	22a	22d	5-	5a	5b	5c	5d	5e	5f	5g	13b	16-	16b	16c	16d	16f	17a	Lugs	Sq. Bot.	Drill Holes	Total Clas.	Un-class.
CUT 1																														
SECT.1 5"	No.		6	21		5	6					2	-						-		-						3	1	48	3
	Pct.		12	44		10	12					5	2						2		2						6	2		
SECT.2 12"	No.		17	13	1	2	2																				3		40	1
	Pct.		42	32	2	5	5																				7			
SECT.3 15"	No.		3	12	2	2																						1	20	
	Pct.		15	60	10	10																						5		
CUT 2																														
SECT.1 4"	No.	-	4	11		2	3	2				-	-		4	-			3			3							36	2
	Pct.	3	11	31		6	8	6				3	3		11	3			8			8								
SECT.2 8"	No.	3	7	13		-	4						-						-										34	
	Pct.	9	20	38		3	12						3						3											
SECT.3 12"	No.		4	4		-			2	2											-			-					12	
	Pct.		33	33		8			6	6											8			8						
SECT.4 16"	No.		2	10																									12	
	Pct.		10	85																										
SECT.5 20"	No.			5																									5	
	Pct.			100																										
CUT 3																														
SECT.1 4"	No.	2		2		-			2		-	2	3	-	3	-	14	3	2	-	-	2	-	-	-		-		35	2
	Pct.	6		6		3			6		3	6	9	3	9	3	40	9	6	3	5	6	3	3	3		3			
SECT.2 10"	No.	-		3								2	3	-	3	2	14		2	2			-		-	1			34	4
	Pct.	3		9								7	9	3	9	6	41		10	7			3		3					
SECT.3 15"	No.		2	2		-		-		-					2	-	5			-			-	-	-	1			20	
	Pct.		10	10		5		5		3					10	3	25			5			5	3	5					
SECT.4 20"	No.		2	12		-				-					4	-	7			-				-			2	-	32	2
	Pct.		10	36		3				3					12	3	21			3				3			6			
CUT 4																														
SECT.1 5"	No.	-	3			2					4	4	-		5		6		-	-			2	-	-		-		28	3
	Pct.	4	11			7					14	14	4		8		21		4	4			7	4	4		4			
SECT.2 11"	No.	2	2	-		3					2	2	2		-		12						2	2			-		28	1
	Pct.	7	7	4		11					7	7	7		4		42						7	7			4			
SECT.3 16"	No.	8				4	3				3											-			-				28	-
	Pct.	28				14	11				11											4			4					
SECT.4 22"	No.	2	3	6													2												13	
	Pct.	15	23	46													15													

Fig. 4.   Table showing number and percentage of sherds of each decoration type in the sections of the cuts into Peck Village site.

not distinguish the precise nature of "large triangular punctates used singly in connection with curvilinear incised decoration" (type 16d, Plate IV).

In classifying the Peck Village collections, the serial number of sherds from each cut section was listed on a "type sheet" with the designation of the index card representing the decoration type to which the sherd was referred. Unusual combinations of recognized decorations on an individual sherd were described by the use of both type designations separated by a (+) sign. However, as given in the summary table (Fig. 4), these infrequent combinations have been broken down into the established types. The only combinations that occurred at Peck Village were within the "5" types—5a, b, c, e or f combined with 5d (see type list, pages 13 and 14). The few unrecognizable or unusual decorations which did not occur often enough to indicate their adoption as definite styles were figured and described on the type sheets. Although their number for each cut section is given in the summary table (Fig. 4), they are not considered in the proportional graphs. When a sherd bore so small a portion of a decoration that although the general idea was recognized the details were not apparent, it was designated by the number of the appropriate decoration group followed by a dash.

The limitations and crudity of this means of classifying potsherd decoration are obvious. Increasing understanding of the chronology will doubtless demonstrate the stages of southeastern ceramic evolution and make possible a more analytical classification, which at present promises to be the result of rather than the means to prehistoric chronology.

DECORATION INDEX

The decorated potsherds found at the Peck Village site were classified according to the types in the Mississippi-Louisiana regional survey index listed below. The sherds from this site fall into four divisions:

11

1. Decorations, because of their consistent occurrence
   on typical Marksville sites, can be recognized as belonging to the Marksville Complex.
2. Sherds typical of the Deasonville Complex.
3. Sherds belonging to the Coles Creek Complex.
4. Unusual decorations which cannot with certainty be assigned to any of the above complexes.

Types represented in the general classification index
that occur at Peck Village are included in the first three
headings. Decorations falling into the fourth class are described, but from their nature have no type numbers. Sherds
representing each of these classes are illustrated in Plates
I to V. The complex presented is indicated in the legend to
each plate. Type numbers identify each individual sherd
with reference to the following list and the various tables
and graphs.

Types of the Marksville Complex

Type 12a:

Criteria:

Decoration: Closely spaced, deeply incised, wide
lines. In cross section lines are semicircular.
Complex curvilinear designs are usual although
rectangular arrangements sometimes occur.
Execution: Always neat. Lines smooth and regu-
lar.
Paste: Smooth.
Color: Grey to brown.
Temper: Grit, sand, possibly crushed pottery.

Usual Accompanying Characteristics:

Application: Decoration usually is separated
from rim by undecorated border. Decoration
may form a band around the upper part or be
applied to the entire exterior of the vessel.
Shape: Usually "potshaped" or straight-sided
vessels with wide mouths.

Bottoms: Flat, either square or round in shape.

Rim: Sometimes vessel walls thickened in decoration border space, though often walls rise straight to a flat rim.

Handles: Absent.

Size: Small, not over 8″ in diameter.

Type 14a:

    Criteria:

Decoration: Curving bands of rouletting; either zigzagged perpendicular to axis of band, or running in lines parallel to band. Rouletting enclosed by wide, deep lines. These bands often branch.

Other characteristics similar to type 12a.

Type 14d:

    Criteria:

Decoration: Curving bands of punctates made by the end of a small cane held at an oblique angle; enclosed by wide, deep lines.

Other characteristics similar to type 12a.

Types of the Deasonville Complex

Type 9a:

    Criteria:

Decoration: Cord-wrapped paddle imprints applied without regularity.

Execution: Usually very poor.

Paste: Coarse, medium hardness.

Color: Brown and dark brown.

Temper: Sand and grit.

Application: Decoration generally covers entire exterior of vessel.

Shape: Cup-like, nearly vertical sides.

Bottom: Usually convex.

Rim: Uneven, sometimes strap of clay applied on exterior.

Handles: Absent.

Size: Usually not over 12″ in diameter.

Type 11c:

>> Criteria:

>>> Decoration: Red slip applied to either or both exterior and interior of vessel with no other attempt at ornamentation.

>> Usual Accompanying Characteristics:

>>> Shape: Generally bowl-shaped vessels.

Type 8e:

>> Criteria:

>>> Decoration: Incised lines made with pointed instrument enclosing curving or angular bands of punctates made with a point. Bands often branch.
Execution: Usually neat.
Paste: Medium texture and hardness.
Color: Mottled black, brown or grey.
Temper: Grit.
Shape: Usually "potshaped"—bulging sides, wide mouth.
Handles: Absent.

Type 20a:

>> Criteria:

>>> Decoration: Curvilinear scrolls formed by a number of incised lines made with a pointed instrument.
Execution: Usually mediocre.
Paste: Medium hardness; medium quality.
Color: Buff to dark brown.
Temper: Grit, sand.
Remarks: Shell, which is often found as tempering in this type at other sites, does not appear here. Handles, another typical feature, are also absent.

Type 22a:

>> Criteria:

>>> Decoration: Small raised areas, pinched up between two fingers; irregularly spaced over exterior of vessel.
Execution: Rough.
Paste: Medium quality and hardness.
Color: Dark brown, black.
Temper: Grit.
Shape: Bulging sides, wide mouth.

Type 22b:

    Criteria:

        Decoration: Rough ridges parallel to one another down the sides of the vessel; apparently pinched up with the fingers while the vessel was plastic. Other features similar to type 22a.

Types of the Coles Creek Complex

Type 5a:

    Criteria:

        Decoration: A number of lines, spaced less than one centimeter apart, incised in the peculiar "overhanging[7]" manner, encircling the vessel parallel to the rim.

        Execution: Usually neat; lines evenly spaced.

        Paste: Smooth, fine texture, hard.

        Color: Usually grey, interiors often blackened.

        Tempering: Grit, possibly crushed potsherds.

    Usual Accompanying Characteristics:

        Application: Decoration starts at rim and extends halfway down sides of the vessel.

        Vessel Shapes: Straight, nearly vertical sides.

        Bottoms: Usually flat, either square or round in shape.

        Rim: Usually flat on top with no thickening or curving of vessel walls. Lines sometimes incised in top of rim (see type 5d).

        Handles: Absent.

        Size: Small, not over 8″ in diameter.

Type 5b:

    Criteria:

        Decoration: Overhanging lines placed over one centimeter apart which encircle the vessel parallel to the rim.

        Remainder of description is the same as for type 5a.

[7] The term "overhanging" is used to describe lines incised with a flat-pointed instrument held at such an angle to the vessel wall that the top of the line is deeply incised while the bottom rises to the surface of the wall. The effect is similar to weatherboarding on the sides of a wooden building.

Type 5c:

    Criteria:

        Decoration: A row of either triangular or irregularly shaped punctates placed below and parallel to overhanging lines drawn parallel to the vessel rim.

        Remainder of description is the same as for type 5a.

Type 5d:

    Criteria:

        Decoration: The specific feature of one, two, or three lines incised into the flat rim of a vessel. These lines sometimes have punctates spaced in them. In some cases they are formed in the rims of sherds decorated with some other of the "5 group" decorations.

        Other features same as for type 5a.

Type 5e:

    Criteria:

        Decoration: Row of imprints which appear to have been made with one corner of a cube. The row encircles the vessel below and parallel to overhanging lines drawn parallel to the vessel's rim. The overhanging lines of this decoration are usually larger and more deeply incised than those of type 5a.

        Remainder of description is the same as for type 5a.

Type 5f:

    Criteria:

        Decoration: One or two lines which usually, but not always, are incised in the overhanging manner, and are drawn parallel to the rim of the vessel.

        Execution: Often rather mediocre.

        Remarks: Decoration 5f usually occurs on a wide variety of ware which in color, texture, and temper reflects the general trend of the ware in the collection in which it occurs.

Type 5g:

> Criteria:
>
>> Decoration: Band of decoration near rim consisting of closely spaced overhanging lines incised at an angle of forty-five degrees to rim.
>>
>> Execution: Usually neat.
>>
>> Decoration usually starts at rim and extends down one-third the vessel wall.
>
> Usual Accompanying Characteristics: Similar to type 5a.

Type 13b:

> Criteria:
>
>> Decoration: Zigzags made either by a roulette or rocker stamp rocked back and forth as it was moved sideways down the vessel wall. This decoration is usually bordered top and bottom by lines.
>>
>> Execution: Usually very neat.
>>
>> Decoration usually starts below the rim leaving a rim border and extends halfway down vessel.
>>
>> Other characteristics similar to type 5a.

Type 16b:

> Criteria:
>
>> Decoration: Areas filled with trianguar-shaped punctates alternating with straight, parallel line-filled areas. The incised lines in this decoration are sometimes overhanging.
>>
>> Execution: Usually neat.
>>
>> Paste: Hard, smooth texture.
>>
>> Color: Grey to brown.
>>
>> Temper: Grit.
>>
>> Shape: Uncertain.
>>
>> Handles: Absent.

Type 16c:

> Criteria:
>
>> Decoration: Small triangular punctates used to fill in areas in curvilinear decoration. The incised lines in this decoration are either overhanging, have punctates in them, or were made with a point.
>>
>> Other features similar to type 16b.

Type 16d:

Criteria:

Decoration: Large triangular punctates used singly in connection with curvilinear incised designs. In some cases the incised lines of this decoration are overhanging. In others rows of small punctates or punctates in incised lines were used.

Other features similar to type 16b.

Type 16f:

Criteria:

Decoration: Incised lines drawn at forty-five degree angle to rim so as to form diamond-shaped areas. In each diamond is centered a triangular punctate, apparently made with one corner of a cube or the pointed end of a spatula-like implement.

Remainder of description same as for type 16b.

Type 17a:

Criteria:

Decoration: This decorative feature consists of small zigzags or punctates impressed in the top of small thickened areas in the vessel rim. The lines which sometimes show on the sides of type 17a sherds are usually overhanging.

Execution: Neat.

Paste: Fine, hard.

Color: Brown to grey.

Temper: Grit.

UNCLASSIFIED DECORATIONS

One case of a narrow band of fine punctates enclosed by delicately incised lines running around the vessel parallel to the rim. From cut 3, section 3 (Plate V, sherd *c*).

Two cases of short vertical rows of punctates grouped by twos between two incised lines running parallel to the rim. From cut 3, section 3; and cut 1, section 1.

Two cases of triangular punctates in parallel rows on vessel lugs. From cut 3, section 3; and cut 3, section 4 (Plate V, sherd *k*).

Five cases of parallel incised lines decorating interior of bowls. Some of these may be duplicates. From cut 4, section 1; and cut 2, section 1.

One row of punctates below and parallel to thickened rim. From cut 4, section 3.

One case of double row of punctates running just below and parallel to the rim. From cut 1, section 1, (Plate V, sherd *h*).

One case of rows of punctates alternating with incised lines drawn nearly parallel to the vessel rim. From cut 1, section 1, (Plate V, sherd *e*).

Serrated rims, either scalloped or notched, are almost common enough to warrant their becoming a type. In all cases except the one illustrated in the lower right hand corner of Plate IV, they are roughly executed on plain unthickened rims (Fig. 12, sherds *h, k*; Plate V, sherd *d*).

Sherd *j* on Plate V is the only recognizable indication of an extraneous complex involved in the local situation. Its fine hard texture, thinness, curvature, and decoration appear to identify it with the historic Natchez ware. The Natchez are known to have inhabited this region during historic times and this is probably a chance inclusion. Sherd *j* is from cut 1, section 2.

COMPARISON OF TYPES

After completing the classification of the sherds from the Peck Village site according to the above list of types, the total number and percentage of each decoration in each cut section were tabulated (Fig. 4).

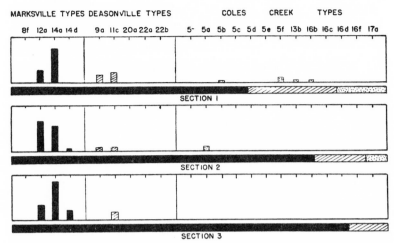

Fig. 5. Graphs of proportions of pottery types in Cut 1.

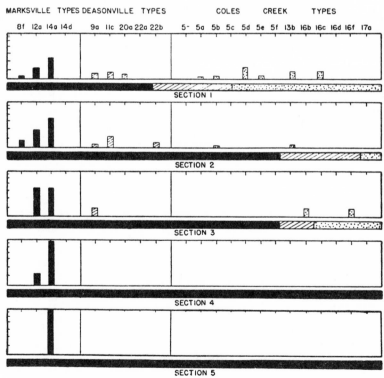

Fig. 6. Graph of proportions of pottery types in Cut 2.

Ceramic Decoration Sequence   113

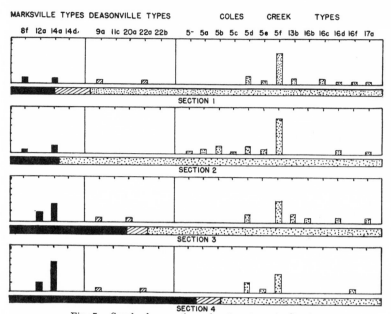

Fig. 7. Graph of proportions of pottery types in Cut 3.

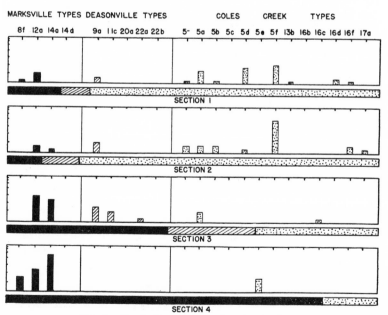

Fig. 8. Graph of proportions of pottery in Cut 4.

In figures 5 to 8 in which these percentages are shown graphically, the types representing the three complexes have been grouped separately and are indicated by vertical bars.ʻ Horizontal bars under each section graph denote the proportion of sherds of each complex. The few unclassified sherds are not considered in these graphs.

From this comparison it is apparent that proceeding from the lower to the upper sections there is in each cut a tendency for decorations of the Marksville Complex to decrease in number, and an almost proportional increase in types of the Coles Creek Complex.

COMPLEX MARKERS

From observations made on a number of village site collections in the lower Mississippi Valley, it has been noted that although each of the several decoration complexes of the area include a number of different and often unrelated types which appear at the various villages typifying any one complex, there are one or two small groups of closely related types peculiar to each complex that statistically dominate to a marked degree. These decorations must be considered as the most typical of their complex, and from the role they play serve as "complex markers".

Prior to the work at Peck Village the markers for the three complexes occurring there were known to be as follows:

Marksville:

Type 12a: Wide, deep, closely-spaced, incised lines forming curving or rectangular figures.

Type 14a: Wide, deep, incised lines bounding rouletted bands which alternate with smooth areas and form curving or rectangular figures.

Coles Creek:

Types 5a, b, c, d, e, and f: Essentially overhanging, incised lines encircling vessel near and parallel to the rim with some accompanying features.

ʻPercentages in these graphs given as Figs. 5, 6, 7, and 8 are plotted according to the sine of a circle quadrant having a radius equal to the height of each graph.

Deasonville:

Type   9a: Cup-shaped vessels of rough ware, covered with irregular applications of cord-wrapped paddle.

Type   11c: Application of red slip to either exterior, interior, or both.

(Type   11a: Polychrome, or red and white painted ware, is characteristic of some typical Deasonville sites but does not occur here.)

When percentages of the markers representative of each complex are directly compared, the tendency toward replacement of the Marksville sherds by Coles Creek as the midden deposit was being accumulated is even more apparent (Fig. 9).

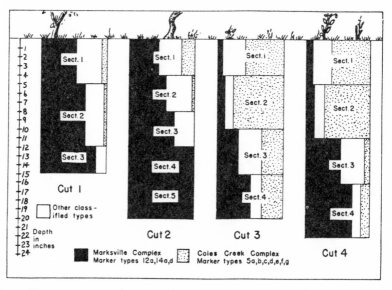

Fig. 9. Graph comparing the proportions of Marksville and Coles Creek marker decoration types in the four cuts at Peck Village site.

Sherds typical of the Deasonville Complex are not present in sufficient numbers in the collections to show definitely the relation in which they stand to this indicated superposition of complexes. As shown by the map given as figure 1, the Peck Village site lies well within the area covered by the Coles Creek Complex, and is a hundred miles south of the Yazoo River Basin where typical Deasonville sites are found. Sherds of this complex occurring at Peck site probably are the result of either trade or influence from the Deasonville area.

RELATIVE AGE OF VILLAGE SECTIONS

Cuts into the midden are too few in number for definite determination, but comparison of the cut graphs (Figs. 5 to 8) considered in the light of their relative positions in the midden (Fig. 3), indicates a difference in age of the eastern and western sides of the village. Cuts 1 and 2 were located adjacent to one another on the southwestern sides of the midden, and yielded the pure Marksville Complex from their lower sections with only a small amount of Coles Creek in the upper sections. The lower sections of cuts 3 and 4, on the eastern side of the midden, show about half Marksville and half Coles Creek, with Coles Creek sherds predominating in the upper sections and Marksville types almost negligible. This seems to mean that the western section of the midden in which cuts 1 and 2 were located was deposited before the eastern section, and ceased growing at about the time the eastern section of the midden pierced by cuts 3 and 4 began to be deposited. If this indicated situation of village "creep" was the case, then in effect, instead of revealing design styles through the time represented by twenty inches of refuse deposit, the cuts into the Peck Village site show the changing trend in design through the period of time required to deposit approximately forty inches of midden. This would tend to augment the evidence of trend toward design change.

The most important implication of the Peck Village situation is that with the passage of time, while deposition of the midden was in progress, the ceramic art of the inhabitants was slowly changing from decorations consisting of wide, deep, closely-spaced lines forming curvilinear and angular designs (type 12a) and curving bands of rouletting enclosed by wide deep lines (type 14a, Plates I and II) to decorations formed with overhanging lines which usually encircled the vessels parallel to the rim (types 5a, b, c, d, e, f,) and curvilinear lines with which triangular punctates were employed (the "16" types, Plates III and IV). As there is no apparent typological connection between the dominant decorations of the two complexes, the change in ceramic art is probably not the result of local evolution of Coles Creek out of Marksville, but rather a replacement. The Coles Creek decorations appear fully developed although in all cases they are not as specialized or as neatly executed as at many sites of the pure complex. Some of the types which form a minor proportion of the Coles Creek Complex do seem to be typologically related to Marksville. They probably resulted from the gradual replacement of complexes, indicated by the smooth changes in proportion in the graphs. This may have allowed a certain amount of Marksville to be absorbed into the Coles Creek.

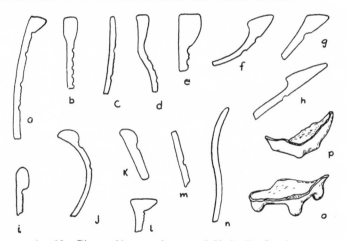

Fig. 10. Rim profiles and features of Marksville Complex pottery. Profiles *a*, *c* and *f* to *n* are of type 14a; *b*, *d*, and *e* are of type 12a. The interiors of these sherds are to the left of the page. Sherd *p* is a fragment of a square bottom; *o* is the bottom of a vessel with four legs.

The most obvious of these forms found at the site is type 13b, rouletted zigzags swung from the rim of the vessel, which may have evolved from the idea of zigzagged rouletting between broad, deep lines (type 14a).

COMPARISON OF VESSEL FEATURES

General observations on vessel features disclosed by sherds in the Peck Village site collections are made in the following table comparing the Marksville and Coles Creek Complexes. The paragraphs that immediately follow are numbered to correspond with the table and are in more detail.

Vessel Feature	Marksville	Coles Creek
1. Area covered by decoration.	Sometimes decoration is in a band near rim. Often entire outer surface including bottom.	Band of decoration near rim extending halfway down vessel sides.
2. Border between body decoration and rim.	Frequent, wide.	Infrequent, narrow.
3. Treatment of rim and neck.	Often thickened, sometimes flat on top, occasionally slightly everted.	Usually unthickened, merely continuation of vessel wall terminating in flat rim. Often line in rim.
4. Vessel mouth shapes.	Round.	Round.
5. Lugs or ears on rim.	Absent.	Frequent, often large, sometimes decorated.
6. Drilled holes near rim.	Absent.	Frequent, two holes on opposite sides of vessel near rim.
7. Handles.	Absent.	Absent.
8. Shape of vessel walls.	Sometimes straight, perpendicular; often convex or pot-like.	Usually nearly straight and perpendicular.
9. Shape of vessel bottoms.	Flat; round, square or four legs. Bowls convex.	Flat, round or square. Bowls convex.
10. Vessel forms.	Wide-mouth pots and convex-bottom bowls.	Wide-mouth pots-, convex-bottom bowls.
11. Vessel size.	Average not over 6″ in diameter; 6″ high.	Average not over 6″ in diameter; 6″ high.
12. Paste.	Smooth soapy texture.	Smooth soapy texture.
13. Temper.	Grit, crushed potsherds.	Grit, crushed potsherds.
14. Color.	Black, brown, light grey.	Black, brown, dark grey, light tan.
15. Thickness.	Average about 5/16 inch.	Average about 3/16 inch.

1. A characteristic of sherds with Marksville decorations from Peck Village is the covering of the vessel exterior from rim to bottom with decoration, which sometimes extends over the bottom of the vessel. However, a few of these vessels resemble the Coles Creek types in that the area decorated was only the upper half of the vessel walls.

2. Frequent use is made of a border between the decoration on the vessel body and the rim on the Marksville decorated sherds. At Peck Village this border is usually unornamented. At other sites which yield collections of the pure Marksville Complex the rim border is highly

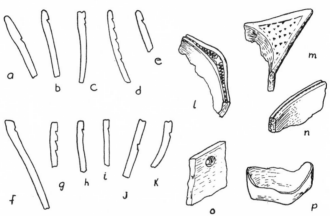

Fig. 11. Rim profiles and vessel features typical of the Coles Creek complex. Drawings *a* to *k* are profiles of sherds with decorations of the "5" types. Sherd *n* is type 5d; *l* is type 17a; *m* is a typical ear; *o* shows a drilled hole near the rim; *p* is a fragment of a square vessel bottom. Sherd interiors are toward the left.

developed and often decorated with delicate cross-hatching. Coles Creek types, on the other hand, in their most highly developed forms as found at pure Coles Creek sites have no decoration border separating body decoration from the rim. At Peck Village simple, narrow borders appear on a few sherds of the latter complex.

3. Frequent tendency toward elaboration of the rim by thickening of the vessel walls is shown in the profiles of some of the sherds of the Marksville Complex (Fig. 10).

Coles Creek rims are usually simple, as shown in figure 11. Note lines in the rims of several of the sherds (decoration type 5d).

4. Although vessels of both complexes often have square bottoms, the shape of the body at and near the rim is almost invariably round.

5. Large, flat, triangular-shaped lugs (Fig. 11, sherd *m*) are common on Coles Creek vessels, usually on bowls. Some of the lugs are decorated with combinations of triangular punctates. The broad base of these lugs is attached to the rim of the vessel. They usually point out and upward at an angle of about twenty degrees to the plane of the rim. Four lugs seem to have been used on each vessel so that the walls form a circle, when viewed from above the rim of the lugs forms a square. Small thickened areas in Coles Creek rims, decorated in their flattened tops with zigzagged rouletting (type 17a, Fig. 11, sherd *l*) are perhaps an extreme form of these lugs.

6. Holes drilled on opposite sides of vessels near the rim, possibly for suspension, are common on Coles Creek sherds (Fig. 11, sherd *o*). These holes were made with a solid point drill after the paste had been hardened.

7. Handles or knobs are entirely absent in the Peck collection. The lugs described in paragraph 5 appear to be ornamental in purpose and not to have served primarily as handles.

8. Some of the sherds bearing the Marksville decorations indicate straight-sided vessels, but pots with sides convex so that body diameter exceeds rim diameter are more common. On the other hand, Coles Creek vessel walls are more nearly straight and perpendicular, so that body and rim diameter are about equal. A few vessel walls bearing decorations of both complexes indicate shallow bowls with convex bottoms. As shown in the profiles of rim sherds (Figs. 10 and 11), the differences in vessel shape although distinct are not great.

9. While a few convex-bottomed bowls are found in both Marksville and Coles Creek, the bottoms of the more common pots are flat. Their shape is either square or round. Three examples of legs on the corners of square bottoms (Fig. 10, sherd *o*) belong to the Marksville Complex.

10. The most common shape of vessels of both complexes is the wide-mouther, straight-sided, beaker. Pots with wide mouths and slightly bulging sides are also found, as well as the convex-bottomed bowls mentioned above. No indications of bottle forms, "casuela" bowls, or effigy vessels appear.

11. Not more than one or two vessels of either complex could have exceeded six by six inches in size. Many were still smaller, about four by four inches.

12. The paste of sherds of both complexes is similar: fine-grained, smooth, hard, and of a "soapy" texture.

13. Grit and possibly also finely crushed potsherds serve as tempering in both the Marksville and Coles Creek sherds. No instances of shell tempering are found.

14. The similarities of the ware extended to the coloring; mottled black, brown, tan, and grey are most common. Some of the Marksville pieces are of a very light grey, almost a dirty white.

15. Although sherd thickness in the whole collection ranges from one-eighth to one-half inches, the Coles Creek ware averages slightly thinner than the Marksville.

From the above comparisons it seems apparent that while there is marked dissimilarity in decoration and rim features of the two complexes, there are basic resemblances in vessel shapes, bottoms, size, absence of handles, and tempering material. These similarities tend to bracket the two ceramic complexes together as contrasted with the more common Lower Mississippi ware described by Clarence B. Moore and other investigators. Although the features of paste, texture, hardness, and color may be interpreted as cultural characteristics, they also just as plausibly may be the result of common use of local clay.

The Deasonville Complex has not been brought into this comparison because its representative types are few in number and do not clearly show their relation to the sequence of decorations.

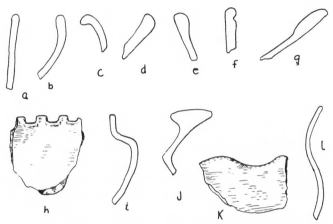

Fig. 12. Rim profiles *a* to *f* are typical of the sherds of the Deasonville-Complex. *a* is type 9a; *b* to *f* are of type 11c. Profile *g* is a sherd decorated on the interior with an unclassified straight line pattern. *i*, *j* and *l* are undecorated sherds. *h* and *k* are plain notched rims. The interior of these sherds are to the left.

Rim profiles of Deasonville sherds, (Plate V, types 9a, 11c) are shown in Fig 12, *a* to *f*. A general description of features of these types follows:

The cordmarked sherds (type 9a) indicate rough, carelessly made vessels with plain, unthickened rims, nearly vertical sides and convex bottoms. Decoration extends over the entire outer surface of the vessel. Grit, sand, and possibly some fibre were used to temper the dark chocolate-colored paste.

Red slip ware (type 11-c) usually forms shallow bowls. The rims of this type are simple though slightly thickened in some cases (Plate V, type 11c). Grit and sand are the usual aplastic material.

The other Deasonville types found here are not sufficient in number to show their characteristics with any degree of certainty. Shell tempering, handles, or bottle forms do not appear in the collection.

RANGE OF THE MARKSVILLE AND COLES CREEK COMPLEXES

The indicated replacement of Marksville by the Coles Creek Complex at the Peck Village site is of general significance only so far as it aids in clearing the problems of chronological dating facing southeastern archaeologists.

As stated above, old village sites yielding Marksville pottery have been found widely scattered through western Mississippi and eastern and southern Louisiana, where most of the field surveys in these two states have been concentrated since the inauguration of such work eight years ago. Pottery decorated in practically an identical manner comes from the mounds of the Hopewell Culture in southern Ohio. It seems fair to assume that there is cultural connection between these two areas, and that further investigation will discover sites yielding this pottery in the intervening states of Arkansas, Tennessee, and Kentucky.

A line drawn east and west through Jackson and Vicksburg, Mississippi, and Monroe, Louisiana seems roughly to delineate the northern extent of Coles Creek sites. To the east they are found in Mississippi not more than fifty miles from the line of bluffs marking the eastern edge of the Mississippi flood plain. Coles Creek villages are widely spread over the flood plain area west of the river, and there are indications that they occur up the valley of the Red River as far as Shreveport. To the south they have been found near Baton Rouge, Louisiana. From an old village on the Veasey Place, Pecan Island, on the Louisiana coast, Henry Collins, Jr. collected pottery showing definite Coles Creek characteristics although with slight local variations. Some of the decoration types that form a minor proportion

in the Coles Creek in the Louisiana area were found by
Clarence B. Moore[9] along the northwest coast of Florida,
i. e. large triangular punctates used with curving, scroll-
like lines, small triangular punctates filling line-enclosed
areas alternating with plain areas, punctates in lines, and
rim lugs.

In addition to these villages in southern Louisiana that
yield pottery decorated solely in the types of either the
Coles Creek or Marksville Complexes, there are other villages whose collections show mixtures of the two complexes
in various proportions. Since most of the deposits do not
extend below plow level and have been thoroughly mixed by
cultivation, stratigraphic study is impossible. It appears
plausible that these mixed sites, like the Peck Village, represent the transitional period from the older Marksville to the
later Coles Creek time.

---

[9] Moore, C. B., "Certain Aboriginal Remains of the Northwest
Florida Coast", Parts I and II, *Journal of the Academy of Natural
Sciences of Philadelphia*, Vols. XI and XII.

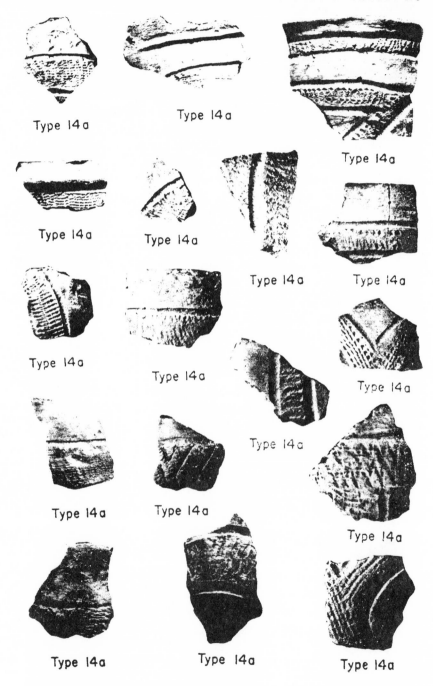

Type 14 a

Type 14 a

Type 14 a

Type 14 a

Type 14 a

Type 14 a

Type 14 a

Type 14 a

Type 14 a

Type 14 a

Type 14 a

Type 14 a

Type 14 a

Type 14 a

Type 14 a

Type 14 a

Type 14 a

Plate I. Potsherd decorations typical of the Marksville Complex from the Peck Village site.

35

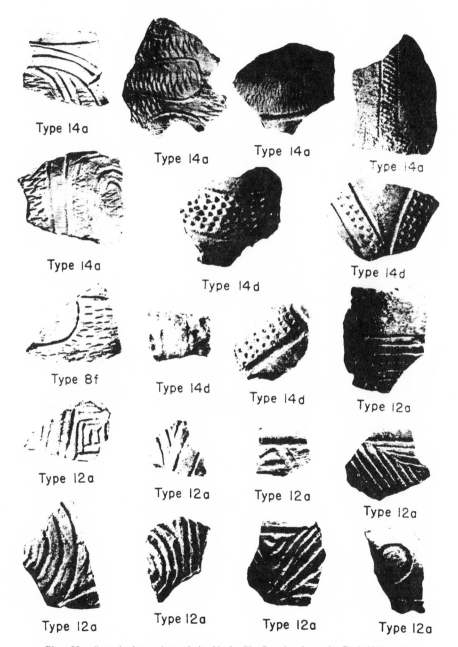

Type 14a

Type 14a

Type 14a

Type 14a

Type 14a

Type 14d

Type 14d

Type 8f

Type 14d

Type 14d

Type 12a

Type 12a

Type 12a

Type 12a

Type 12a

Type 12a

Type 12a

Type 12a

Type 12a

Plate II. Ceramic decorations of the Marksville Complex from the Peck Village site.

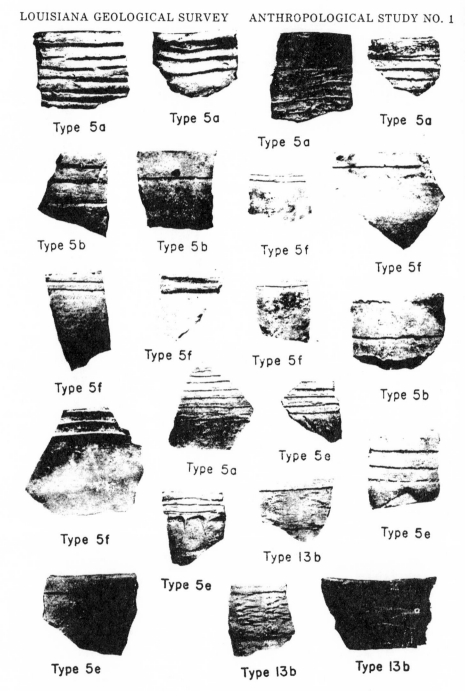

Plate III.   Pottery decorations typical of the Coles Creek Complex from Peck Village site.

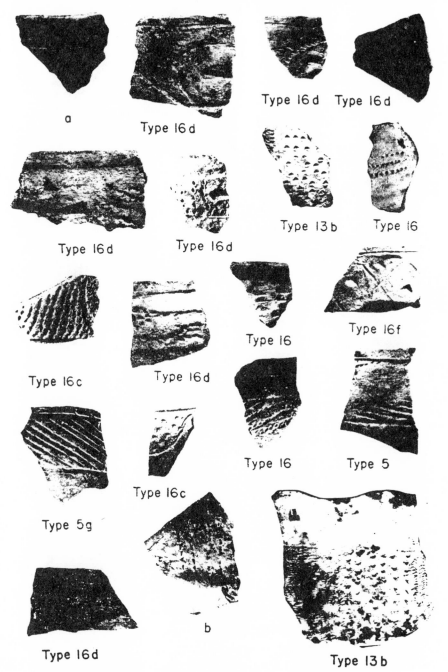

Plate IV. Potsherds of the Coles Creek Complex from Peck Village site.

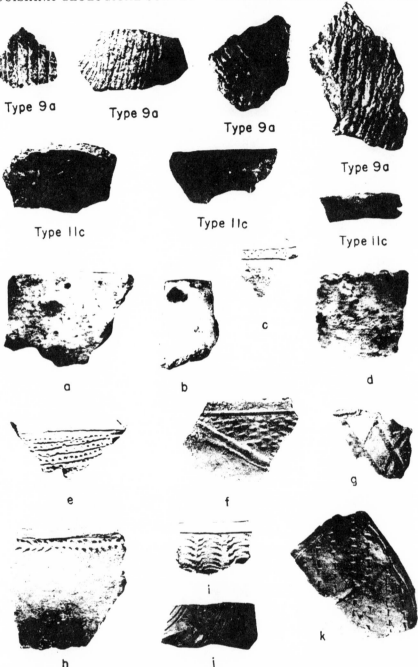

Plate V. The classified sherds at top of this plate are typical of the Deasonville Complex. Sherds *a* to *i* are unclassified but appear to be related to the Coles Creek Complex. Sherd *j* may belong to the Natchez Complex.

5

Analysis of Indian Village Site Collections From Louisiana and Mississippi

by

JAMES A. FORD

School of Geology, Louisiana State University

TABLE OF CONTENTS

VII

VIII

ILLUSTRATIONS

IX

Foreword

The field-work of which this report is a result was initiated under the auspices of the Mississippi Department of Archives and History in 1927. In the summers of that and the succeeding years of 1928 and 1929,[1] Moreau B. Chambers and I excavated and made surface collections from sites in west-central Mississippi. Chambers continued the work of the state survey in the summers of 1930, 1932, 1933, and 1935. During this period he examined the larger part of the southern half of Mississippi. In 1930 Chambers determined the historic pottery types of the Natchez Tribe by excavating a site near Natchez, Mississippi. The collections from the Yazoo River valley were gathered in the 1932 field season. Part of Chamber's work in 1933 and 1934 is represented by the material from eastern Mississippi, from Nanih Waiya, Lyon's Bluff, and Bran's Camp sites.

Financed by a Grant-in-Aid from the National Research Council, I extended the collecting surveys into the Mississippi River valley region of northern and central Louisiana in 1933. Most of the sites from this area were first visited in that year. The stratigraphic study of the Peck Village site which provided the material for the first study of this series was part of that season's work. Additional material from the same part of the state was collected in the course of the 1935 survey sponsored by Louisiana State University.

Several individuals in both states have taken an active interest in the work and have rendered invaluable assistance. Mr. Edward F. Neild of Shreveport has located the sites and made all the collections from the Caddo territory in northwestern Louisiana. Without his work it would be impossible to treat the ceramic features of this important group.

---

[1] The work of these two seasons was financed jointly by the Mississippi Department of Archives and History and the Bureau of American Ethnology, Smithsonian Institution.

1

Mr. and Mrs. U. B. Evans of Alexandria, Louisiana, located sites and secured material from the Catahoula and Larto Lake regions. They made it possible for me to make several trips into the region, and in many other ways added materially to the success of the two summers' work.

I am indebted to Miss Caroline Dormon, of Chestnut, Louisiana, for assistance in investigations in the northern part of the state. Several of the village sites listed were discovered and collected from by Miss Dormon.

Mr. W. M. Crawford of Sicily Island, Louisiana, has made some of the collections from that vicinity. Especially useful were his collections from the Natchez Fort site.

Collections of material from several sites near Starkville, Mississippi, were made by Mr. L. L. Long, agronomist at Mississippi State College. These are in the National Museum at Washington, D. C., and were examined there.

Messrs. Emerson Perdue, Casimir Ehret, and Stanley McDonald, students in the University and part-time laboratory assistants, did much of the work involved in preparing collections and computing and checking percentages for tabulations.

My wife, Ethel Campbell Ford, and Mr. Walter Beecher have done their best to reform the grammar and spelling in this paper. All cases in which these happen to be correct are due directly to them.

I am indebted to Mr. H. B. Collins, Jr., and Mr. Frank Setzler, of the United States National Museum, for opportunities to acquire field experience and theory under their immediate direction. Dr. John R. Swanton, of the Bureau of American Ethnology, has been most helpful in providing information and advice, as well as encouragement.

Dr. Henry V. Howe, and Dr. Fred B. Kniffen of the School of Geology, and Major Fred Frey, Dean of the

College of Arts and Sciences of Louisiana State University, have all made possible the last two winters of almost uninterrupted laboratory work. Dr. Kniffen has provided office space. His constant encouragement, advice, and frank and penetrating criticism have been invaluable.

I am indebted in part to all of these men for the development of the fundamental theories that underlie this study. However, for the detailed applications, which undoubtedly will be questioned by many, I must take full responsibility. The collecting surveys were not started with these ideas in mind. Only the idea that midden material might prove useful in some way motivated the work at the start. Theories and methods developed in the course of, and as a result of, the field-work.

The nature of this analysis of surface collections demands that deductions be based on the weight of the evidence. There are so many possibilities of error that few isolated situations or sites can stand alone. All conclusions must be probabilities. Yet, without a tentative beginning such as this, it is believed that systematic archeology in the southeast will be impossible.

The methods presented here have been largely ignored by those working in the area. The material dealt with has received only passing mention in reports. For these reasons it appears advisable to give in detail the pertinent methods and underlying theories in the hope that they may prove applicable in other parts of the southeast. It must be pointed out that a study of this type, with so many unavoidably subjective elements, is full of pitfalls and possibilities of error. And, even if the student is able to avoid the many tempting false trails, the result of his best efforts is still merely a theory.

J. A. F.

School of Geology, Louisiana State University,
Baton Rouge, Louisiana.

THEORY AND METHODOLOGY

Chronology

At the conference on Southern Pre-history held at Birmingham, Alabama, in 1932, the point was stressed that no program of archeological field research is warranted that is not directed toward the solution of some problem. Unsolved problems are not difficult to find in the south. In fact, to become acquainted with the archeology of the area at present is to realize how little of the great mass of available data has been critically compared and arranged. For analysis and synthesis the south is practically a virgin field.

Work of various degrees of excellence has been done in all the southern states. Unfortunately the programs of the serious investigators have been limited at most to one or two seasons of excavation at sites chosen more or less at random. No sustained, clearly defined program has been attempted. This has resulted in a large conglomerated mass of data that appears to defy all attempts at analysis.

Possibly this state of affairs has caused some observers to fall into the habit of visualizing the cultures that formerly existed in the south as a flat picture—a picture without perspective or time differentiation. That this cannot be the case even a casual survey of the available literature will show. In numerous instances adjacent sites present materials and situations differing to such a degree that there can be slight probability of contemporaneity.

The writer's impression of the general outline of the history of prehistoric southern cultures will perhaps assist in comprehending the reasons for the methodology applied in this paper. The impressions are partly the results of work and general observation in southeastern arche-

4

ology; partly they are derived from experience and reading in other fields where cultural histories have been more thoroughly determined.

It seems that most of the country was inhabited by a semi-sedentary population that derived at least half its subsistence from agriculture. Small village communities with outlying farmlands were the rule. Every village was more or less a self-sustained unit, but a certain amount of trade and other intercourse was carried on. Probably some of the town sites which today show large ceremonial earthworks were the religious centers of the surrounding areas. The lives of these early people were comparatively tranquil. The frequent mass movements with consequent friction, which are recorded at the dawn of written history, are probably due to the disturbing influence of the invading white man. Though the population was probably very conservative culturally, there is little doubt but that all through the relatively undisturbed prehistoric period the insidious phenomenon of cultural change was in operation. This process is at work in even the most "static" of cultures. The peoples involved were not necessarily aware of what was occurring. Slow evolutionary changes were probably usual, but marked changes occurred in certain areas through wholesale adoption of foreign styles or the actual replacement of populations either through gradual infiltration or conquest.

Territorial distinctions in cultural features were developing as the result of geographic isolation of groups. Probably some shifting of population brought widely variant cultural groups into proximity. A certain amount of merging and refocalizing might be expected along the lines of contact.

As the cultures moved on in a restless everchanging flow through time, local communities were undergoing certain geographic changes. At various times new village sites were occupied and some old ones abandoned. Possibly part of this shifting might be accounted for by depletion of the land through primitive agricultural methods or changes in natural features, that is, movements of rivers, silting up of lakes, etc. It is futile to guess at the causes. The large number of old villages found in uninhabited areas at the time of the coming of the white man indicates that there was a constant shifting. A few of these were pointed out by the Indians as sites from which their groups had recently moved.

With this sketch in mind, it is apparent that no true treatment of materials in an area can ignore temporal relationships. The results of careful research will not be a closely knit, flat picture of everything found, but must be a series of such pictures, each representing a sample taken at a definite time horizon.

This concept leads directly to what has been called the historic method of attack. A plan applicable to the southeast may be outlined as follows:

I. Develop a measure of time in terms of cultural changes.

    A. By working from the historic period back into the prehistoric.

    B. By using the most practical means available, preferably a cultural element (or elements) which:

        1. Is available in quantities sufficient for adequate comparison without extensive excavation,

        2. Is least subject to a logical form dictated by the materials of manufacture,

        3. Is least likely to be subject to possible conservative influences of religion or taboo.

II. With the cultural time scale at hand, excavate sites which will elaborate the details of the cultures at the various time levels. At the same time test, and if possible subdivide, the time scale.

This paper is an attempt to carry out the first part of this program in portions of Louisiana and Mississippi. If this is successful and a fairly reliable time scale can be determined, the archeologist is placed in somewhat the same enviable position as the geologist who collects fossils from different strata of known comparative ages. In this way the true relationships of cultural materials may be expected to appear.

A fundamentally different approach to relationship problems is being applied by McKern, Deuel, and other investigators to the Indian remains in the northern United States. On the basis of taxonomy, they are arranging the cultural complexes into a biological-like system of general culture bases which are subdivided into patterns, aspects, foci, and most specific divisions of components. This method appears to be most valuable in clarifying the degree of relationship between the various cultural complexes. Finally it may solve, or assist in solving, temporal relations.

The nature of the McKern method demands a comprehensive number of carefully excavated sites to determine the cultural characteristics from which comparisons must be made. The southeast is lacking in a sufficient number of such sites to permit a very significant analysis of this kind. That the next step should be a program of excavation to secure this data is very doubtful. Situations and material are disturbed in excavating and cannot be duplicated. More intelligent observation may be expected if this can be done with a knowledge of the significance of the material.

Effective attack demands method. Underneath the methodology must lie a foundation of theory. Our problem has already been presented: to determine chronological relationships. The methods used in the work and the theories which led to the adoption of these methods will be discussed in the following pages.

Sherd collections

In the Lower Mississippi Valley, the requirements for a cultural factor suitable for an analysis of time change appear best to be met by the fragments of domestic pottery which have been broken and unintentionally deposited on the sites of the old villages. The specific advantages are that: (1) potsherds are available in almost unlimited quantity without disturbing the sites; (2) clay, the material of which pottery is made, has a great range of possible and practical shapes and ornamentations; and (3) conservative influences retarding changes of style were probably at a minimum on these domestic utensils. Comparison is facilitated and made more profitable by the fact that southeastern ceramic art was in a rather complicated and specialized stage. No midden deposits have been found in the local area that lack decorated potsherds.

As has already been demonstrated in the archeology of the southwest, it may be expected that the ceramic art of this region will be held stylistically within fairly definite bounds of time and space, will show influence from neighboring contemporaneous areas, and will have evolved or changed with time. Concentric diffusion may also be expected. However, the relatively small area under consideration probably is not sufficient to measure this phenomenon. The writer has the impression at present that the entire eastern United States is closely involved in the diffusion of ancient pottery styles.

There are certain material limitations to potsherds as the basis of ceramic study. The sites of the old villages in the local area are generally excellent for purposes of modern agriculture, and usually have been in cultivation for a number of years. As a consequence, the vessel fragments are reduced through breakage to very small sizes. This makes difficult the significant correlations of decoration with vessel appendages and shapes, and, in a number of cases, obscures the plan of the decoration.

These failures of sherd collections should eventually be corrected by the supplementary evidence of entire vessels secured from burials.

In the past, burial collections have been given major emphasis by archeologists working in the Lower Mississippi Valley. The intact condition of the material is a distinct advantage, and, when the sites are properly excavated, it is often possible to determine directly the relative age of specimens at any one site. However, burial collections are subject to possibilities of selection, peculiar mortuary styles, and possible lag due to ceremonial conservatism. There is also the possibility that some of the mound building peoples did not inter their dead, or at least buried only a few. This may explain why no pottery of the exceedingly common Coles Creek types was secured in the local area by Clarence Moore or other investigators. As a matter of fact the writer does not know of a single entire vessel representative of some of the common Coles Creek types.

Several of these objections are material and are the sources of some of the errors that have been made in attempting to visualize the relationships of southeastern ceramics. No attempt is being made to minimize the usefulness of burial collections. When the degree to which they reflect the real trends of domestic ware is determined, invaluable supplementary evidence is provided. At the same time the burial ware may present a special set of cultural features which will be parallel to, and will assist in checking the relations evident from, the domestic ware.

There is another very evident possibility of limitation of the diagnostic value of surface sherd collections for determining the relative age and period of time covered by a site. This lies in the chance that the midden deposit at a site may be of such a thickness that the oldest material, laid down in the lower strata, will not appear on the surface. This would result in an incorrect impression as to the extreme age of the site. The chances that this will have happened frequently are slight. Few sites have refuse dumps of greater thickness than the depth to which plowing penetrates, and most of the sites are in cultivation. Many villages are on slightly rolling ridges. Cultivation has taken most of the surface soil off the highest part of the ridge, exposing the top of the subsoil; and, in making collections, special attention is paid to washes and gullies that have eroded into the site. There is usually a concentration of material in such places. Except in cultures which either accumulated garbage very rapidly, or which remained static for long periods of time, such a thing as completely buried strata is improbable. Although super-position may be found at definite spots at some village sites, almost certainly a shifting of the houses, or of the village sites as a whole will have occurred during the period of deposition, leaving the older stratum exposed in some places.

The possibility of a buried stratum at any one site is not a matter of great importance. In this study the desired results are not the ages of individual sites, but the relative ages of the different schools of ceramic art. It is not probable that there could be a buried stratum, representing an old time period, buried at every site at which that stratum occurs. Considering the large number of sites found in this area, there should be many villages which were abandoned during each period, and which were not reoccupied, thus leaving the pottery characteristic of each period on the surface.

After the foregoing, it is hardly necessary to mention that the theories in this study are based upon the assumption that the collecting surveys have succeeded in obtaining a sample of all of the schools of pottery art that have been used in the region. In view of the intensiveness of the surveys, especially in certain parts of the area, this assumption seems fair.

It is also evident that no conclusions can be based on the collection from an individual site. Since comprehension of the stylistic periods and areas is the object of the study, the conditions on any one site must be compared and checked by others in order to be certain of the true conditions that obtain.

Collecting methods

The methods of collecting the material were practically uniform. In all cases, unless otherwise stated, collections were not excavated, but came from the surface. Most of the old village sites are found in plowed fields. Since the middens are not ordinarily more than six to eight inches deep, the material has been thoroughly mixed by years of cultivation.

The collectors have tried to secure as much material as possible from all parts of the village dumps. Collecting conditions vary at different times of the year, and many of the collections used have been obtained by making repeated visits to a site.

Careful surface examination of a number of sites has shown no tendency for certain types or combinations of types to be segregated in different parts of the area covered by village refuse. Such segregation might be expected in some cases from shifting of individual houses, or the entire village, while styles were changing. This phenomenon is often observed in carefully excavated sites. Possibly long cultivation of most of the old villages, with the consequent dragging and washing of surface material has destroyed evidence of this nature.

Either while making the collection, or later in the laboratory, the sherds were sorted. Only those pieces were retained which promised to yield information concerning vessel decoration, shape, tempering material, or appendages. All rim sherds and all pieces that showed untypical texture or thickness were saved.

Detailed descriptions of sites, including maps where desirable, were made on mimeographed form sheets. As much information as possible has been obtained on the few sites not visited by the survey parties.

The collections presented here represent only a very small portion of all sites located and examined. Many other collections which are not considered ample for quantitative study are on file. All have been examined, and appear to substantiate the situations outlined in this paper.

Necessity for quantitative analysis

Quantitative analysis of site collections is necessary in order to evaluate correctly the relative popularity of different decoration types. Such evaluation is of paramount significance in comparing sites for the following reasons:

(1) It may be expected that two sites occupied through the same period of time, under the sway of the same school of ceramic art, will yield nearly identical decorations in about the same proportions.

(2) The assumption is usually possible that, while decorations characteristic of a school of art will form a major proportion of the material at their native sites, on contemporaneous sites of different modes to which they might have been traded or were the results of imitation, they will be in the minority.

(3) Provided the factor of population had remained nearly constant, a village inhabited through two style periods could be expected to show a majority of the material characteristic of the period in which it existed the longer. This assumption involves the very uncertain population factor; hence, it is fortunate that it is not essential in building a relative time scale.

Quantitative reliability of random collections

There follow certain possibilities, inherent in the method of collecting, of quantitatively misrepresenting the prevailing modes at any one village site.

One source of error might be the possibility that the collection would contain duplicate sherds from the same vessel. This is rather improbable because a very small percentage of the total amount of the material on any site is exposed on the surface and recovered by the collector. In a few cases, when sherds from the same vessel are found among excavated material, they are readily detected due to identity of decoration, execution, paste, thickness, curvature, and color.

A more important problem is the extent to which random surface collections actually represent the different types of material present on the surface of the deposit. An attempt has been made to determine this reliability by comparing collections made at different times from thirteen sites.

The percentage of the different types in each collection was first determined. Then the average differences between type percentages in collections from the same sites were computed. This is called average variation. Where three collections were involved, the difference between the largest and smallest percentage of each type was taken as the variation of the type. If a type appeared in one collection but not in the other, the variation was considered to be from zero to the percentage to which the type was present.

The range is the greatest variation found in comparing any one type.

In the following table, repeated collections from thirteen sites are arranged in order of increasing average variation:

Site	No. Sherds Coll. A	Coll. B	Coll. C	No. Types Involved	Average Varia- tion	Range: Ex- treme Varia- tion
Prichard Landing	64	118	....	32	.016	.05
Coles Creek	77	98	....	38	.021	.14
Churupa Place	97	101	89	12	.024	.06
Mazique Place	95	70	....	24	.024	.09
Harrison Bayou	99	74	....	23	.028	.12
Sidney Biggs	48	76	....	31	.030	.104
Wilkinson Place	68	84	....	18	.030	.105
Smith Creek	60	87	203	23	.034	.08
Old Rhinehart	31	111	....	15	.034	.085
Pocahontas	129	73	....	25	.036	.155
Chase Place	32	115	....	26	.041	.27
Colbert Place	61	44	....	21	.05	.23
Alphenia Landing	25	38	....	14	.073	.29

Extreme variation increases in the same order, but at a somewhat faster rate. Both of these factors are in rough inverse proportion to the number of sherds comprising the collections; the larger the collections, the smaller the variations, and vice versa.

It is very improbable that the types in several collections from a site should differ from the true conditions on the site in the same numerical direction. It seems more probable that the type percentages in different collections are both more and less than the true percentage, so that the difference between the percentages in two collections will not be greater than the difference between either collection and the true conditions.

If this is correct, the average and extreme variations shown above may be accepted as marking the probable degree to which random collections of different sizes will reflect the true conditions on a village site.

Qualitative reliability

Obviously a consideration of ceramics solely on the basis of decoration and such notable features as square bottoms, handles, lugs, and peculiar rim types is not giving a complete picture of the original ceramic complex. There are certain types of ware, which are often discovered at excavated sites, that are marked by simple though distinctive shapes and peculiarities of paste. These have certainly been overlooked in this study. This is regrettable, but is not particularly material to the real objective. A comparison must be based on specific features. The information that may be gleaned from these is intended to serve as a guide to more detailed investigation. This will give fuller information on the pottery complexes as well as on the many other cultural elements that are also neglected in this work.

Discussion of classification

In order to facilitate minute comparisons, the large mass of material composing the village site collections made necessary a uniform system of classification. Empirical classifications, such as must be used for this material, are not simple, and always must leave much to be desired in the way of objectivity.

Limitations of village site collections of potsherds as sources of information concerning vessel shape, size, and associated features have been discussed. Decoration is the most variable factor of vessel design that can be consistently determined to any degree of certainty. For this reason, it must serve as the principal basis of the classification system. Peculiarities of shape, size, and appendages must be determined wherever possible and treated in a more general manner. They appear to correlate more or less with particular decorations; hence it is possible to describe these features as the "usual accompanying characteristics".

The ordinary difficulties inherent in all attempts to categorize cultural phenomena are present in potsherd decoration classification. While specific types are apparent around which most of the material clusters, there are cases of intergradation of types and of unusual combinations of features. It is a difficult matter to try to describe as well defined types the remains of what once were living artistic styles. Fortunately the few rebels practically never succeeded in entirely divorcing themselves from their artistic background. Relationships of unconforming sherds can usually be determined by peculiarities of the decoration elements and by characteristic combinations of these elements. However useful such diagnosis may be to the worker in the field or laboratory who has developed a "feel" for the material, naturally it cannot be used as the basis for a comparative study. Fortunately widely divergent pieces are rare.

The fragmentary nature of potsherds demands an intimate knowledge of the different parts of the decorations. Two pieces from separated parts of the same decoration may appear entirely different, and it is only through thorough knowledge that they can be correctly identified. Certain types of decoration are more readily and certainly identified than others. For example, cord marking is apparent from a very small sherd, but even a large piece of a decoration with a complicated motif sometimes will not give a clue to its nature. In the work of classifying, where there is any possible doubt as to the identification of a type, the type is not allowed unless it occurs in easily recognizable form on other sherds in the same collection.

There is still another way in which errors are bound to occur in classification. In types which are formed by the combination of two or more elements, and where the isolated elements also form decoration types, there is the possibility that only one of the elements may appear on a sherd. The other element may have been present in the original decoration, but through its loss the sherd will be referred to the wrong type. For example, the combination of a number of overhanging lines drawn parallel to the vessel rim with a single row of triangular punctates just below and parallel to the lines forms a common decoration. Another type consists of the arrangement of overhanging lines without the row of punctates. It is clear that if a sherd of the first described decoration is broken so that it does not include the lower part, it will be included in the second described type. This is usually not a very serious mistake, and no great errors are likely to come of it. The types that can be mistaken for others are generally very closely related, and occur in the same groups of decorations.

In each site collection, there are always a few sherds that have so small a part of some decoration that they cannot be used. Often this is nothing more than a single incised line. Such pieces have been ignored in presenting tabulations of classified material; they can add nothing. Introducing them into the tables would only result in upsetting the percentages of the serviceable material. None of the collections examined show as much as ten per cent of such pieces; the average is more like two or three per cent.

Proper orientation of a potsherd will often aid materially in determining the decoration of which it is a part. Orientation is generally possible because of the tendency of fractures to occur along coil lines. All of the pottery of the region, except an occasional very small bowl, was made by the coiling process. The flattened coils are from one to two inches wide, and the lines along which they have been joined are weak places in the vessel walls. Coil line breaks run almost parallel to the vessel rim, and can be recognized by their straightness and the concavity or convexity of the broken surface. From vessels whose coil junctures are weak, sherds break out as fairly regular rectangles.

Classification systems

A system of classification that will deal satisfactorily with such an elastic and variable thing as art is yet to be found. The writer has considered and tried several different plans.

Noteworthy among the discarded methods is a morphological, biological-like arrangement of decorations into orders, suborders, families, etc. This proved unsatisfactory because of the extreme flexibility of pottery types, as well as doubt as to their generic relationships. The frequent migration of decoration elements from what seemed to be their native types was of significance, and could not be indicated by the method. Zoological classification is not embarrassed by such anomalies as would result from the frequent crossing of different species.

An analytical system of classification was tried on collections from twenty-seven sites. It attempted to record specific decoration features, combinations of these features, execution, temper, paste, texture, thickness, hardness, vessel shape, and vessel appendages. The impracticability of this plan developed in attempts to detect significant correlations.

The system which was finally applied was very simple and uncomplicated. In effect, it was merely a list of decorations recorded on index cards and arranged under general headings to facilitate filing and reference. The index was expanded as new types were found. Unusual specimens were sketched. Later, if they conformed to newly determined types, they were classified. From time to time, as the general characteristics—temper, execution, vessel shape, etc.— became apparent, they were noted on the type cards.

This method is highly subjective; much is left to the judgment of the classifier. This was limited as much as possible by having only one classifier, by expanding the index freely to accommodate minute type variations, and by excluding all doubtful specimens from detailed classification.

The "index" method, dependent as it must be on the classifier's acquaintance with the material, was not suitable for presentation. It was only semi-systematic, was non-analytical, was meaningless unless memorized in detail, and was not capable of logical expansion.

Near completion of the work of classification, another system was developed which overcame some of these objections. Since all of the collections were not readily available for direct reclassification, and the types could easily be transferred to the improved method, this was done directly.

The present system is analytical in nature. Two components are considered to be present in every decoration: motifs and elements. Motif is the plan of the decoration: scroll, parallel features, herringbone, etc. Elements are the means used to express the motif, i. e., incised lines, rows of punctates, rouletting, etc. Another significant factor which deserves consideration is the specific and peculiar manner of using the elements to form the motif.

Motifs, elements, and specific applications occurring in this study are listed below.

Decoration motifs

Symbols in this list occupy the first position in the type expressions.

00 Motif uncertain.
    01 Too small a fragment to permit identification.
10 Irregular application.
    11 Elements arranged without order over the vessel surface.
20 Regular application.
    21 Elements spaced at regular intervals over surface of vessel.
30 Features arranged in bands.
    31 Curving bands from one to two inches wide. Bands often branch.
    32 Straight bands that turn at right angles; one to two inches wide.
    33 Straight bands dropped at right angles to the rim; one to two inches wide.
    34 Bands forming curving, unconvoluted, compressed scrolls.
40 Scroll and scroll-like arrangements.
    41 Convoluted scrolls formed by a number of lines.
    42 Guilloche, or rope-like arrangement.
    43 Curvilinear meander.
    44 Scroll figures formed by straight lines with right angle turns.
    45 Curving scroll-like lines that often branch.
50 Chains of triangles or flags.
    51 Chain of isosceles triangles in a row parallel to the rim. Alternate triangles are inverted and nested so that a solid band of decoration is formed.
    52 V-shaped flags in a row parallel to the rim and hung either from the rim or from a line just below and parallel to the rim.
    53 U-shaped flags arranged in a row parallel to the rim.

54 Features arranged in zigzags; similar to a "worm fence" made of rails.

60 Features arranged parallel to one another or in parallel rows.
    61 Arranged parallel to the vessel lip.
    62 At forty-five degree angle to the vessel lip.
    63 Perpendicular to vessel lip.
    64 Series of herringbone arrangements parallel to vessel lip.
    65 Series of herringbone arrangements perpendicular to lip.

70 Crosshatching.
    71 Features run forty-five degrees to vessel lip.
    72 Lines run forty-five degrees to vessel lip. A punctate is centered in each diamond formed.
    73 Lines run forty-five degrees to vessel lip. Alternate diamonds are filled with features.

80 Features applied to the vessel lip.
    81 In the flat top of square lip.
    82 On the inside of outflaring lip.
    83 In flattened, outward-slanting lip.
    84 Features applied to rounded or pointed lip.

Decoration elements

Symbols in this list occupy the second position in the type expression.

20 Incised lines.
    21 Lines incised with a pointed instrument. These were made while the paste was still soft.
    22 Lines made with a blunt instrument. As much as one-fourth inch wide. Usually rough. Made while vessel paste was soft, so that the lines are plowed with uneven and ragged edges.
    23 Wide, deep lines, semicircular in cross section. Apparently made with a cane held at an acute angle to vessel surface. Paste was firm enough to result in clean cut (not plowed) lines.
    24 Overhanging lines. Incised with a flat, pointed instrument, held at such an angle that the tops of the lines are deeply incised, while the bottoms rise flush with the surface of the vessel wall. Made when paste was firm.
    25 Incised lines made with a pointed instrument. Small punctates are spaced in lines at short intervals.
    26 Lines, either incised with a pointed instrument before firing, or scratched after firing. Sometimes even incised after the surface was polished. Small spurs are spaced at short intervals on one side of the lines. Where the decoration was made in soft paste, the spurs are short lines; where scratched, they are often tiny triangles.
    27 Scratched lines. These were made after the vessel was fired.

28 Fine crosshatching made with delicate lines. This is either incised or scratched.

30 Combed lines.
   31 Narrow bands of lines made with a comb-like instrument. From four to six lines are usual. Lines are fine, and were incised in firm paste before firing.

40 Brushed decoration.
   41 Brushed with a bundle of fibers while vessel surface was plastic.
   42 Brushed by fingers held side by side while paste was plastic.

50 Rim notches.
   51 Deep notches cut into lip. Rough finish.
   52 Shallow scallops cut from outside edge of lip.
   53 Large scallops cut into rim.

60 Finger tip markings.
   61 Fingernail imprints.
   62 Rough areas raised by pinching between two fingers.
   63 Modeled teats or small nodes. Made with fingers, rough.
   64 Rough ridges raised by pinching between the fingers.

70 Punctates.
   71 Punctates made with a pointed instrument. Rough.
   72 Imprints made with the end of a cane cut at right angles.
   73 Semi-conical punctates, made with the end of a cane held at an acute angle to the vessel wall.
   74 Triangular punctates, shaped as though made with the corner of a cube. These are both large and small.

80 Fabric and cord imprints.
   81 Imprints of a cord wrapped paddle.
   82 Imprints of coiled basketry.

90 Stamp impressions.
   91 Check stamp (Louisiana coast types).
   92 Curvilinear stamp (Atlantic coast types).
   93 Zigzag stamp.

100 Rouletting.
   101 Large zigzag made either by an unnotched wheel or rocker stamp.
   102 Linear rouletting made with a notched wheel. Teeth about .1 inch square.
   103 Linear rouletting. Delicate. Made with a notched wheel with pointed teeth.
   104 Rows of delicate punctates that are almost indistinguishable from the delicate rouletting described as element 103.

110 Paint.
   111 A brick red, applied as a wash, before firing.

Adaptation and arrangement of features

Where used, these symbols occupy the third position in the type expression.

1   Motif brought out in negative. Inferior elements are used to fill or stipple the background so that the motif is formed by the undecorated surface.

2   Positive motif. Elements are used to fill the area of the motif so as to differentiate it from an unmarked background.

3   Bands an inch or more wide formed by a number of lines.

4   Four to six lines used to form bands not over half an inch wide.

5   Narrow bands not over half an inch wide formed of three lines; less often of four lines. This is usually accompanied by small circles used as nucleuses, and triangles made with a three-line band that serve as fillers in the vacant parts of the decoration.

6   Elements placed closely together; generally touching.

7   Elements placed over three-eights of an inch apart.

8   Only one or two lines used.

9   Single row of the feature described by the lower numbers in type used below the main decoration.

10 Features described by the lower numbers in the type used at the ends of lines.

11 Described features alternate to form pattern.

12 Features are used in the top of a short thickened area in the lip. Viewed from above this area is triangular in shape.

13 Decoration is on the vessel interior.

14 Decoration is applied to the entire exterior of the vessel.

In the above list, it will be noted that motifs and elements are arranged in typologically related groups. Each item is given two numbers: the first designates the group to which the motif or element belongs; the second specifies the particular members of each group.

Simple vessel decorations are expressed in terms of this classification by three sets of numbers which are separated by semicolons. These represent respectively: motif, element, and combination (example: type 45;23;6). Where no peculiarities of combination need be expressed, this designation is omitted; the index then consists of only two sets of figures (example: type 11;63).

Cases of two motifs or two elements involved in the same decoration are described by placing the most essential feature over the less important (examples: type $\frac{53}{61}$;21;2 and type 61;$\frac{24}{74}$;11). Body motifs are over motifs applied to the lip. Elements which outline motifs take precedence over those used as stippling.

Where two motifs are used in the same decoration and each is expressed by a different element, the dominant motif with its element is placed over the inferior. If the manner of combination applies specifically either to the superior or inferior features, it also is placed either above or below the line (example: type $\frac{61;24;6}{81;25}$).

In some cases the old classification included two sets of elements or modes of application, either of which was allowed in the same type. To transfer these it is necessary to show that either one or the other comprises the type. This is effected by listing both feature designations and separating them by a slanting line to signify "or" (examples: type 63;$\frac{24/21}{71}$;10, and type 53;111;1/2). Where two elements were used to express the same motif, their designations were divided by commas (example: type 34;$\frac{26,27}{21/28}$;1).

The principal advantage of this system is the facility with which specific parts of the different types may be compared from a list of the type symbols. Thus, if it is desirable to know how often overhanging lines (element 24) or triangular punctates (element 74) appear in the list of types used in the table given as figure 1, all that is necessary is to note where the appropriate numbers are used in the element column.

Decoration complexes

As the work of classifying the village site collections progressed, it became apparent that on the basis of decorations the sites could be placed in several different categories. This tendency is clearly shown in the comparative table, figure 1. The types found at sites thus differentiated were so very dissimilar that it appeared probable that they were the results of the sway of distinct and separate schools of ceramic art styles. The term "decoration complex" will be used to refer to each of these groups of peculiar artistic styles.

Nearly all the decorated material conforms to the types of seven different complexes. Four have been associated with historic tribes and from these have received their names: Choctaw, Natchez, Caddo, and Tunica. The other three appear to be entirely prehistoric in the local area and are named for sites at which they were first recognized: Deasonville, Coles Creek, and Marksville.

The few scattered types that cannot be associated with any of these complexes are of two classes: either they are found so infrequently that their association is uncertain, or they are commonly found in more than one complex. These are listed in the comparative table as "unrelated" types (see Figure 1).

The seven complexes that have been found in the Louisiana-Mississippi area have rather well defined geographical limits along the boundaries that occur within the region studied. In dealing with semi-sedentary cultures this development of localized areas is to be expected. The few cases where isolated villages are found far outside the normal range of their particular pottery complex can be attributed to the white man's interference with the normal life of the people. Such examples are the Choctaw site found in Louisiana on the Marksville prairie (Site No. 4, Nick Place, page 48), and the Natchez Fort site, near Sicily Island (Site No. 7, page 65).

As far as historical evidence goes, the types of pottery determined for the various tribes found by the European explorers are very consistently associated with those tribes, and are confined to the areas they are known to have held. This is true in all except one case—the late Tunica site at the mouth of Red River (see page 129). In view of this usual correlation, it seems best to attach the names of the different groups to the types of ware with which they are associated. It is recognized that back of the historic period there can be no certainty that the historic Choctaw type of material was always and only made by the Choctaw tribe. However, it is as simple to keep this fact in mind as to associate a different name for the material with the historic groups of Indians. As used here, the tribal names have become archeological terms that describe certain decoration complexes. All attempts to project political or linguistic groups back into the prehistoric era are questionable; archeology can only speak with confidence in terms of a small part of the material culture.

The names of the complexes refer only to ceramic styles. It is intended that they serve for this purpose only until all recoverable evidence of the old cultures has been secured. Then appropriate names, arranged according to some accepted system, may be adopted for the cultural divisions.

Internal characteristics of decoration complexes

All the complexes in the area except the Choctaw are made up of several decoration types. In the Coles Creek, there are as many as thirty-six distinct types. Of course, every type is not found on each site where any one of the complexes dominates. This probably results from the smallness of some of the collections. That a type appears on a majority of the sites representing a complex must be accepted as evidence that it is associated with that complex of types.

The numerical proportion of the different types in their respective complexes proves to be of special significance. In each complex one or more decorations form a strikingly large proportion of the site material. These are the decorations that are more likely to be found in small site collections. From their role as the most typical features, they have received the name of "marker types". The marker types are identified in the type descriptions that follow, and on the table comparing the percentages of types at the various sites (Figure 1) they are marked by asterisks. The percentages of these types are indicated by bolder figures.

Type sites

In geological field-work a new horizon is presented by fully describing the characteristics of a type site. All subsequent finds of a comparable nature are measured by this standard.

Cultural complexes cannot very well be introduced by this method. The features are more flexible than the products of organic evolution, and variation is the rule rather than an exception. For this reason it seems best to present descriptions of several type sites for each new complex. Only in this way is it possible to demonstrate that specific features are products of real styles spread over certain areas, and are not local variations or inventions.

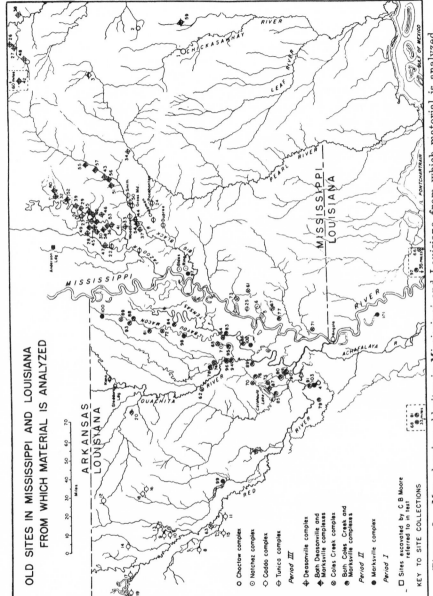

Figure 2.   Map showing old sites in Mississippi and Louisiana from which material is analyzed.

GEOGRAPHICAL DESCRIPTION

Northwestern Louisiana midden deposits are generally found on the tops of fairly high, red, sandy ridges overlooking small streams, or on the lakes that connect with Red River. Black soil, quantities of sherds, animal bones, and other evidence of occupation mark the sites. They usually cover from three to five acres, but, at a few places along the shores of the Red River lakes, the refuse deposits extend for a mile or more. Mounds are found at only a few sites in the valley of the Red. Small truncated pyramids and conical forms are both represented.

Few sites are found in the hills that form the divide between the Red and the Ouachita Rivers. Typical Mississippi Valley conditions appear along the Ouachita. The highest locations available in the valley floor were chosen in the attempt to keep above spring floods. On the map (Figure 2) it will be noticed that almost no sites are found in the active flood plain between the Tensas and the Mississippi in Louisiana, or between the Yazoo and the Mississippi in the Yazoo-Mississippi Delta of Mississippi. Sites are located along the higher natural levees that border the more ancient courses of the Mississippi—the Tensas or the Yazoo for example. Maçon Ridge, between the Ouachita and the Tensas, was thickly settled at one time. Its elevated position and arable land, near the swamps stretching to the east, must have been ideal for the native economy. The country around Catahoula and Larto Lakes and the Marksville Prairie offered favorable situations which appear to have been used advantageously.

Along the bluffs that border the Mississippi River on the east, old sites are scattered every few miles. Some lie in the valleys of streams that cut down through the bluffs to the valley floor; others are on talus fans at the foot of the bluffs; still others occupy the edge of the tableland, a hundred or more feet above the river.

Sites in the Mississippi Valley are rather compact. Rarely do they cover more than four or five acres. Even where there is an extensive mound group, the midden refuse is generally confined to a small section of the site. The middens are distinctive and can be easily detected. Usually the soil is darker than normal, and sometimes is quite black. Potsherds, charcoal, ashes, and fragments of animal bones are abundant. In spite of this concentration, the deposits rarely reach an appreciable depth. Four to ten inches is average.

Mounds are found near approximately three-fourths of the middens. From one to four or five mounds are not uncommon. Few sites have more than ten. Truncated pyramids are usual. In height they range from barely perceptible elevations to forty-five and fifty feet. Some of the higher ones have ramp approaches. At some of the sites, the mounds are arranged as though grouped about a large rectangular or rounded court. The structures do not seem to have any consistent orientation. Small steep conicals not over fifteen feet high accompany the truncated pyramids at a few sites. At others they are the only form of earthwork. Perhaps ten sites have been found where there are mounds associated with an enclosure formed by an earth wall. These are of two general types: fairly small, rounded enclosures with mounds spaced at intervals along the earth walls; and larger enclosures with gaps at intervals in the walls, and most of the mounds arranged inside the enclosed space.

A few groups of mounds, in other ways apparently normal, are not accompanied by midden deposits. It seems probable that at some of these the camp debris has been overlain by alluvium deposited by the annual overflows. Excavation at three of such sites has discovered a stratum of midden soil buried as much as five feet beneath the present surface.

Most of the old villages in the Yazoo-Mississippi Delta are marked by a large accumulation of fresh water mussel shells. This is so distinctive that the sites are referred to locally as "shell ridges". Four to five feet is by no means an unusual depth for these deposits. They often cover several acres. Potsherds and other camp refuse are scattered throughout, so there is no doubt that these are normal midden deposits.

EARLY HISTORY

The area described was included in the French province of Louisiana. Except for the meager narratives of the DeSoto expedition, it was first made known to Europeans through French explorations in the latter part of the seventeenth and the early eighteenth centuries. Soldiers and missionaries penetrated trails and streams of the region, and left fairly good accounts of their work in letters, reports, and maps that have been preserved in the archives of France.

The best recent summaries and syntheses of this material are found in the publications of Dr. John R. Swanton of the Bureau of American Ethnology (BAE Bull. 43), "Indian Tribes of the Lower Mississippi Valley and Adjacent Coast of the Gulf of Mexico", and "Early History of the Creek Indians and their Neighbors" (BAE Bull. 73). Excellent additional material is given in the bibliography.

For practical purposes, the year 1700 may be considered as the beginning of the historic period. At this date the distribution of the tribes was known, but they had not been seriously disturbed by the whites.

This area was the meeting point of four large, widespread linguistic stocks: the Muskhogean, Siouan, Caddoan and Attakapan. A fifth stock, the Tunican, is included in the area, and appears to have no direct outside connections (map, Figure 3).

The large Creek confederacy of Georgia and Alabama was the most powerful unit of the Muskhogean linguistic family. In Mississippi, Muskhogean languages were spoken by the large tribe of Choctaw, who occupied the east central

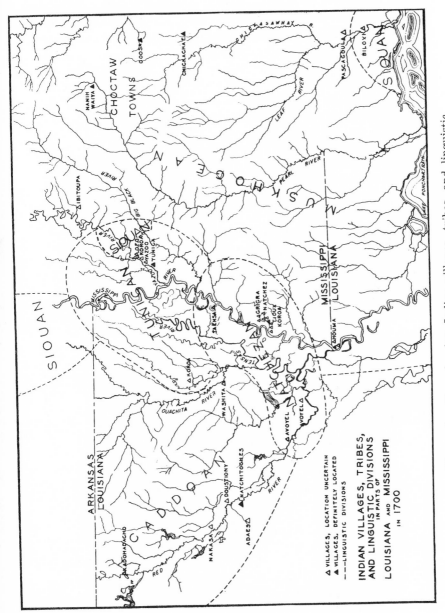

Figure 3. Map showing Indian villages, tribes, and linguistic divisions in parts of Louisiana and Mississippi in the year 1700.

and southeastern parts of the state; the small group of
Houma, who were settled on the east side of the Mississippi
River opposite the mouth of the Red; the Chocchuma, north
of the Choctaw on the Yazoo and Pearl Rivers; the Ibitoupa,
on the upper Yazoo River; and to the north, beyond the
range of this study, the Chickasaw in northern Mississippi.
Linguistically, the Natchez, Tensas, and the Avoyel were
slightly apart from the other members of the Muskhogean
family, and are assigned by some students to a distinct family called "Natchezan". However, Swanton has recognized
that properly the Natchez language is a member of the
Muskhogean family. The Natchez tribe was situated near
the present town of Natchez, Mississippi, on the east side
of the Mississippi River and forty-two miles above the
mouth of the Red. The Tensas were on Lake St. Joseph,
thirty-eight miles higher up on the west side of the river;
and the Avoyel were located on the Marksville prairie, in
the Louisiana parish which has taken their name.

The tribes of the isolated Tunican family occupied the
lower Yazoo River valley in Mississippi and extended westward into Louisiana to the Tensas and Ouachita Rivers. On
the Yazoo were the Yazoo, Tunica, and part of the tribe
of Koroa. Another band of Koroa was on the Ouachita in
northern Louisiana, and still another group was settled
near the Natchez.

The Siouan languages were represented by the small
tribe of Ofo. Part of these people were settled near the
Natchez towns, and the rest on the Lower Yazoo River with
the Tunican speaking tribes. The nearest linguistic rela-
tives of the Ofo were the Quapaw of the Arkansas River
country, beyond whom an expanding wedge of Siouan speaking people extended to the north. Southward there was another small group of this same stock, the Biloxi. These had
evidently passed down the lower Mississippi at a recent
date and reached their place on the Mississippi Gulf coast
where they formed a small isolated group among the Muskhogean Choctaw. The French settlement of Biloxi received
its name from this tribe.

North and northwest of the Avoyel, up the Red River valley, and extending over all the country to the Ouachita River were tribes of the Caddoan linguistic family. The Washitas were on the Ouachita River not far above its junction with the Tensas. On Red River, near the present town of Natchitoches, Louisiana, were the Natchitoches and Doustiony groups. A few miles to the southwest, on a small branch of the Red, were the Adai. The Kadohadacho, from whom the name "Caddo" is derived, was a large tribe centered around the present town of Shreveport and around Caddo Lake, one of the raft-formed lakes on the Louisiana-Texas border. Other Caddo speaking people were found in Texas and in Oklahoma.

Properly the Attakapan peoples do not belong in this discussion since they did not occupy part of the area in historic times. They were the southern neighbors of the Caddo, and the western neighbors of the small groups of Muskhogeans who lived near the mouth of the Mississippi River. The Attakapa were settled on the rivers flowing into the Gulf of Mexico in southwestern Louisiana. Westward they extended along the Texas coast.

This, then, is a rough picture of the distribution of the tribes found by the French in 1700. A difficult problem of local archeology is the identification of the material cultures of each of these groups in historic times. The records are too scarce, the historic sites too modest, and the large prehistoric sites too tempting to have insured much work of this nature. However, the pottery types at least of the Choctaw, Natchez, Tunica, and Caddo have been determined. Further discussions of the history of these tribes accompany the section devoted to describing their sites.

MATERIAL TO BE PRESENTED

All of the collections from the Louisiana-Mississippi area that are large enough to promise a true picture of the conditions on their respective sites will be considered in this study. Size has been the only criterion used in selecting these collections. Where possible, collections of more than fifty decorated sherds were used. In some instances this was not practical; smaller collections had to be included to show particulars of geographic range. This is especially true with the Deasonville sites.

The surveys have secured many collections that are too small to permit statistical analysis. These will not be considered, but as far as can be determined they all conform to normal conditions as outlined here.

The impossibility of illustrating representative material from all the sites is obvious. Several sites scattered over the geographical area of each complex have been selected. The sites from which material is illustrated are described in the text.

Sherds that best conform to and illustrate the different types have not been selected for illustration. An attempt is made to show something of the latitude that was allowed in classifying material. Often certain sherds are illustrated for no better reason than that they fit the space in the plate and allow more material to be included. Explanations are placed on the pages facing the plates. The descriptions of the sherds are grouped according to complexes.

This study is centered about the information contained in the table comparing percentages of decoration types at the different sites (Figure 1). Sites are arranged down the side of the table, and are grouped according to complexes. Across the top, the decoration types are also arranged by complexes. The map (Figure 2) shows the location of these sites. Numbers identifying the villages on the map correspond to those before the site names in the table. A few villages are beyond the limits of the area included in the map. Around the border will be found arrows pointing in their direction with distances indicated.

Excavated material from burials is presented from several localities. This is not included in the comparative table for reasons already given (page 9). The material illustrated from these sites should make their relationships apparent. On the distribution map (Figure 2), burial sites are identified by name.

The exact locations will be given of only the village sites that are described in the text. These are spaced over the areas covered by the various complexes, and are intended to serve as type sites. They can be easily located by anyone who wishes to examine them through the use of the detailed quadrangles issued by the Mississippi River Commission or county and parish maps. Locations of all sites dealt with in this paper, as well as a number of other sites from which inadequate collections have been made, are on file at the School of Geology, Louisiana State University, Baton Rouge, Louisiana. This information is available to all responsible parties who may be interested in research in the region.

The foregoing has been chiefly concerned with a description of the methods, theories, and geographic and historical background of this study. The following sections are devoted to a description of the material. Theory will be avoided as much as possible. In the interest of orderly arrangement, however, it is necessary to introduce the principal conclusions of the study, chronological order, as an outline. This order consists of three time periods, which, with the included decoration complexes are as follows:

Period III   Choctaw, Natchez, Caddo, and Tunica decoration complexes.

Period II   Deasonville and Coles Creek decoration complexes.

Period I   Marksville decoration complex.

PERIOD III

Choctaw complex

History of the Choctaw tribe

Inland from their settlements on the Gulf coast the French found a large tribe of Muskhogean-speaking people, the Choctaw, occupying approximately sixty towns situated on the streams that form the headwaters of the Pearl and Pascagoula Rivers. The location of these towns is shown by four maps dating between 1715 and 1770 which are published by Swanton in his "Early History of the Creek Indians and their Neighbors" (BAE Bull. 73, Pls. 4, 5, 6, 7). Present purposes do not demand that all the Choctaw towns be listed. The particular ones with which we are concerned will be mentioned later.

The Choctaw became attached to the French at an early date. By means of unceasing and delicate diplomacy, the young colony used them as a bulwark against the machinations of the English, who controlled the Chickasaw and other tribes to the north and east. Numerically the Choctaw were the most powerful group under French control. Bienville, in 1702, estimates that they could provide between 3,800 and 4,000 warriors. On the basis of three and a half people to each warrior, Dr. Swanton has estimated that the total population would be about thirteen or fourteen thousand[2]. In view of the figures given by several later travellers through the Choctaw country, this does not seem to be exorbitant[3].

The southernmost Choctaw town was Yowani, situated on the Chickasawhay River in what is now the southern part of Wayne County, Mississippi. At the northern border of the territory is the Nanih Waiya mound. This moderately large earthwork is a truncated, pyramidal structure similar

---

[2]Swanton, BAE bull. 73, p. 452.
[3]Idem.

40

to those so common in the Mississippi valley. The mound was sacred to the Choctaw and played a prominent part in the different versions of their creation legends.[4] Apparently there was no large permanent village at the site. However, at least one important general council of the nation was held there in historic times[5].

After France relinquished the colony of Louisiana, the Choctaw came for a while, in the latter part of the eighteenth century, under Spanish dominion. Their holdings were not seriously disturbed, however, until they had passed into the hands of the United States government and the state of Mississippi was formed in 1817. The Treaty of Doak's Stand (1820), which resulted from the pressure ot a rapidly increasing white population, secured the removal of most of the tribe from the state. The majority of the Indians went to land ceded to them along the Red River in Oklahoma. Some scattered into Alabama and Louisiana; others remained in their ancestral territory and finally became citizens of the state of Mississippi. Today many are still to be found in Neshoba and Winston Counties.

One of the bands that moved to Louisiana settled in the Bayou Lacomb region, near the north shore of Lake Pontchartrain. Here they were visited and described by Bushnell in 1909[6]. At present only two or three individuals are left.

Another band moved to the pine covered hills in La Salle Parish and their descendants are found not far from Jena, Louisiana. Others, until fifteen years ago, lived near Alexandria, in Rapides Parish. This last band left a cemetery near the Woodward Forest Nursery which is still pointed out by local people. It seems very probable that Choctaws were also responsible for the historic burials that were found on the Marksville prairie at the Nick plantation site (Site No. 4, page 48).

---

[4]Swanton, BAE bull. 103, pp. 5-37.
[5]Idem, p. 36.
[6]Bushnell, David I., BAE bull. 48.

Identification of Choctaw ceramics

Professor H. S. Halbert, who lived and studied among the Mississippi Choctaw in the latter part of the nineteenth century, has contributed largely to the ethnology and recent history of the Choctaw. Among his accomplishments is the location of several of the more important villages[7]. Basing his work largely on Halbert's information, H. B. Collins, Jr., of the United States National Museum, made collections in 1925 from four historic Choctaw villages: Ponta (Coosa), Halunlawasha, Chickachae, and Yowanee[8]. Although all the material was basically similar, only two sites yielded what can be considered adequate collections: Ponta (Coosa) and Chichachae.

Choctaw pottery complex

Collins found that the historic Choctaw pottery complex consisted of only one very distinctive type. This is described as follows:

Type 40;31;4 (Marker type)

40 Motif: Uusually curvilinear scroll or scroll-like figures. Less often, angular zigzagged figures are employed. Generally a band of lines runs parallel to the rim, one-fourth to one-half an inch below it, to form a top border for the decorated area.

31 Elements: Bands of lightly incised lines made with a comb-like instrument. Generally there are four to six fine lines in each band. In width the bands vary from two-eighths to three-eighths inches. A few sherds appear to have been decorated free hand but in close imitation of the comb technique.

4 Arrangement: Four to six lines forming bands that are about three-eighths of an inch wide.

---

[7]Halbert, H. S., Bernard Roman's Map of 1772, pp. 415-439.
[8]Collins, H. B. Jr., Potsherds from Choctaw Village Sites in Mississippi.

This decoration was applied after the paste had hardened so that the incised lines are clean cut, and did not plow up the surface. The area of the vessel that is decorated appears to be a band about the upper part of the walls. Decoration did not extend under the bottom.

Usual Accompanying Characteristics:

All of the shapes of the vessels decorated in this manner are not known. Apparently the most common was a small food bowl not more than six to eight inches in diameter, and three to four inches in height. Bottoms were rounded, and

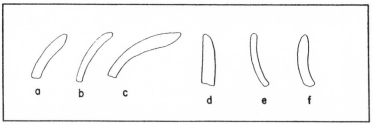

Figure 4.   Profiles of rim sherds of the Choctaw complex.

rims were slightly incurving and never thickened. Lips are either rounded or form a rounded point in profile. This last feature is formed by the sherds having straight exterior walls to which the interior walls curve (Figure 4). Appendages, such as handles or lugs, are not found on the Choctaw ware.

Choctaw pottery from eastern Mississippi is fine grained, but decidedly sandy. Sand appears to have been the only tempering used. The ware is of medium hardness and ranges from .2 to .7 inches in thickness. About .4 inches is average. Paste colors are of various shades of salmon, buff, and grey, mottled with black. Light red and salmon colored slips are rare.

The texture of the ware from the Nick Plantation (Site No. 4) in the Marksville Prairie of Louisiana is decidedly different. Here the paste is uniformly grey in color, .2

inches thick, hard, and contains no sand. The sherds have a very good polish, but, in all other features, resemble the Mississippi material.

Sites of the Choctaw complex

Site No. 1, Chickachae, and Site No. 2, Coosa

Chickachae and Coosa are two historic village sites of the Choctaw tribe from which Collins secured enough decorated material to permit statistical analysis. In support of the documentary evidence identifying these sites, gunflints, lead bullets, and blue glass beads were found on each[9]. In a personal communication, Mr. Collins writes that mounds were not found near the sites. Both were located in plowed fields near small streams. Surface material was scanty.

A cemetery found at Coosa was the only burial arrangement determined for any of the historic sites. This appeared to date between the years 1800 and 1830, at a time when the Indians had lost much of their own culture. The use of burial furniture—cooking utensils, porcelain, and beads—was all that differentiated the graves from those of the whites[10].

In the region of the Choctaw towns, Collins investigated a site on the farm of Mr. Lawrence Slay near Crandall, in Clark County, at which there were eight small, conical burial mounds. Human bones were found arranged in layers that strongly suggested the early Choctaw method of exposing the dead on scaffolds, cleaning the bones, and then erecting a mound over a number of individuals at one time[11].

Site No. 3, Nanih Waiya

The survey party of the Mississippi Department of Archives and History has done very little work in the region of the historic Choctaw villages. In the summer of 1933,

---

[9]Collins, H. B. Jr., Potsherds from Choctaw Village Sites in Mississippi.

[10]Collins, H. B. Jr., Archeological and Anthropometrical Work in Mississippi, pp. 93-94.

[11]Idem, pp. 90-91. See also Swanton, BAE bull. 103, pp. 173-177.

M. B. Chambers secured a collection from the field about Nanih Waiya mound, which is located in the southern part of Winston County, Mississippi.

The site consists of a large pyramidal mound; a small flattened, round structure; and an enclosing earth wall, the greater part of which has been plowed away. Dr. Calvin S. Brown gives an excellent description of the large mound:

> It is a typical rectangular mound, 218 feet long by 140 feet wide at the base, thus covering seven-tenths of an acre. The axis is north-west by south-east. The dimensions of the flat top are 132 feet by 56 feet, the area being one-sixth of an acre. The height is 22 feet, in some places nearly 25 feet. The slopes of the mound are covered with trees; the top seems to have been cultivated[12].

According to Dr. Brown, the small mound 250 yards northeast of the large one has been spread out by cultivation, and is now seven or eight feet high. He also notes a short section of the earth embankment that formerly surrounded the site. Earlier accounts by Dr. Lincecum, 1843; B. L. C. Wailes, 1854; and S. S. Halbert, 1877, describe the enclosure before its almost complete obliteration. These accounts are summarized by Swanton in Bulletin 103, Bureau of American Ethnology, pages 6-9.

Surface material from Nanih Waiya is illustrated in figure 5. The percentages of the different types found there are shown in the comparative table given as figure 1. A very noticeable fact is that not only is the historic Choctaw complex of pottery present here, but there is also material from the Deasonville complex of Period II, and a small proportion of Marksville sherds, Period I.

If a guess may be hazarded, it is that, when the site is thoroughly examined, the results will agree with one version of the Choctaw origin myths, which states that the Choctaws did not build the structure, but found it already there when they moved into the region. The site appears to be a typical

---

[12]Brown, C. S., Archeology of Mississippi, p. 24.

DESCRIPTION OF SHERDS IN FIGURE 5

Sherd	Type	Color of Paste	Finish (Good, Medium Poor)	Temper	Hardness (Hard, Medium Soft)	Thickness (inches)	Remarks
				PERIOD III.—CHOCTAW			
a	40;31;4	Black	M	Grit	M	.3	Rim of bowl
b	40;31;4	Black	M	Grit	M	.3	Rim·
c	40;31;4	Black	G	Sand	M	.3	Rim
d	40;31;4	Black	M	Sand	M	.2	....
e	40;31;4	Black	M	Sand	M	.2	Rim
f	11;81;14	Light grey	P	Vegetable	M	.2	....
				PERIOD II.—DEASONVILLE			
g	11;81;14	Black	P	Grit	S	.4	....
h	11;81;14	Tan	P	Vegetable	M	.2	....
i	11;81;14	Grey	P	Vegetable	M	.3	....
j	11;81;14	Grey	P	Sand	M	.3	....
				PERIOD I.—MARKSVILLE			
k	$31;\dfrac{23}{101/102};\frac{1}{2}$	Light Green	M	Grit	M	.2	....
l	$31;\dfrac{23}{101/102};\frac{1}{2}$	Tan	M	Grit	M	.2	Thickened rim
m	51;23	Black	M	Sand	M	.3	Thickened rim

Material from Nanih Waiya (Site No. 3).

47

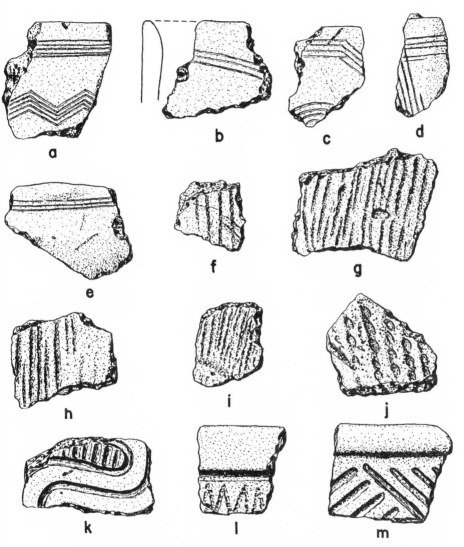

Figure 5. Selection of representative material from the fields
about the Nanih Waiya mound (Site No. 3).

Mississippi Valley mound, but it is one hundred fifty miles east of its natural setting. The strangeness of such a great earthwork in the country occupied by the Choctaws probably accounts for the great veneration it received from that tribe.

Site No. 4, Nick plantation

Irreg. S 71, T2N, R4E

On the Nick plantation, one mile south of Marksville, Louisiana, a conical mound was located by the writer in 1933. It is situated near the eastern escarpment of the Marksville Prairie on the south side of Coulie des Grues, a small stream that empties into Old River. At present the mound is eighty feet in diameter, and ten feet high. It has been cultivated for some time. Earth held in place by the roots of small trees shows that the mound has lost at least three feet in height as a result of plowing.

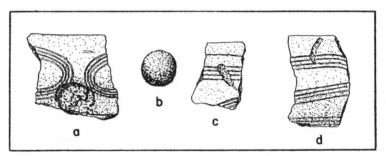

Figure 6. Material from site No. 4, Nick place.
a. type 40;31;4, brown, grit temper, 0.2 inch thick, shallow bowl.
b. lead musket ball.
c. type 40;31;4, grey, grit temper, 0.2 inch thick, shallow bowl.
d. type 40;31;4, brown, grit temper, 0.2 inch thick, shallow bowl.

No material could be found in the surrounding field, but in the furrows running across the structure were human bones, blue glass beads, fragments of iron, a brass turkey bell, and sherds of the typical Choctaw pottery (Figure 6).

Probably these burials were deposited by one of the bands of Indians that left Mississippi after the treaty of

Doak's Stand. These may have been the same people who lived in the vicinity of Alexandria, Louisiana, forty miles to the northwest, until about 1920 (page 41).

Another probable conclusion is that the Choctaw burials were merely shallow interments in the top of a structure built much earlier than the period of their occupation. The size and shape of the mound are very similar to those at the Marksville site located only one mile to the north (page 226).

More evidence that seems to point to a former occupation of the area by the Choctaw within recent times was found in 1932 by a negro tenant in the southern end of the Marksville enclosure. He found a burial a few feet under the surface in his garden. Accompanying it were iron, C-shaped bracelets, glass beads, and an undecorated hemispherical bowl very similar in shape, paste, and finish to the vessels indicated by the sherds from the Nick place.

DESCRIPTION OF CHOCTAW COMPLEX SITES

Site No.	Site Name	Cemetery	Mound	Conical Low —10'	Conical Tall +10'	Pyramidal Low —10'	Pyramidal Tall +10'	Ramp	Enclosures	Approximate Area	Thin —10"	Thick +10"	Collection Analysis	Minimum Date
1	Chickachae									4A	X		Choctaw	1830
2	Coosa	X								3A	X		Choctaw	1830
3	*Nanih Waiya			1			1	X	X	3A	X		Choctaw, Deasonville, Marksville	
4	*Nick place..		X†			1†								

†Burials appear to be intrusive into the mound, and properly should be classed as surface burials. Mound is probably much older than the period of Choctaw occupation.

*Sites which are described in the text and from which material is illustrated.

Natchez complex

Historical sketch of the Natchez tribe

The early history of the Natchez fared exceptionally well at the hands of the French explorers. Not only was this the strongest group with whom they had to deal in traffic up the lower Mississippi, but their highly developed religious customs and tragic end made good copy.

At the end of the seventeenth century, the Natchez were situated on the east side of the Mississippi River, forty-two miles above the mouth of the Red, near the site of the present town of Natchez, Mississippi. They occupied nine[13] villages scattered along St. Catherine's Creek, which for most of its course lies approximately three miles east of and parallel to the high bluffs along the Mississippi. Cabins forming the villages were strung out to such an extent that all the towns in reality formed one long community.

From the figures given by various observers, Dr. Swanton has estimated that the total population of the Natchez about the year 1698 was approximately 3,500. One thousand warriors are estimated, and four hundred cabins.[14] Native tradition recorded by De la Ventre says that formerly the people were much more numerous—at least five thousand.[15]

The history of the Natchez begins in 1682, with the visit of La Salle and Tonti. On their journey down the river, they stopped at the landing and La Salle visited the Natchez villages:

M. de la Salle went with seven men to their village 3 leagues distant from the river on rising ground.[16]

---

[13]This is Iberville's figure. De Montigny says "ten or twelve", see Swanton, BAE bull. 43, p. 45.

[14]Swanton, BAE bull. 43, p. 43.

[15]Ibid., p. 39.

[16]Swanton, BAE bull. 43, p. 187, from Margry, Découvertes, I, pp. 602-603.

The central village of the Natchez appears to have been the "Grand Village" or "the village of the Chief" to which Iberville was conducted on his visit in 1700.

> The 11th [of March 1700] I reached the landing place of the Natchez, which I find to be 18 leagues distant from the Oumas . . . I sent a man to inform the chief of my arrival. The brother of the chief with 20 men came to bring me the calumet of peace, and invited me to go to the village. Two hours after midday I was

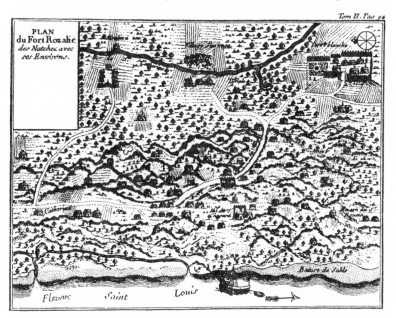

Tom II. Pao 94

PLAN
du Fort Rozalié
des Natchez avec
ses Environs.

Fleuve   Saint   Louis

Courtesy of Dr. John R. Swanton

Figure 7. Map of the French settlement at the Natchez about 1725. This shows landing, Fort Rosalie, and the concessions of St. Catherine and White Apple with the Grand Village of the Natchez between them.

(From Dumont, Mémoires Historiques sur La Louisiane, II, p. 94).

> at this village which is a league[17] from the edge of the water. Half way there I met the chief who came before me accompanied by twenty men very well built. The

---

[17]At this time a French league was approximately equal to three modern English miles.

chief was very sick of a flux, a sickness of which the
savages almost always die . . . We repaired to his [the
chief's] cabin, which was raised to a height of 10 feet
on earth brought thither, and is 25 feet wide and 45
long. Near by are 8 cabins. Before that of the chief
is the temple mound, which forms a round, a little oval,
and bounds an open space about 250 paces wide and 300
long. A stream passes near, from which they draw their
water [St. Catherine's Creek] . . . From the landing
place on the river one ascends a very steep hillside about
150 fathoms high covered completely with woods. Being
on top of the hill one finds a country of plains and
prairies filled with little hills, in some places groves of
trees, many oaks, and many roads cut through, going
from one hamlet to another or to cabins.[18]

After a difficulty with the Natchez in 1714, which was
referred to as the "First Natchez War", Bienville established a fort on the high bluff over the natives' landing
place. The post was named Fort Rosalie. In 1718 Le Page
du Pratz came to the Natchez, and acting as agent for a
M. Hubert of New Orleans, purchased two grants from the
Indians located on both sides of the Grand Village. One of
these was for M. Hubert, and the other for the Western
Company. M. Hubert's grant was situated north of the
village, and was called St. Catherines; the one for the company was immediately below, and received the name of
White Earth. A map from Dumont's "Mémoires Historiques
sur La Louisiane", II, page 85, (see Figure 7) shows the
landing on the river, Fort Rosalie, and the concessions of
St. Catherines and White Earth. Between the concessions
is a native village which, from the description of Du Pratz,
must be the Grand Village.

A number of smaller concessions were occupied in the
neighborhood and at least two hundred fifty Frenchmen had
arrived at the station by the latter part of the second decade.
Relations with the natives, however, continued to be somewhat precarious. In 1722 the "Second Natchez War" occurred and was followed by a third skirmish in the autumn
of the following year.

[18]Swanton, BAE bull. 43, pp. 190-191, from Margry, Découvertes, IV, pp. 410-412.

In 1729 the Natchez suddenly attacked the post thinking that the Tunica, Choctaw, and other tribes under French dominion would act in concert with them. Nearly all the garrison and habitants were killed. The few survivors fled down the river, and reached New Orleans with news of the massacre.

But the Natchez had acted too soon. The Choctaw avoided antagonizing the French and instead joined them in their revenge on the Natchez. Revenge was not unanticipated. The Natchez constructed two forts on each side of St. Catherines: Fort Valour and Fort Farine. Here they were attacked early in 1730 by the French and Choctaw. The engagement settled into a siege from which the entire Natchez nation soon escaped through the negligence of their attackers.

They fled westward across the Mississippi to the western border of the swamp country along the Tensas River, where they constructed another fort. After receiving slight reinforcements from France, the French and their Indian allies, under the personal direction of Governor Perier proceeded up the Red River to the mouth of the Black, then up the Black and the Tensas until they found the Natchez. The Natchez fort was surrounded with entrenchments and shelled with mortars. Once again, owing to the negligence of the French and their reluctant allies, most of the Natchez succeeded in escaping. They broke up into bands and scattered to the other tribes. A large number joined the Chickasaws; others attached themselves to the Cherokees and the Washitas.

This ends the history of the Natchez as a tribe. The French took over their territory near the river while the back country became the hunting ground of the Choctaw.

Discussion of Natchez pottery

The prevailing ceramic decoration types of the Natchez are less distant from the general background of southeastern pottery than the Choctaw. Though specialized to a lesser degree, they are almost as distinctive. Bands of three or four lines drawn freehand forming scroll and meander figures are the prominent features. With all their attendant peculiarities, these have been found only on sites near the historic territory of the Natchez. Most of these sites show evidence of European contact. The few which do appear to be prehistoric are probably not of any great age.

The common rim profiles of the Natchez pottery types are shown in figure 8.

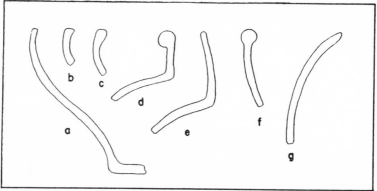

Figure 8.   Profiles of rim sherds of the Natchez complex.

Historic Natchez pottery types

Type 41;21;5 (Marker type)

41   Motif: Curvilinear interlocking scroll.

21   Elements: Incised lines made with a pointed instrument.

5   Arrangement: Lines are arranged in narrow bands which usually consist of three lines, but in some cases only two lines. Incised triangles are often used to fill in the vacant spaces above and below the bands of lines which join the whorls formed where the scrolls meet. Small circles are sometimes utilized as nucleuses or centers for the junctional whorls of the scrolls.

   The lines of the decorations were incised after the paste had become fairly hard so that they are cleanly cut with no jagged edges or plowed effect.

Usual Accompanying Characteristics:

The decoration is usually applied to the body of the vessels in an encircling panel which may or may·not extend to the vessel bottom. A single line, or a band of lines, is used to mark the top and bottom of the decorated panel. On pots or bottles with necks, the decoration starts at the base of the neck; on vessels without necks, a narrow undecorated border is left between rim and decoration.

Vessel shapes: The narrow-band scroll and meander decorations, characteristic of the historic Natchez, occur on a number of different vessel shapes which appear to be peculiar to the ware. These are illustrated in figure 9.

The rims of the vessels are usually unthickened and have rounded edges. None of the vessels have outflaring rims. Several bottles have beaded edges which project slightly outward (Figure 8, sherds d, f).

Handles and lugs are entirely lacking on this ware.

Paste: The paste of the Natchez marker types is of smooth, fine texture. It is hard, and takes a high polish. Thickness, which averages .2 inches, is very uniform in the vessel walls. Bottoms are generally slightly thicker than the side walls.

Very fine sand and sometimes finely ground charcoal were used to temper the paste.

The color of the pottery is a fairly uniform light chocolate, which is darker in the pieces that are highly polished.

Slips are unusual, and generally there is slight difference in color between the interior and exterior paste of sherds. One scroll-decorated vessel (Figure 9 l) was covered with a reddish slip that had been scraped from all the vessel surface except that enclosed between the lines outlining the decoration.

Type 43;21;5

43   Motif: Curvilinear meander (Figure 9 c, e).

21   Elements: Neatly incised lines, made with a pointed instrument.

DESCRIPTION OF MATERIAL IN FIGURE 9

Sherd	Type	Color of Paste	Finish (Good, Medium Poor)	Temper	Hardness (Hard, Medium Soft)	Thickness (inches)	Remarks
				PERIOD III.—NATCHEZ POTTERY TYPES			
a	43;21;5	Brown	G	Grit, Charcoal	....	.2	....
b	Iron axe	....	....	....	....	....	....
c	43;21;5	Grey	G	Charcoal	....	.2	....
d	42;21;5	Brown	G	Grit	....	.2	....
e	43;21;5	Brown	G	Shell, Grit	....	.3	....
f	....	Grey	P	Sand	....	.2	....
g	43;21;5	Mottled, Brown and Black	M	Grit	....	.2	....
h	Iron Bracelets	....	....	....	....	....	....
i	43;21;5	Brown	M	Charcoal, Grit	....	.2	....
j	41;$\frac{21}{28}$;2 (1)	Grey	M	Grit	....	.2	....
k	Brass Turkey Bells						
l	Red slip in line enclosed bands forming scroll	....	....	Grit	....	.2	....
m	"Teapot" vessel	....	....	Grit	....	.3	Red slip
n	Cast Iron Kettle			....	....	....	....

Material found accompanying burials in Fatherland mound C.

Figure 9. Material found accompanying burials in mound C, Fatherland plantation.

5   Application: Lines are arranged in narrow bands which are usually formed of three lines.

Triangles are sometimes used as fillers in the vacant spaces left above and below the band of lines connecting the units of the decoration. Small circles often serve as nucleuses about which the reverse curves of the meanders turn.

Usual Accompanying Characteristics are similar to type 41;21;5.

Type 64;41

64   Motif: Herringbone running parallel to the rim of the vessel.

41   Elements: Surface of vessel brushed while plastic with bundle of fibre.

Decoration is carelessly applied.

Usual Accompanying Characteristics: (The description of the vessels of this type depends mainly upon two examples found in Fatherland mound C).

Decoration is applied to upper half of vessel.

The rim is unthickened, and slightly everted. The lip is rounded.

In shape the vessels are jars with height greater than body diameter. The body bulges slightly toward the base, but diameter at the rim is only slightly less than body diameter.

The vessels have no appendages.

Since the bottoms of both the vessels found in the Fatherland mound are missing, it is uncertain whether the bottoms are flat, round, or convex.

Paste: The texture of this ware is fairly coarse and soft. The sherds average about .4 inches thick. The usual tempering material is small lumps of clay and some finely ground charcoal. The color is a yellow or a light buff, and no slips are used.

Sites yielding the Natchez complex

Fatherland plantation

The ceramic types of the Natchez Indians were first determined by M. B. Chambers in 1930. In the course of the investigation program of the Mississippi Department of Archives and History, a historic site of this tribe was excavated on Fatherland plantation, in Adams County, Mississippi. The old village is situated three miles southeast of the town of Natchez. It consists of three mounds in the

Figure 10. Map of Natchez, Mississippi and environs showing St. Catherines Creek, mounds A, B, and C on Fatherland plantation and the village site on the east side of the creek. Compare with figure 7. (Reproduced from Natchez quadrangle, U. S. Geological Survey).

flat bottom land on the west side of St. Catherines Creek (Figure 10). One of the structures, A, is almost completely cut away by the stream but appears to have been a low pyramid. The second mound, B, one hundred yards south of the first, is pyramidal, eighty feet square at the base and seven feet high. Another hundred yards southward is mound C. It was a low rounded structure fifty feet in diameter and four feet high. Surface midden material was not found in the wooded bottom land about the mounds but occurred sparsely on the low bluffs east of the creek.

The Fatherland plantation site is recognized as a site of the Natchez Indians by the European trade material found there. There is additional evidence of a historical nature that makes its identification even more specific. Apparently it was the site of the Grand Village described by Iberville (page 51). The native village shown in Dumont's map (Figure 7) must be this village on the basis of the position of the concession of White Earth shown to the south of it. The "Temple" and another house are both on the west side of the creek and appear to be raised on mounds. This answers Iberville's description of the village that he visited in 1700. The arrangement of the Fatherland mounds and midden deposit corresponds to the old map and Iberville's description. The location and size of the two mounds on the west side of St. Catherine's, with the main village to the east across the stream, also correspond to the situation found at the Fatherland plantation site.

The geographic position of the village shown by Dumont may be compared with that of the Fatherland site by comparing figure 7 and figure 10. The latter figure is copied from a portion of the Natchez quadrangle issued by the Mississippi River Commission. If the present ferry landing of the city of Natchez is in approximately the same location as the landing for Fort Rosalie, then the two sites are practically identical.

Fatherland mound C

Mound C, the southernmost of the Fatherland group, was entirely excavated by Chambers. It proved to be a burial mound. Fifty-nine skeletons were found lying on the mound base. They were orientated in various directions and were extended, flexed, or bundled after removal of the flesh. Two children were buried in wooden chests, outlined by iron nails, hinges, and hasps with locks. Although the skeletal material was in very poor condition, a few skull fragments showed that some of the heads had been flattened.

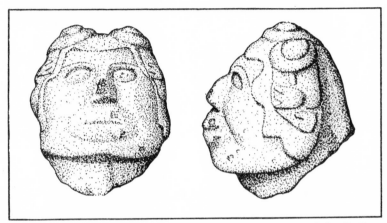

Figure 11. Effigy head made of limestone found in Fatherland mound C.

Large quantities of European material accompanied these bodies: glass and porcelain beads which were white blue or striped, glass bottles, crockery, pocket knives, C-shaped iron bracelets, brass turkey bells, metal buttons, a flintlock pistol, and short sections of coil spring about one inch in diameter. Le Page du Pratz says that the Natchez men used the coil springs as plugs in the lobe of the ear.[19]

---

[19] Swanton, BAE bull. 43, p. 55, from du Pratz, Histoire de la Louisiane, ii, p. 200.

DESCRIPTION OF SHERDS IN FIGURE 12

Sherd	Type	Color of Paste	Finish (Good, Medium Poor)	Temper	Hardness (Hard, Medium Soft)	Thickness (inches)	Remarks
				PERIOD III.—CHOCTAW			
k	40;31;4	Black	M	Charcoal	M	.3	Rim, wide-mouth pot
				NATCHEZ			
a	41;21;5	Grey	M	Charcoal	M	.2	Rim, shallow bowl
b	41;21;5	Black	G	Grit, Shell	H	.2	....
c	41;21;5	Grey	M	Grit	M	.2	....
d	41;21;5	Grey	M	Vegetable	M	.2	....
e	41;21;5	Tan	M	Grit	M	.2	....
				CADDO			
j	41;$\frac{21}{28}$;2	Grey	M	Grit	M	.2	....
				TUNICA			
g-g	80;20	Grey	G	Charcoal	H	.2	Interior view of rim sherd Also shown in profile.
				INDETERMINATE			
h	....	Black	M	Grit, Shell	M	.2	Interior decoration
i	51;21	Grey	P	Grit, Shell	S	.2	Rim
f	11;41	Grey	P	Grit	M	.3	....

Material from Fatherland Village Site (Site No. 5)

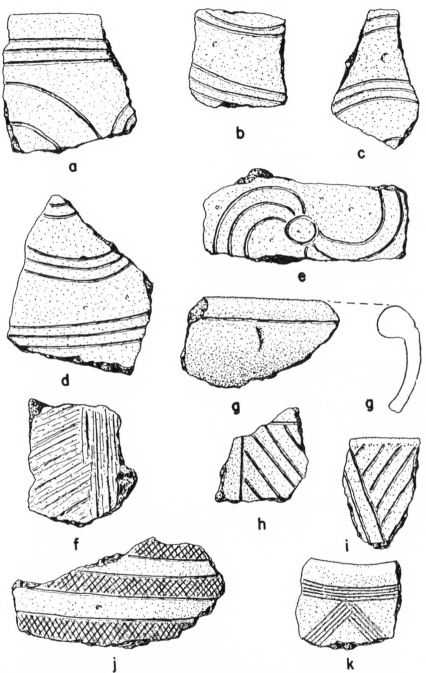

Figure 12.   Selection of representative material from the Fatherland village site collection (Site No. 50).

63

A large amount of material of native manufacture was also deposited with these burials. It consisted mostly of pottery. The prevailing types were bowls, jars, and bottles of peculiar and characteristic shapes. Nearly all of these were decorated with some variations of either the scroll or meander, which were formed by narrow bands of three incised lines. Examples of this ware are shown in figure 9.

Other ceramic types accompanying the burials were fragments of two large urn-shaped vessels decorated with a herringbone pattern of brush marks running parallel to the rim; two vessels decorated with scrolls formed by bands of line-enclosed, delicate crosshatching; a bottle with a line-enclosed scroll, formed by a band of red pigment; a "teapot" vessel undecorated but covered with a red slip; and a plate-shaped vessel with an incised star-like design.

With one of the burials was found the remarkable human effigy head shown as figure 11. On the hair will be noticed one of the curious three-pronged ornaments that so often appear on effigy pieces from the sites at Moundsville, Alabama, and Etowah, Georgia.

Three sherds with the peculiar rim that serves as a marker type of the Tunica complex were found in mound C (Figure 12 g). As these were not associated with burials there is the possibility that they were included in the earth used in constructing the mound.

Fatherland village site

The site of the village that was connected with the group of mounds on Fatherland plantation was found in 1931 by Chambers, Collins and the writer on the bluffs east of St. Catherine's Creek. This is across the creek from the mounds. The potsherds and flint chips comprising the midden refuse were thinly scattered over about five acres of plowed fields. A cut formed in the building of a plantation road that winds down the bluffs, revealed a six-inch stratum of undisturbed black midden soil. In this were found potsherds decorated with the typical curving bands formed by three lines. Intermingled with these sherds were several pieces of glass bottles, iron nails, and lead musket balls.

Classification of the sherds obtained on this and subsequent visits is shown in figure 1. Typical sherds are illustrated in figure 12.

The percentage of ware brushed in the herringbone pattern (type 64; 41) was much higher on the village site than in the mound. Possibly this was a utilitarian type considered unsuitable for burial furniture.

Several sherds from the village site were of recognizable foreign provenance: one Choctaw type (Figure 12 k), and seven of the Tunica markers (Figure 12 g). No material related to any of the other complexes that occur in the region is found. This argues that the site had not been inhabited any great length of time before the European invasion, and identifies all the ware found as having been used in a period close to the historic horizon.

Site No. 6, Foster site

Chambers secured a collection from about the large pyramidal mound at Foster, Mississippi, in 1930. The site is ten miles northeast of the town of Natchez. The collection is very small and is included only because of the dearth of Natchez sites. Tunica types, as well as Natchez, are included in the collection. There is no assurance that the mound itself is a product of the period that produced this material. No European material was found about the site.

Site No. 7, Natchez Fort

SE corner of irreg. S38, T11N, R8E

Green has succeeded in locating the site of the fort which the Natchez Indians constructed after fleeing from their old villages in Mississippi in 1729.[20] This fort was situated on the eastern side of the area called Sicily Island,

---

[20]Green, John, Governor Perier's Expedition Against the Natchez Indians.

DESCRIPTION OF SHERDS IN FIGURE 13

Sherd	Type	Color of Paste	Finish (Good, Medium, Poor)	Temper	Hardness (Hard, Medium, Soft)	Thickness (inches)	Remarks
				PERIOD III—NATCHEZ			
a	41;21;5	Grey	G	Vegetable	M	.2	Rim of shallow bowl
c	41;21;5	Black	M	Grit	M	.2	....
d	41;21;5	Grey	G	Vegetable	S	.2	....
e	41;21;5	Grey	M	Vegetable	S	.2	Rim of shallow bowl
f	41;21;5	Black	M	Grit	S	.2	Rim of shallow bowl
g	41;21;5	Grey	P	Vegetable	S	.2	....
h	64;41	Black	P	Vegetable	S	.2	....
i	41;21;5	Grey	G	Vegetable	M	.2	....
j	41;21;5	Black	M	Grit	M	.2	....
l	—;21;5	Black	M	Vegetable	H	.2	Rim
m	41;21;5	Black	M	Grit	M	.2	....
n	41;21;5	Black	M	....	H	.2	....
				PERIOD II—DEASONVILLE			
p	11;81;14	Buff	P	Vegetable	M	.3	Rim
				COLES CREEK			
o	63;101	Light blue	M	Vegetable, grit	H	.2	....
				INDETERMINATE			
b	Piece of hollow, spherical, cast iron projectile, .6″ thick						
k	....	Black	P	Grit	S	.2	....
q	Celt made of light tan chert						

Material from Natchez Fort (Site No. 7).

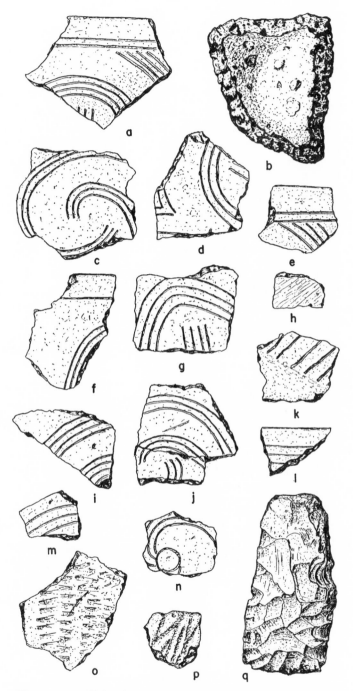

Figure 13. Selection of representative material from the Natchez Fort village site collection.

in Catahoula Parish, Louisiana.. It is not far west of Tensas River. Fool River, a short branch of the Tensas, reaches nearly to the bluffs on which the fort was built.

Green bases his identification of the site upon maps drawn by an engineer who accompanied Perier's expedition. One of these shows the route of the army from the Mississippi River up the Black, the Tensas, and through Fool River to the Natchez Fort. The other is a minute detail of the disposition of the forces in the siege of the fortress. This last agrees exactly with the geographical features of the site. Tradition, and the more concrete evidence of quantities of lead balls, fragments of shells, and guns found on the site are given by Green as supplementary evidence.

The site was brought to the writer's attention in 1935 by Mr. W. M. Crawford of Sicily Island. Crawford already had a collection of surface material from the site and very kindly assisted in collecting more.

The decorated sherds were nearly all of the marker types of the Natchez complex as found at Fatherland plantation (see Figure 1, material illustrated in Figure 13). A few of the more indeterminate types that occurred at Fatherland were present. Also, small percentages of two types of pottery that belong to the Coles Creek complex were found. These are probably accidental inclusions, as a site with typical material of this complex is found only one-half mile to the north (Site No. 65, Ditto place).

European material at Natchez Fort is fairly abundant. The collection includes blue glass beads, a number of lead bullets, a brass turkey bell, and a number of fragments of hollow cast iron shells (Figure 13 b). These last indicate balls about four and one-half inches in diameter with walls one-half an inch thick. They were found at the spot where the fort of the natives stood and may have been thrown by the cannon used by Perier.

Ring cemetery

NE¼ S27, R3E, T14N

In the summer of 1929 the writer excavated a pre-historic Indian cemetery on the farm of Mr. William Ring, in Warren County, Mississippi. This cemetery occupied the top of a high round-topped hill of the loess formation, three miles back from the edge of the bluffs along the east side of the Mississippi River. No mounds were found near the cemetery.

The hill top has been in cultivation in the past, and the burials all lay within fifteen inches of the surface. They were in very fragmentary condition, but it was ascertained that most of them were extended. Burial furniture consisted of pottery. Three or four vessels accompanied each skeleton and were clustered both at the head and feet. No European material was found.

In both decoration and shape the pottery resembles very closely the material from Fatherland plantation. There seems to be little doubt but that this is a recent burial site of a people connected with the historic Natchez. This pottery is not illustrated. It will be found on display in the museum of the Mississippi Department of Archives and History, Jackson, Mississippi.

Glass site

W½ irreg. S36, T14N, R3E

In 1910 Moore found pottery of the Natchez types accompanying intrusive burials in the summit plateau of a pyramidal mound situated one mile north-northeast of the railroad station of Glass, Warren County, Mississippi.[21] This structure is one of a group of four. They lie in the Mississippi flood plain adjacent to the Yazoo and Mississippi Valley Railroad and are not more than one-half mile from the high bluffs that form the eastern border of the valley.

---

[21]Moore, C. B., Some Aboriginal Sites on Mississippi River, pp. 381-388.

The burials were in shallow graves. All were in very fragmentary condition and some skeletons had entirely disappeared.

Thirty-five vessels were recovered with the burials. They were so near the surface that most of them had been broken by cultivation. Moore describes the general features of the ware as follows:

> The ware from this place contains little if any shell tempering. It is fairly thin, and, as a rule, of medium excellence. Various forms of the bowl predominate. The ·principal feature in connection with the pottery uncovered from this place is the great proportion of decorated vessels. In point of fact, but one wholly undecorated vessel, or part of a vessel, was met with in the mound.
>
> With the exception of a vessel having a design of red and of cream-colored pigments upon it, all others from this mound bear incised or trailed decoration to a greater or less extent. This decoration is largely conventional and often based on the scroll, as is so frequently the case with pottery in the Lower Mississippi region.[22]

Moore illustrates seven vessels. The shapes and decorations of six are similar to the material from Fatherland mound C. The vessel illustrated by Moore as figure 12 (vessel No. 36) was presented to Moore and was represented as coming from the site. It is reminiscent of sherds from the Tunica complex sites. Similar inward-facing animal heads on the rims were found on the village site at Pocahontas (Site No. 24; Figure 21 r).

Other artifacts which Moore found with these burials were polished pebbles, one discoidal stone, powdered hematite, and two peculiar spade-shaped objects of clay about fifteen inches long.

No European material was found accompanying these burials. On the basis of the material which Moore illustrates, these intrusive burials are assigned to the Natchez pottery complex.

---

[22] Ibid., pp. 382-383.

The mound in which the burials were found and the others forming the group probably antedate this pottery. Such large mounds are not a usual feature of Natchez sites, and graves appear to have been used quite commonly. As a surface collection has not been obtained from the site, positive evidence of its age is lacking.

About one mile east of the Glass site the survey party in 1930 found a small historic cemetery on the top of the bluff (NW¼ NW¼ irreg. S6, T14N, R3E). Shallow burials had been exposed previous to the visit, and the farmer on whose place they were located had recovered a small amount of material. This included glass beads, small cones made of sheet copper, and C-shaped iron bracelets. Four pieces of pottery, which had been preserved, were identical with the common Fatherland types. None of this material could be obtained by the survey.

DESCRIPTION OF NATCHEZ COMPLEX SITES

Site No.	Site Name	Burial		Mounds							Midden				
		Cemetery	Mound	Conical		Pyramidal		Ramp	Enclosure	Approximate Area	Thin —10"	Thick +10"	Collection Analysis	Minimum Date
				Low —10'	Tall +10'	Low —10'	Tall +10'							
5	*Fatherland place		X	1		2				5A	X		Natchez	1730
6	Foster place					1				3A		X	Natchez	
7	*Natchez Fort									2A	X		Natchez	1731
	Ring place	X								2A			Natchez	
	Glass site	X†											Natchez	
	Cemetery on bluff above Glass	X											Natchez	Circa 1730

*Sites from which material is illustrated.

†Burials intrusive in top of mound.

Caddo complex

History of the Caddo tribes

The most complete summary of historical information concerning the Caddoan people of northwestern Louisiana is contained in an article by William B. Glover, "A History of the Caddo Indians," published in the Louisiana Historical Quarterly, Vol. 18, No. 4, October, 1935. Other information is contained in the historical section of Winslow Walker's report on a burial site at Natchitoches, "A Caddo Burial Site at Natchitoches, Louisiana," Smithsonian Miscellaneous Collections, Vol. 94, No. 14. The brief treatment given here is taken principally from these two sources.

The name Caddo is generally used to indicate the group of tribes which formed the large Caddoan linguistic family. The Caddoan family occupied northwestern Louisiana, and extended into the present states of Arkansas and Texas. This large group extended far to the north and included such distant tribes as the Wichita, Pawnee, and Arikara. Four groups of Caddo were in Louisiana at the beginning of the eighteenth century: the Kadohadacho and Natchitoches located on Red River; the Adai located south of the Red on one of its branches not far above the Natchitoches; and the village of the Washita which was west of the Tensas on the Ouachita River.

Early visitors to the country of the Caddo in Louisiana neglected to give much information as to the location of their villages. Henri de Tonti in 1690 was the first to give a clear account, although De Soto may have visited some of them earlier.[23] After a five day journey overland from the village of the Tensas on Lake St. Joseph, Tonti arrived at three villages named Natchitoches, Ouachita, and Capiche.[24] These seem to have been situ-

---

[23]The Elvas narrative mentions a village called "Nacacahoz" which may have been a settlement of the Natchitoches, see French, B. F., Historical Collections of Louisiana, vol. II, p. 199, 1850.

[24]French, B. F. Historical Collections of Louisiana, vol. I, p. 72.

ated on the Ouachita River. Cadadoquis, Natchitoches, and Nasoui villages are mentioned as being on Red River.

Under the command of St. Denis a post was established at the village of the Natchitoches on Red River in 1712. Three years later a garrison was added. Through St. Denis' influence most of the Caddoan peoples were attached to the French interests.

Some of the remnants of the Natchitoches remained near the site of their old village (the present day town of Natchitoches) until as late as 1805. Soon afterwards they were driven westward by the white settlers.

The Adai group were located near the present town of Robeline, Louisiana. These people were generally under the control of the Spaniards and it was at their village that the mission of Los Adaes was established. These people are first mentioned by Cabeza de Vaca about 1530. According to John Sibley there were only twenty men remaining at their village in 1805. Soon after this they ceased to exist as a separate tribe.[25]

The Cadohadacho traditions relate that they migrated from the lower Red River country in ancient times. Pénicaut reported that the Cadohadacho lived one hundred and seventy leagues above the Natchitoches in 1701. Glover estimates that this would place them a little above the Big Bend region near the present towns of Fulton and Texarkana, Arkansas. In 1800, Sibley found them on the south bank of the river, near Caddo Lake in Louisiana.[26]

White settlers thronged into the fertile valley of the Red in the first quarter of the nineteenth century. In a treaty with the United States in 1835 the Caddos sold what remained of their land to the government and moved to Texas.

---

[25]Glover, W. B., A History of the Caddo Indians, p. 7.
[26]Idem, p. 98.

There seems to be no information concerning the exact position of the Washita group along the Ouachita River. On a map Swanton places them at about the point where Harrisonburg, Louisiana now stands.[27] This is where the southern edge of the Kisatchie wold touches the Ouachita River. No evidence has been found in that vicinity of historic village sites that might be attributed to this group.

Identification of Caddo ceramic types

The ceramic complex of the Caddo tribe as presented here is not as well identified with that group historically as is desirable. Some of the pottery types that consistently occur on the different village sites have been identified as Caddoan, in burials deposited within the historic period. One such site is documented, but others are identified only by the European material found in them and by the fact that they are near or in the country known to have been inhabited by the Caddoan tribes.

The burials found at the Fish Hatchery site near Natchitoches, Louisiana, provide the most authentic case.[28] These appear to have belonged to the village of the Natchitoches which was first visited by Henri de Tonti in 1690. St. Denis established a fort at this village about 1712. In reality this was the founding of the present town of Natchitoches, Louisiana. Toward the end of the eighteenth century, the post became an important center of trade for the Caddoan people of the upper Red River. The Natchitoches occupied their village as late as 1805, but soon afterward they were forced westward into Texas by the increasing white population.

St. Denis describes the old village of the Natchitoches as being on an island which had been formed by the stream flowing both through the present channel and through the old channel that bends around to the south.

---

[27]Swanton, John R., BAE bull. 43, pl. 1.
[28]Walker, Winslow, A Caddo Burial Site at Natchitoches, Louisiana.

This latter channel is now abandoned by the river and is called Cane River. These detour channels are common on the upper Red. They are not meanders but were formed by the Raft impounding the stream.

Other features which Walker associates with the Natchitoches group of Caddo are: flattened skulls; stemless pottery pipes; notched, stemmed, and concave-base projectile points; grooved stone axes; and both long and short stone celts. The material of European derivation consists of porcelain and blue glass beads, metal scissors, a few brass turkey bells (hawk bells), brass bracelets, and an iron spike.

Walker points to marked similarities of the ware at the Natchitoches site and that found by Clarence B. Moore at two sites along the Ouachita River: Glendora plantation, a short distance up the Ouachita River from the town of Monroe, in Ouachita Parish; and Keno place, a short distance to the north on a small tributary stream, Bayou Bartholomew. Both of Moore's sites were cemeteries. Further significance of the similarities lies in the fact that at both sites European trade material was found.[29]

Other finds of ware of these types are cited. Beyer illustrates a vessel from a mound near Campti, Louisiana, a few miles up the Red River from Natchitoches.[30] Jones figures two vessels from a burial site near Shreveport.[31] Moore found material very similar to this at the Haley, Battle, and Foster places on the Red River in southwestern Arkansas.[32]

Most of the village site of the Natchitoches has been cut away into the river. Apparently all that remains is the portion of the cemetery investigated by Walker.

---

[29]Moore, C. B., Antiquities of the Ouachita Valley, pp. 27-80, 120-151.

[30]Beyer, G. E., The Mounds of Louisiana, pl. 10.

[31]Jones, C. C., Antiquities of the Southern Indians, pl. 28, Figures 3, 4.

[32]Moore, C. B., Some Aboriginal Sites on Red River.

Most striking of the features of the Natchitoches burial ware is the decoration. One polished shell-tempered bowl with high sides, of modified carinated shape, is decorated on the body with two series of encircling, curvilinear scrolls formed by negative bands. These bands are an inch wide, and are delineated by scratched lines. Through the center of the bands run two closely spaced lines with many short cross lines between them. The spaces outside of the bands are filled with round or oval undecorated discs. Outside these disc-shaped areas the surface of the vessel is roughened by closely spaced scratched lines. A similar band forms a zigzag around the outcurving wall. The space outside the band is filled with the negative discs similar to those on the body of the bowl (see Walker, pl. 5a). According to the present classification, this is a decoration type $34 ; \dfrac{26, 27}{21/28} ; 1$.

Another vessel illustrated from this site is a shell-tempered bottle with a short neck (Walker, pl. 5b). The lower half of the body is plain, but the upper part is decorated with two tiers of interlocking scrolls. The figures are formed of narrow, undecorated bands bordered by lines incised with a pointed instrument. In the background are a number of parallel lines, almost perpendicular, but curving so they fit against the circular units formed by the junctions of the scrolls. (This decoration is type $34 ; \dfrac{21}{21/64} ; 1$). A comparatively tall, almost spittoon-shaped bowl appears to be a modification of the carinated form. Other characteristic vessels are globular bottles with short necks, bottles with long necks (these have a decided bulge in the neck), and shallow round-bottomed bowls.

It should be kept in mind that all of these are burial collections. These investigators have given a very good idea of the types of material that the Caddoan peoples of northwestern Louisiana buried with the dead. Apparently these are only a portion of the domestic types.

Discussion of Caddoan village sites

The collections from northwestern Louisiana were made by Mr. Edward F. Neild, of Shreveport, from 1932 to 1935. They include types not found in the burial collections described above, but several conditions tend to identify them as Caddo:

1. The consistent occurrence in these collections of small amounts of the recognized Caddoan burial wares.

2. The occurrence of trade beads, gun flints, and turkey bells on two village sites which produced typical Caddo complex material.

3. The fact that only village sites yielding this complex are found in the regions known to have been thickly settled by the Caddo, near Natchitoches, and around Caddo Lake.

Attempts have been made by the writer to collect from some villages connected with the historic Caddoan burial sites. The village site at Natchitoches has been washed into the river. At Glendora plantation a power plant now occupies the site. A few sherds were secured from Keno place in 1936. There were too few for statistical analysis, but they agreed in every way with Neild's collections. An old negro living at this latter site reported that when his grandfather came as a boy to this plantation, over a hundred years ago, the place was in woods and that ruined huts of the Indians stood at that time in the field where he himself watched Clarence Moore excavate in 1909.

Since this paper has been in press the writer has excavated a village site at Allen, Natchitoches Parish, Louisiana. This village was accompanied by a cemetery in which the burials were accompanied by European material, principally glass beads. The site is only twenty miles from the town of Natchitoches where St. Denis' post stood and doubtless represents a historic village of the Caddo peoples. The pottery accompanying the burials and scattered through the midden deposit at the site removes any doubt as to the proper identification of the decoration types described as Caddo in this article.

Types of the Caddo complex

Type 11/21;61 (Marker type)

11/21   Motif: Either irregular arrangement (11), or regular arrangement (21), of elements.

  61   Elements: Fingernail imprints, or else imprints made with the end of a reed, which resemble very closely those made by the fingernails. The execution of this type is generally very careless.

Usual Accompanying Characteristics:

This decoration is applied to the body of the vessel. It usually extends up very near the lip, from which it may be separated by a narrow undecorated border and an incised line. How much of the vessel area is covered by the imprints is not certain. Beakers and urn-shaped pots with slightly outflaring rims appear to be the most common vessel forms. No appendages have been noted on these sherds. Rim pieces are usually quite unmarked in profile. In a few cases they show a slightly outflaring lip.

The paste of this ware is fairly hard. Color ranges from grey to dark brown, and the average thickness is about .3 inches.

21

Type 32;—;2
      71

32   Motif: Bands of features which make right-angle turns.

21   Element: Narrow lines made with pointed instrument used to mark the confines of the motif.

71   Element: Punctates made with a point.

2   Arrangement: Sub-element is used as stippling to bring out the motif in positive. Often this decoration is arranged to form step-like zigzags from the vessel rim.

Usual Accompanying Characteristics:

This decoration is found on the vertical side
walls of convex-bottomed bowls. These bowls
are usually about ten inches in diameter. In shape
they approach the typical carinated form, differing only in that the side walls are straight rather
than outcurving. Their rims are undifferentiated
and have rounded lips. There are no appendages. Bottoms are usually convex, or, in a few
cases, slightly flattened. The texture of the ware
is rather fine and hard. It averages .2 inches in
thickness. Color varies through grey and buff
to reddish brown. Grit, sand, and occasionally
shell, serve as tempering.

26, 27

Type 34;———;1 (Marker type)
     21/28

34   Motif: Compressed meander formed by line-
enclosed band which is from one-half to one inch
in width. Infrequently the scroll is the motif.
Seldom is the motif simple. Two tiers of decoration, as well as other variations, are common.

26, 27   Elements: The decoration is generally built up
entirely of fine, scratched lines (27). Usually
the lines which outline the band forming the
motif are plain, but in some cases, like the line
that is generally found centered in the motif
band, they have numerous small spurs attached
(26). Sometimes the center line is formed by
two closely spaced lines with numerous short
cross lines between them. Arrangements of
spurred lines are often found encircling the vessel both above and below the decorated area,
where they serve as borders.

21/28   Elements: In the angles that occur outside the
band of the motif, small triangular areas are
formed that are filled either with fine lines
drawn parallel to one another (21), or delicate
crosshatching (28). These areas have a concave
side opposite the angle which they are used to
fill. At regular intervals outside the motif, bars
of either of these features are used to connect
lines which are almost parallel. These bars have
two concave sides so that the resulting effect is

that the only plain areas left in the background are the plain, round, or oval areas between these connecting bars and the angle fillers.

This very characteristic decoration shows many variations and elaborations on the motif described above; however, the elements used are practically always those given. Probably this is the most peculiar and characteristic of the Caddo types. It is marked by very careful execution. Lines are delicately scratched, and were made after the paste had hardened either before or after it was fired or, in some cases, even after a high polish had been applied. Red pigment was rubbed in the lines of a few vessels, found by Walker at the Natchitoches site.

Usual Accompanying Characteristics:

This decoration is applied to the bodies of vessels. It extends to the lip on wide mouthed vessels, and only to the base of the neck on the bottle forms. The side walls are decorated all the way to the bottom and in rare instances even the bottoms are decorated.

The most common shape is the bottle with globular body, concave bottom, and a small neck. Often these necks do not have straight walls, but are swelled in a manner peculiar to ware of this type. Deep bowls with hemispherical bodies and short outflaring rims are decorated in this manner as well as shallow bowls of a more definitely carinated form (Figure 17).

Rims are typically unthickened. The sherds become thinner toward the lip. No appendages have been found.

Paste is generally hard and of a fine texture. In color it ranges from grey to black. The surface of sherds has been finished with unusual care. Either they have a polished black surface or red slip was applied which may or may not be polished. On a few pieces of poorer grade ware, grey in paste color, the red slip is not firmly fixed and tends to flake off.

Grit and large flakes of crushed shell are the usual tempering material.

Thickness ranges from .2 to .4 inches.

$$\text{Type } 34; \frac{21}{21/64}; 1$$

34   Motif: Compressed meander formed by line-enclosed band.

21   Elements: Narrow lines incised with a pointed instrument.

21/64   Elements: Either narrow, incised lines (21), or small ridges raised by pinching with the finger tips (64), arranged parallel to one another and perpendicular to the lip. These cover all the decorated space outside the undecorated band that forms the motif.

1   Arrangement: Motif is brought out in negative by the shading formed by either the lines or pinched ridges that occupy the background.

This decoration was usually rather carelessly applied while the paste of the vessels was moist. However, a few examples have the lines scratched after the paste had hardened. These are generally more neatly executed.

This type is found most often on squat bottles with short necks which have outflaring mouths. The bottoms are generally convex. The decorated area extends from the base of the neck half way down the side walls or to the bottom, and is bordered top and bottom by lines.

Carinated bowls also bear this type of decoration on side walls only. It is on these that most of the scratched lines forming this type are found.

No appendages were used.

Texture of the paste is usually rather coarse. The material is often porous, light, and not very hard. In color it shows different shades of grey, buff, light brown, salmon, and sometimes is mottled with black. Crushed shell is commonly used as tempering material. Slips are very infrequent. The few that have been noted are red.

$$\text{Type } 41; \frac{21}{28}; 2$$

41   Motif: Scroll, scroll-like, and angular figures. In this case the motif is formed by bands from one-half to one inch in width.

21   Element: Narrow lines made with a pointed instrument. These are used to outline the bands which form the motif.

28   Element: Delicate crosshatching used to fill in the bands forming the motif.

2   Arrangement: Since the motif is shaded with crosshatching while the background of the figures is undecorated, this decoration is positive.

       Neat execution is usual. Ordinarily the lines were incised before the paste had hardened, but there are a few cases where the lines were scratched after drying.

Usual Accompanying Characteristics:

       The decoration is generally found on bottles of different characteristic Caddo forms. It either extends all the way from the base of the neck to the bottom, or forms a band that occupies the upper half of the vessel walls.

       The ware is generally rough, of a porous texture, and rather soft; black, grey, or salmon in color; and is often tempered with ground shell. While red slips are sometimes found, they are not common.

$$\text{Type } 60; \frac{61/64}{41/21} \text{(Marker type)}$$

60   Motif: Parallel arrangement of features; that is, the elements are arranged in rows or lines that are parallel.

61/64   Elements: Fingernail imprints (61) arranged in rows, or low ridges raised by pinching with the ends of the fingers (64). In some cases these ridges are formed into small nodes; in others impressions have been made at an angle in the ridges to give a "rope" effect. The ridges and rows of imprints are spaced one to two inches apart.

41/21   Elements: Either brush marks made with the ends of a bundle of fibres (41), or incised lines made with a pointed instrument and drawn parallel to one another. These last two elements are used to fill in the areas between the ridges or rows of imprints mentioned above. The brush marks or lines may either parallel the more prominent features, or be arranged at angles to them.

Some of the entire vessels found by C. B. Moore at the Haley Place in Arkansas show that the ridges in this type sometimes appear to represent a large mesh cord net in which the vessel is enclosed.[33]

Usual Accompanying Characteristics:

The decoration of this type extends entirely up to the lip of the rim sherds on which it is found. These lips sometimes are marked with shallow notches. The vessel is nearly always decorated entirely to the bottom; in some cases decoration extends over the bottom.

Urns with slightly pointed convex bottoms, globular bodies, slightly constricted necks, and wide outflaring rims, appear to be the usual shape.

The paste is fairly coarse in texture. Its colors are grey, salmon, or black. The exterior color is often grey, as a result of firing. Slips are not noted.

Tempering material consists of a small amount of sand and fine grit. No shell has been noted.

Type 61;21;6

61   Motif: Features arranged parallel to the rim and parallel to one another.

21   Element: Narrow lines incised with a pointed instrument.

---

[33]Moore, C. B., Some Aboriginal Sites on Red River, figs. 43, 51, 53, 57.

6   Arrangement: Lines spaced less than three-eighths of an inch apart. The execution of this type is generally rather careless. The lines are uneven and wavy. The pointed instrument used in making them often has plowed up the vessel surface leaving uneven ridges on each side of the lines.

     The decoration starts at the lip, and usually covers one to three inches of the side walls of the vessel.

Usual Accompanying Characteristics:

     There is generally no border space between the decoration and the lip of the vessel.

     Beakers, wide mouthed pots with slightly bulging sides, and bowls with convex bottoms and short vertical sides appear to be the typical shapes.

     The rims are straight continuations of the vessel walls. Many show the peculiarity so common in the Coles Creek complex: very thin lip with vessel walls gradually thickening to a maximum at one to one and a half inches below the lip. This gradual thickening takes place on the interior of the sherds; the outside maintains a straight wall.

     The texture of these sherds is hard, but they are finished carelessly. Sand and grit are used as temper. In color they are similar to the others in the collections in which they are found. At the Caddo sites most of them have a decidedly reddish tinge.

     It must be pointed out that although this decoration type belongs with the Caddo types on the basis of occurrence, typologically it is only a slight variant of the Coles Creek type 61;24;6 (see page 179).

Type 63;42 (Marker type).

63   Motif: Features arranged perpendicular to lip of vessel.

42   Elements: Vessel surface decorated with the fingers placed side by side and drawn down the

sides of the vessel while the paste was still plastic. This results in shallow furrows about one-half inch wide with small, low ridges between them. Necessarily the execution and finish of this type is rough. The decorated area extends from the lip to the bottom of the vessel.

Usual Accompanying Characteristics:

The usual shape is that of the urn with only slightly bulging sides, gently outflaring lips, and tall for the diameter. The shape of the bottom is uncertain. Rim and lip are unthickened. No appendages are found. The paste is rather rough in texture, and is colored mostly in browns and black. Average thickness is .3 inches. A small amount of sand and grit is used as tempering materials. No slips are found.

Summary of Caddo Village Site Collections

The following summary of the typical features of collections from sites of the Caddo complex is intended to assist in the ready identification of collections. In addition to the decoration types described in the foregoing, the collections are likely to include types that refer to the complexes of the contemporaneous Natchez and Tunica groups. Coles Creek types are persistently present on these sites. In the following, no attempt is made to differentiate the types representative of the various complexes. This is done in the various chapters on type description.

Ceramic decorations:

Irregular or regular arrangements of fingernail imprints.

Angular bands of punctates arranged in various decorations.

Compressed meanders made with scratched lines; spurred lines; negative round or oval areas in background.

Compressed meanders with background filled with nearly vertical, parallel, curving lines.

Scroll and scroll-like figures of bands of delicate crosshatching.

Surface either brushed or covered with parallel lines, interrupted at intervals by rows of fingernail imprints or ridges raised by pinching.

Marks of fingers placed side by side and drawn down side of vessel.

Large crosshatching formed by incised lines; some red slip.

Curving bands of punctates forming scroll-like figures.

Scroll formed by numerous incised lines.

Overhanging lines arranged parallel to the rim.

Overhanging lines arranged parallel to the rim with a single row of triangular punctates below and parallel to the lines.

Irregular arrangements of punctates made with a point.

Irregular brushing with bundle of fibres; sometimes the rims are notched.

Chain of line-filled triangles.

Lines parallel to one another arranged at forty-five degree angle to the rim.

Paste:

The Caddo collections from northwestern Louisiana are striking in the large amount of reddish or pink paste pottery that they contain. This is due to the large iron content of the Red River soils. The material also occurs in different shades of grey, buff, brown, and black which in appearance is similar to the material from the Mississippi Valley. Grit and shell are used as tempering material. There is a good deal of sand in the wares and it probably is inherent in the clays from which they were made. The interiors of some of the sherds are intentionally blackened.

Vessel shapes:

Carinated bowls.
Spittoon-shaped vessels with outflaring lips.
Beakers.
Globular bottles with bulging necks.

Vessel appendages:

Uncommon; a few strap handles are present in the collections.

Other features in the Caddo collections

Besides the characteristic pottery, the collections from these northwestern Louisiana sites are marked by

peculiar types of stone work. Projectile points are
either stemmed or notched, or have concave bases (Figure 15 a-h. Some points are as long as eight or ten
inches. Small cylindrical beads of fine-grained red and
grey stone are common. A few of these are carved in
what appear to be effigy forms (Figure 15 e). Other
artifacts are fragments of boatstones (Figure 15 k), a

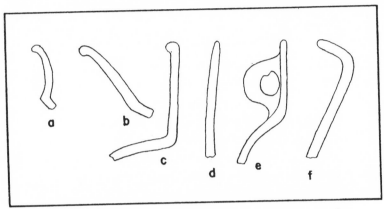

Figure 14.   Profiles of rim sherds of the Caddo complex.

pierced, banded slate tube that may be a type of bannerstone (Figure 15 j), and a fragment of a thin bar gorget
of greenstone (Figure 15 i).

Village sites with the Caddo pottery complex

Most of the village sites in northwestern Louisiana,
which by their material are identified with the Caddo
complex, are scattered along the lakes and small streams
which empty into Red River. A few others are found in
the hill country north and east of the Red. High ridges
rising above small streams or lakes are the locations
usually chosen for the villages. Where recent cultivation
with the consequent erosion has occurred, the sites are
marked by a large amount of surface material.

DESCRIPTION OF ARTIFACTS IN FIGURE 15.

Artifacts from Caddo sites

a   Large rough spear head of grey chert

b   Notched point of grey shert

c   Concave-base point of black chert

d   Concave-base and notched point of black chert

e   Y-shaped point of brown chert

f   Triangular point of grey chert

g   Concave-base point of brown chert

h   Concave-base point of brown chert

i   Half of gorget made of green stone.   Specimen is ¼ inch
      thick

j   Broken head of banded brown slate, oval in profile

k   Two views of boatstone of grey granite
      Material from Site No. 19, Harrison Bayou.

l   Two views of carved bead of grey slate

m   Two views of stone mask of brown chert
      Material from Site No. 9, Jim Sinner Place.

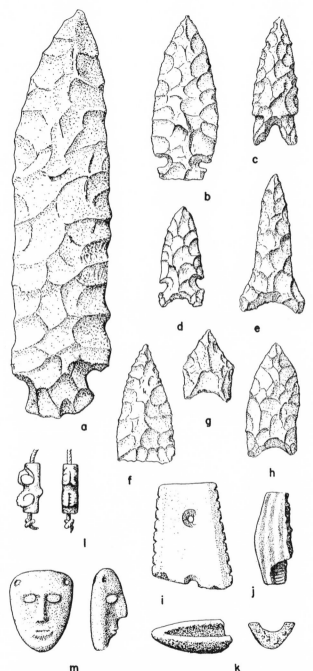

Figure 15. Stone artifacts from Caddo complex
village site collection.

DESCRIPTION OF SHERDS IN FIGURE 16

Sherd	Type	Color of Paste	Finish (Good, Medium, Poor)	Temper	Hardness (Hard, Medium, Soft)	Thickness (inches)	Remarks
				PERIOD III—CADDO			
a	34;$\frac{26,27}{21/28}$;1	Black	G	Grit	M	.3	Rim, carinated bowl
b	34;$\frac{21}{21/64}$;1	Black	M	Vegetable	M	.2	Scratched lines, rim carinated bowl
c	41;$\frac{21}{28}$;2	Black	M	Shell	S	.2	....
d	11/21;61	Black	R	Vegetable	S	.3	Carinated bowl
e	32;$\frac{21}{71}$;2	Light brown	R	Vegetable	M	.3	Carinated bowl
g	11/21;61	Black	M	Vegetable	M	.2	Carinated bowl
h	60;$\frac{61/64}{41/21}$	Black	P	Grit	M	.2	....
j	63;42	Black	P	Vegetable	M	.2	Outflaring rim
n	60;$\frac{61/64}{41/21}$	Buff	P	Grit	M	.2	....
				PERIOD II—COLES CREEK			
l	71;21	Black	M	Grit	H	.3	Rim
m	61;24;7	Grey	P	Vegetable	H	.3	Rim
				INDETERMINATE			
f	....	Black	M	Grit	S	.2	....
i	11;41	Tan	P	Grit	S	.3	Rim
k	11;41	Black	P	Vegetable	M	.2	Rim
o	51;21	Grey	P	Mica	M	.2	Wide mouthed pot with handles

Material from Wilkinson plantation (Site No. 15).

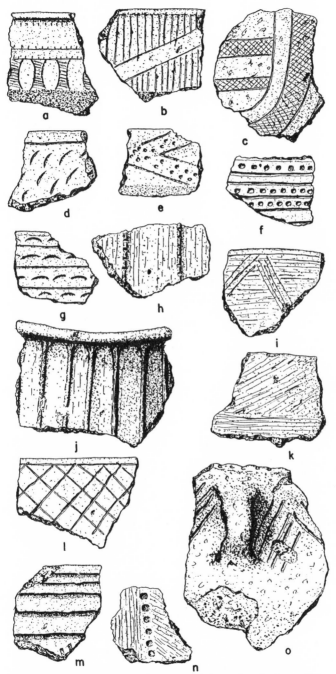

Figure 16.   Selection of representative sherds from the
Wilkinson village site collection (Site No. 15).

The usual repositories for the dead were cemeteries located in or near the villages. Cultivation of the sites often exposes quantities of human bones. In excavations at the Wilkinson place (Site No. 15), Mr. Neild found skeletons from two to four feet beneath the surface. They were extended on their backs and had pottery vessels placed around their heads.

Mounds are found at only one site: Mound place (Site No. 17). They are all low, truncated, pyramidal structures. No particular arrangement is apparent, and they have no uniform orientation.

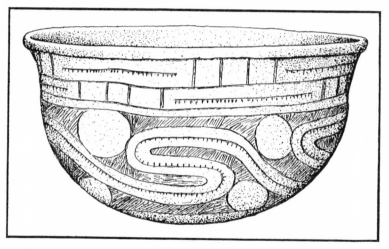

Figure 17. Site No. 15, Wilkinson place, Neild collection. A typical example of the Caddo burial ware. Type 34; $\frac{26, 27}{21/28}$;1. Brown paste, good finish, medium hardness, 0.2 inch thick.

Site No. 15, Wilkinson place
S18, T11N, R10W

The village site on the Wilkinson place is situated south of the Red River in a northwestern projection of Natchitoches Parish, ten miles west of the town of Hanna, Louisiana. It covers about five acres on the top of a low ridge. At the foot of the ridge lies a small stream that empties into James River. Along this latter stream, several of the lakes formed by the Red River Raft still remain.

The site has been under cultivation for some time and perhaps has eroded some. Potsherds and flint chips are found in abundance. A profusion of fragments of human bones suggests that the spot was also utilized as a cemetery.

A very significant point is the number of gun flints and glass beads found on the site. These indicate that the village was occupied after 1722. The town of Nachitoches is only twenty miles to the southeast. Possibly the Indians secured this material at the post that was established there by St. Denis.

Figure 15 shows a selection of representative sherds from the site. In figure 1 the results of classification of the collection are given. It will be noted that the spurred line scroll, the decoration that is usually thought of as typically Caddoan (type 34; $\frac{26, 27}{21/28}$;1), forms only a small percentage of the collection from the surface. However, at the head of an extended skeleton buried in a shallow grave in the field, Mr. Neild found the typical example of Caddo burial ware shown in figure 17. A small amount of the less diagnostic types of the Deasonville complex is included in the surface collection. As the marker type of this complex (type 11;81) is found at none of the Caddo complex sites, these other types cannot be accepted as very significant. The Coles Creek complex is plainly responsible for some of the types that are found in the collection. Not only are there typical Coles Creek pieces, but some appear to be Caddoan modifications of Coles Creek ideas (Figure 16 f, g). In all of these features this collection may be considered typical of those found in the Caddoan territory.

DESCRIPTION OF SHERDS IN FIGURE 18

Sherd	Type	Color of Paste	Finish (Good, Medium Poor)	Temper	Hardness (Hard, Medium Soft)	Thickness (inches)	Remarks
			PERIOD III—CADDO				
a	34; $\frac{26;27}{21/28}$;1	Black	G	....	M	.2	Carinated bowl
b	41; $\frac{21}{28}$;2	Tan	M	Charcoal	M	.2	Scratched lines
c	Same as a	Black	M	Grit	S	.2	Carinated bowl
d	60; $\frac{61/64}{41/21}$	Black	M	Sand	S	.2	Bottle
f	Same as d	Black	P	....	S	.2	....
g	Same as d	Buff	P	Grit	M	.3	Rim
i	63;42	Grey	M	Shell	M	.2	....
k	11/21;61	Black	P	....	S	.4	....
o	11/21;61	Black	M	Sand	M	.2	Rim of beaker
			TUNICA				
h	63;64	Black	M	....	M	.2	....
			PERIOD II—COLES CREEK				
j	71;21	Black	M	Grit	M	.2	Rim
m	61;24;7 (?)	Black	M	Sand	S	.2	....
n	01;74	Black	M	Grit	M	.2	....
p	61;24;6	Black	M	Vegetable	M	.3	Rim of beaker
q	61; $\frac{24}{74}$;9	Black	M	Grit	S	.3	....
r	61;24;6	Brown	P	Vegetable	M	.2	Rim of beaker
			INDETERMINATE				
e	52;21;2	Black	M	Sand	S	.3	Scratched lines
l	....	Black	P	Sand	M	.2	....

Material from Harrison Bayou (Site No. 19).

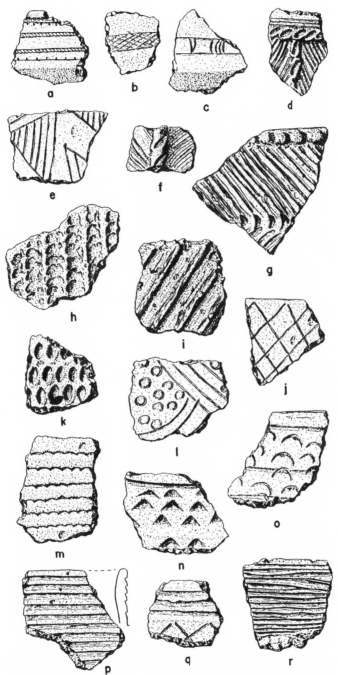

Figure 18.   Selection of representative material from Harrison Bayou village site collection (Site No. 19).

95

Site No. 19, Harrison Bayou

The Harrison Bayou site is on the eastern side of the small stream of that name, three miles west of the point where the Texas-Louisiana boundary line touches the south side of Caddo Lake. The site is located in the state of Texas, due west of Caddo Parish, Louisiana.

The midden deposit is rather extensive and occupies the side of a steep hill on the eastern side of the bayou. Cultivation and the resulting erosion have exposed quantities of refuse material. Results of the classification of the one hundred and seventy-one decorated sherds secured from the site by Neild are shown in figure 1. Representative types are illustrated in figure 18. Most of the material can be referred to the Caddo complex. Small percentages of Coles Creek are found. Deasonville is present in even smaller percentages and less determinate types.

The collection best shows the variety of stone artifacts that characterize Caddo collections. Most of the material illustrated in figure 15 has come from this site

DESCRIPTION OF CADDO COMPLEX SITES

Site No.	Site Name	Burial Cemetery	Mound	Conical Low −10'	Conical Tall +10'	Pyramidal Low −10'	Pyramidal Tall +10'	Ramp	Enclosure	Approximate Area	Midden Thin −10"	Midden Thick +10"	Collection Analysis	Minimum Date
8	Smithport landing ..	X								5A		X	Tunica, Caddo	
9	Jim Sinner Pl.	X								5A		X	Caddo, Tunica	
0	Ed Pease....	X								10A		X	Caddo	
1	Rock Bayou									5A		X	Caddo	1835, trade beads
2	Bob Hardy												Caddo	
3	Hy. Edwards									10A		X	Caddo, Coles Creek	
4	Maddox Place									10A		X	Caddo, Tunica, Coles Creek	
15	*Wilkinson Place	X								5A		X	Caddo, Tunica, Deasonville, Coles Creek	1835, trade beads, gun flints.
16	Arch Green	X								5A		X	Caddo, Tunica	
17	Mound Pl.....						4			10A		X	Caddo, Tunica, Coles Creek	
18	Colbert Pl...									5A		X	Caddo, Tunica, Deasonville, Coles Creek.	
19	*Harrison Bayou									8A		X	Caddo, Tunica, Deasonville, Coles Creek.	
20	Point Post Office												Caddo, Tunica, Coles Creek, Marksville.	

*Sites from which material is illustrated, and which are described in text.

Tunica complex

History of Tunica, Yazoo, Koroa, and Ofo tribes

At the beginning of the eighteenth century the larger part of the Tunica, Yazoo, Koroa, and Ofo tribes were living in villages along the Yazoo River in Mississippi. Another village of Koroa lived in Louisiana on the Ouachita River above the Washita tribe. The Ofo belong to the Siouan linguistic family of which the Quapaw, located to the northwest on the Arkansas River, are the nearest representatives. Swanton places the tribes of the Tunica, Yazoo, and Koroa in a distinct linguistic group which is designated as the Tunican linguistic family.[34] It has already been mentioned that there were three towns of Tunican people settled at the Natchez: a village of Koroa, and the small tribes of Tioux and Grigra.

The best described village, composed principally of members of the Tunican family, was situated four leagues (approximately twelve miles) up from the mouth of the Yazoo River on the east bank. The first record seems to be from the visit of La Source who accompanied Father Davion, the missionary, in 1698.

> On the 11th we arrived at the Tonicas, about 60 leagues below the Arkanseas. The first village is four leagues from the Mississippi inland, on the bank of a quite pretty river [the Yazoo]; they are dispersed in little villages; they cover in all 4 leagues of country . . . . The village of the great chief is in a beautiful prairie.[35]

Father Davion became a missionary to the Tunicas and remained with them for more than twenty years. He was visited by Le Sueur in 1700 who writes:

> I sent to beg M. Davion, a missionary priest at the Tonicas, 7 leagues up the river, to come and say mass for us. The first settlements of the savages

---

[34]Swanton, J. R. BAE. Bull. 43, pl. 1.
[35]Swanton, BAE bull. 43, p. 308, from La Source in Shea, Early Voy. Miss. pp. 80-81.

are 4 leagues up the river, and M. Davion is established 3 leagues higher up, on the branches of the same river.[36]

Pénicaut, who accompanied Le Sueur, names six tribes living on the right of the river, four leagues from its mouth: "the Yasoux, the Offogoulas, the Tonicas, the Coroas, the Ouitoupas, and the Oussipés."[37]

Father Gravier also visited the "River of the Tounika" in 1700. He mentions the village four leagues from the mouth of the river, and gives a rough census of Davion's charges:

> There are three different languages in his mission . . . the Jakou [Yazoo], of 30 cabins; the Ounspik [Ofo], of 10 or 12 cabins; and Toumika [Tunica], who are in 7 hamlets and who comprise in all 50 or 60 small cabins. He devotes himself only to this last language, and the Toumika being the most numerous give the name to the mission.[38]

Pénicaut records that a small fort was established on the lower Yazoo River in 1718. This was named Fort St. Peter.

> At this same time M. De Bienville sent M. de la Boulaye, lieutenant, with thirty men, many munitions, and much merchandise to establish a fort near the village of the Yasoux. When he arrived there he selected one of the most elevated situations which he could find on the borders of their river, four leagues from its mouth on the right, two gunshots distant from their village where he had his fort built.[39]

M. de La Tour, acting as agent for M. Le Blanc, in 1722 with sixty men established a plantation near the fort. A detail map showing the location of the fort and

[36]Swanton, BAE bull. 43, p. 308, from Margry, Découvertes, IV, pp. 179-180.

[37]Swanton, BAE bull. 43, p. 308, from Margry, Découvertes, V, p. 401.

[38]Swanton, BAE bull. 43, p. 309, from Shea, Early Voy. Miss. pp. 132-136.

[39]Swanton, BAE, bull. 43, p. 333, from Margry, Découvertes V, p. 554.

plantation in relation to the river is given in Dumont "Mémoires Historiques sur la Louisiane" and reproduced by Swanton, BAE bull. 43, plate 7.

Between 1718 and 1721 the command of Fort St. Peter must have changed for in 1721 Father Charlevoix mentions M. Bizort as commandant and says:

> He had chosen a bad situation for his fort and was preparing when he died to remove it a league higher in a very fine meadow where the air was more healthy and where there was a village of Yazoos mixed with Couroas and Ofogoulas [with] at most 200 men fit to bear arms.[40]

The above descriptions give a very good idea as to the location of at least one of the villages of the Yazoo River people—the village situated four leagues up the river on the right. Also, it appears that this village was a short distance above Fort St. Peter. Since a league at this period was equal to about three English miles, the site should be about twelve miles (by river) from the mouth of the Yazoo. This distance is correct for the position of the Haynes Bluff site.

Fort St. Peter seems to have stood on the bluff on the east side of the river, near the present Haynes Bluff bridge over the Yazoo.

Soon after 1706 the Tunica, who were friendly to the French, were threatened with attacks from the Chickasaw and other tribes to the north who were under English influence. Not feeling able to resist, the Tunica left their home on the Yazoo and moved southward to settle on the east bank of the Mississippi River opposite the mouth of the Red River. Originally this was the home of the Houmas. La Harpe says that the Tunicas forcibly drove out the Houmas, but Pénicaut represents it as a simple occupation of the Houma village after its abandonment by the former owners.[41] The old village of the Houmas

---

[40]Charlevoix, Histoire de la Nouvelle France, III, p. 413.
[41]Swanton, BAE bull. 43, p. 311, from Margry, Découvertes V, p. 483.

was located on the bluffs. Apparently the Tunicas did not settle on the exact site but preferred situations nearer the river.

The final migration of the Tunicas westward to the Marksville prairies in Avoyelles Parish, Louisiana, occurred sometime between 1784 and 1803. A small group of their descendants still live just south of the town of Marksville.

Identification of Tunica ceramic types

Determination of the historic Tunica ceramic decoration complex rests primarily on the identification of the Haynes Bluff site (Site No. 21) as the village of Tunica mixed with Yazoo, Koroa, and Ofo situated "two gunshots distant" above the French fort, St. Peter. Fort St. Peter is pointed out by certain historians as having been on the bluff over Haynes Bluff Landing about one-half mile down the river from the site. Some old tile drains found there by Mr. Otto Maganus, of Vicksburg, are supposed to have belonged to some of the buildings attached to the post. Considering the map of the establishment given by Dumont, this appears probable.[42] Haynes Bluff is the only point in the lower course of the Yazoo where the line of bluffs bordering its eastern side approaches the river closely enough to allow the fort to be placed on the bluff as close to the river as is shown on the map.

It is probable that this village above Fort St. Peter is the one that is referred to by several travelers of the same period as being four leagues up the river on the right. The distance, approximately twelve miles, is almost exactly correct.

Still this does not definitely identify the site. Its earthworks are much more extensive than those found in connection with historic Choctaw and Natchez sites. This gives rise to a suspicion that this village is of a greater antiquity. This seems to be the case, as is pointed

---

[42]Swanton, BAE bull. 43, pl. 7b.

out later. But the occurrence of sherds of the marker
pottery type, characteristic of the complex at the Haynes
Bluff site, found in the entirely historic Fatherland
mound and on the village site, indicates that those pottery types existed up to the historic period.

Clarence B. Moore's[43] find of a shallow burial accompanied by glass beads, and the collection of trade material secured by Calvin Brown,[44] are supplementary
evidence of a dubious nature as applied to the age of
the midden deposits.

The writer is not entirely satisfied that this complex
is the most recent in the lower Yazoo River valley. However, considering the resemblances of some of the pottery
to the other historic types, particularly the Caddo, there
can be little doubt that the complex considered as Tunica
belongs very near the historic period, and is in its proper
place in the time scale. If it should later develop that
the real Tunica complex was something different (more
like the Natchez, for example) it would fit in as a very
thin veneer over these types in the lower Yazoo valley.

Doubts of the proper identification of this complex
have arisen as a result of excavations recently made at
Angola farm. On Angola farm is located the village opposite the mouth of the Red River to which the Tunicas
moved after driving out the Houmas about 1706. Cemetery burials were found there accompanied by trade material. The native pottery was definitely of Natchez
and Caddo types (See Angola farm, page 129). None
of the dominant type of ware found at Haynes Bluff accompanied the burials. Only a few sherds of this type
were discovered in the surrounding soil. It is possible
that by this time the tribe had abandoned their original
pottery types in favor of the more ornamental wares of
the Natchez and Caddo. This has occurred in some

[43]Moore, C. B. Certain Mounds of Arkansas and of Mississippi,
p. 570.
[44]Brown, C. S. Archeology of Mississippi, p. 56.

cases, notably the adoption of the Catawba ware by the Cherokee, and may be the explanation in this case. As usual a decision must await further field-work.

Types of the Tunica complex

Type 11;62.

11   Motif: Irregular spacing of elements to cover all of decorated area.

62   Elements: Small nodes carelessly pinched up between two fingers while the paste was plastic.

    The decoration is very carelessly applied. There is no attempt to make the nodes uniform or of any particular shape.

Usual Accompanying Characteristics:

    The decorated area generally covers the upper half of the vessel. The lower parts of the walls and the bottom are smooth.

    The usual shape of vessels of this type is the globular pot-shaped round body, slightly constricted mouth, and perhaps, outflaring rims. Two knobs or handles, placed on opposite sides near the lip, are on some of these sherds. A general peculiarity is that the bottoms are thinner than the side walls.

    Another shape is a cylindrical vessel which may either be the beaker form or might, if it had a bulging bottom, form an urn. Handles are not present. Decoration is confined to a more narrow band than on the pots.

    Texture of the ware is rough, of moderate hardness, and averages about .2 of an inch in thickness. Sand, shell, and occasionally crushed charcoal are used as tempering material. Color varies from black (which is usually shell tempered and very friable) through brown, buff, and grey. Many pieces are mottled from uneven firing. Smoke stains indicating use over the fire are common.

Type 53;21;2

53   Motif: Large U-shaped flags filled with concentric, progressively smaller flags.

21 Element: Lines incised with a pointed instrument.

2 Arrangement: Motif brought out in positive. The flags are concentrically arranged inside one another in order to form a positive area against an undecorated background. Two methods of arranging these festooned lines are noted: (a) flags swung from a line bordering the rim and spaced at intervals around the vessel, (b) more flags are added in rows down the side of the vessel, each row swinging from the one above it. Decorations of this type are usually confined to the upper two-thirds or half of the vessel walls.

Usual Accompanying Characteristics:

Vessels of this type seem usually to have been rather large pots. Exact shapes and other features are not clear. The paste is usually grey or buff in color and is tempered with sand, grit, and shell.

Type $\frac{53}{61}$; 21; 2

53 Dominant Motif: U-shaped flags filled with concentric, progressively smaller flags.

61 Submotif: Lines running parallel to the rim.

21 Elements: Narrow lines incised with a pointed instrument.

2 Arrangement: The lines arranged parallel to the rim connect the line-filled, U-shaped flags spaced about the vessel so as to form a solid band of decoration encircling the vessel.

Usual Accompanying Characteristics:

The shape of these vessels is not definitely known. In some cases they were round bowls with low sides. The average sherd thickness is .2 of an inch. Paste is generally buff to grey in color; it is grit, sand, or shell tempered.

Type 63; 64

63 Motif: Arrangement in rows perpendicular to the rim.

64   Element: Small rough ridges raised by pinching. These pinched ridges are arranged down the side walls of the vessels from near the lip to the bottom. The execution is very rough and irregular. The marks of the fingers can be plainly seen.

Usual Accompanying Characteristics:

The vesels are generally small pots with convex bottoms, low necks, and outflaring rims. A few examples have strap handles. The paste is soft and porous; grit, charcoal, and shell are used as tempering. Thickness is about .2 of an inch. Color varies from grey through brown to black.

Type 64; 21

64   Motif: Herringbone design, running parallel to rim of the vessel.

21   Element: Incised lines made with a pointed tool. In some cases these lines are wider than the ordinary 21 lines. Almost invariably the decoration is very poorly executed. Often a line passes through the angles of the herringbone.

Usual Accompanying Characteristics:

The shape of these vessels is uncertain. The type is found on a rough ware which is tempered with grit, sand, and shell. Thickness is about .3 of an inch. Colors are grey, buff, to black.

Type 82; 20 (Marker type)

82   Motif: Decoration is on the inside of the lip of an outflaring thickened rim.

20   Element: An incised line, either narrow or wide. These rims usually have peculiar and easily recognized profiles as shown in figure 19.

Usual Accompanying Characteristics:

Typically this rim is found on carinated bowls; diameter greater than height, convex bottoms, and low, curving sides. In a few cases it is found on the outflaring rims of globular bottles with wide necks. The paste of these bottles is grey. It is porous and soft. Grit and shell are used as tempering. The more typical carinated bowls range from a hard, flinty, bluish paste with grit tempering, through buff and brown, to soft grey ware with grit and shell tempering. These rims are generally the only ornamentation found on vessels of this type.

Type 82; 52 (Marker type)

82   Motif: Decoration is on the outside edge of an outflaring thickened rim.

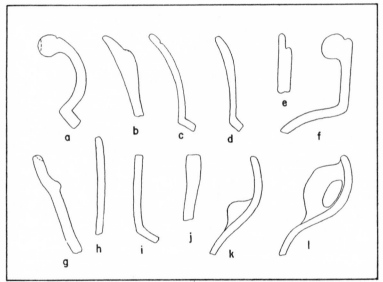

Figure 19. Profiles of rim sherds of the Tunica complex.

52   Element: Shallow notches on the outside of the lip. These notches are sometimes quite wide, so that the rim is scalloped. In other cases cord or fibre string has been impressed in the lip at an angle of 45 degrees to the tangent of the sherd.

Usual Accompanying Characteristics:

       These are the same as for the above type.

Type 82; $\dfrac{52}{20}$ (Marker type)

82   Motif: Decoration is on both the outside and inside of the lip of an outflaring, thickened rim.

52   Element: Shallow notches, scallops, or cord marks on the outside of the lip.

20   Element: A line drawn on the inside of the lip.

Usual Accompanying Characteristics:

These are usually the same as for the two above types. In a few cases where this rim appears on the lips of bottles the necks do not flare outward but are vertical. However these rims are also thickened and have the graceful profiles peculiar to these types.

Summary of Tunica village site collection features

In addition to the decorations peculiar to the complex of the Tunicas, the collections from sites which show the complex are likely to include pottery types characteristic of the Natchez, Caddo, and usually pottery of the Coles Creek complex. The significance of this trade material is obvious as far as the Natchez and Caddo are concerned. It is somewhat surprising that only one site, Pocahontas, shows any Choctaw pottery. The presence of Coles Creek is another matter and will be considered in the conclusions.

The following brief summary of characteristics is to assist in the recognition of a Tunica collection.

Pottery Decorations:

Outflaring lips with lines incised in them.
Outflaring lips, notched or scalloped.
Small nodes raised by pinching with two fingers.
Small ridges raised by pinching.
U-shaped festoons of incised lines.
Herringbone design.
Scroll formed by numerous lines.
Interior decorations of straight lines.
Various regular arrangements of punctates made with a point.
Chain of line-filled triangles.
Red slip on a few sherds.
Brush markings made with bundles of fibres.
Natchez type: three-line scroll with circle nucleuses.
Caddo type: scrolls formed of bands of delicate cross hatching.
Coles Creek type: incised lines, either plain or overhanging, running parallel to rim. Sometimes line in top of straight rim.

DESCRIPTION OF SHERDS IN FIGURE 20

Sherd	Type	Color of Paste	Finish (Good, Medium Poor)	Temper	Hardness (Hard, Medium Soft)	Thickness (inches)	Remarks
				PERIOD III—NATCHEZ			
n	41;21;5	Brown	M	Grit	M	.2	....
				CADDO			
r	41;$\frac{21}{28}$;2	Blue	G	Charcoal	M	.2	Rim of shallow bowl
				TUNICA			
a	82;$\frac{52}{20}$	Grey	G	Charcoal	H	.2	Rim
b	82;$\frac{52}{20}$	Dark blue	G	Grit	H	.2	Profile, carinated bowl
c	82;20	Dark blue	G	Grit	H	.2	Rim, profile
d	82;20	Grey	G	Charcoal	H	.2	Rim, profile
f	82;$\frac{52}{20}$	Dark blue	G	Shell	M	.2	Carinated bowl
g	Profile of sherd f						
h	82;$\frac{52}{20}$	Grey	M	Charcoal, grit	H	.2	Profile of carinated bo rim
i	....	Black	P	Shell	S	.2	Handle
j	82;52	Dark blue	G	Charcoal, grit	H	.2	Carinated bowl
l	53;21;2	Grey	P	Shell	S	.3	....
m	63;64	Black	P	Shell	S	.2	Rim
				PERIOD II—COLES CREEK			
k	71;21	Grey	D	Shell	S	.2	Rim
q	61;24;6	Dark blue	M	Vegetable, grit	M	.2	Rim
				INDETERMINATE			
e	Undecorated	Brown	G	Grit	M	.2	Profile of rim of pot
o	11;41	Grey	P	Charcoal	M	.2	Rim
p	51;21	Dark blue	P	Grit	M	.3	Rim

Material from Haynes Bluff (Site No. 21).

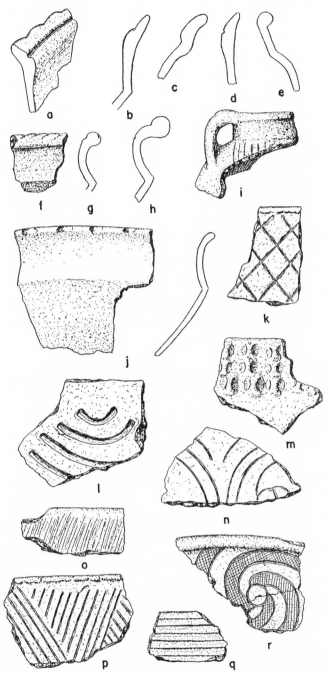

Figure 20. Selection of representative material from Haynes Bluff village site collection (Site No. 21).

Paste:

> Light porous grey or black ware.
> Fairly hard grey or blue ware.
> Shell tempering.
> Charcoal tempering.
> Interiors sometimes blackened.

Vessel Shapes:

> Carinated bowls.
> Shallow, concave bowls.
> Globular, wide mouthed pots with handles.
> Beakers.
> Bottles.
> Effigy vessels.

Vessel Appendages:

> Strap handles.
> Knobs (sometimes twin knobs side by side).
> Effigy heads facing inward on vessel rims (rare).

Sites yielding the Tunica Complex

Site No. 21, Haynes Bluff
SE¼ NW¼ S23, T18N, R4E

The mound group referred to by this name is actually about one-half mile northeast of Haynes Bluff; the point where U. S. highway 61 crosses the Yazoo River. This site was first visited and described by Clarence B. Moore in 1907.[45] It was again visited and described by Calvin Brown.[46]

The site is located on the eastern side of the Yazoo River at the foot of the bluffs that border the lower course of the river. It occupies a talus fan that rises slightly above the level of the annual inundations of the river.

The largest mound stands on the south bank of a small stream that flows from a spring at the foot of the bluffs. The mound is a truncated pyramid one hundred eighty-five feet square at the base and about thirty feet

---

[45]Moore, C. B., Certain Mounds of Arkansas and of Mississippi, pp. 569-570.
[46]Brown, C. B., Archeology of Mississippi, p. 55 ff.

high. It has a summit plateau seventy-five feet square. Three small mounds that have almost been obliterated by plowing lie to the south of the large mound. It was in one of these that Moore found a shallow burial with glass beads.[47]

The surface collection comes from the plowed field between the mounds. Classification of the decorated sherds is shown in figure 1. Representative pieces are illustrated in figure 20.

Site No. 25, Anna site

The Anna group of mounds in Adams County, Mississippi, is situated on the edge of the bluff overlooking the Mississippi River about ten miles north of Natchez, Mississippi. Four large pyramidal mounds comprise the central group. The largest, about fifty feet tall, stands directly on the edge of the bluff. A graded approach, or ramp, descends its eastern side toward another pyramid, about twelve feet high, situated about three hundred feet distant to the east. Two other truncated pyramids of the same size as the latter are arranged three hundred feet to the north of these two. Deep ravines almost surround the mounds. Five other mounds belonging to the same group are reported to lie a short distance north of these but have not been examined by the writer.[48]

Midden material is scattered on and around the four mounds. Basically the pottery is related to the Tunica complex and is closest to that found at Pocahontas (Site No. 24). Classification of the material from Anna is shown in figure 1. Sherds are illustrated in figure 22 k-s.

There is nothing to indicate that the Anna site was occupied within historic times.

---

[47]Moore, C. B., Certain Mounds of Arkansas and of Mississippi, p. 570.

[48]Described by Brown, Archeology of Mississippi, pp. 40-42.

DESCRIPTION OF SHERDS IN FIGURE 21

Sherd	Type	Color of Paste	Finish (Good, Medium, Poor)	Temper	Hardness (Hard, Medium, Soft)	Thickness (inches)	Remarks
				PERIOD III—CADDO			
i	32;$\frac{21}{71}$;2	Light blue	M	Veg., Grit	M	.2	Carinated bowl, blacken interior
o	34;$\frac{21}{21/64}$;1	Grey	G	Grit	M	.2	Square lip, carinated bow black interior, scratche lines
				NATCHEZ			
k	41;21;5	Black	M	Grit	M	.2	....
				TUNICA			
a	82;20	Dark blue	M	Charcoal, Grit	M	.2	Interior view
b	82;52	Black	G	Grit	M	.3	Interior view
c	82;52	Dark blue	M	Charcoal, Grit	M	.2	Interior view
e	53;21;2	Black	M	Grit	S	.2	....
f	82;5?	Light blue	G	Char., Grit	M	.2	Drilled hole
g	11;62	Black	R	Shell, Grit	M	.3	....
h	52;71;2	Grey	R	Shell	S	.2	Outcurving lip
p	Handle	Grey	R	Shell	M	.3	....
q	Twin Knobs	Grey	R	Shell	M	.2	Near lip
r	Effigy head from rim of vessel:						
		Grey	R	Grit	M	.3	Faces inward
				PERIOD II—COLES CREEK			
j	63;64	Grey	R	Grit	S	.3	....
				INDETERMINATE			
d	....	Buff	G	Grit	S	.2	Interior view
m	51;21	Grey	R	Grit, Shell	M	.2	Beaker
n	....	Grey	R	Shell	M	.2	Shallow bowl
l	01;71	Grey	R	Shell	S	.2	....

Material from Pocahontas (Site No. 24).

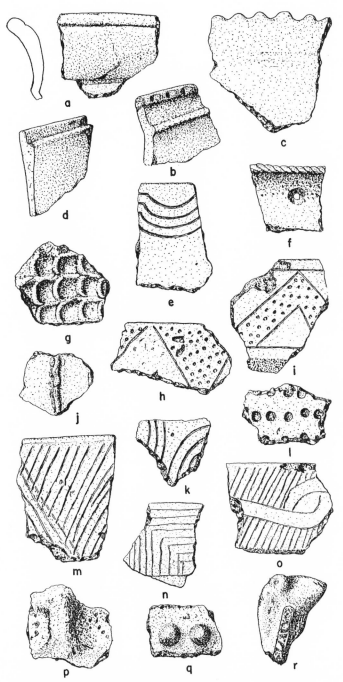

Figure 21.   Selection of representative material from the Pocahontas village site collection (Site No. 24).

DESCRIPTION OF TUNICA COMPLEX SITES

Site No.	Site Name	Burial		Conical		Pyramidal		Ramp	Enclosure	Midden			Collection Analysis	Minimum Date
		Cemetery	Mound	Low —10'	Steep +10'	Low —10'	Tall +10'			Approximate Area	Thin —10"	Thick +10"		
21	*Haynes Bluff	X	X	3			1	X		2A		X	Tunica, Coles Creek	Circa 1730
22	Lake George			18			2	X	X	10A		X	Tunica, Coles Creek	
23	Fort Place			4			1			4A	X		Tunica, Coles Creek, Deasonville	
24	*Pocahontas	X	X		1		1			2A		X	Tunica, Coles Creek	
25	*Anna						4	X		5A		X	Tunica, Coles Creek	

*Sites described in the text and from which material is illustrated.

Excavated burial mounds in the Valley of the Big Black river

The six sites which will be discussed were excavated by M. B. Chambers and the writer for the Mississippi Department of Archives and History in the summers of 1927, 1928, and 1929. Owing to regrettable inexperience, the records of the work were not kept as carefully and fully as could be desired.

Five of the sites, the Dupree, Gross, Smith, Chapman, and Pocahontas mounds, lie in the Big Black Valley east of the river in Hinds and Madison counties, Mississippi. Woodbine mound is west of the river in Yazoo county (see map, Figure 2). From north to south all the sites are spaced within forty miles.

As far as historical records reveal, the region in which these mounds are located was not inhabited when the French first explored the country in the early eighteenth century. Presumably, at least a few scattered families of Choctaws had moved into the area in the early eighteen hundreds. There was a Choctaw agency a short distance east of the Pocahontas site on the Natchez Trace where the treaty of Doak's Stand was signed in 1820.

These sites are included under the heading of the Tunica complex because they appear to be most closely related ceramically to that group. It is true that the marker types of Tunica (the notched rim with a line incised inside the outflaring thickened lip) are not found except on the Pocahontas village site, yet there are resemblances in more general and less diagnostic features such as carinated bowls, bottles, handles, shell tempering, punctate-filled flags, chains of line-filled triangles, festooned lines, and scroll decorations. These are all features that have a wide distribution to the north, east, and west, yet, within the area covered by this study, they point more directly to Tunica than to anything else.

DESCRIPTION OF SHERDS IN FIGURE 22

Sherd	Type	Color of Paste	Finish (Good, Medium, Poor)	Temper	Hardness (Hard, Medium, Soft)	Thickness (inches)	Remarks
				PERIOD III.—TUNICA COMPLEX			
b	Handle	Light Tan	P	Shell	M	..	....
				PERIOD II.—COLES CREEK COMPLEX			
e	Triangle lug	Brown	M	Grit	M	.4	At right angles to vessel wal
f	61;24;6	Brown	M	Grit	M	.3	Rim of beaker
h	61;24;6	Black	M	Grit	M	.2	....
i	61;—24;9 / 71	Light Tan	M	Shell	M	.2	....
j	34 / —;24;1 / 61	Grey	M	Charcoal	M	.3	Rim, scratched lines
				INDETERMINATE			
a	....	Black	M	Grit	M	.2	Rim of beaker
c	Impressed decoration	Grey	M	Sand	M	.2	Bottle with small neck
d	Scratched decoration	Black	M	Sand	M	.3	Interior view
g	Scratched lines	Grey	M	Charcoal	M	.3	Square lip beaker

Material from Pocahontas (Site No. 24)

Sherd	Type	Color of Paste	Finish	Temper	Hardness	Thickness	Remarks
				PERIOD III.—NATCHEZ COMPLEX			
r	41;21;5	Black	G	Grit	M	.2	Rim
				PERIOD III.—TUNICA COMPLEX			
k	52 / 82;—20	Brown	G	Grit	S	.3	Out-flaring rim; interior view
l	82;20	Grey	M	Charcoal	M	.3	Interior view, thickened out-flared rim
m	82;20	Black	M	Grit	M	.2	Thick, outflaring rim
n	82;20	Grey Light	M	Shell	M (int. view)	.2	Interior view, outflaring rim
o	41;21;3	Brown	M	Charcoal	M	.3	....
q	53;21;2	Grey	P	Charcoal	S	.2	....
				INDETERMINATE			
p	51;21	Grey	P	Grit	M	.3	....
s	11;41	Grey	P	Charcoal	M	.3	Rim

Material from Anna (Site No. 25).

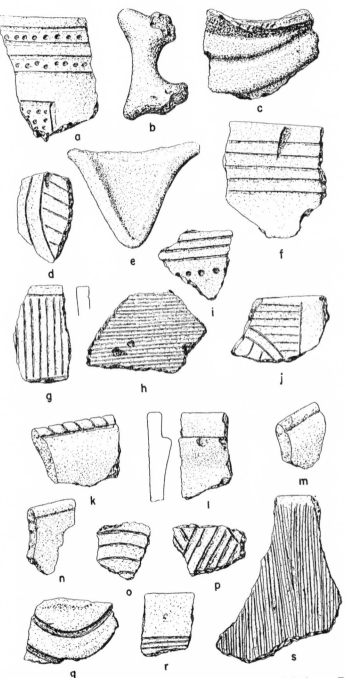

Figure 22. Selection of representative material from Pocahontas (Sherds a-j) and Anna (Sherds k-s) village site collections.

Part of the difficulty probably lies in the fact that
we are attempting to compare burial collections from the
Big Black mounds with surface material from the Tunica
sites. The exact relationships may be clearer when Tunica
burial collections are available for comparison. Because
they are burial collections, the pottery from the Big Black
sites has not been classified in the survey index. These
sites do not affect the problems of relative dating and
are included here only to complete the picture of Mississippi archeology as it stands at present.

Dupree plantation site

SE¼ NW¼ S2, T15N, R3W

The Dupree site consists of only a single conical
mound, sixty feet in diameter and twelve feet high. It
is located on the south side of a branch of Fourteen Mile
Creek on the old Dupree plantation, six miles west of
Raymond, Hinds County, Mississippi. The mound was
excavated in the summers of 1927-1928 by Chambers and
the writer. Thirty-five burials were found. There was
no particular plan to the arrangement of the burials in
the mound. They were variously oriented and scattered
from the top to the base. The skeletons were in several
different positions: extended on the back, lying on the
side with knees drawn up, or tightly flexed on the back.
Several cases were found of skull burials. These were
accompanied by the usual burial furniture, but the rest
of the bones of the skeletons were missing. Two of these
skulls had the atlas and axis sections of the vertebral
column in their correct positions. This may mean that
these isolated skulls were decapitated heads which were
buried with the flesh still on them.

The burials were accompanied by a liberal amount
of furniture. Most of this was pottery vessels of varied
though simple shapes.

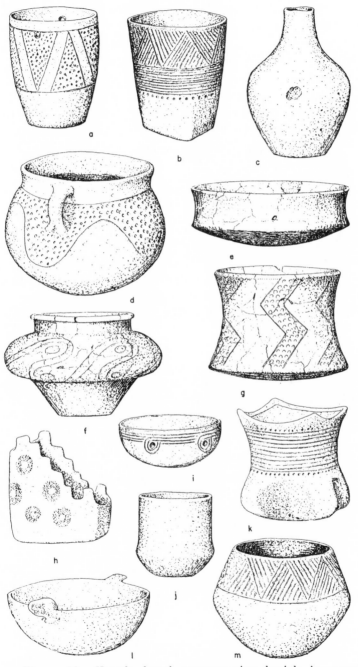

Figure 23. Vessels found accompanying burials in mounds located in the Big Black River valley, Mississippi.

These are listed in the table of comparisons given on page 127. The first column in the table refers to the drawings of the different types given as figure 23. A brief description of the various vessel shapes is given in the following paragraphs.

Two bowls are convex in shape, shallow, and undecorated. They are roughly finished, mottled grey to reddish, and the paste is tempered with grit and sand. The size is small, being not over seven inches in diameter.

One square bowl has low vertical sides and a flat bottom.

A deep round bowl with convex bottom and vertical sides is grey in color, undecorated, and seven inches in diameter.

Eight carinated bowls have convex bottoms, sharp angles between the bottoms and side walls, and low vertical sides with a distinct inward camber. Most of these are of a hard, thin, steel blue or light grey ware and are mottled with dark areas caused by uneven firing. None are decorated. Shell tempering is present in some of this ware but grit is more usual (Figure 23 e).

Beakers comprise the second most numerous class of vessels in the collection. They are all marked by straight walls and flat bottoms. While the bodies and the rims of the beakers are all round, the bottoms of ten are round, and nine are square with well marked corners. Several are decorated with zigzagged bands of punctates, enclosed by lines, which extend from the rim to the bottom (Figure 23 g), and wide bands of nested triangles shaded with straight lines drawn at two angles (Figure 23 b, m).

Gross plantation

The single mound on the Gross plantation, nine miles northwest of Flora, Madison County, Mississippi, was situated on the edge of the second terrace on the east side of the Big Black River. It was conical in shape, eighty feet in diameter, and thirteen feet high. Thirty-seven burials were scattered through the mound. These were extended, flexed, and bunched. Several disassociated skulls were found. One of these had shell ear pins near the mastoid processes indicating that it had been covered with skin when interred.

Fourteen pottery vessels were found, (see table, page 127). Other finds are listed on page 128.

Unlike all the other Big Black sites except Pocahontas, there is a midden deposit in the field just west of the mound. However, judging from the pottery, the village site is not connected with the mound, but is earlier. The collection from this is treated in figure 1, (Site No. 24). As will be noted, this is a typical site of the Deasonville complex, and is characterized by cord marked pottery. None of the types found in Big Black mounds occur in the village site collection. Neither is there any of the typical village site ware accompanying burials in the Gross mound. However, there are sherds of cord marked pottery scattered through the mound. This argues that these sherds were gathered with the dirt that was taken to build the structure, and that the village site was already there when the mound was constructed. Deasonville decorations are not found in any of the other Big Black mounds.

No evidence could be found of a village site which appeared to belong to the mound.

Smith plantation

The Smith mound is only about one and one-half miles east of the Gross site. It is another conical mound, sixty feet in diameter and ten feet high. Burials were scattered through the mound without any particular arrangement. One burial in the top of the mound was accompanied by an unusual amount of material which included a square vessel. This piece of pottery has terraced sides and is covered with a white slip on which red circles are painted (Figure 23 h). Other finds are tabulated on pages 126 to 128.

No refuse indicative of habitation could be found in the surrounding fields.

On the Woodbine plantation, eight miles southwest of Bentonia, Yazoo County, Mississippi was another small conical mound which measured sixty feet in diameter and nine feet high. The mound is located on a low ridge near a small stream. Two miles to the west this stream empties into Big Black River.

Twenty-eight burials were scattered from the top to the bottom of the mound with apparently no plan or orderly arrangement. Only five pottery vessels were found. These and other finds are tabulated on pages 126 to 128. Very little village site refuse could be found in the fields about the mound.

Chapman plantation

NE¼ NW¼ S3, T7N, R1W

The Chapman mound was located on the south side of the Chapman's store-Brownsville highway, on a hillside west of Straight Fence Creek, in Hinds County, Mississippi. The mound was so close to the road that part of it had been cut away by road machinery. But for this chance it probably would have escaped discovery as the structure is very flat. The remnant of the mound was about fifty feet in diameter and three feet high. The site is now in woods and probably has not been in cultivation. Fifteen burials were found in the mound. Accompanying them were the eight vessels tabulated on page 127. Other finds are listed on page 128. No indications of a village site could be found.

Pocahontas site

NE¼ NW¼ S3, T7N, RLW

The Pocahontas site, located at the small town of Pocahontas in the northeastern part of Hinds County, Mississippi, has two mounds. The burial mound is conical in shape and steep; seventy-five feet in diameter and ten feet high. It is located on the property of the public school. For this reason the excavators were not able to obtain permission to examine it thoroughly. However, a number of artifacts have been recovered through the efforts of the school children, and some have been presented to the state museum. Available material is compared on page 126. One remarkable fragment was part of a vessel which represented a bird, possibly a duck. Only a part of the body, including one wing, was preserved. Another find was a clay pipe representing a kneeling human figure. The connecting holes for the bowl and stem are formed in the back and posterior of the figure (Figure 24).

The larger mound of the two is situated about four hundred yards southeast of the burial mound. It is a pyramidal truncate three hundred and fifty by two hundred and fifty feet at the base and twenty-five feet high. The sides of the mound are very steep and the only approach is a winding path up the western side. Trees cover the slopes of the mound and only the plateau on top has been cultivated.

The fields about the pyramidal mound are profusely covered with fragments of pottery, flint chips, briquettes, fragments of animal bones, and human bones that have been plowed from shallow field burials.

The pottery from the village site is illustrated by representative pieces in figures 20 and 21 a-j. The collection has been classified and in the table, figure 1, is listed with the Tunica complex to which it appears to be related. Comparison of the illustrations will show that the same types are found at this site that occur in other mounds in the Big Black valley: carinated bowls, bottles,

Figure 24. Effigy pipe made of pottery found in the burial mound at Pocahontas, Hinds County, Mississippi (Site No. 24).

seed bowls, beakers, square bottom forms, globular pots with handles or knobs, effigy heads on vessel rims, shell tempering, pinched decorations, zigzagged bands of lines enclosing punctates, chains of line-filled triangles, festooned lines, U-shaped flags filled with punctates, lines drawn parallel to the rim; artifacts such as copper covered earspools of stone, chipped and ground celts, triangular, leaf-shaped and stemmed projectile points, and grooved sandstone abraders.

Usual types of pottery decoration which do not occur in the mounds but are found on the Pocahontas village site include rims of the typical Tunica type (Figure 21 a);

straight rims that have been cut away to form a shelf inside the lip which is a type peculiar to this village site collection (Figure 21 d) ; a red and white painted sherd (Deasonville complex) ; scratched decorations on vessel interiors; and a single sherd decorated with the band of five combed lines—a type that is peculiar to the historic Choctaw-sites.

Relationship of Big Black pottery to the Coles Creek complex

The pottery from the mounds in the Big Black River valley shows certain relationships to the Coles Creek complex. This is also apparent on the Pocahontas village site, where sherds occur decorated with several lines drawn parallel to the vessel rim and with a row of punctates below and parallel to the lines (type $61 ; \frac{24}{71 ; 9}$). The same plan of ornamentation is found on two vessels from the Dupree mound. The lines parallel to the rim, but without the row of punctates (type 61 ;21 ;6) is found on vessels from Dupree, Gross, and Pocahontas burial mounds. Other features which indicate relationship are the beaker form of vessel, found at Dupree, Smith, Chapman, and Pocahontas; the flat, square shape of vessel bottoms that occurs at the same sites; and the holes drilled on opposite sides near the rims of vessels found in Dupree, Smith, and Pocahontas mounds.

TABLE COMPARING VESSEL DECORATIONS FROM BIG BLACK SERIES OF MOUNDS IN WEST-CENTRAL MISSISSIPPI

DECORATIONS	DUPREE	GROSS	SMITH	WOODBINE	CHAPMAN	POCAHONTAS
Flags:						
Punctate filled, U-shaped	2	1			2	2
Punctate filled, V-shaped	3					
Line filled, V-shaped	1			1		
Festooned lines					1	
Chain of line-filled triangles	1		2			
Chain of line-filled squares					1	1
Line bordered, zigzagged punctate band	1					
Chain of punctate-filled diamonds	1		1			
Lines drawn parallel to rim	2	1				1
Scrolls		3	1		1	1
Meanders		3				
Notched rims	1		1			
Painted: red and white			1			
Pinched nodes	1					1
Drilled holes	X*		X			X
Band of lines with loops encircling depressed area						X
Effigy heads on rim	X			X		X

*X indicates presence of characteristic named.

TABLE SHOWING NUMBER OF VESSELS OF DIFFERENT SHAPES FROM
THE BIG BLACK SERIES OF EXCAVATED MOUNDS IN
WEST-CENTRAL MISSISSIPPI

	Illustrated in figure 23	DUPREE	GROSS	SMITH	WOODBINE	CHAPMAN	POCAHONTAS
Bowls:							
Convex, shallow	i	2			1		
Convex bottoms, vertical sides, deep	—	1	1		1		2
Square, flat bottoms	—	1					
Carinated	e	8	4		1		1
Cups	j		2	2			1
Beakers:							
Flat, round bottoms	a	10		2		1	
Flat, square bottoms	b	9		1			
Seed Bowls	m	4	1	2	1	2	
Pots:							
With Handles:							
Convex bottoms	d	6	1			1	2
Round, flat bottoms	—	1	1			2	
Square, flat bottoms	—	1					
Without Handles:							
Convex bottoms	—	4	2	1			
Round, flat bottoms	—	1				1	1
Square, flat bottoms	—	1					
Vase, carinated	g	3		1			
Bottles	c	3	2	2	1	1	1
Toy Vessels*	—	X				X	X
Unusual forms		2		1			

*These vessels are reproductions of usual forms and are counted under those
forms. Their presence is indicated by "X".

FEATURES AND ARTIFACTS, EXCLUSIVE OF POTTERY, FROM THE
BIG BLACK SERIES OF SITES

	DUPREE	GROSS	SMITH	WOODBINE	CHAPMAN	POCAHONTAS
Mounds:						
Small, steep, conical burial mounds	x	x	x	x	x	x
Large rectangular truncate						x
Burial:						
Liberal burial furniture	x	x	x	x	x	x
Skeletons extended	x	x	x	x	x	x
Skeletons flexed	x	x	x	x	x	x
Isolated skull burials	x	x		x	x	x
Bunched burials	x	x	x	x	x	x
Skulls capped with bowls	x	x				x
Ceremonial and Ornamental:						
Biconcave discoidal stones	x	x			x	x
Quartz crystals		x		x		x
Elbow pipes	x	x				x
Stone earspools, plated with copper	x	x		x		x
Fossil sharks' teeth	x					
Unshaped lumps of galena	x	x	x			
Plummets of iron ore	x			x		
Lens-shaped masses of green clay	x					
Masses of red ochre	x	x			x	x
Ear pins of Busycon columella	x	x				
Disc-shaped beads of shell	x	x		x	x	x
Tubular beads of shell			x			x
Beads of Marginella shells	x	x		x		x
Tubular beads of stone	x					x
Utensils:						
Smooth ground celts, usually greenstone	x	x	x	x	x	x
Chipped celts of flint	x	x		x		x
Grooved sandstone abraders		x				x
Chert knives or side scrapers		x				x
Leaf-shaped flints	x	x		x		
Triangular-shaped projectile points		x				x
Stemmed projectile points	x	x		x		x
Flint awls or hand drills	x	x				
Terrapin carapaces				x		

Angola farm

N½ irreg. S52, T1S, R5W

The village of the Houmas lay in the hills on the eastern side of the Mississippi River, opposite a narrow neck formed by the river swinging in a great bend to the west. The Red River emptied into the Mississippi in this bend. La Salle and Tonti mentioned the tribe when they descended the river in 1682, but they did not stop. Iberville was the first to visit the village:

> The 20th [of March, 1699], I reached the landing place of the Ouma village, at half-past 10 in the morning, distant from my camp about 3 leagues, where I found five men, three Oumas and Quinipissas [Acolapissas], who awaited me with the peace calumet, having come from the village when they heard the report of the swivel gun. As far off as they discovered us they sang, and the Bayougoulas whom I had sang for me. Landing, we embraced and caressed each other after their manner, and smoked together. At 11 I set out for the village, the Bayougoulas and these people escorting us the entire way. The deputies of the Oumas walked in front, singing continually, although we had to pass along a very bad road, filled with very steep hills or little mountains for almost the whole distance. One hour after midday we came in sight of the village, where, at 400 paces, I met three men deputed to bring me the calumet. It was necessary to smoke in form, seated on a mat, which fatigues me very much, I never having smoked. These three new singers conducted me up a height, where there were three cabins, at 300 paces from the village, where they had me stop and sent to inform the chief of my arrival, waiting a reply as to what we should do.[49]

---

[49]Swanton, John R., BAE, bull. 43, p. 285, from Margry, Découvertes, IV, pp. 174-177.

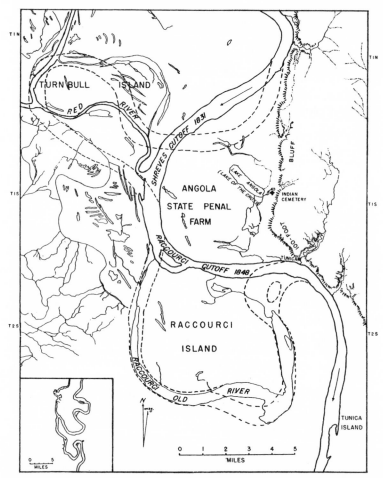

Figure 25. Map showing present course of the Mississippi River near the mouth of the Red River (solid line). Dotted line indicates the Mississippi channel in 1731. The inset map in lower left corner represents the same part of the channel and is from the chart probably drawn by M. Baron, showing route of Perier's army in expedition against Natchez Fort.

Gravier visited the Houmas the next year, and has left a better description of the village:

We left the village of the Natchez on the 24th, and on the 25th of November [1700] we discovered the hills of the Houmas to the south of the Mississippi [in the great bend descending the stream to the westward], which forms a bay that one enters by leaving the main channel to the right. There is a good league and a half from the point of disembarkation to the village of the Houmas, over a very bad road, for one has to ascend and descend, and walk half bent through the canes. The village is on the crest of a steep mountain, precipitous on all sides. There were 80 cabins in it, and in the middle of the village is a fine and very level space, where, from morning to night young men exercise themselves.[50]

According to La Harpe, the migration of the Tunicas from their home on the Yazoo River to the site of the Houma village occurred in 1706, as the result of the capture of an English trader, who later set the Chickasaws upon them.

The Tonicas, not feeling themselves strong enough to resist, abandoned their villages and collected again among the Houmas, who received them trustingly. While [the latter] were reposing on their good faith the Tonicas surprised them and killed more than one-half of their nation.[51]

Although the Tunicas took over the old village of the Houmas, they appear also to have formed other settlements nearer the river.

The 12th of [January, 1719] we descended the Mississipy; at 10 o'clock we entered the lake of the Tonicas, to the right of the river going up; at 11 o'clock we arrived at the village and proceeded to the cabin of M. Davion, of the foreign missions, who was pastor there.[52]

---

[50]Swanton, BAE bull. 43, p. 288, from Margry, Découvertes, IV, p. 418.
[51]Swanton, BAE bull. 43, p. 311, from La Harpe, Jour. Hist. pp. 100-101.
[52]Swanton, BAE bull. 43, p. 312, from La Harpe in Margry, Découvertes, VI, pp. 246-248.

Father Charlevoix's account of his visit to these villages is similar.

> The 28th [of December, 1721], after having gone 2 leagues, we arrived at the river of the Tonicas, which appeared to me at first to be but a brook; but at a musket-shot distance from its mouth it forms a very pretty lake. If the Mississippi continues to throw itself as it does on the other side, all this place will become inaccessible. The river of the Tonicas has its source in the country of the Tchactas, and its course is very much obstructed by falls. The village is beyond the lake on a pretty high ground, yet they say that the air here is bad, which they attribute to the quality of the waters of the river; but I should rather judge that it proceeds from the stagnation of the waters in the lake. The village is built in a circle, round a very large open space, without any enclosure, and moderately peopled.[53]

Swanton has the following to say about the locations of the Tunica villages at this time:

> When the French first came to Louisiana the Mississippi bent far around to the westward opposite the place where these Tunica villages were then located, but where were then the Houma, leaving a narrow neck of land, which, from the circumstance of a cross having been erected there by Iberville, was called 'the portage of the cross'. In time the river cut partly through this, sending a narrow, rapid stream directly across, and this was the condition of affairs in Poisson's time [circa 1727]. At the lower end was a landing and village called 'the little Tonicas', and at the upper end the landing and village of 'the great Tonicas'. Subsequently this neck was cut entirely through and the old channel abandoned by the river.[54]

Some time between 1784 and 1803 the Tunicas purchased some land from the Avoyel and removed westward to the Marksville Prairie near the Red River.[55] A

---

[53]Swanton, BAE bull. 43, p. 312, from Margry, Découvertes V, p. 519.

[54]Swanton, BAE bull. 43, pp. 313-314. Gives reference to Jesuit Relations, LXVII, p. 309.

[55]Swanton, BAE bull. 43, p. 315.

few Indians that identify themselves as Tunicas are still living near the town of Marksville. They point to Tunica Island in the Mississippi River, a short distance below the mouth of the Red, as their ancestral home. The impressive mound group at Marksville (see page 226) has been adopted into their mythology, and they tell how in old times Tunica women built the structures while their men fought a great battle, and how the blood that flowed cut deep ravines.

The map given in figure 25 is made from portions of the Batchelor and Artonish Quadrangles constructed by aerial surveys for the Mississippi River Commission. It shows the Mississippi from below Tunica Island to Point Breeze and includes the mouth of the Red River coming in from the west. The insert in the lower left corner contains the corresponding section of the river taken from a map probably drawn by M. Broutin, the engineer who accompanied Governor Perier's expedition to attack the Natchez in the last Natchez war. According to the legend of the map, the course of the Mississippi was taken from the earlier map of M. Pauger. This insert map probably dates from very near 1731, the date of the expedition.[56] On the large map the probable course of the Mississippi about the year 1731, based both on the inset map and the old scars shown by aerial photographs, is shown by broken lines.

The old stream bed marked "Lake Angola" on modern maps was named "Lake of the Cross" on the Lockett map of Louisiana made in 1872. Possibly this is reminiscent of the original name for the portage across the neck of land—"Portage of the Cross". The lake appears to have been formed by a stream meander prior to the date of the French exploration. Probably it was the bay referred to by Gravier, and the "Lake of the Tunicas" through which La Harpe, and later, Father

---

[56]A photostatic copy of the entire map will be found in the Karpinsky collection of maps in the Library of Congress. This copy was obtained through the courtesy of Mr. William Green.

DESCRIPTION OF SHERDS IN FIGURE 26

Sherd	Type	Color of Paste	Finish (Good, Medium Poor)	Temper	Hardness (Hard, Medium Soft)	Thickness (inches)	Remarks
				PERIOD III—NATCHEZ			
i	43;21;5	Dark blue	M	Grit	S	.2	Deep bowl
				CADDO			
c	34;$\frac{21}{21/64}$;1	Black	P	Shell	S	.2	....
d	Same as c	Black	P	Shell	S	.2	....
j	41;$\frac{21}{28}$2	Black	G	Grit	M	.2	....
k	Same	Grey	M	Grit	M	.2	....
				TUNICA			
a	82;20	Black	M	Charcoal	S	.3	Thickened outflaring rim
b	82;20	Terracotta	M	....	M	.2	Carinated bowl, interior v
				INDETERMINATE			
e	Scratched decoration	Black	M	Shell, sand	M	.3	Interior of plate-shaped v sel
f	11;41	Black	P	Grit	S	.3	Thickened rim
g	Scratched decoration	Grey	M	Grit	M	.2	Interior of shallow bowl
h	11;41	Black	P	Grit	M	.2	Rim
l	11;91	Buff	M	....	M	.2	....
m	Gun flint						

Material from Angola farm.

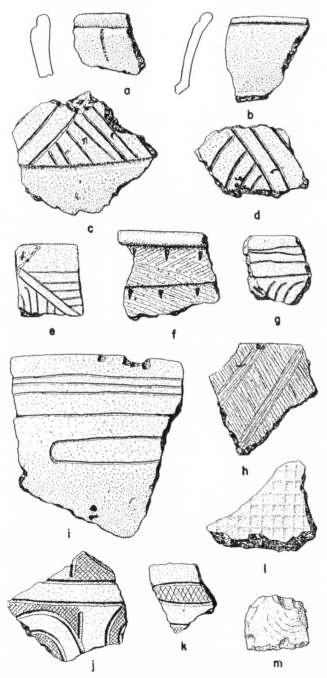

Figure 26. Selection of representative sherds of the material found scattered through the soil in the excavations at Angola farm.

135

Charlevoix, passed in approaching the Tunica villages. On the reconstruction of the 1731 channel of the Mississippi it is apparent that the Indian cemetery marked near the eastern end of Lake Angola is the logical position of the village of "the great Tonicas" at the upper end of the portage.

The rich bottom land surrounding Lake Angola is now included in the Louisiana State Penal Farm which is also named Angola. In April, 1934, burials were discovered in plowing a broad talus fan spread out from the mouth of a small stream that flows out of the hundred-foot bluffs which border the eastern side of the Mississippi. The burials were located six hundred yards from the bluffs at a point where the fan had been carved by the Mississippi in former times. The old, filled-in stream channel was very apparent. A half mile to the south it opened up to form Lake Angola.

Through the courtesy of Mr. R. L. Himes, Superintendent of the State Penitentiary, the writer was provided with a crew of men and was allowed to excavate the site for the Louisiana State University. The net result of eight days excavation was ten burials. Two had been disturbed by plowing. The remaining seven were the skeletons of adults, orientated in various directions, and extended on their backs approximately three feet beneath the present surface. Four males were accompanied by the metal parts of flintlock muskets. Masses of round lead balls with a few gunflints and a black substance which probably was powder lay over the stocks of two of the guns. Beads were found with almost every burial, and were clustered about the neck, chest, and ankles. A number of small cones, crudely bent from sheet copper, lay at the ankles of one male (Figure 27 g). Small turkey bells lay near the feet of two others. In the abdominal region of one male was a small metal pipe and the iron blade of a halberd (Figure 27 f). Another had an iron axe blade. Three of the males had flat-bottomed, straight-sided copper kettles about fifteen inches in diameter placed above their shoulders. Two pottery vessels of native manufacture were near the skulls of two different burials.

The three other adults appeared to be females. Compared with the males, the burial furniture in their graves was scanty. Two of them had three native vessels each near their heads; the other had one. About the ankles of one of the females were a few porcelain beads.

An infant was buried in a wooden chest, nineteen inches deep, nineteen inches wide, and forty-three inches long. The wood had decayed. Nails, hinges, and a hasp showed its outlines. The small skeleton lay on the bottom of the box. Over the pelvis was inverted a copper kettle similar to the ones that accompanied the adults. At the feet lay a crockery bottle of European manufacture, eight inches in diameter, and eleven inches tall. A few fragments of red ochre were found under the left side of the skull.

Except that these are burials in excavated graves rather than in a low mound, this site shares several striking features in common with the Natchez burials in Fatherland mound C (page 61). The European trade material used as burial furniture is practically identical, except that at the Natchez site the only firearm found was one pistol. The beads, brass turkey bells, axe, and native-made copper cones used as ornaments are exactly similar to material found there. The infant buried in a wooden box is identical with two found in Mound C interred in similar chests.

Of the nine pieces of native-made pottery found, only seven were decorated. Five are shown in figure 27 with some of the European material from the site. The description of this plate appears on the page opposite.

DESCRIPTION OF SHERDS IN FIGURE 27

Sherd	Type	Color of Paste	Finish (Good, Medium Poor)	Temper	Hardness (Hard, Medium Soft)	Thickness (inches)	Remarks
			PERIOD III—NATCHEZ				
e	43;21;5	Buff	M	Grit	M	.2	
			CADDO				
c	....	Yellow	M	Shell	S	.2	Red slip, flaking off
b	34;$\frac{21}{21/64}$;1	Tan	M	Shell	M	.2	
			INDETERMINATE				
a	....	Tan	P	Grit, charcoal	M	.2	
d	51;21	Black	P	Shell	S	.3	
f	Iron halbert						
g	Cones made from sheet copper. Used as ornaments.						

Material from graves at Angola farm, historic Tunica cemetery.

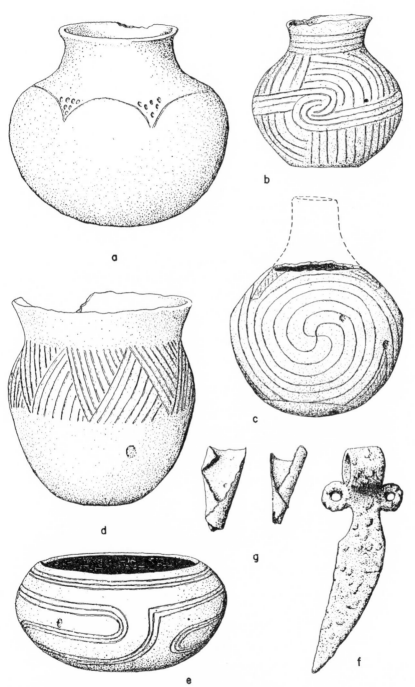

Figure 27. Material found accompanying the burials in the
historic Tunica cemetery at Angola farm.

139

None of the burial vessels show the peculiar rim type that serves as the marker decoration for the Tunica site at Haynes Bluff on the Yazoo River. However they are definitely historic types. Figure 27 e is a Natchez type vessel (Figure 9 a). Figure 27 b and c are Caddo types (see page 81). While figure 27 a is not identical with any of the recognized historical types, it has a shape approaching the bottle, which is only found in the historic horizon. Its decoration is similar to that of pottery found in the Big Black series of mounds (Figure 23 d).

Sherds found scattered through the soil in the process of excavating the site are slightly more illuminating. Figure 26 c-h are Caddo types. 26 i is Natchez. Two sherds, 26 a and b, are one of the Tunica marker types.

If Tunica ware has been correctly identified on the Yazoo River in Mississippi, then at the date of the occupation of this village (1706 to about 1800) the Tunica had taken over the pottery types of the Caddo and Natchez rather thoroughly. Only two sherds of the old type of Tunica pottery were found. Possibly the process of adopting the Natchez and Caddo wares had already been underway in some of the villages on the lower Yazoo River.

PERIOD II

Deasonville complex

Discussion of the Deasonville complex

The pottery complex herein called Deasonville was first recognized at an old village site near Deasonville, Yazoo County, Mississippi, which was excavated by Collins, Chambers, and the writer in 1929-1930 (Site No. 51).[57] The site consisted of midden debris scattered over the top of a low ridge near a small stream known as Ellison's Creek. A group of six mounds, a half mile to the north, could not with certainty be connected with the village site. Excavation in the village revealed the floor plan of three circular houses, sixty, forty-five and thirty-eight feet in diameter. The house walls had been formed by posts set in the bottoms of shallow trenches. Openings in the western sides of the structures indicated the locations of doorways. The black midden soil which covered the surface and filled the house wall trenches contained mussel shells, animal bones, flints, and potsherds. A list of the artifacts recovered besides pottery includes: beamers made from deer metapodial bones, awls of deer ulna and bird bones, arrow points of antler tines (uncertain), stemmed arrowheads of flint, triangular arrowheads, asymmetrical flint knives, small chipped celts, larger ground celts, pitted hammer stones, elbow pipes of clay, small discs cut from potsherds, briquettes showing impressions of cane, and charred corncobs.

Collins describes six classes of pottery ware: plain, cord marked, painted, incised, punctated, and rouletted or stamped. Part of the material obtained from the excavations of the houses has been reclassified according to the system used in this article. Results are shown in figure 1. The material has not been illustrated here since

---

[57]Collins, H. B. Jr., Excavations at a Prehistoric Indian Village Site in Mississippi, pp. 1-22, pls. 1-13.

141

it is well represented in the plates accompanying Collins' article. It will be noted that the proportions of the wares differ slightly from those given by Collins. This is especially true of the painted ware. It is probable that the present collection is in error on this point; the Deasonville site is remembered by the writer to have a much higher proportion of this type than is usual at sites of the complex. Collins' incised ware, illustrated on plate 4, is correctly identified as relating to prehistoric sites to the south, which have later been identified as typical of the Coles Creek complex.

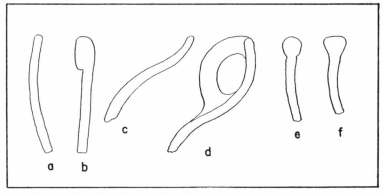

Figure 28. Profiles of rim sherds of the Deasonville complex.

Deasonville is slightly atypical of the complex that bears its name in that all of the types found there do not occur on every site that must be assigned to the same complex. Cord marked pottery, red slip ware (which Collins did not differentiate from painted, or red and white slipped ware), and the incised overhanging lines of the Coles Creek types, reoccur most persistently. Red and white ware, incised scrolls, and punctates in bands between incised lines with their accompanying shell tempering and handles, are found at occasional sites. Perhaps this may be due to the unfortunate smallness of most of the collections representing these other sites. The Phillipi plantation site, the only other village of the typical complex that has been excavated, shows the same types that are found in the Deasonville village collection (see page 167).

As intimated above, the marker types of the Deasonville complex are: red slipped ware (type 11;111;14;, and cord marked ware (type 11;81). The small proportion of Coles Creek types noted for the Deasonville site is usual. Villages yielding this complex have been found in the lower part of the valley of the Yazoo River, and to the east they occur in the valleys of the Pearl and Chickasawhay rivers. The eastern and northern extent of the complex is not known since the sites have been found in those directions as far as surveys have been conducted. There seems to be an unusual concentration of sites in the lower Yazoo valley and most of the collections used in this study have come from there. The collections are the results of a survey conducted for the Mississippi Department of Archives and History by M. B. Chambers and D. J. Ford in 1932.

Types of the Deasonville complex

Type 01:111

01   Motif: Uncertain. The details of these decorations cannot be determined, but the type always shows contrasting areas of red and white (sometimes grey) pigment. These may or may not be separated by incised lines.

111   Element: Red pigment applied as a slip.

At only four sites have the details of decorations of this type been determinable. U-shaped flags filled with bright red slip, swung from the rim in the interiors of shallow bowls, were identified at the Deasonville and Taylor sites. Bars of alternate red and white extending from the rim to the flat bottoms of shallow bowls on both exteriors and interiors were found at Phillipi and Deasonville. The type designation does not separate these different decorations, it intends only to signify the occurrence of sherds decorated with contrasting areas of red and white pigment.

The pigments seem to have been applied as a wash before the ware was fired. They are firmly fixed, and show no tendency to rub or flake off.

Usual Accompanying Characteristics:

In most cases, the decorations extend up to the rim and there is no separate rim border as is common on many of the incised types. On shallow bowl forms, the pigments are applied to the interiors as well as to the exteriors.

All the shapes which bear this decoration have not been determined. One that has been identified is the small, shallow, flat bottomed bowl. This type was found at Deasonville.

Drilled holes near the lip are frequently found, but no handles or knobs have been noted. Typical rim profiles are shown in figure 28 e-f.

Bottoms are usually flat, and often are painted in solid colors.

The texture of the paste is rather hard and fine; the surface finish is smooth, but not polished. The ware is not more than .3 inches thick, and is tempered with sand, grit, and sometimes small quantities of finely ground shell. Much of the paste is grey or tan in color, but a salmon pink is not uncommon.

Type 11;111;14 (Marker type)

11   Motif: Irregular application of elements covering entire surface of vessel.

111   Element: Red slip applied as a wash before the vessel was fired.

14.   Application: Decoration covers entire exterior of the vessel. In this case, the wash is applied to the interior as well.

Usual Accompanying Characteristics:

This particular decoration covers the entire exterior area of the vessel, and there is no differentiated border around the lip. Usually the lips of this type are plain. They are merely rounded edges of the unthickened vessel walls.

The shapes of these vessels have not been determined. No appendages have been found. Bottoms of some of the larger sherds are flat.

The ware is not more than .3 inches thick in most cases and is grey or light brown in color. Sand, grit, and very little shell were used as tempering.

Type 11;81;14 (Marker type)

11　Motif: Irregular spacing of elements to cover entire exterior area of vessel.

81　Elements: Impressions of cord wrapped paddle. Although there is no definite arrangement of the markings demanded of this type, many of the sherds show that the cord impressions are nearly vertical. This indicates that the paddle was held horizontally. The impressions are sometimes partially smoothed over, but more often this has not been done.

14　Arrangement: Decoration covers entire exterior of vessel.

Usual Accompanying Characteristics:

This decoration is found on cylindrical, concave-bottomed pots; on deep concave-bottomed bowls shaped like half a cocoanut; and on globular vessels with walls curving in toward the rim to form slightly restricted openings. On vessels of the above shapes, the decoration extends over all the exterior of the vessel, but a few sherds indicate flat bottoms which were undecorated.

The rims are usually merely undifferentiated terminations of the vessel walls (Figure 28 a). Little care was expended in making the edges smooth and straight; they are often rather irregular. In some cases a strap of clay has been added to or folded over the rim so that a thickened rim one-half to one inch wide is formed (Figure 28 b). This is not always decorated. The paste of this type is usually brown or grey in color like the surface of the sherds. Mottled areas of black and grey, caused by uneven firing, are not unusual on the sherd surface.

Sand and grit are the tempering materials commonly used. A few sherds are slightly porous as though from the burning or leaching out of some tempering material.

The ware is fairly hard, rough, and carelessly finished. It varies from .2 to .4 inches in thickness.

No appendages are found. Very seldom do sherds show drilled holes. Slips were not applied.

Type 11;82

11   Motif: Irregular spacing of elements to cover exterior of vessel. In this type it is not certain that all of the vessel exterior was entirely covered. The sherds observed appear to come from side walls so the treatment of the bottoms is not known.

82   Elements: Impressions of coiled basketry. These impressions show that the basketry foundations were perhaps a quarter of an inch in diameter, and that the fibres forming the stitches passed around and between the coil foundations. Since the sherds of this type are small, it cannot be determined whether the impressions are applied by forming the vessel in a coiled basket or by applications of the impressions by a sort of stamp.

The sherds resemble very much the cord marked ware described above, type 11;81. They are either brown or grey in color, are fairly hard, vary from .2 to .3 inches in thickness, and are tempered with sand and grit. Sometimes so much sand is present in the clay, or else is added as tempering, that a definitely sandy texture results.

The characteristic features of shape, size, appendages, etc., cannot be determined from the sherds at hand.

Type 31;$\frac{21}{71}$;2

31   Motif: Curving bands of features. These bands often branch, indicating that they form parts of some decoration more complicated than the simple scroll.

21   Element: Narrow lines roughly incised with a pointed instrument. These are used to mark the confines of the bands of features forming the motif.

71 Elements: Punctates made with a pointed instrument. These are irregularly spaced, and are used as stippling to fill in the areas of the curving bands outlined by the incised lines.

2 Arrangement: Punctates are used as stippling to bring out the bands as positive areas of the decoration.

This type is usually rather carelessly executed. The lines are uneven and wavy, and plow up the surface of the vessel. Punctates are applied in a similar careless fashion.

Usual Accompanying Characteristics:

This decoration is most often applied to the bodies of vessels, and does not come near the rim. In the few instances where it does approach the rim, a line is used to separate the decorated area from the undecorated rim border. In most cases, the decoration covers all the side walls of the vessel; there is no attempt to confine it to a band about the upper part of the vessel wall.

It is not very clear just what shapes are correlated with this decoration. Probably there are some pot forms, and one or two of the sherds have handles (Figure 28 d).

The paste is rather rough in texture. Its color varies from a light grey to dark brown. Grit, sand, and sometimes a large proportion of shell are used as temper. The ware varies from .2 to .4 inches in thickness, and is of a medium hardness. Slips of different colored clays have not been noted.

Type 41;21;3

41 Motif: Scroll, or scroll-like arrangement.

21 Elements: Lines incised with a pointed instrument. Several sherds show lines a little wider than usual, as though made with a blunt point.

3 Arrangement: Numerous lines used to form the motif.

These usually number from four to eight or nine. They are spaced fairly widely apart, perhaps one-half inch. Incised triangles are sometimes found used as fillers between the units of the scrolls. In a few cases small circles are used as nucleuses for the scrolls.

The execution of this type is rather careless. The lines are uneven and wavy.

Usual Accompanying Characteristics:

The decoration is applied to the side walls of vessels, and does not often extend up near the rim. The common vessel shape is a wide mouthed pot with globular body, short, vertical neck, and with either knobs or strap handles attached to the lip and to the shoulder. The lips of rim sherds are plain, unspecialized terminations of the vessel walls or neck. Bowl forms are also found.

Average diameter of these pots is about eight inches, but it appears that some are as large as twelve or fifteen inches.

The shapes of the vessel bottoms cannot be stated with certainty. Probably most of them were flat and round; others may have been convex.

The paste is rough and is either grey, buff, or light brown in color. Sometimes the ware is porous as though firing or leaching had removed some tempering material. Temper usually consists of grit and crushed shell. Average thickness is .2 to .3 inches. The material varies from rather soft to medium hardness. Slips are not found.

Type 84;52

84 Motif: Features placed on the outside of straight rim.

52 Elements: Shallow notches spaced from one-quarter to one-half inches apart.

These notches are usually found on sherds which bear no other decoration, although in rare cases they occur on the other types of the Deasonville complex. However, the combinations are not considered as belonging in this type. The rims bearing these notches are usually straight unthickened terminations of the vessel walls.

Usual Accompanying Characteristics:

This ware is generally grey, buff, or light brown in color, .2 to .3 inches in thickness, grit tempered, fairly hard, and has only a mediocre finish. Nothing can be said as to the shapes of the vessels on which this type is found.

Types 84;63

84   Motif: Features placed on outside of lip. In this case the features are often found arranged in a row about one-half inch below the lip on the exterior of the rim sherds.

63   Elements: Small teats or short oblong nodes.

These are arranged on the outside of straight, unthickened lips. The sherds are not decorated in any other way.

Usual Accompanying Characteristics:

The vessels with which this rim type are connected appear usually to have been large pots with slightly constricted mouths and short vertical or out-flaring rims. Other forms have nearly vertical side walls.

The ware is grey, buff, or light brown in color. Some of the sherds are rather sandy in texture. This may be due to sand tempering or to the inclusion of that material in the clay. From .2 to .3 inches is the usual thickness. The ware is fairly hard.

This type is particularly numerous and almost peculiar to Lyon's Bluff Site in eastern Mississippi. There is a possibility that the decoration is not part of the Deasonville complex; in fact, it may form part of an entirely new complex. For a further discussion refer to the item on the Lyon's Bluff Site, page 151.

Summary of Deasonville village site collection features

Collections from the sites of the Deasonville complex in central Mississippi are readily recognized. Cord marked and red slip ware form the major proportion of the material in the collections. When the red and white painted ware is present, it provides a very striking determinant.

All the Deasonville collections that are of sufficient size to be considered representative of the sites from which they come, contain other decorations than those listed as Deasonville in the type list. The proportion of these types is small, and usually they are readily recognized. A few scattered and rather indeterminate types can be questionably referred to historic (Tunica or Caddo) complexes. Types of the Coles Creek complex, however, are very persistent.

A number of other Deasonville sites yield Marksville pottery also. Strangely enough these latter collections tend to have few types representative of the Coles Creek complex. An attempt will be made to show the significance of these conditions in the conclusions.

The following list of ceramic features should assist in quick identification of a Deasonville village site collection:

Pottery Decorations:

Red and white painted ware (not always present).
Red slip ware (large percentage).
Cord marked pottery (large percentage).
Impressions of coiled basketry.
Curving, line-bordered bands of punctates.
Many line scrolls, lines incised with a point.
Straight rims with shallow notches.

Cord marking and basket imprint is often applied to entire exterior of vessels. Paint is used on exteriors of vessels, and interiors of shallow bowls. Other decorations are applied only to vessel bodies or are confined to a band occupying one-half to one-third body area near the rim.

Types and features of the Coles Creek complex which are found on Deasonville sites (rims of these types are generally straight and vertical):

Lines incised with a point drawn parallel to the rim.
Overhanging lines drawn parallel to the rim.
Lines incised in the squared lip.
Row of punctates made with a point, parallel to rim.
Large triangular ears on bowls.

Types and features of the Marksville complex that are found on some Deasonville sites: (where these are found, Coles Creek types are generally absent):

Bands of rouletting between broad, deep lines.
Closely spaced, broad, deep lines that are semi-circular in cross section, forming curving and angular designs.
Flat, square vessel bottoms. (Both Coles Creek and Marksville).

Vessel shapes in Deasonville collections:

Shallow bowls with concave bottoms.
Flat bottomed bowls.
Cocoanut-shaped vessels (usually cord marked).
Pots with globular bodies and slightly constricted mouths, vertical or slightly outflaring lips, and often strap handles.
Bottles with wide mouths.
Beakers.

The sherds are fairly uniform in thickness, averaging from .2 to .3 inches. Shades of grey, buff, brown, and black are the usual colors. Pink paste is fairly common in the painted ware. Grit, sand, vegetable matter, and ground shell serve as tempering material.

Other artifacts founds in Deasonville village-site collections:

Small discs cut from potsherds.
Notched projectile points.
Stemmed projectile points.
Triangular projectile points.
Elbow pipes of clay.
Bone and antler arrow points.

Sites of the Deasonville complex

Site No. 27, Lyon's Bluff

NE¼ S33, T2ON, R15E

The old village site at Lyon's Bluff is situated nine miles northeast of the town of West Point, in Oktibbeha County, Mississippi. It is twenty miles from the Alabama state line. The midden deposit is about twenty-five acres in extent, and occupies a point formed by a horseshoe bend on the south side of Line Creek. A conical mound approximately seventy feet in diameter and fifteen feet high stands about in the center of the site.

According to H. S. Halbert, who spent many years working among the Choctaws, this was the site of a Chocchuma fort. The Chocchuma were a small group of Muskhogean-speaking people who lived between the Choctaw and the Chickasaw.

> . . . According to Choctaw tradition, it was these hostile acts of the Chocchumas, together with their frequent horsestealing inroads into the Choctaw and Chickasaw countries, that aroused the warlike wrath of the latter tribes and caused the war that terminated in the destruction of the Chocchuma nationality. I here append the following traditions regarding this war. The most noted stronghold of the Chocchumas was built on Lyon's Bluff on the south side of Line Creek, about 8 miles northeast of Starkeville. The creek here makes a bend to the north, forming a horseshoe containing about 8 acres. In the center is an artificial mound. A rampart, some traces of which could still be seen a few years ago, extended across this neck of land, connecting, as it were, the two ends of the horseshoe. This inclosure, known as Lyon's Bluff, strongly fortified, was occupied by a large band of Chocchuma warriors with their women and children. The place was besieged by the allied tribes. The Choctaws occupied the south, in front of the rampart, while the Chickasaws were posted on the north side of the creek, so that there was no chance of escape for the Chocchumas. For several days and nights was the siege kept up, until the last Chocchuma warrior fell, and the women and children yielded to the mercy of the conquerors.

> The late venerable Mr. Howell Peden, of Clay County, from whom several years ago I received many Chocchuma traditions, informed me that in 1830 there was living near Plymouth, on the Tombigbee, an old Chocchuma woman who was a girl or young woman during the Chocchuma war, and who was the last survivor of the massacre on Lyon's Bluff. She had been a cook in Jackson's army during the Creek war of 1813. This fact is noted, as it

gives a clue to the approximate date of the Chocchuma war. A woman over 50 would hardly be apt to serve as an army cook. Assuming this woman to be 7 in 1770, she would have been 50 in 1813; 1770, then, may be accepted as the approximate date of the Chocchuma war.[58]

In the summers of 1934 and 1935, Chambers made extensive excavations at this site for the Mississippi Department of Archives and History. His attention was mainly centered on the midden deposit. This was found to be from two to six feet deep in places. Stratified cuts showed no vertical difference in the material recovered. In his work Chambers found no evidence pointing to contact of the Indians and Europeans. If the site had been occupied by the Chocchumas as late as 1770, such evidence ought to be plentiful.

Whether or not this site was occupied in historic times is still an open question. The evidence that it was is traditional; all indications to the contrary are purely negative.

The collection from the site differs from that typical of the Deasonville complex in the Yazoo River Delta. A small percentage of Deasonville types was found, but the largest percentage of any one type was of the type 11;62 (small areas raised by pinching with the finger tips, scattered irregularly over the vessel surface). On the basis of its occurrence at two Tunica sites, this type has been placed in the Tunica complex. This identification is doubtful. Possibly it is the marker type of an entirely different complex that lies in eastern Mississippi and western Alabama. It will be noted that other sites from eastern Mississippi (Site No. 26, Brans Camp, and Site No. 48, Reynolds place) show percentages of this decoration. At the same time, they suggest more strongly the usual Deasonville situation of a marked proportion of Deasonville types with a small proportion of Coles Creek.

---

[58]Swanton BAE bull. 43, p. 295, quoting Halbert: The Small Indian Tribes of Mississippi, Publs. Miss. Hist. Soc., Vol V., pp. 302-8.

Another decoration type found at Lyon's Bluff, as well as at Site No. 48, is type 84;63 (a row of small nodes placed outside of and about one inch below the vessel lip). Although found in small proportions at two other Deasonville sites, this type also may be part of an unknown complex located to the east.

Some features of the Lyon's Bluff collection suggest material found at Moundville, Alabama: a few sherds of a fine, black, polished ware with scratched scroll decorations, and one piece having the outline of a human hand scratched on the interior.

Other finds are: small tubular beads of both clay and shell, a ladle made from part of a conch shell, perforated deer teeth, a broken celt, and stemmed and triangular projectile points.

The exact relationship of the Lyon's Bluff site can only be solved by more field work in eastern Mississippi and the adjacent part of Alabama.

Site No. 32, Gamewood plantation

N½, SE¼, S28, T15N, R1E

This is an old village situated in Holmes County, Mississippi, on the north side of Black Creek, a short distance northeast of Howard Station. The midden is about eight acres in extent, and occupies the top of a low bluff over the creek. The deposit is very rich in refuse material, and is three feet deep in the thickest part. Mussel shells are so profuse that the site is locally known as a shell ridge. A low conical mound stands near the edge of the bluff. Both mound and village site are in cultivation. Chambers' collection consists of 105 decorated sherds, the majority of which are cord marked (classification, figure 1). Only one sherd of a Coles Creek type was found. The material is illustrated in figure 29 a-g.

Site No. 39, Quafalorma plantation

NW¼, NE¼, S5, T14N, R1W

The Quafalorma site is located on the dividing line between Quafalorma plantation and Good Hope plantation, one and one-half miles northeast of Thornton, Mississippi, in Holmes county. It lies in flat land on the southwestern edge of Horseshoe Brake, and has been under cultivation for some time. There are no mounds at the site. Occupation is apparent from refuse scattered over an area of about three acres. The collections made at the site include a mixture of sherds, flint chips, and mussel shells.

Forty-eight decorated sherds were found (classified in Figure 1; illustrated in Figure 29 h-m). The larger proportion of the material is the cord marked and red slip ware, typical of the Deasonville; overhanging line decorations of the Coles Creek complex are present in smaller proportions.

Site No. 46, York Hill plantation

SW¼, SE¼, S22, T12N, R2W

The site on York Hill plantation is situated on the edge of the escarpment east of the Yazoo River, two miles northeast of Yazoo City, Mississippi. It has been in cultivation for some time. At present it is indicated by midden material scattered for a quarter of a mile along a low ridge. Four conical mounds are found on the site. Mound A is thirty-five feet in diameter and seven and one-half feet high. B, C, and D are each about twenty feet in diameter and two and one-half feet high. The mounds are arranged as though placed about a court or open square.

The collection from York Hill consists of only twenty decorated sherds. The greater number of these are cord marked. There is a small proportion of Coles Creek sherds (classified in Figure 1; illustrated in Figure 29 h-s).

DESCRIPTION OF SHERDS IN FIGURE 29

Sherd	Type	Color of Paste	Finish (Good, Medium, Poor)	Temper	Hardness (Hard, Medium, Soft)	Thickness (inches)	Remarks
			PERIOD II—DEASONVILLE				
a	11;81;14	Dark blue	R	Vegetable	H	.3	Rim
b	11;81;14	Dark blue	R	Veg., Grit	H	.2	....
c	11;81;14	Dark blue	R	Vegetable	M	.3	Notched rim
d	11;111;14	Buff	R	Vegetable	M	.3	Red slip
e	11;81;14	Black	R	Veg., Grit	M	.2	....
f	11;111;14	Buff	M	Vegetable	M	.4	Slightly thickened rim
			COLES CREEK				
g	61;24;7	Dark blue	M	Grit	M	.3	Rim

Material from Gamewood plantation (Site No. 32).

Sherd	Type	Color of Paste	Finish	Temper	Hardness	Thickness	Remarks
			PERIOD II—DEASONVILLE				
h	11;81;14	Dark blue	R	Vegetable	M	.3	Rim
i	11;81;14	Blue	R	Vegetable	M	.3	....
k	11;81;14	Dark blue	R	Grit, Veg.	M	.2	Thickened rim
l	01;111	Black	M	Grit	M	.3	Rim, red slip
			COLES CREEK				
j	51;24;6	Dark blue	M	Grit	M	.2	....
m	61;24;8	Grey	M	Grit	M	.3	Rim

Material from Quafalorna plantation (Site No. 39).

Sherd	Type	Color of Paste	Finish	Temper	Hardness	Thickness	Remarks
			PERIOD II—DEASONVILLE				
n	11;81;14	Brown	R	....	S	.3	....
o	11;81;14	Brown	R	Grit	S	.3	....
p	41;21;3	Dark blue	R	Shell	M	.3	....
s	11;111;14	Dark blue	M	Grit, Veg.	M	.2	Thickened rim
			COLES CREEK				
q	61;24;7	Black	M	Grit	M	.3	Rim
r	61; 24/79;9	Light Brown	R	Grit	M	.3	....

Material from York Hill plantation (Site No. 46).

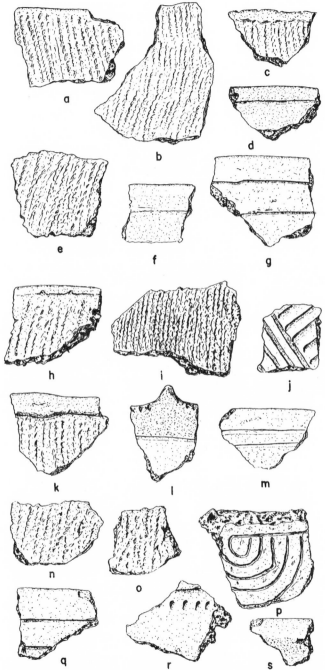

Figure 29. Selection of representative material from Gamewood
plantation (Sherds a-g) Quafalorma plantation (Sherds h-m) and
York Hill plantation (Sherds n-s).

157

Site No. 43, Taylor place

S6, T11N, R3E

The site on the Taylor place, Yazoo County, Mississippi, is situated two miles north of the small town of Vaughn Station. It is in a field on the west side of the Illinois Central Railroad about one hundred yards south of Big Cypress Creek which flows into Big Black River.

There are two mounds at the site. Both are low conicals. One is ninety feet in diameter and nine feet high; the other has been plowed over and has a diameter of one hundred feet and a height of six feet. Midden material is thinly scattered over the field between the mounds. A surface collection, made in 1929 by Collins, Chambers and the writer, consists of only twenty-nine decorated sherds. The decorations identify the site with the Deasonville complex (Figure 30 a-h) Cord marking, red and white paint, red slip, curving bands of punctates, and many-line scrolls are all found. The usual small proportion of Coles Creek types is present.

Site No. 45, Wilzone plantation

NW¼, S34, T13N, R3W

The site on Wilzone plantation is on the west bank of Wolf Lake, three-quarters of a mile northwest of Lake City, in Humphries County, Mississippi.

The midden is situated in cultivated lowland on the bank of Wolf Lake. Actually Wolf Lake is an abandoned channel of the Yazoo River. The deposit covers an area three hundred feet long by one hundred fifty feet wide. Nearby, in a pasture which has not long been out of cultivation, is a small rise two hundred twenty-five feet in diameter and six feet high. This is probably the remnant of a mound.

As is usual on the Yazoo basin sites, the midden is characterized by a large quantity of mussel shells. A collection of only twenty-seven decorated sherds was secured from the site. Both the Deasonville and Coles Creek complexes are represented. Coles Creek material forms the larger proportion of this collection (see Figure 1). This is unusual for sites in the Yazoo River valley; Coles Creek is usually a minor element and Deasonville predominates. Probably this case can be attributed to the small size of the collection. In appearance the material is similar to that from typical Deasonville sites (Figure 30 i-p).

160

DESCRIPTION OF SHERDS IN FIGURE 30

Sherd	Type	Color of Paste	Finish (Good, Medium Poor)	Temper	Hardness (Hard, Medium Soft)	Thickness (inches)	Remarks
			PERIOD II—DEASONVILLE				
a	11;82	Grey	P	Grit, vegetable	M	.4	Rim, wide-mouthed pot
b	11;81;14	Dark blue	P	Vegetable	M	.3	....
c	11;111;14	Light blue	M	Vegetable	M	.2	Rim, interior view, red and white slip
d	84;52	Grey	P	Grit, vegetable	S	.4	Rim
e	41;21;3	Dark blue	M	Shell, vegetable	M	.3	Rim
f	41;21;3	Grey	P	Grit, vegetable	S	.3	....
g	31;$\frac{21}{71}$;2	Grey	P	Shell	S	.2	....
			INDETERMINATE				
h	52;21;2	Grey	P	Shell	S	.3	Wide-mouthed pot

Material from Taylor Place (Site No. 43).

Sherd	Type	Color of Paste	Finish	Temper	Hardness	Thickness	Remarks
			PERIOD II—DEASONVILLE				
i	11;81;14	Dark blue	P	Vegetable	H	.2	....
j	11;81;14	Light blue	P	Vegetable	H	.2	....
			COLES CREEK				
k	61;24;8	Black	P	Grit	H	.2	Rim
l	$\frac{61;24;8}{81;21}$	Grey	M	Vegetable	M	.2	Rim
m	61;24;8	Grey	M	Grit, vegetable	M	.3	Rim
n	01;74	Buff	M	Grit	M	.2	Corner of square bottom
o	Lug	Dark blue	M	Grit	M	—	
p	34;$\frac{24}{74}$;1	Dark blue	M	Grit	H	.2	Polished

Material from Wilzone plantation (Site No. 45).

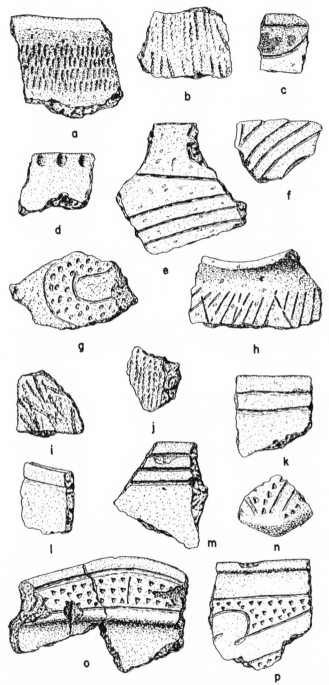

Figure 30. Selection of representative material from Taylor place (Sherds a-h) and Wilzone plantation (Sherds i-p) village site collections.

161

Description of Deasonville Complex Village Sites

Site No.	Site Name	Burials		Conical		Pyramidal		Enclosure	Approximate Area	Midden		Collection Analysis
		Cemetery	Mound	Low -10"	Tall +10"	Low -10"	Ramp +10"			Thin -10"	Thick +10"	
26	Brans Camp								4A		x	Deasonville
27	*Lyons Bluff						1		25A		x	Deasonville, ?
28	Godfrey Smith								1A		x	Deasonville, Coles Creek
29	Bee Lake Pl.								3A		x	Deasonville, Coles Creek
30	Cary Pl.					1	1		6A		x	Deasonville, Coles Creek
31	Crump Pl.			1					5A		x	Deasonville, Coles Creek
32	*Gamewood Pl.			1					8A		x	Deasonville
33	Hancock Pl.								4A		x	Deasonville, Coles Creek
34	Hoag Pl.				3	1			5A		x	Deasonville
35	Ingersoll Pl.								3A		x	Deasonville, Coles Creek
36	Lightcap Pl.								2A		x	Deasonville, Coles Creek
37	Lee Pl.								4A		x	Deasonville
38	Plymouth Bluff				Uncertain							Deasonville
39	*Quafalorma Pl.								5A		x	Deasonville, Coles Creek
40	Robinson Pl.								5A		x	Deasonville
41	Rugby Farm								4A		x	Deasonville, Coles Creek
42	Ky. Q. Smith				One, Uncertain							Deasonville
43	*Taylor Pl.			2					5A		x	Deasonville
44	Walker Pl.			3					6A		x	Deasonville, Coles Creek
45	*Wilzone Pl.			1					2A		x	Deasonville, Coles Creek
46	*York Hill Pl.			4					10A		x	Deasonville, Coles Creek
47	Tanglewood Pl.						2		5A		x	Deasonville, Coles Creek
48	Reynolds Pl.				Uncertain							Deasonville, Coles Creek

*Sites which are described in the text and from which material is illustrated.

Sites yielding both Deasonville and Marksville complexes

As can be seen from the table given as figure 1, there are village sites scattered over the lower Yazoo basin and eastward, which are characterized by types of the Deasonville complex, and which also show pottery types characteristic of the Marksville ware. The geographical position of these Marksville plus Deasonville sites is shown in figure 2. There appears to be no geographical segregation of these sites; they are scattered among the pure sites. In some cases mixed and pure sites are within one or two miles of one another.

The ceramic features that comprise the Marksville complex are described later. The marking features of the pottery are rouletted bands bounded by wide, deep, smooth lines, alternating with plain, undecorated bands (type 31; $\frac{23}{101/102}$; $\frac{1}{2}$) ; and wide, deep, smooth lines which form curvilinear decorations, placed closely together (type 45;23;6).

It will be noted that types of the Coles Creek complex are not found as consistently on these mixed sites as they are on the pure Deasonville sites.

Site No. 53, Pete Clark place

SE¼, SE¼, S13, T12N, R3W

The Pete Clark village site is situated on the "Old Clark Place" six miles northwest of Yazoo City, Mississippi, on the Silver Creek road. The site consists of one mound with a surrounding accumulation of kitchen midden material. It lies in the lowland on the west bank of the Yazoo River, and has been in cultivation for a number of years. The mound, conical in shape, is sixty feet in diameter and ten feet high. It is covered with a growth of trees and bushes, and is badly pitted with holes dug by the curious.

DESCRIPTION OF SHERDS IN FIGURE 31

Sherd	Type	Color of Paste	Finish (Good, Medium, Poor)	Temper	Hardness (Hard, Medium, Soft)	Thickness (inches)	Remarks
				PERIOD II—DEASONVILLE			
a	11;81;14	Grey	R	Veg., Grit	M	.2	Straight rim
b	11;81;14	Black	R	Grit	M	.2	....
c	11;111;14	Buff	M	Grit	M	.3	Rim
				COLES CREEK			
d	61;24;8	Light Blue	M	Vegetable, Grit	M	.2	Rim
				PERIOD I—MARKSVILLE			
e	31;$\frac{23}{101/102}$;½	Black	M	Grit	M	.4	....
f	Same as e	Black	M	Grit	M	.3	Thickened rim
g	45;23;6	Black	P	Grit	M	.3	....
		Material from Coody plantation (Site No. 54).					
				PERIOD II—DEASONVILLE			
h	11;81;14	Buff	R	Vegetable	S	.3	Straight
i	11;81;14	Grey	R	Vegetable	M	.3	Thickened rim
k	01;111	Black	M	Grit	M	.2	Interior view
				COLES CREEK			
j	61;71;9	Buff	M	Grit and Veg.	M	.3	Rim
l	61;24;7	Grey	R	Veg., Grit	M	.4	Square lip
				PERIOD I—MARKSVILLE			
m	31;$\frac{23}{101/102}$;½	Blue	M	Grit, Veg.	M	.3	Square lip
		Material from Pete Clark plantation (Site No. 53).					
				PERIOD II—DEASONVILLE			
n	11;81;14	Grey	R	Vegetable	M	.3	Rim
o	11;81;14	Grey	R	Vegetable	M	.2	....
p	11;111;14	Grey	M	Vegetable	M	.2	....
q	11;111;14	Buff	M	Sand, Veg.	M	.2	Rolled rim
				COLES CREEK			
r	34;$\frac{24/104}{104}$	Grey	M	Grit	M	.3	Square lip
				PERIOD I—MARKSVILLE			
t	31;$\frac{23}{101/102}$;½	Black	R	Grit	M	.2	....
u	45;23;6	Black	M	Veg., Grit	M	.3	Rim
v	31;$\frac{23}{101/102}$;½	Grey	R	Sand & Veg.	M	.2	....
w	31;$\frac{23}{101/102}$;½	Black	R	Sand, Grit	M	.2	....
				INDETERMINATE			
s	....	Black	M	Grit	M	.3	....
		Material from Old Hoover plantation (Site No. 57).					

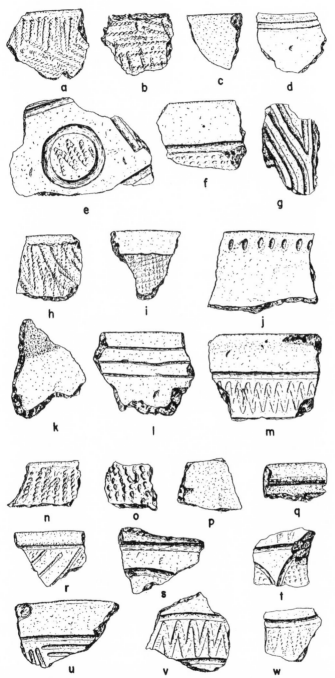

Figure 31. Selection of representative material from the L. M. Coody (Sherds a-g), Pete Clark (Sherds h-m), and Old Hoover (Sherds n-w) village site collections.

The village refuse extends about two hundred yards both north and south of the mound. The plowed field is thickly covered with potsherds and mussel shells. In fact, mussel shells occur in such profusion that this and other sites along the Yazoo are referred to as "shell ridges".

Eighty-five decorated sherds were secured from the site. Most of the material is cord marked. A few Coles Creek and Marksville types are present. The results of classifying this material are shown in figure 1. A selection of sherds is illustrated in figure 31 h-m.

Site No. 54, L. M. Coody place

S20, T8N, R3W

The village site on the plantation of Mr. Lewis M. Coody of Phoenix, Mississippi, is located in the southern part of Yazoo County. It occupies a low ridge on the west side of the Big Black River, just above the mouth of Sibley Creek. There is no mound at the site. Kitchen debris indicates the location. The site has been under cultivation for a long time, and because of the large proportion of mussel shells in the refuse it is locally known as a "shell ridge". The depth of the deposit was not determined by the survey party, but appeared to be at least several feet in thickness.

A collection of seventy-two decorated sherds was secured, and from them decorations of two complexes are apparent: a large proportion of Deasonville, and a smaller percentage of Marksville. The classified results are shown in figure 1, and typical sherds are illustrated in figure 31 a-g.

Site No. 57, Old Hoover place

A village site with one mound is situated on the Old Hoover place, three miles north of Pickens, Holmes County, Mississippi. The site stands between the Illinois Central Railroad and the Big Black River. The midden is about four acres in extent and is not deeper than the depth to which plowing has extended. A single truncated pyramid, one hundred twenty-five by eighty feet at the base, and seven feet high, is located in the center of the deposit.

Surface collections from this place were made by Chambers in 1931. Owing to the scarcity of material, only nineteen decorated sherds were found. These included two types of the Deasonville complex, red slip ware and cord marking; and two of the Marksville complex with bands of rouletting and closely spaced curving lines. The collection is classified with the results shown in figure 1. Representative pieces are illustrated in figure 31 n-w.

Site No. 60, Phillipi plantation
Common corner S's 5, 6, 7, 8, T16N, R2E

In 1932 Chambers and D. J. Ford discovered and excavated a village site on Phillipi plantation in Holmes County, near Cruger, Mississippi. Four small mounds and a midden deposit comprised the site, which is located on Jordan Branch one-half mile north of Chicopa Creek. It is on the high ground, one mile from the sixty-foot bluffs that form the eastern edge of the Yazoo-Mississippi flood plain.

The midden deposit is on the west side of the creek and covers about thirty acres. Over most of its area it is about twelve inches deep. Part of the site is in cultivation; other sections are pasture and woods. Two mounds stand in the midden area. The largest is pyramidal, forty-five by twenty-seven feet at the base and eight feet high. The other is slightly smaller. Approximately three hundred yards east of these structures and across the creek are two small conical mounds, each about twenty-five feet in diameter and five feet high.

In the course of their examination Chambers and Ford excavated the floor of a house in the midden. It was rectangular in shape, about ten by fifteen feet. The floor was formed of hard packed clay and the walls had been constructed by setting posts, six inches in diameter, into the ground about a foot apart. Burned clay briquettes showed that wattle and daub construction had been used.

DESCRIPTION OF SHERDS IN FIGURE 32

Sherd	Type	Color of Paste	Finish (Good, Medium Poor)	Temper	Hardness (Hard, Medium Soft)	Thickness (inches)	Remarks
				PERIOD III—TUNICA			
h	11;62	Black	R	....	M	.3	Thickened rim
				PERIOD II—DEASONVILLE			
a	11;81;14	Grey	R	Small amt. Sand	H	.3	
b	11;81;14	Black	P	Vegetable	H	.4	Rim sherd
c	11;81;14	Grey	P	Vegetable	H	.3	
d	11;82	Cream	R	Sand	M	.4	Rim sherd
e	11;111;14	Dark blue	M	Shell	M	.2	Thickened rim Red and white slip
f	11;111;14	Dark blue	M	Shell	M	.3	Red and white slip
g	11;111;14	Dark blue	M	Shell	M	.3	Thickened rim Red and white slip
i	31;$\frac{21}{71}$;2	Tan	R	Vegetable	M	.2	
m	41;21;3	Dark blue	M	Shell	M	.2	Rim
s	11;111;14	Grey	M	Finely ground Shell	H	.3	Drilled potsherd disk Red and white slip
				PERIOD I—MARKSVILLE			
k	81;$\frac{28}{73}$;9	Buff	M	....	M	.2	Part of rim decorated
l	31;$\frac{23}{101/102}$;½	Dark blue	M	Vegetable	M	.2	....
n	31;$\frac{23}{101/102}$;½	Tan	M	Grit	M	.2	....
o	45;23;6	Black	M	Grit	M	.2	....
p	45;23;6	Black	M	Grit	M	.2	....
q	45;23;6	Grey	M	Vegetable	M	.3	Rim slightly thick
r	45;23;6	Light blue	M	Vegetable	M	.3	....
				INDETERMINATE			
j	81;51	Grey	R	Vegetable	H	.3	Rim sherd. Orange slip

Material from Phillipi plantation (Site No. 60).

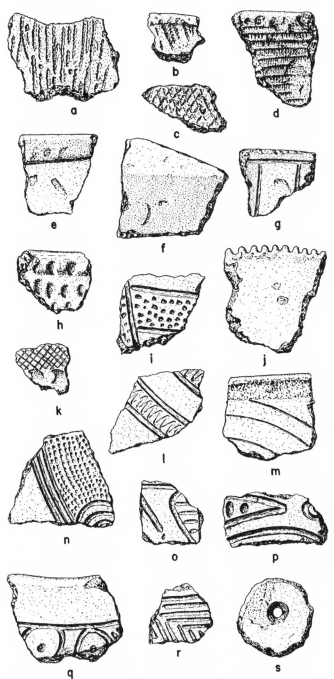

Figure 32. Selection of representative material from Phillipi
plantation village site (Site No. 60.)

169

The collection of 287 decorated sherds was secured from the surface and in the course of the above excavation (Figure 32). Predominantly the types are those of the Deasonville complex. The ware from the site, except in certain proportions, is practically identical with that from the Deasonville village. More red and white painted ware was found here than is usual at most of the Deasonville sites. Cord marked pottery, of course, predominates. Other types are red slip ware, curving bands of punctates between incised lines, many line scrolls, and a substantial percentage of a type that is rare in this part of the area—coiled basketery imprints. Coles Creek is represented by only two sherds. Marksville types form small percentages.

DESCRIPTION OF DEASONVILLE PLUS MARKSVILLE COMPLEX SITES

Site No.	Site Name	Burial		Mounds Conical		Mounds Pyramidal		Ramp	Enclosure	Midden Approximate Area			Collection Analysis
		Cemetery	Mound	Low −10'	Tall +10'	Low −10'	Tall +10'				Thin −10"	Thick +10"	
49	Love Pl.			Uncertain									Deasonville, Coles Creek, Marksville
50	Gross Pl.				1					4A		x	Deasonville, Coles Creek, Marksville
51	Deasonville v.s.									8A		x	Deasonville, Coles Creek, Marksville
52	Christmas Pl.			3						5A	x		Deasonville, Coles Creek, Marksville
53	*Clark Pl.				1					4A		x	Deasonville, Coles Creek, Marksville
54	*L. M. Coody									—		x	Deasonville, Coles Creek, Marksville
55	Cowsert Pl.			1—Uncertain						5A		x	Deasonville, Marksville
56	Exum Pl.									4A	x		Deasonville, Marksville
57	*Old Hoover					1				4A	x		Deasonville, Marksville
58	Lake View Pl.			2						—		x	Tunica, Deasonville, Coles Creek, Marksville
59	McRae Pl.			1						—			Deasonville, Marksville
60	*Phillipi Pl.			2		2				80A		x	Deasonville, Coles Creek Marksviile

*Sites described in the text and from which material is illustrated.

Coles Creek complex

Discussion of the Coles Creek complex

The pottery complex described under the name of Coles Creek first came to the attention of the writer as a result of its occurrence on what a number of historians have described as the White Apple village of the Natchez Indians (Site No. 67, Mazique plantation). At the time only this collection and the one from the Coles Creek site (Site No. 61) were available for comparison with the excellent Natchez site at Fatherland plantation (page 59). The obvious difference between the complexes appeared to preclude the possibility that the historians could be correct. Investigation in the courthouse records at Natchez showed that the identification of the White Apple village rested on a map drawn by the county surveyor rather than on early documentary evidence.

The complex was identified with the name of the less historically involved of the two sites, Coles Creek, and was first recognized in print by Henry B. Collins in his report on the excavations at Deasonville, Mississippi.[59] Perhaps this name is a little unfortunate. Neither of the two original sites is quite typical of the many that have been located in southwestern Mississippi and east-central Louisiana. They differ in that they each yield a few sherds of the Tunica complex. Despite this fact there is no evidence that any of the Coles Creek sites retained their inhabitants until the time of contact with Europeans. The entire complex may be regarded as prehistoric.

Most of these sites were located and collected from by the writer in the summers of 1933[60] and 1935[61] (see map, Figure 2).

---

[59]Collins, H. B. Jr., Excavations at a Prehistoric Indian Village Site in Mississippi.

[60]This survey was financed by a "Grant-in-Aid" from the National Research Council. L. L. Lovell was field assistant.

[61]Survey financed by a grant from the Louisiana State University.

Collections from the Chevalier and Gorum sites, as well as other supplementary material, were secured by Mr. and Mrs. U. B. Evans of Alexandria, Louisiana. Mr. E. F. Neild of Shreveport provided the material from the Biggs site, and additional material from the Neal and Larto Lake sites. Mr. W. M. Crawford made the collection from Ditto plantation.

The combination of ceramic decoration designated by the name Coles Creek characterizes a number of villages, most of which are situated south of a line running east and west through the mouth of the Yazoo River. However, a few sites are found up the course of Bayou Maçon in Louisiana, almost to the Arkansas border. Southward they occur all through the Mississippi Valley and along the tributary streams all the way to the Gulf Coast. Twenty sites have been selected for presentation in the comparative table (Figure 1). It would be tedious and probably profitless to describe each of these old villages at length. Therefore, only the sites from which material is illustrated will be described in the text. Several other villages of the complex which present unusual features will be considered in those details.

The types of pottery that mark the sites of this complex are described in the list that follows. It must be pointed out that, in the northern part of the Coles Creek area and as far south as the mouth of the Red river, all of the village-site collections of significant size contain a minor proportion of the Deasonville types. This is shown in the table given as figure 1. These Deasonville sherds are generally of the marker types, and especially is the characteristic cord marked pottery found.

Many of the Coles Creek village sites are characterized by accumulations of midden debris which cover rather small areas. Potsherds form a large proportion of this material; hence, collecting is comparatively easy. Both pyramidal and conical mounds accompany these village sites, but there are no known earthwork enclosures that appear to be related to them. The mounds, where more than one is found, appear to be arranged about a square or open court.

Decoration types of the Coles Creek complex

Type 01;74:

01   Motif: Uncertain

74   Element: Triangular shaped punctates. This type, which is usually distinguished on small sherds, may be part of any of the decorations employing the element 74.

Type 34; $\dfrac{21}{111/28}$;1/2:

34   Motif: Compressed meander formed by a line-enclosed band of moderate width.

21   Element: Incised lines made with a pointed instrument and used to enclose the band forming the motif.

      Often large triangular punctates are found at the ends of the lines which separate the recurving band of the motif. In these positions they serve as nucleuses about which the bends on the meander turn (Figure 49).

Either:

111   Element: Red slip used to differentiate motif and background

Or:

28   Element: Fine crosshatching made with a pointed instrument used to differentiate motif and background.

1/2   Arrangement: The motif is either: (1) brought out in negative (the elements used to mark the background while the band forming the meander is plain); or, (2) the motif is brought out in positive, that is, the elements are used to contrast the meander with the plain background.

      The execution of this decoration varies from very neat to careless.

Usual Accompanying Characteristics:

This decoration is applied in a line-enclosed panel that occupies the upper half or third of the vessel walls. Generally a narrow border, which may or may not be occupied by a thickened rim, is left between the decoration and the lip.

The sherds bearing this decoration generally indicate round, shallow bowls with convex bottoms.

The texture of the paste varies considerably from a hard, fine grained, thin, slaty-blue ware (found in central Louisiana) to a thicker, coarse, buff colored ware (more common along the coast). Thickness ranges from .2 to .4 inches. The tempering is grit, vegetable, and sand. Exterior color of the ware ranges through black, buff, and grey to cream. Red slips were applied in some cases as has been indicated.

In some instances bowls bearing this decoration have large lugs on the rim. Four triangular-shaped lugs, which are spaced about the rim, are generally used (see Figure 37).

Type $\dfrac{34;24;1}{61;24;6}$

34   Dominant Motif: Compressed meander formed by line-enclosed band, ½ to 1 inch in width.

24   Element: Motif is outlined by overhanging lines.

1   Arrangement: Motif is brought out in negative by use of sub-motifs to shade the background.

61   Sub-motif: Features running parallel to vessel rim.

24   Element: Overhanging lines, usually parallel to rim.

6   Arrangement: Lines are placed closely together.

Remainder of the features of this type is the same as for the preceding type.

Type 34; $\dfrac{24}{74}$;10

34   Motif: Compressed meander formed by a line-enclosed band, ½ to 1 inches in width.

24   Element: Overhanging lines used to outline the motif. In a few cases element 25 (punctated lines) is used.

74   Element: Triangular punctates. In this case large punctates are used.

10   Arrangement: Large punctates are placed singly at the ends of lines. They often serve as the centers about which the recurving bands of the meander motif are swung. The background is plain and undifferentiated from the area enclosed in the bands.

    Remainder of description is the same as for the above types.

Usual Accompanying Characteristics: Same as for preceding type.

Type 34; $\dfrac{24/104}{104}$;1 (Marker type)

34   Motif: Compressed meander formed by a line-enclosed band.

24/104   Elements: Either overhanging lines (24) or rows of punctates (104) used to outline motif. In a few cases punctated lines are used.

104   Elements: Rows of delicate punctates used as shading to fill in the background of the decoration. In a few instances, this resembles rouletting with a notched wheel, but all examples included here are executed freehand.

1   Arrangement: The last mentioned elements are used to fill in the area outside of the undecorated band which forms the motif. In this way the motif appears as a negative or undecorated area.

Usual Accompanying Characteristics: Same as for preceding types.

Type 51;24:

51 Motif: Band of isosceles triangles with the alternate triangles inverted and nested in the others. Alternate triangles are filled with straight lines drawn parallel to one of the ascending sides of the triangles. The other triangles have their parallel lines parallel to the other ascending leg.

24 Elements: Overhanging lines used to form as well as to fill in the figures.

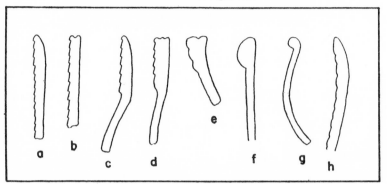

Figure 33.   Profiles of rim sherds of the Coles Creek complex.

Usual Accompanying Characteristics:

The description of this particular decoration is applicable to nearly all the pottery decorated with motifs 51, 52, 61, 62, 72, 81, and 83.

These decorations are applied to the vessel walls and usually form a band around the upper part of the vessel. In width these bands sometimes cover from one-third to one-half of the vessel wall, but more often they are only two or three inches in width. A few examples have a narrow border, not over half an inch wide, between the top of the decorated area and vessel lip. Sometimes this border is thickened by adding a strap of clay to the outside of the lip. On most of the sherds, however, especially those with the 61 motifs, the decorations extend up the straight vessel wall to the lip.

The most common type of rim sherd has a peculiar and characteristic profile. This is especially true of the 61 motif decorations. The outside of the sherd is straight. The inside curves slightly, so that maximum thickness is reached about one inch below the lip, and then gradually it becomes thinner up toward the lip (figure 33 a). The lip is flattened to the plane of the vessel mouth.

Another common type of rim is a plain, straight wall proceeding up to a square lip, or a lip flattened to the plane of the mouth. Rarest perhaps is the exterior-thickened lip, which is described above. Occasionally one or more lines are found incised in these flattened rims (Figure 33 b-e).

The greater part of the sherds with these decorations indicates beaker-shaped vessels with slightly outward-slanting, vertical, or slightly inward-slanting walls. These vessels are compactly proportioned and in height are very little more than the greatest diameter. They vary in size from four inches to twelve inches in diameter. Bottoms are flat, and in shape are either round or square with four definite corners.

Another less common vessel shape is a large globular-bodied pot with a slightly constricted neck. This neck is generally short (2 to 3 inches), and rises vertically from its junction with the body wall. Decoration is placed on the neck of these vessels. Shapes of the lower part of the body and of the bottoms are not certain.

Most of the ware is of a good quality, is hard, and has a soapy texture. A mottled dirty grey is the usual color. Occasionally shades of buff shading to a light brown are found. Uneven firing often has mottled the surfaces with dark patches.

A small amount of sand or grit may have been mixed into the paste as tempering material, and there are small, black, discolored spots that appear to owe their discoloration to carbonized vegetable matter.

Sherd thickness varies according to the size of the vessel. The common beaker forms are often thin (.2 of an inch); some of the larger globular vessels are as much as .4 of an inch thick.

Intentionally applied slips or washes are not found. Some interiors have been blackened. This was probably achieved by some smoking process.

Type 52; $\dfrac{24}{74}$;2

52 Motif: A row of triangular or V-shaped flags suspended from near the lip of the vessel.

24 Element: Overhanging lines used to outline the V-shaped flags of the motif.

74 Element: Small triangular-shaped punctates used to stipple the areas enclosed in the V-shaped flags.

2 Arrangement: The motif is made to stand out in a positive manner by means of the triangular-punctate stippling.

Usual Accompanying Characteristics: Same as for type 51;24.

Type 61;24;6 (Marker type)

61 Motif: Features parallel to one another and to the vessel lip.

24 Element: Overhanging lines.

6 Arrangement: Elements placed closely together.
   This decoration starts at the lip of the vessel. The effect of the closely spaced overhanging lines running parallel to the lip is similar to weatherboarding on a building.

Usual Accompanying Characteristics: Same as for type 51;24.

Type $\dfrac{61;24;6}{81;21}$

Body Decoration:

61 Motif: Features parallel to one another and to vessel lip.

24 Element: Overhanging lines.
6 Arrangement: Elements placed closely together.

Rim Decoration:
81 Motif: Features placed in top of the flat,
squared lip.
21 Element: One or more lines incised with a
pointed instrument.
This decoration is especially characteristic
of the northern part of the Coles Creek area,
which is central-western Louisiana and southwestern Mississippi.

Usual Accompanying Characteristics: Same as for type
51;24.

Type $\dfrac{61;24;6}{81;25}$

Body Decoration:
61 Motif: Features parallel to one another and to
vessel lip.
24 Elements: Overhanging lines.
6 Elements: Placed closely together.

Rim Decoration:
81 Motif: Features placed in the top of flattened
lip.
25 Element: One or more lines incised with a
pointed instrument.
In these lines closely spaced punctates are
placed at regular intervals. This type most often
occurs in south Louisiana.

Usual Accompanying Characteristics: Same as for type
51;24.

Type 61;24;7 (Marker type)
61 Motif: Features parallel to one another and to
vessel lip.
24 Elements: Overhanging lines.
7 Arrangement: Elements placed more than one-
fourth of an inch apart. Sometimes the lines are
as much as an inch apart. At least four or five
lines running parallel to the rim are characteristic of this type.

Usual Accompanying Characteristics: Same as for type 51;24.

Type $\dfrac{61;24;7}{81;21}$

Body Decorations:

61 Motif: Features parallel to one another and to vessel lip.

24 Elements: Overhanging lines.

7 Arrangement: Lines placed more than one-fourth inch apart.

Rim Decoration:

81 Motif: Features placed in top of flattened lip.

21 Elements: One or more lines incised with a pointed instrument.

Usual Accompanying Characteristics: Same as for type 51;24

(The decoration which would be described as

type $\dfrac{61;24;7}{81;25}$ occurs so infrequently that it has

not been included in the list).

Type 61;24/21;8 (Marker type)

61 Motif: Features parallel to one another and to vessel lip.

24/21 Elements: Overhanging lines (24), or lines made with a pointed instrument (21).

8 Arrangement: Only one or two used. These are close to the lip, and may be placed closely together or widely apart. On Coles Creek sites, they are generally found on the low concave-shaped bowls, and are usually closely spaced, overhanging, and neatly executed. Some of these rims are thickened, and the lines are incised in the applied strap. As found at the Deasonville sites, this type is more carelessly executed. The lines are often made with a point, and the spacing between them is irregular. They occur on a number of different vessel shapes: concave bowls, beakers, and near the lip of wide mouthed pots.

Type $\dfrac{61\,;24\,;8}{81\,;21}$

Body Decoration:

- 61 Motif: Features parallel to one another and to vessel lip.
- 24 Element: Overhanging lines.
- 8 Arrangement: One or two lines are used. These are either closely spaced or are separated by more than a quarter of an inch.

Rim Decoration:

- 81 Motif: Features placed on top of flattened lip.
- 21 Element: One or more lines incised with a pointed instrument.

Usual Accompanying Characteristics: Same as for type 51;24

Type 61; $\dfrac{24}{71\,;9}$

- 61 Motif: Features parallel to one another and to vessel lip.
- 24 Element: Overhanging lines. These are usually placed closely together as in arrangement 6, although in some pieces fewer lines are used and are spaced wider apart.
- 71 Element: Punctates made with a pointed instrument.
- 9 Arrangement: Punctates are arranged in a single row just below and parallel to the incised lines.

    Rare examples have an additional row of punctates between the incised lines and the vessel lip. Other sherds are obviously of this type, but the lines are incised with a pointed instrument and not overhanging.

Usual Accompanying Characteristics: Same as for type 51;24.

Type 61;71;9

- 61 Motif: Features parallel to one another and to vessel lip.

71 Element: Punctates made with a pointed instrument.

9 Arrangement: A single row of the punctate elements, placed just below and parallel to the rim. Sometimes they are separated from the rim by a single incised line, but more often this is not the case.

Usual Accompanying Characteristics: Same as for type 51;24.

$$\text{Type } 61;\frac{24}{74};9$$

61 Motif: Features arranged parallel to one another and to vessel lip.

24 Element: Overhanging lines. A number of these are arranged parallel to the lip, either closely together or spaced.

74 Element: Large triangular punctates. These punctates are essentially similar in execution, but differ in a detail from the usual triangular punctates. That is, the flattened, pointed instrument was in this case held at an acute angle to the vessel walls, with the point directed toward the upper part of the vessel, so that, while the upper two sides of the punctates are impressed with vertical walls, the floor of the feature slopes gently out to the plane of the vessel wall on the third side of the triangle.

9 Arrangement: A single row of these triangular punctates is used below and parallel to the overhanging lines.

Usual Accompanying Characteristics: Same as for type 51;24

Often the incised lines are larger than is usual for the less complex overhanging line decorations.

$$\text{Type } 61;\frac{24}{74};11$$

61 Motif: Features parallel to one another and to vessel lip.

24 Element: Overhanging lines.

74 Element: Triangular punctates (in this case arranged in rows).

11 Arrangement: Elements alternate; that is, an overhanging line is incised parallel to the lip; below that is a row of triangular punctates, and placed below them is another overhanging line, etc.

Usual Accompanying Characteristics: Same as for type 51;24.

Type 61;25;6

61 Motif: Features parallel to one another and to vessel lip.

25 Element: Incised lines dotted with punctates. These lines are usually not overhanging. The punctates are made with a pointed instrument, and are regularly spaced, close together, along the lines.

6 Arrangement: Elements (punctated lines) are placed close together; not more than one-fourth inch apart.

Usual Accompanying Characteristics: Same as for type 51;24.

Type 61;25;7

61 Motif: Features parallel to one another and to vessel lip.

25 Elements: Punctated lines. Incised lines with punctates spaced in them at short intervals, made with a pointed instrument.

7 Arrangements: The punctated lines are spaced over one-fourth inch apart.

These last two decorations are noted especially on sites from southern Louisiana. They are not found as often in the northern parts of the Coles Creek area. A few cases occur in the Caddo collections.

Usual Accompanying Characteristics: Same as for type 51;24.

Type 61;74;9

61 Motif: Features parallel to vessel lip.

74 Elements: Triangular punctates. In this case they are used in a row.

9   Arrangement: The triangular punctates are arranged in a row parallel to and a short distance below the lip. In a few cases a single incised line separates them from the lip, but this is not usual.

Usual Accompanying Characteristics: Same as for type 51;24.

$$\text{Type } 62; \frac{21}{71}; 10$$

62   Motif: Elements arranged parallel to one another at a forty-five degree angle to the lip. This applies to the superior element.

21   Element: Lines incised wtih a pointed instrument.

71   Element: Punctates made with a pointed instrument.

10   Arrangement: The lines are parallel to one another and are placed closely together. They form a band about the upper part of the vessel wall. The punctates are used at both ends of each of the incised lines.

Usual Accompanying Characteristics: Same as for type 51;24.

$$\text{Type } 62; \frac{21}{71}; 11$$

62   Motif: Elements arranged parallel to one another at forty-five degree angle to the lip.

21   Element: Lines incised with a pointed instrument.

71   Element: Punctates made with a pointed instrument. Punctates are arranged in rows.

11   Arrangement: The incised lines alternate with rows of punctates. These are usually spaced very closely together, and are all arranged at forty-five degree angle to the vessel lip.

Usual Accompanying Characteristics: Same as for type 51;24.

Type 62;24;6

62   Motif: Elements arranged parallel to one another at a forty-five degree angle to lip.

24   Elements: Overhanging lines.

6   Arrangements: Lines are spaced closely together—less than one-fourth inch.

This condition is usual, but is not always the case. A few examples of this type have a row of the large triangular punctates similar to those found in type 61; $\dfrac{24}{74;9}$, arranged in a row immediately below the band of slanting lines.

Usual Accompanying Characteristics: Same as for type 51;24.

Type 63;24/21

63   Motif: Elements arranged parallel to one another at right angles to the lip.

24/21   Elements: Either overhanging lines (24), or lines incised with a pointed instrument (21).
Often punctates are found at the ends of the vertical lines.

This arrangement usually forms a narrow band about the upper part of the vessel wall. It may or may not be bordered top and bottom with confining lines.

Usual Accompanying Characteristics: Same as for type 51;24.

Type 63;64

63   Motif: Elements arranged parallel to one another at a ninety degree angle to the vessel lip.

64   Elements: Ridges raised on the surface of the vessel by pinching with two fingers while the paste was plastic.

This is usually roughly executed, and the imprints of the finger tips and nails are visible.

Type 63;71

63   Motif: Elements arranged parallel to one another at a ninety degree angle to the vessel lip.

71   Elements: Punctates made with a pointed instrument.

These are arranged in rows that run perpendicular to the lip of the vessel. In a number of cases, the rows are grouped closely in pairs, and a wider space separates each pair from those adjoining.

Type 63;101 (Marker type)

63   Motif: Elements arranged parallel to one another at a ninety degree angle to the vessel lip.

101   Elements: Roulette or rocker stamping. The instrument was usually unnotched. It was rocked back and forth as it was moved sideways down the vessel wall, giving a zigzagged effect. These figures are arranged parallel to one another about the upper part of the vessel, and form a band from two to three inches wide. Generally this band is bordered top and bottom with incised lines, which may or may not be overhanging.

Usual Accompanying Characteristics: Same as for type 51;24.

Type 71;21

71   Motif: Large crosshatching.

21   Element: Narrow incised lines made with a pointed instrument. The lines forming this motif are drawn at an angle of forty-five degrees to the vessel lip. Small squares formed in this manner are from one-fourth to one-half inch wide on each side.

The decoration is carelessly executed. The lines are generally uneven, wavy, and plow the vessel surface. They were evidently incised while the paste was quite soft.

Usual Accompanying Characteristics:

The decoration is generally applied to the upper one-third to one-half of the vessel walls. Often a line confined the decorated space above and below. A narrow undecorated border separates the area of decoration from the lip. Vessels with this type are either pot-shaped with globular bodies and a slightly constricted, low outflaring mouth; or beakers with flat bottoms and straight, slightly outflaring sides. The lip is not differentiated from the vessel wall except on the pots where it curves outward. Handles and knobs sometimes occur on the pots, where found in Caddo collections. The paste is usually rough in texture and of medium hardness. It averages about .2 to .3 of an inch in thickness. Grit, sand, and shell are found as tempering material.

Type 72; $\dfrac{24}{72/74}$

72 Motif: Diamonds formed by large crosshatching made with lines running at forty-five degree angle to the lip.

24 Element: Overhanging lines used as crosshatching to make the diamonds. In all cases, these lines are not definitely overhanging. Element 21 (lines incised with a pointed instrument) is not uncommon.

72/74 Elements: Either imprints of the end of a hollow tube (perhaps a piece of cane or bone) held nearly vertically to the vessel surface (72), or triangular punctates (74). The last element is most commonly used.

This decoration forms a rather wide band about the upper part of the vessel walls. It is bordered both top and bottom by an incised line.

Usual Accompanying Characteristics: Same as for type 51;24.

Type 81;21/25

81 Motif: Features in the flat top of square lip. Rim rises straight to lip.

21/25 Elements: Lines incised with a pointed instrument (21); or incised lines with punctates made with a pointed instrument spaced in them (25). One line is most common, but two or even three are found in some examples.

Generally this rim is unthickened, but the decoration does occur in the various types of thickened Coles Creek rims. A few fragments of the shallow spherical bowls have small projections on the inside of the lip which provide a wider lip surface to accommodate two or three of these lines. This type is often found in connection with the decorated lugs described below.

The incised lines serve to connect the decorations which appear on the four lugs.

Usual Accompanying Characteristics: Same as for type 51;24.

Type 81;101/74;12

81 Motif: Features in the flat top of squared lip. In this case the features occur in a small thickened space in the lip. These appear to be a rudimentary form of the lugs described below. Four probably occur on each vessel so decorated.

101/74 Elements: The decorations that are found in these thickened areas are usually either zigzagged stamping (101) which adapts itself to the triangular-shape dtop of the thickened lip, or triangular punctates which are impressed in the top of the lip (74). Usually there is either a large triangular punctate, or a punctate made with the end of a tubular instrument, in the widest part of the flat lip.

A single overhanging line is occasionally found on the outside of sherds of this type, a short distance below and parallel to the sherd lip.

Usual Accompanying Characteristics: Same as for type 51;24.

Type 83;25

83 Motif: Features placed in the top of flat, outward-slanting lip. The flattened lip of this motif is not leveled in the plane of the lip of the vessel walls, but has a definite outward slant.

25 Elements: Incised lines, made with a pointed instrument, which have punctates in them at regular short intervals. Two or four of these lines are usual.

This decoration is most common on the south Louisiana sites near the Gulf coast.

Usual Accompanying Characteristics: Same as for type 51;34.

Type 83;74;12

83 Motif: Features placed in thickened areas in the top of flat, outward-slanting lip. These

areas appear to be rudimentary forms of the lugs described below. This type is very similar to type 81;101/74;12 described above. The essential difference lies in the decided outward slant to the top of the lip.

74 Elements: Triangular punctates used to decorate the area formed by the flat top of the enlarged area in the lip.

This type is most frequently found in southern Louisiana.

Usual Accompanying Characteristics: Same as for type 51;24.

Lugs:

These appendages are triangular shaped projections that extend outward from the vessel rim at a slight angle above the plane of the vessel mouth. The broad bases of these lugs are attached to the lip of the vessel, and vary from three to four inches along the line of junction. The appendages are usually about the same thickness as the walls and project outward from two to three inches. Usually lugs have a small part of the vessel wall attached to them so that there is no doubt as to their identification. Four of these features seem to have been used on each vessel (Figure 37). The effect is that of a large, square, almost flat plate, with the body of the vessel attached in the middle of it.

Lugs are decorated with different combinations of triangular punctates: with punctates at the ends of incised lines, with punctates in incised lines; and with zigzagged stamping or rouletting.

Shallow bowls with concave bottoms are the usual shape of vessels bearing these peculiar rim appendages. However, deeper beaker forms are not uncommon. In texture, temper, thickness and color this ware is similar to that described as the 'Usual Accompanying Characteristics' of type 51;24.

Square Bottoms:

The corners of square, flat bottoms from vessels with sides and round body cross section are common features of both Marksville and Coles Creek collections. As they usually do not include enough of the body wall to indicate the particular decoration type to which the vessels belong, it is an easy matter to handle them as independent features.

Summary of features in collection from Coles Creek sites

The Coles Creek complex in central-western Louisiana and southwestern Mississippi is marked by a number of very distinctive features. No difficulty should be encountered in recognizing a typical collection.

A feature of nearly all the pure collections is the admixture of a small amount of Deasonville types. Rather indeterminate types that have been ascribed to the historic complexes occur infrequently and in small proportions. Most of these latter refer either to Tunica or Caddo. In a few instances, the marker types of these two complexes have been found.

Certain Coles Creek sites are analogous to some of the sites in the Deasonville, in that they also yield a varying percentage of Marksville types.

The following list will assist in quickly identifying collections of this complex:

Pottery Decorations:

Overhanging lines drawn parallel to the vessel rim. This includes several variants, and is the numerically dominant type.

Overhanging lines parallel to vessel rim with a single row of triangular punctates (or less often punctates made with a pointed instrument) below and parallel to the lines.

Closely spaced overhanging lines drawn at a 45-degree angle to rim, forming a band about vessel.

Closely spaced overhanging lines perpendicular to rim, which form a band about the vessel.

Alternate lines and rows of triangular punctates drawn parallel to vessel rim.

Lines, sometimes with punctates in them, drawn in the square lip of sherds with other of the body decorations.

Meanders formed by negative bands ½ to 1 inch wide, with a background of either overhanging lines, triangular punctuates, roulette-like punctating, or delicate crosshatching. Large triangular punctates often used at ends of lines.

Chains of triangles or triangular shaped flags filled with closely spaced overhanging lines or small triangular punctates.

Large crosshatching with a punctate, usually either triangular or made with the end of a cane, centered in each diamond.

Roulette or rocker stamp zigzags arranged vertically to form a band about vessel.

Punctates used in incised lines are common in the southern part of the area.

The decorations usually form a band around the vessels that includes less than half the height of the walls. Often the band of decoration is quite narrow—one to three inches. In the overhanging line types, the decoration extends all the way to the lip; other types may have a narrow border between the lip and top of the decorated area.

Features of the Deasonville complex usually found in small proportions in collections from Coles Creek sites:

Cord marked pottery.

Red slip ware.

Red and white painted ware.

Types and features of the Marksville complex that are found on some Coles Creek sites:

Bands of rouletting between broad, deep lines.

Closely spaced, broad, deep lines forming curvilinear and angular designs. Lines are semi-circular in cross section.

Flat, square bottoms on many of the vessels decorated with these types.

Vessel shapes and features found in Coles Creek collections:

Rims with straight exterior walls and interior walls that curve so that sherds become thinner toward the lip.

Rims that are thickened on the exterior by the addition of a strap of clay.

Lines incised in square lip.

Beakers with nearly vertical sides and flat, square, or round bottoms are the most common type.

Large pots with wide mouths, low vertical necks, and globular bodies.

Shallow, round-bottomed bowls with four large, triangular lugs spaced around the rim. These are attached to the lip, and project outward almost at a ninety degree angle to the vessel walls.

The ware is usually between .2 and .3 inches thick. It is neatly finished but not polished. Paste is often dark blue in color and is moderately hard. Sherd exteriors are generally grey. Grit and vegetable matter are used as temper. The ware has a soapy texture. Vessel interiors are often blackened.

Sites of the Coles Creek complex

Site No. 71, Smith Creek site

N. end of irreg. S21, T2N, R4W

This site may properly be considered a typical and pure Coles Creek village. The only extraneous complex represented in the entire collection of 457 classified sherds is Deasonville in a very small percentage which is a proportion entirely consistent with the distance of this site from the Deasonville area in the lower Yazoo River valley.

The site is situated on the bluffs bordering the eastern side of the Mississippi River in extreme southwestern Mississippi. It is on the south side of Smith Creek, a small stream that has cut a deep channel through the border of the escarpment as it descends into the valley from the high tableland to the east.

Three mounds with a fairly profuse accumulation of midden debris, not over ten inches deep, mark the site of the old village. The largest mound, A, is a pyramidal truncate approximately two hundred feet square at the base, twenty feet high, and with a summit plateau ninety feet square. It stands upon the highest part of the ridge that the site occupies. This ridge lies between the creek to the north and the Mississippi bottoms to the south.

About two hundred feet northeast of the large mound, down slope and near the creek, are two smaller truncated pyramids, B and C. Both have been cultivated but still retain something of their original shape. Mound C stands on the edge of the low bluff bordering the creek

DESCRIPTION OF SHERDS IN FIGURE 34

Sherd	Type	Color of Paste	Finish (Good, Medium Poor)	Temper	Hardness (Hard, Medium Soft)	Thickness (inches)	Remarks
				PERIOD II—COLES CREEK			
a	61;24;6	Dark Blue	M	Grit	M	.3	Rim
b	61;24;6	Dark Blue	M	Grit, Vegetable	M	.2	Rim
c	61;24;7	Dark Grey	M	Vegetable	M	.3	Rim
d	61;24;6	Light Grey	G	Vegetable	M	.2	Slightly thickened rim
e	61; $\frac{24}{74:9}$	Dark Blue	M	Grit	M	.2	....
f	61; $\frac{24}{74;9}$	Dark Blue	M	Grit	H	.2	Rim
g	61;24;8	Dark Blue	G	Vegetable	H	.2	Thickened rim
h	61;24;6	Buff	M	Grit, Vegetable	M	.3	Rim
i	61;71;9	Grey	P	Grit	M	.3	Rim
j	51;24	Dark Blue	P	Grit, Vegetable	H	.2	Thickened rim
k	63;64	Black	P	Grit	M	.2	....
l	62;24;6	Dark Blue	M	Vegetable	M	.3	Rim, beaker
m	63;101	Grey	M	Vegetable, Grit	M	.3	Rim
n	63;24/21	Light Blue	M	Vegetable, Grit	M	.2	Slightly thickened rim
o	63;101	Grey	M	Grit, Vegetable	M	.2	Two drilled holes

Material from Smith Creek (Site No. 71).

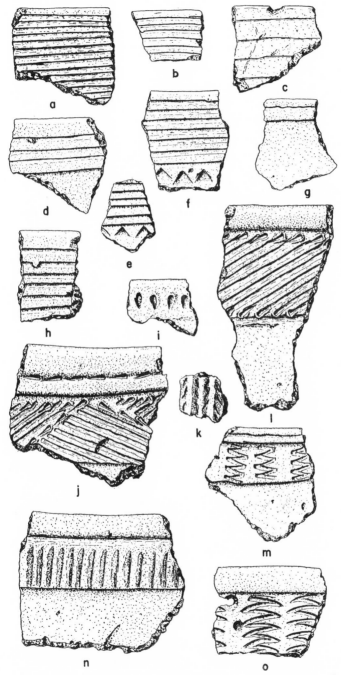

Figure 34. Selection of representative material from Smith Creek village site collection (Site No. 71).

DESCRIPTION OF SHERDS IN FIGURE 35

Sherd	Type	Color of Paste	Finish (Good, Medium, Poor)	Temper	Hardness (Hard, Medium, Soft)	Thickness (inches)	Remarks
				PERIOD II—DEASONVILLE			
k	11;81;14	Grey	M	Vegetable	M	.3	....
m	11;111;14	Light Brown	M	Vegetable	M	.2	Interior view, red slip
				COLES CREEK			
a	34;$\frac{24/104}{104}$;1	Light Brown	M	Grit and Vegetable	H	.2	Small rim lug
b	34;$\frac{24/104}{104}$;1	Black	M	Grit	H	.2	....
c	63:24/21	Buff	G	Grit	H	.2	Rim
d	81;101/74;12	Buff	M	Grit	M	.2	Small rim lug
e	Triangular Lug	Light Blue	M	Grit	M	.3	....
f	34;$\frac{24/104}{104}$;1	Dark Blue	G	Grit	M	.1	Rim
h	34;$\frac{21}{101/28/74}$;1/2	Black	M	Vegetable	M	.2	Red slip, interior decoratio
j	72;$\frac{24}{74/72}$	Black	P	Grit	M	.2	Rim
l	Triangular Lug	Black	M	Grit	M	.3	Small fragment
n	Combination of 61;24;8 and 11;81	Grey	M	Vegetable	H	.2	Thickened rim
o	Triangular Lug	Light Tan	M	Vegetable	M	.3	Interior view
p	Combination of 61;$\frac{24}{74;9}$ and 11;81;14	Grey	M	....	H	.2	Rim
q	Square bottom	Black	M	Vegetable	M	.3	Polished black interior
				INDETERMINATE			
g	....	Brown	G	Grit	H	.2	Line in rim
i	....	Brown	M	Grit	M	.3	Rim

Material from Smith Creek (Site No. 71).

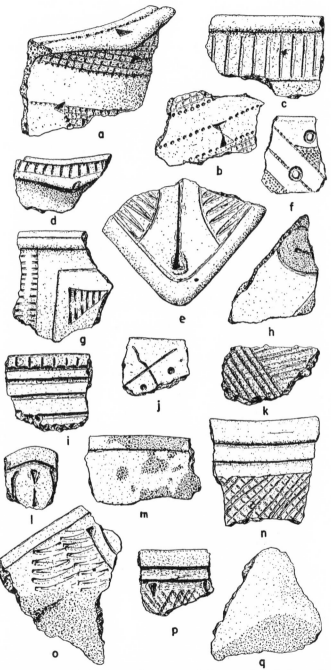

Figure 35.   Selection of representative material from Smith
Creek village site collection (Site No. 71).

197

and is half cut away. It measures five feet in height and is ninety feet along the remaining side. Mound B, situated near a small ravine that cuts back toward Mound A from the creek, is slightly smaller than C. It is seventy feet square at the base and six feet high.

All three of the mounds have about the same orientation. They are within a few degrees of being set square with the cardinal points.

Sherd collections have come from around Mound A, from between B and C, and from an eighteen-inch midden deposit exposed in the bank of a road that descends the bluffs two hundred feet east of C.

The sherds from Smith Creek have been classified with the results shown in figure 1. Representative sherds are shown in figures 34 and 35.

The sherds shown in figure 35 k,n, and p illustrate the intrusive Deasonville influence. Note that on sherds n and p of this figure, cord marking, more neatly applied than at typical Deasonville sites, has been added below typical Coles Creek decorations.

Site No. 73, Truly place

Irreg. S 18, T10N, R1W

This site is a group of mounds that stand on the edge of the hundred foot escarpment that marks the eastern extent of the Mississippi River valley, and is twenty miles north of Natchez. The group is located in Jefferson County, Mississippi. A short distance to the north of the mounds, Coles Creek cuts a deep gash in the escarpment as it descends to the valley floor.

At present there are four large mounds. One stands on the edge of the bluff. It is a truncated pyramid approximately two hundred by two hundred and fifty feet at the base and twenty feet high. The three other mounds are smaller and are located to the south of this one.

Closest is an irregularly shaped structure approximately one hundred feet in diameter and eight feet high. One hundred yards to the south is a flat topped pyramid two hundred feet square at the base and twenty-two feet high. A short distance further is another pyramidal mound which is slightly smaller in size. In the fields surrounding these mounds are quantities of potsherds and animal bones.

The site was first recorded by Culin, who reported on the collections made there by Dr. Dickson in 1846.[62] The site was then known as the "Ferguson Mounds". Dickson described an arrangement of seven conical mounds that are no longer to be found. The height that he gives for the mound standing on the bluff, fifty-six feet, is evidently an error.

In the course of excavations Dr. Dickson found a stone effigy pipe depicting a flat headed Indian holding an elbow pipe between his knees.[63]

"Three finely finished vases" are mentioned in the report but are not described.

Surface material from the site was secured by Chambers in 1930 and by the writer in 1935. The collections show a majority of typical Coles Creek decorations (Figure 36 a-l). Several of the Deasonville types are present (Figure 36 l).

[62]Culin, Howard, The Dickson Collection of American Antiquities.

[63]Idem, pl. 12. Reproduced in Brown, Archeology of Mississippi, pl. 227.

DESCRIPTION OF SHERDS IN FIGURE 36

Sherd	Type	Color of Paste	Finish (Good, Medium, Poor)	Temper	Hardness (Hard, Medium, Soft)	Thickness (inches)	Remarks
			PERIOD II—DEASONVILLE				
l	11;81;14	Buff	P	Grit	M	.2	....
			COLES CREEK				
a	61;24;6	Dark Blue	G	....	H	.2	Rim
b	61;24;6	Dark Blue	M	Vegetable	M	.2	Rim
c	61;24;6	Dark Blue	M	Vegetable	H	.2	Rim
d	61;$\frac{24}{74;9}$	Black	M	....	M	.2	Rim
e	61;$\frac{24}{74;9}$	Light Blue	M	Vegetable	M	.3	Rim
f	51;24	Dark Blue	G	Vegetable	H	.2	Rim, polished exterior
g	Lug	Dark Blue	M	Vegetable	M	.2	....
h	63;101	Dark Blue	M	Vegetable	M	.2	Rim
j	34;$\frac{24/104}{104}$;1	Black	M	....	M	.2	....
k	Same type	Black	M	Grit, Veg.	M	.3	Rim, polished
			INDETERMINATE				
i	$\frac{61;24;8}{81;25}$	Light Blue	M	Vegetable	M	.2	Slightly thick rim

Material from Truly plantation (Site No. 73).

Sherd	Type	Color of Paste	Finish	Temper	Hardness	Thickness	Remarks
			PERIOD II—DEASONVILLE				
s	11;81;14	Dark Blue	R	Grit, Veg.	M	.2	Thickened rim
			COLES CREEK				
m	01;74	Light Blue	M	Vegetable	M	.2	Rim, shallow bowl
n	61;24;6	Tan	M	Grit	M	.2	....
o	51;24	Black	M	Grit	M	.2	Thickened rim
p	$\frac{61;25;6}{81;25}$	Black	M	Grit	S	.2	Wide mouth pot
q	63;24/21	Dark Blue	M	Vegetable	M	.2	Rim
r	51;24	Dark Blue	M	Grit	H	.3	....
t	62;$\frac{21}{71}$;11	Black	P	....	M	.2	Rim
u	63;101	Dark Blue	M	Grit	M	.2	Rim

Material from Chevalier place (Site No. 75).

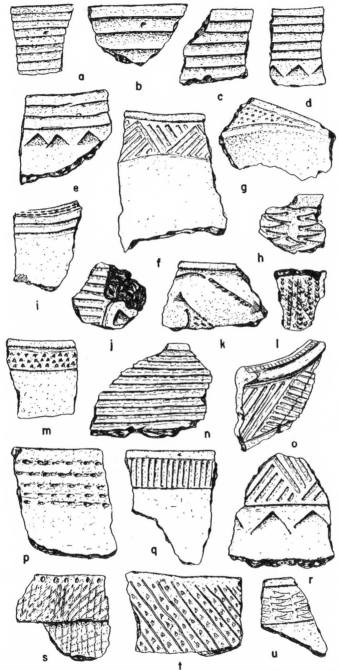

Figure 36. Selection of representative material from Truly plantation (Sherds a-k) and Chevalier plantation (Sherds l-u) village site collections.

201

Site No. 75, Chevalier mound

NE¼ S10, T6N, R4E

The mound on the Ed Chevalier place is situated in LaSalle Parish, Louisiana. It is two and one-half miles up from the mouth of French Fork, a small stream that flows into the eastern side of Catahoula Lake. The surrounding country is low swamp, and the site is located on the slight elevation provided by an ancient natural levee. The Gorum site (Site No. 87) is down this old levee, two miles toward the mouth of French Fork. Higher up the stream there are several other sites which are not represented by collections.

Moore visited the Chevalier site in 1908. He reports that the single mound at the site then had a height of twenty-one feet. Moore's excavations in the structure and the neighboring woods produced no results and he seems to have spent little time there.[64]

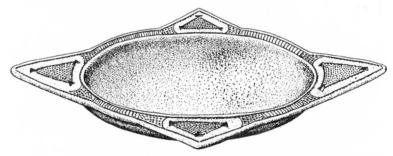

Figure 37. Reconstruction of bowl from Chevalier site (Site No. 75).

In 1933 the mound had been reduced to a height of five feet and was very much spread. A house and garden occupied most of it. Mr. Chevalier, the resident, reports finding human bones in the garden. The material which comprises the present collection came from the garden and the nearby fields.

---

[64]Moore, C. B., Antiquities of the Ouachita Valley, p. 103.

The collection is classified in the table given as figure 1. Selections of the material are shown in figure 36 l-t.

This collection includes most of the significant Coles Creek types. A small proportion of Deasonville material is present and is illustrated by figure 36 s. A reconstruction of a bowl shows the use of the triangular lugs which are so common in Coles Creek collections (Figure 37). Three of the lugs, most of the rim, and part of the bottom of this vessel were secured by Mr. Chevalier from his garden.

One piece (one per cent) of Marksville decoration was found. Although this proportion is significant, it is not enough to warrant placing this site with the Coles Creek and Marksville sites which are considered in the next section.

DESCRIPTION OF COLES CREEK COMPLEX SITES

| Site No. | Site Name | Burials | | Mounds | | | | | Enclosure | Midden | | | Collection Analysis |
| | | Cemetery | Mound | Conical | | Pyramidal | | | | Approximate Area | Thin −10" | Thick +10" | |
				Low −10'	Tall +10'	Low −10'	Tall +10'	Ramp					
61	Coles Creek	x		1	1					6A	x		Tunica, Coles Creek, Deasonville
62	Billy Ldg.			(washed into river)						3A	x		Coles Creek, Deasonville, Caddo, Tunica
63	James Smith									—			
64	Hedgland Pl.			1		1				6A	x		Coles Creek, Deasonville
65	Ditto Pl.									4A	x		Coles Creek, Deasonville
66	Marmande Pl.									—			Coles Creek
67	Mazique Pl.						2	x		4A		x	Coles Creek, Deasonville
68	Morgan Pl.									—			Coles Creek, Deasonville
69	C. H. Neely Pl.			2	1					2A		x	Coles Creek, Deasonville
70	Rhinehart Site									½A		x	Coles Creek
71	*Smith Creek			1		1	1	x		4A		x	Coles Creek, Deasonville
72	Stark Pl.			2			2	x		1A		x	Coles Creek, Deasonville
73	*Truly Pl.									2A		x`	Coles Creek, Deasonville
74	White Oak. Ldg.			2						3A		x	Coles Creek, Deasonville
75	*Chevalier Md.	x		1						—			Coles Creek, Deasonville

*Sites described in the text and from which material is illustrated.

Sites yielding both Coles Creek and Marksville complexes

In the same parts of east-central Louisiana and southwestern Mississippi in which the sites with the Coles Creek complex are found, there are other old villages, the collections from which show varying proportions of both Coles Creek and Marksville ware. The situation is analogous to the Deasonville-Marksville sites in the Yazoo River country. Varying proportions of the two groups of decorations appear on the different villages. There is no geographical segregation of these sites; they are often found within a mile or two of villages yielding collections that are either pure Coles Creek, or pure Marksville in character.

There is a noticeable tendency for some of the Marksville decorations to be less neatly executed than those from the pure Marksville sites. This is especially true of type 31; $\dfrac{23}{101/102}$;1/2 (rouletted bands confined by wide lines and contrasted with undecorated bands of about the same width). The tendency is for the rouletted bands to be wider, for the confining lines to be less firmly drawn, and for zigzagged rouletting to be carelessly applied with more space between the imprints than usual.

The Peck site discussed in the previous bulletin of this series belongs in this classification.[65] Stratigraphic studies made in the twenty-inch midden there demonstrate that the Marksville complex of decorations underlay and therefore was earlier than the Coles Creek. This direct evidence of sequence was discovered as a result of the comparative analysis presented in this paper, and serves as supplementary evidence.

The Peck collection used here consists of all the decorated material recovered in the course of excavation.

---

[65]Ford, J. A., Ceramic Decoration Sequence at an Old Indian Village Site Near Sicily Island, Louisiana.

as well as supplementary material gathered from the surface. It will be treated as an ordinary surface collection. See comparative chart, figure 1.

While discussing direct evidence of the temporal relation of Marksville and Coles Creek, it should be stated that in the National Museum at Washington the writer has examined the material secured by Walker in the course of his excavation of the base of the large mound at Jonesville, Louisiana, in 1932.[66] The sherds which he found on the surface were of both Marksville and Coles Creek types. The twenty-three decorated sherds from the interior of the large mound and the fifty-two from the base were all of the Marksville complex. Walker's forthcoming report should make this clear.

Site No. 90, Hudson place

SW¼ SW¼ S26, T5N, R5E

This old village is situated on the Hudson Place, on the east bank of Larto Lake, in the extreme southern part of Catahoula Parish, Louisiana. Larto Lake is an old Mississippi River channel, horseshoe-shaped, one-half mile wide, and seven miles long.[67] The site occupies the slight elevation provided by the natural levee on the interior bank of the curve. There are four mounds, irregular in shape, and not over six feet high. Three of them have been subject to cultivation but the original shapes appear to have been pyramidal. A dwelling occupies the one nearest the bank of the lake. Midden material is found in typical black soil along the bank of the lake, and many sherds have been washed down to the water's edge.

The site was first described by Dr. Beyer of Tulane University in 1896.[68]

---

[66]Walker, Winslow, Trailing the Mound Builders of the Mississippi Valley.

[67]Russel, R. J., "Larto Lake, An Old Mississippi River Channel," Louisiana Dept. Consv., La. Consv. Review, July 1933.

[68]Beyer, George E., The Mounds of Louisiana.

Clarence Moore visited the site in 1912. In his report he refers to this site as the Wiley place. He did not excavate.[69]

The collection used in this paper was secured partly by Mr. and Mrs. U. B. Evans and Dr. Fred B. Kniffen in the spring of 1933, and partly by the writer later in the same year.

The decoration types are mostly those of the Coles Creek and Marksville complexes (compared in chart, Figure 1; illustrated in Figure 38). There is a scattering of rather indeterminate material from the historic complexes. The usual small proportion of Deasonville is found (Figure 38 k).

Two of the peculiar clay objects that are illustrated from the Neal site (Figure 40 v) were found here.

---

[69]Moore, C. B., Some Aboriginal Sites in Louisiana and in Arkansas, pp. 31-32.

DESCRIPTION OF SHERDS IN FIGURE 38

Sherd	Type	Color of Paste	Finish (Good, Medium, Poor)	Temper	Hardness (Hard, Medium, Soft)	Thickness (inches)	Remarks
			PERIOD II—DEASONVILLE				
k	11;81;14	Buff	P	Grit	M	.4	....
			COLES CREEK				
a	61;24;6	Light Blue	M	Vegetable	M	.2	Square lip, beaker
b	63;101	Grey	M	Vegetable	M	.3	Thickened rim
c	$61;24;8 \over 81;21$	Dark Blue	G	Grit	H	.2	Punctated line in rim
d	61;24/21	Dark Blue	M	Vegetable	M	.2	Square lip, beaker
e	63;24;6	Grey	M	Vegetable	M	.3	Square lip
g	$61;{24 \over 74;9}$	Buff	M	....	M	.3	Beaker
h	61;71;9	Black	M	Grit	M	.3	Square lip
f	81;101/74;12	Black	M	Vegetable	M	..	....
j	$34;{24/104 \over 104};1$	Dark Blue	M	Vegetable	H	.2	........................;1
			PERIOD I—MARKSVILLE				
l	$31;{23 \over 101/102};1/2$	Grey	M	Vegetable	H	.3	Rim
m	$31;{23 \over 101/102};1/2$	Black	M	Grit	M	.2	....
n	$31;{23 \over 73};2$	Grey	M	Vegetable	H	.2	....
o	45;23;6	Grey	M	Vegetable	H	.2	....
p	45;23;6	Black	M	Vegetable	M	.3	Square lip
q	45;23;6	Black	M	Vegetable	H	.2	....
			INDETERMINATE				
i	01;72	Grey	M	Vegetable	M	.3	....

Material from Hudson place (Site No. 90).

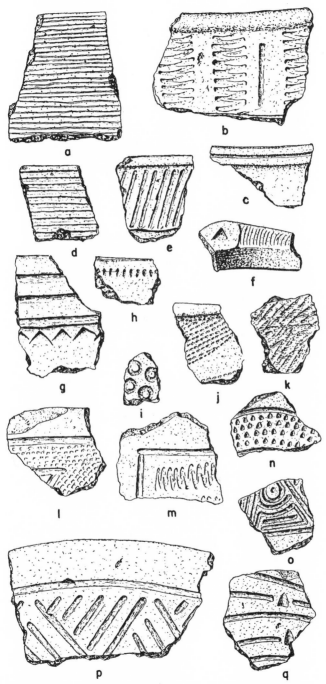

Figure 38. Selection of representative material from the Hudson village site collection (Site No. 90).

DESCRIPTION OF SHERDS IN FIGURE 39

Sherd	Type	Color of Paste	Finish (Good, Medium, Poor)	Temper	Hardness (Hard, Medium, Soft)	Thickness (inches)	Remarks
			PERIOD II—DEASONVILLE				
m	11;81;14	Grey	P	Vegetable, grit	H	.3	....
o	11;111;14	Black	G	Grit	M	.2	Polished, thickened rim, red slip
			COLES CREEK				
a	61;24;6	Grey	M	Vegetable	H	.2	Beaker
b	61;24;6	Grey	P	Grit, Vegetable	M	.2	Beaker
c	61;$\frac{24}{71;9}$	Black	P	Vegetable	M	.2	Beaker
d	62;24;6	Black	M	Vegetable	M	.2	Beaker, square lip
e	63;101	Grey	M	Vegetable	M	.2	....
f	63;24/21	Dark Blue	M	Grit, Vegetable	M	.3	Rim
g	63;101	Dark Blue	M	Grit	M	.3	Small lug on lip
h	72;$\frac{24}{72/74}$	Buff	M	Grit, Vegetable	M	.2	Beaker
i	34;$\frac{24}{74}$;1	Grey	M	Vegetable	M	.2	Rim
j	61;71;9	Black	M	Vegetable	S	.3	Square lip
k	64;21;6	Grey	R	Grit	S	.3	....
l	61;24;6	Dark Blue	R	Vegetable	M	.3	Punctates in line
			PERIOD I—MARKSVILLE				
n	45;23;6	Grey	M	Vegetable, Grit	M	.3	....
q	31;$\frac{23}{101/102}$;1/2	Tan	P	Sand, Vegetable	S	.3	....

INDETERMINATE

p   Clay discoidal .5 inches thick

Material from Gorum plantation (Site No. 87).

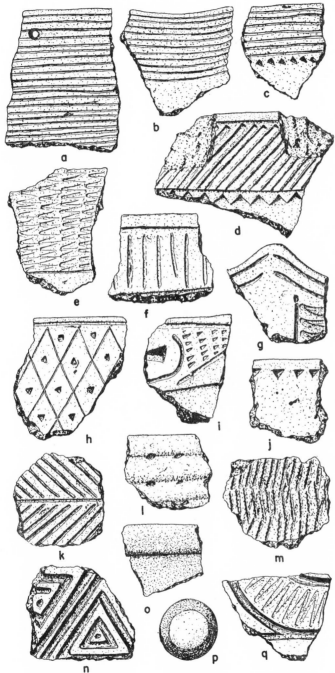

Figure 39. Selection of representative material from Gorum place (Site No. 87).

211

Site No. 87, Gorum place

E½ S8, T6N, R4E

At the Gorum site in LaSalle Parish, Louisiana, there are two mounds. Both are steep conical structures about eight feet high. They are arranged on either side of French Fork, not far from the point where that stream empties into Catahoula Lake. A large pit dug into the top of one of the structures shows that it was constructed of clay. Local residents report that the excavator, a school teacher, found nothing to reward him for his efforts.

The midden debris at this place is about eight inches thick and lies under a foot of alluvium. It is exposed for a half mile by the ditches along the uncompleted state highway No. 471 that runs to the east of the mounds.

This collection of surface material was made by Mr. and Mrs. U. B. Evans and forms part of the Neild collection. Results of classification are shown in the table given as figure 1. Representative material is illustrated in figure 39. Most of the decorations belong to the Coles Creek complex. The small amount of Deasonville usually found on Coles Creek sites is present. A few recent types appear but none are marker types. The Marksville complex is represented by two sherds. These are markers and there can be no doubt as to their identification.

Site No. 93, Neal place

Corners S 13, 14, 23, 24 T19N, R10E

The group of six mounds on the Neal place in West Carroll Parish, Louisiana, stands on the low fifteen-foot bluffs that border the western side of Bayou Maçon. Clarence Moore visited the location and excavated in 1912.[70] Moore gives a map of the group and lists measurements of the mounds.

Three of the structures are truncated pyramids, and a fourth one is irregular in shape. They stand near the bank of the bayou and are arranged as though placed on the four sides of a small court. Two other larger pyramids stand a short distance to the south. Moore's map shows a section of earthen wall connected with one of these large mounds. This cannot be seen today. It has probably been destroyed by cultivation.

Two miles to the north, up Bayou Maçon, are the large peculiar structures on the Poverty Point and Motley plantations. Moore describes and gives maps of these mounds.[71]

The collection from the midden at the Neal place that is classified here was made at different times by Mr. Edward F. Neild and the writer. The material is almost equally divided between Coles Creek and Marksville decoration types (Figure 1.) Representative sherds are illustrated in Figure 40. A peculiar type of artifact is found here in great numbers, both entire and broken. These are irregularly shaped clay balls squeezed into a number of shapes with the fingers and hand. They are well fired, and are usually not over two or three inches in greatest diameter (Figure 40 v). Moore considers these objects at some length and illustrates a plate of the different

[70]Moore, Clarence B., "Some Aboriginal Sites in Louisiana and in Arkansas", pp. 64-66. Moore refers to this site as the Jackson Place.

[71]Idem, pp. 66-69.

DESCRIPTION OF SHERDS IN FIGURE 40

Sherd	Type	Color of Paste	Finish (Good, Medium, Poor)	Temper	Hardness (Hard, Medium, Soft)	Thickness (inches)	Remarks
				PERIOD III—CADDO			
h	11/21;61	Brown	P	Grit, Veg.	S	.3	Rim
				PERIOD II—DEASONVILLE			
l	11;81;14	Dark Blue	M	Vegetable	M	.3	....
o	11;81;14	Grey	M	Vegetable	H	.2	....
p	01;111	Black, Red	M	Grit	S	.3	Red interior
				COLES CREEK			
a	61;24;6	Grey	M	Grit	M	.3	Rim
b	61;24;6	Light Blue	P	Grit	S	.3	Rim
c	61;24;7	Light Blue	M	Grit, Veg.	M	.3	Rim
d	$\frac{61;24;8}{81;21}$	Dark Blue	M	Grit, Veg.	M	.3	Thickened rim
e	$61;\frac{24}{74;9}$	Black	P	....	S	.3	....
f	61;74;9	Dark blue	P	Vegetable	M	.3	Rim
g	63;101	Grey	M	Grit	M	.3	Rim
i	63;24;21	Grey	M	Grit, Veg.	M	.3	Rim
j	$\frac{61;24;8}{81;21}$	Grey	M	Grit	M	.3	Rim
m	$72;\frac{24}{74/72}$	Dark blue	M	Grit	M	.3	....
n	Same as m	Brown	M	Grit, Veg.	M	.3	....
q	$34;\frac{21}{111/28/74};1/2$	Dark Blue	M	Grit, Veg.	M	.2	....
r	$\frac{34}{61};24;1$	Grey	M	Vegetable	S	.3	....
				PERIOD I—MARKSVILLE			
s	45;23;6	Dark blue	M	Grit	S	.3	....
t	$31;\frac{23}{73};2$	Dark blue	M	Grit	M	.3	....
w	45;23;6	Black	M	....	S	.2	....
x	45;23;6	Buff	M	Vegetable	M	.3	....
y	$31;\frac{23}{101/102};1/2$	Grey	M	Grit	M	.2	Thickened rim
z	Same as y	Black	M	Vegetable	M	.3	
				INDETERMINATE			
k	$\frac{84;52}{11;41}$	Grey	M	Grit, Veg.	M	.3	Rim
u	....	Light Grey	M	Grit	M	.3	....
v	Object of burned clay	....					

Material from Neal place (Site No. 93).

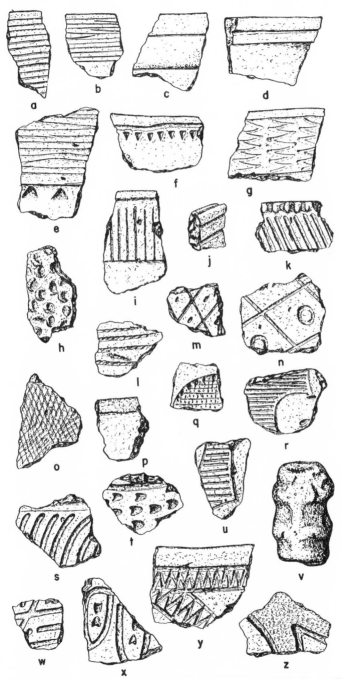

Figure 40. Selection of representative material from Neal
plantation village site collection (Site No. 93).

215

types.[72] His interpretation of their use as charms for the benefit of crops is a possibility.

Similar objects have been collected at other sites in central Louisiana, notably the Hudson place (Site No. 90), Prichard's Landing (Site No. 94), and the Gorum site (Site No. 87). It will be noted that all these sites yield both the Marksville and Coles Creek types of pottery.

---

[72]Moore, C. B., Some Aboriginal Sites in Louisiana and in Arkansas, pp. 72-74, pl. II.

DESCRIPTION OF COLES CREEK PLUS MARKSVILLE COMPLEX SITE

Site No.	Site Name	Burials		Mounds Conical		Pyramidal			Enclosure	Midden Approximate Area	Thin -10"	Thick +10"	Collection Analysis
		Cemetery	Mound	Low -10'	Tall +10'	Low -10'	Tall +10'	Ramp					
76	Picketts I.									2A		x	Coles Creek Deasonville, Marksville
77	Chase Pl.									3A		x	Coles Creek, Deasonville, Marksville
78	Barfield Pl.									4A		x	Coles Creek, Deasonville, Marksville
79	Beldoin Pl.				1					6A		x	Coles Creek, Deasonville, Marksville
80	Wild Hog Md.	x			1								Coles Creek, Deasonville Marksville
81	Marsden Pl.				1					4A		x	Coles Creek, Deasonville, Marksville
82	Veasey Pl.												Coles Creek, Deasonville, Marksville
83	Alphenia Lldg.						3	x		7A	x		Coles Creek, Deasonville, Marksville
84	Sidney Biggs Pl.												Coles Creek, Deasonville, Marksville, Tunica
85	Camp Bayou Md.				1							x	Coles Creek, Marksville
86	Dunbarton Pl.				1(?)					2A		x	Coles Creek, Deasonville, Marksville, Tunica
87	*Gorum Md.				2					4A		x	Coles Creek, Deasonville Marksville
88	Johnson Pl.				2					4A		x	Coles Creek, Deasonville Marksville

DESCRIPTION OF COLES CREEK PLUS MARKSVILLE COMPLEX SITE
(Continued)

| Site No. | Site Name | Burials | | Mounds | | | | | Enclosure | Approximate Area | Midden | | Collection Analysis |
| | | Cemetery | Mound | Conical | | Pyramidal | | | | | Thin −10″ | Thick +10″ | |
				Low −10′	Tall +10′	Low −10′	Tall +10′	Ramp					
89	Jonesville			1	(20 mds.)				x	10A		x	Coles Creek, Deasonville, Marksville
90	*Hudson Pl.				4					3A		x	Coles Creek, Deasonville, Marksville
91	Greenhouse Pl.												Coles Creek, Marksville
92	Melancon Pl.												Coles Creek Deasonville Marksville
93	*Neal Pl.					3	3	x				x	Coles Creek, Deasonville, Marksville
94	Prichard Ldg.									8A		x	Coles Creek, Deasonville Marksville
95	Peck Site			2						1A		x	Coles Creek, Deasonville Marksville
96	King Pl.									3A		x	Coles Creek, Deasonville Marksville

*Sites described in text and from which material is illustrated.

PERIOD I

Marksville complex

Discussion of the Marksville complex

The Marksville complex of pottery decorations derives its name from the site one mile east of the town of Marksville, in Avoyelles Parish, Louisiana, that was first excavated and reported on by Gerard Fowke of the Bureau of American Ethnology.[73] Later it was recognized by F. M. Setzler of the U. S. National Museum that the material recovered by Fowke closely resembled certain of the types of ware that have been found in the mounds of the Hopewell Culture (also known as the Central Basin phase of the Woodland Basic Culture). This culture has been recognized in Ohio and adjacent states. Setzler's investigations of the Marksville site have been partially reported, and a complete analysis is now in preparation.[74]

The Marksville village site will be described briefly later, but for a more detailed discussion the reader is referred to the publications cited.

It has already been mentioned that the pottery types of the Marksville complex are found on certain sites in central and northeastern Louisiana in association with the types of the Coles Creek complex and also in the Yazoo River Valley of Mississippi with the Deasonville complex. Under the present heading the relatively pure village sites that show little or no mixture of any other complex with the Marksville will be considered. Unfortunately the number of such sites represented by adequate collections is very limited. There are only six and all are lo-

---

[73]Fowke, Gerard, Explorations in the Red River Valley in Louisiana, pp. 405-434.
Archeological Work in Louisiana, pp. 254-259.
[74]Setzler, F. M., Hopewell Type Pottery from Louisiana, pp. 1-21.
A Phase of Hopewell Mound Builders in Louisiana, pp. 38-40.

cated in Louisiana (see Figure 2). Since the Marksville complex plays an important part in the history of southern ceramics, it is advisable to describe each of the six sites in detail. However, material from only three will be illustrated.

Pottery decoration types of the Marksville complex

Type 31; $\dfrac{23}{73}$; 2 (Marker type)

31   Motif: Curving, line-bordered bands of features. Bands often branch. The entire plan of this decoration cannot be determined from the usual small sherds.

23   Elements: Wide, deep, smooth lines, probably made with a small cane or reed, and used to border the bands of features that form the motif.

73   Elements: Semi-conical punctates. These are well defined impressions of about the same depth as the incised lines. They appear to have been made with either a small cane, reed, or hollow bone, with an end cut off at a right angle. This implement was held at an angle of about fifteen degrees to the vessel wall to impress the punctates. The hollow center of the tool often has left small projections of clay in the deep and wide end of the punctates, so that the impression is heart shaped.

2   Arrangement: The line-enclosed punctated band appears to have formed the decoration, while the background of the figures was the plain surface of the vessel.

    Execution of this decoration was neat and careful. The incisions were made after the vessel paste had become firm, so there was no tendency for the tools to plow up clay along the sides of the lines. The lines are firmly and boldly drawn.

Usual Accompanying Characteristics:

    The ware upon which the different types of the Marksville complex are figured is remarkably homogeneous. This discussion of usual ac-

companying characteristics applies equally well
to all decorations, except a few that are specified
in the following.

This group of decorations appears to have
been applied to the bodies of the vessels in three
ways: covering the sides and the bottoms, cover-
only the sides, or confined to a band that extends
from near the rim half way down the vessel sides.

In a few cases the figured area extends up
to the lip of the vessel, but more often there is
an undecorated border from one-half to one inch
wide separating decoration and rim. These rims
are either straight, unthickened, ending in a
square lip, or else are thickened in the border
space with a strap of clay applied to the outside
of the vessel wall. The cross sections of these
thickened rims are rectangular, triangular, or
rounded. The straight, unthickened rims are
sometimes notched. A few sherds, from the
Marksville site especially, have lightly crosshatched rims which are often separated from the
body decoration by a line of semi-conical punctates (treated as a separate decoration
type 84; $\frac{28}{23}$; 9). These are thinner than the body
walls and generally have a decided outward camber.

Fragments bearing these decorations usually
indicate very simple vessel shapes. Beakers with
straight, slightly-outflaring sides and flat, circular or square bottoms, are most common. Other
forms are pots with bulging sides, flat square or
circular bottoms, and slightly constricted mouths.
Some of these have four distinct bulges or lobes
in the body walls. A small proportion is bowls
with flat bottoms and low upward-curving walls.

Appendages are very rare on sherds of these
types. On a few pieces from the sites which yield
both the Marksville and Coles Creek complexes,
small triangular lugs are found attached to the
outside of the vessel lip. No handles or knobs are
found.

Bottoms are generally flat with well marked angles between bottom and side walls. In shape they are either round or square with distinct corners. Four short teat-like legs are found on the corners of some of the square bottoms.

The texture of the vessel paste is smooth and "soapy" to the touch. Usually the ware is not polished, but has a smooth finish. Sherd thickness varies considerably, but appears to average about .2 inches. It is fairly hard and firm and tends to break along the lines of the coil junctions. All of the ware appears to have been made by the coiling method.

Grit, a small amount of sand, and small masses of carbon that probably result from the firing of organic matter, form the tempering material.

The color of the paste is usually grey or black. The outside surface is usually oxidized to a dirty white, grey, or brown.

Often uneven firing has mottled the surface with black. The interiors of a number of sherds appear to have been intentionally blackened. No slips are found.

Type 31; $\dfrac{23}{101/102}$; ½ (Marker type)

31   Motif: Curving, line-bordered, bands of features. Bands often branch. The plan of the motif of this decoration can not be determined from the small sherds that are gathered in surface collections. However, several entire vessels with this type of decoration, recovered from mound 4 in Fowke's and later Setzler's excavations at Marksville,[75] demonstrate the fact that in some cases, at least, the entire figures represent conventionalized birds.

23   Element: Wide, deep, smooth lines used to outline the bands of features that form the motif.

---

[75]Setzler, F. M., Pottery of the Hopewell Type from Louisiana.

101/102 Elements: Either rocker or roulette impressions zigzagged at right angles to the axis of the band (101) or running along the axis of the band (102). In both cases these markings are crowded closely together so that the entire surface of the band is roughened. Where the instrument was impressed parallel to the band, it was always notched. Many of the zigzagged markings show the negative markings of a notched tool; others are plain and unnotched.

1/2 Arrangement: Usually it is impossible to determine whether the motif of the decoration is formed positively by the roughened band (2) or negatively by the plain bands that separate the roughened areas, (1). In the majority of cases the former appears to have been the case. The undecorated bands are of about the same width as the decorated and the entire area occupied by the decoration is utilized.

This decoration is neatly and carefully executed. The markings were made after the paste had hardened sufficiently for the incisions to be clean and definite.

Usual Accompanying Characteristics:
They are the same as the preceding type.

Type 45; 23; 6 (Marker type)

45 Motif: Curvilinear scroll-like figures (less often rectangular figures involving right angles).

23 Elements: Wide, deep, smooth lines.

6 Arrangements: The lines used as elements in this decoration are placed closely together. Usually the small ridge that separates neighboring lines is of the same width as are the lines themselves. In some cases the spacing is wider. In this type a special effort appears to have been made to cover all of the area treated with decoration. Small triangles are used in the angles, and in the smaller spaces punctates, which are often hemiconical in shape, were used.

Usual Accompanying Characteristics:

Similar to type 31; $\dfrac{23}{73}$; 2.

Type 51; 23.

51 Motif: Chain of triangles. Alternate triangles arranged base up and base down and nested together so that a solid band is formed around vessel. All the triangles with the bases down are filled with straight lines drawn parallel to one of the ascending legs of the figure; the alternate triangles, with the bases up, are filled with lines similarly arranged, but parallel to the opposite ascending leg.

23 Element: Wide, deep, smooth lines of a semi-circular cross section. These are used to outline the triangles as well as to fill the included areas. The spaces between the lines filling the figures are usually about the same width as the lines.

Usual Accompanying Characteristics:

$$\text{Same as for type } 31; \frac{23}{73}; 2.$$

Type 84; $\frac{28}{73}$; 9

84 Motif: This decoration is found only on rim sherds and is confined to the outside of the rim.

28 Elements: The decoration consists usually of a single row of hemi-conical punctates arranged in a line that runs parallel to the rim from one to two inches below it (arrangement 9). The area between the punctates is most often filled with crosshatching formed by fine lines drawn at 45 degrees to the vessel edge. In some cases the crosshatching has not been completed, and the fine lines are all at an angle of 45 degrees to the rim.

9 Arrangement: Refers to the single row of punctates that is described above.

Usual Accompanying Characteristics:

  This decoration is generally found on the vertical cambered rim characteristic of the typical square bottomed, four-lobed pots with slightly constricted mouths. It does not extend below the neck of the vessels. The vessel body is often covered with decorations of the other Marksville types.

The rest of the description for this ware is identical with that of type 31; $\frac{23}{73}$; 2.

This is the least common of the Marksville types. Although it is found in small proportions at some of the other sites of the complex, it occurs most abundantly at the Marksville village site.

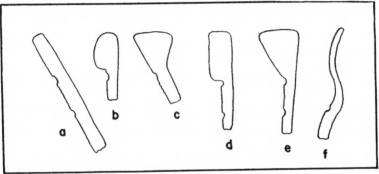

Figure 41.   Profiles of rim sherds of the Marksville complex.

Summary of features in Marksville village site collections

No difficulty should be encountered in identifying a typical Marksville complex collection from the Lower Mississippi Valley. The decoration types are few and distinctive and the paste and technique are uniformly smooth and neatly executed.

The features usually found in these collections are listed below:

Pottery decorations:

Wide, rounded lines bordering curving or angular bands of hemiconical punctates.

Wide, rounded lines bordering curving or angular bands of rouletting, either zigzagged or linear.

Wide, rounded lines placed closely together and forming either curvilinear or angular figures.

Band of nested triangles shaded by straight lines. These lines are of the usual type being wide, and semi-circular in cross section.

Delicate crosshatching or fine straight lines used on the outside of a cambered rim. There usually is a single band of hemi-conical punctates at the base of this decoration to separate it from the decoration used on the vessel body. Except for a wide rim border, these decorations are usually applied to the entire exterior area of the vessels. In a number of cases the bottom is covered.

Vessel features in Marksville collections:

Beakers with flat bottoms and straight, outward slanting walls.
Pots with globular bodies, flat bottoms, and slightly constricted mouths.
Small rounded lugs sticking straight up from rim. (Rare)
Flat square bottoms common.
Vessels with four legs. (Rare)
Cambered rims. (Rare)
Rims thickened by exterior strap of clay. (Common)
Square lips and lips with a flattened surface in the plane of the mouth of the vessel. (Common)

Other artifacts found in Marksville village site collections:

Pottery platform pipes.
Boat stones.
Notched and stemmed projectile points.
One-flake flint knives.

Sites of the Marksville complex

Site No. 103, Marksville

E½ irreg. S. 64, T2N, R4E

The site from which the Marksville complex of pottery decorations is named is situated one-half mile east of Marksville in Avoyelles Parish, Louisiana. It stands on the eastern edge of the Marksville Prairie. Here the limits of the prairie are marked by thirty-five foot bluffs that run north and south. Against these bluffs lies an old stream channel, Old River, which was probably formed originally by the Mississippi. Later it may have been occupied by Red River. At present Old River is a shallow slough, about a hundred yards wide.

Four mounds, situated in an area that is enclosed with an earth wall or ramp, form the Marksville site proper. The ramp is four or five feet high for most of its course and curves to touch the bluffs with both its ends which are one-half mile apart. The enclosed space is half an elongated oval. There are several openings or gateways in the wall. The mounds are in the northern part of the enclosure. The northernmost one is a large truncated structure about three hundred feet in diameter and ten feet high. A short distance to the south are two conicals: one fifty feet in diameter and four feet high; the other has a diameter of ninety feet and is twenty feet high. Southeast of these and nearer the bluffs is an irregularly shaped structure that approximates ten feet in height and covers about an acre. The most profuse outcrop of midden material is exposed in the field between this last mound and the bluffs. It is mostly from here that the survey collections have come.

The Marksville site was first described and excavated by the late Gerard Fowke in 1927. His report has been published and the map which he included is the source of the measurements given above.[76] Fowke's attention was mainly centered on the steep conical mound (Fowke's mound number 4) which he excavated by means of a twenty-foot trench cut in from the southeastern side. Several burials and artifacts were recovered. These are described in Fowke's reports and later the pottery from mound 4 was given detailed attention by Setzler.[77]

Mound 4 was re-excavated in the fall of 1933 by Setzler assisted by the writer. More material was discovered. It was determined that some of the burials recovered by Fowke had been enclosed in a large square burial vault of earth which was covered by layers of canes and clay. This central chamber occupied the larger part of the mound.

---

[76] Fowke, Gerard, Explorations in the Red River Valley in Louisiana.

[77] Setzler, F. M., Hopewell Type Pottery from Louisiana.

DESCRIPTION OF SHERDS IN FIGURE 42

Sherd	Type	Color of Paste	Finish (Good, Medium, Poor)	Temper	Hardness (Hard, Medium, Soft)	Thickness (inches)	Remarks
			PERIOD I—MARKSVILLE				
a	$81;\frac{28}{73};9$	Grey	M	Grit	M	.2	Cambered rim
b	$81;\frac{28}{73};9$	Black	M	Grit	M	.2	Cambered rim
d	$31;\frac{23}{101/102};\frac{1}{2}$	Black	M	Grit	M	.2	Square lip
e	$31;\frac{23}{101/102};\frac{1}{2}$	Buff	M	Grit, vegetable	M	.3	....
f	$31;\frac{23}{101/102};\frac{1}{2}$	Black	M	Grit	M	.2	Square lip
g	$31;\frac{23}{101/102};\frac{1}{2}$	Black	M	Grit	M	.3	....
h	$31;\frac{23}{101/102};\frac{1}{2}$	Grey	P	Grit	M	.3	Blackened interior
j	$31;\frac{23}{101/102};\frac{1}{2}$	Black	M	Grit	S	.2	....
k	$31;\frac{23}{101/102};\frac{1}{2}$	Grey	M	Vegetable	M	.2	....
l	45;23;6	Black	P	....	M	.1	....
m	$31;\frac{23}{73};2$	Light blue	P	Grit	M	.1	....
n	45;23;6	Grey	M	Vegetable	M	.3	....
p	45;23;6	Grey	M	Grit	M	.2	....
s	45;23;6	Black	M	Grit	M	.3	....
			INDETERMINATE				
c	....	Grey	M	Grit	M	,2	Rim
i	....	Buff	M	Grit	M	.2	Shell imprints
o	....	Grey	M	Vegetable	M	.2	Square lip
q	Small boat stone, rough, made of limestone						....
r	Fragment of square bottom, black, vegetable temper					.3	....

Material from Marksville (Site No. 103).

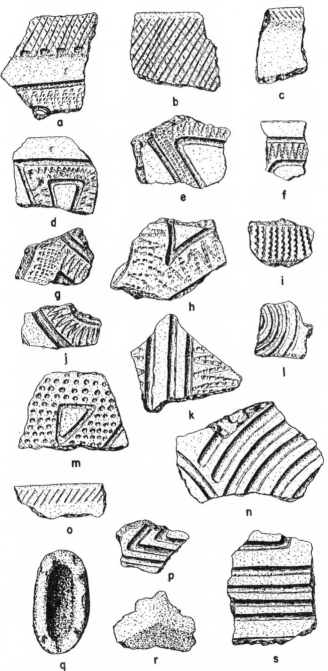

Figure 42. Selection of representative material from the
Marksville village site collections.

229

Further excavations were made in the large truncate mound 6, and in various parts of the village site. In the area of midden exposure east of the irregularly shaped mound, indications of a dwelling were found. It was small, square in shape, and sunken slightly beneath the old surface of the ground. In the middle of the floor was a square pit with postholes in the corners that extended six feet below the floor of the structure.

The shapes of the vessels from mound 4 are very simple. Beakers with flat bottoms, either square or circular in shape are most common. Most of the others are pots with flat, square bottoms, bulging sides that are sometimes four-lobed, and with slightly constricted openings and low necks. Some of the necks are thinner than the vessel walls, and have a slight outward camber. The ware is .2 to .3 inches in thickness, grit tempered, and has a soapy texture that takes a smooth finish and sometimes a polish.

Two types of decoration predominated: (1) wide, deep, smooth lines placed closely together and forming curvilinear patterns of birds, or in one case a true scroll; (2) decorations formed by alternate plain bands, and bands of linear or zigzagged rouletting, bordered by the characteristic lines that usually described the bird motif. A small cup of an unusual shape that might be called two-lobed, bore both types of decoration—one on each lobe. In some cases the decoration covers the sides of the vessels, but in others it extends also under the bottoms. The body decorations generally stop a short distance below the rim. On several of the vessels an upper border is formed by parallel rows of alternate dots and dashes. Some cambered necks are unornamented; others bear crossline patterns formed with lines much finer than those employed in body decorations.

More detailed descriptions of this pottery, from which this rough summary has been liberally borrowed, will be found in the two articles referred to in the footnotes on page 227.

Other material recovered from this mound includes pottery platform pipes.

Setzler's detailed report is now in preparation, and will serve to clarify the picture of this very important site.

The surface collections which are used in this paper were made from the midden exposure in the fields near the bank of Old River. It includes 135 sherds. A representative selection is shown in Figure 42 and is described on the page opposite the figure. Comparison of type percentages is shown in the table, Figure 1. It will be noticed that there is a higher percentage of the delicate cross-lined rims from this location than is found on other sites of the complex.

Site No. 91, Greenhouse place

Four-fifths of a mile north of the Marksville enclosure are seven mounds located on the Alfred Greenhouse place, just east of the Marksville Prairie bluffs, in the flat bottom land along Old River. Fowke's plat shows these as mounds 14 to 20. Four of these structures are truncated pyramids. The other three are conical. They are arranged as though grouped about an open court four hundred feet in diameter.

The few sherds, excavated from mound 18 by Fowke and illustrated by Setzler as plate 6 of "Pottery of the Hopewell Type from Louisiana", are all Coles Creek types. The objects shown as "B" in the same plate are identical with the clay balls found at the Neal place (Site No. 92, Figure 40 v). In 1932 Winslow Walker made a collection of seventy-three sherds from about the Greenhouse mounds which is in the National Museum.[78] This is the material used here. As shown in the comparison table (Figure 1), Coles Creek types are present as

[78]Walker, Winslow, A Reconnaissance of Northern Louisiana Mounds, p. 172.

DESCRIPTION OF SHERDS IN FIGURE 43

Sherd	Type	Color of Paste	Finish (Good, Medium, Poor)	Temper	Hardness (Hard, Medium, Soft)	Thickness (inches)	Remarks
			PERIOD III—CADDO				
a	$34; \frac{21}{21/64}; 1$	Buff	G	Char., Grit	M	.2	Scratched lines, carina bowl
			PERIOD II—COLES CREEK				
f	63;101	Grey	M	Grit	M	.3	Rim
b	11;81	Grey	R	Grit	H	.3	....
			PERIOD I—MARKSVILLE				
g	45;23;6	Black	M	Grit, Veg.	M	.3	....
h	$31; \frac{23}{73}; 2$	Grey	M	Vegetable	M	.3	....
i	$31; \frac{23}{73}; 2$	Black	M	Grit	M	.2	Rim
j	45;23;6	Grey	M	Grit	M	.2	Thickened rim
k	45;23;6	Grey	M	Veg., Grit	H	.3	....
l	$31; \frac{23}{101/102}; \frac{1}{2}$	Grey	M	Veg., Grit	M	.2	....
m	$31; \frac{23}{101/102}; \frac{1}{2}$	Light blue	M	Vegetable	M	.2	....
n	45;23;6	Buff	M	Sand	S	.2	....
o	$31; \frac{23}{101/102}; \frac{1}{2}$	Light blue	M	Vegetable	M	.2	....
p	$31; \frac{23}{101/102}; \frac{1}{2}$	Light blue	M	Vegetable	M	.2	Narrow mouthed pot
q	$31; \frac{23}{101/102}; \frac{1}{2}$	Grey	P	Veg., Grit	M	.3	Square lip, beaker
r	$31; \frac{23}{101/102}; \frac{1}{2}$	Dark blue	M	Grit	M	.2	....
			INDETERMINATE				
c	11;41	Grey	R	Grit	M	.3	....
d	51;21	Grey	R	Grit	M	.2	....
e	51;21	Grey	R	Grit	M	.2	Rim

Material from Yokena (Site No. 97).

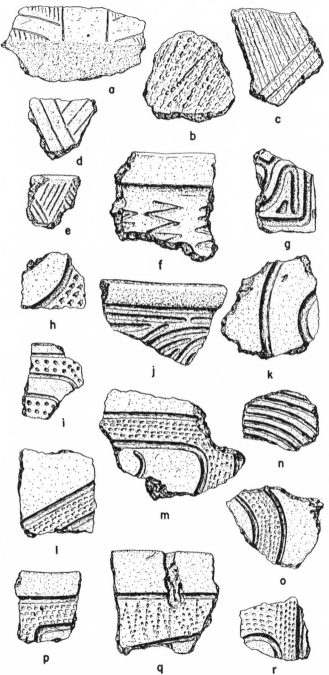

Figure 43. Selection of representative material from Yokena village site collection (Site No. 97.)

233

well as Marksville. On this basis it seems correct to consider this as a separate site from the one enclosed by earthworks at the Marksville site proper.

Site No. 97, Yokena site

W½ irreg. S35, T14N, R2E

This is an old village located at the foot of the bluffs that form the western limits of the elevated prairie east of the Mississippi River. It is situated on talus slopes just above spring flood level. The tracks of the Yazoo and Mississippi Valley Railroad run nearby, and the site is one and one-half miles south of the station from which it is named: Yokena, Warren county, Mississippi. The Glass mound group, excavated by C. B. Moore, is four miles to the north (page 69). Two miles east is the Ring Cemetery, excavated by the writer (page 69).

The group is composed of three mounds. The largest is a pyramidal structure approximately three hundred feet square at the base, twenty-five feet high and with steep sides. It has a summit plateau about one hundred feet square. A graded approach goes up the eastern side of the mound. Part of the western side has been destroyed by an old railroad cut which was abandoned when the tracks were moved to their present location between the mounds and the bluff. The two smaller mounds lie one hundred yards to the west. The largest of these is oblong in shape, and about twelve feet high. While the other has been disfigured by cultivation, it appears to have been a conical and is now seven feet high.

Midden material was found in the plowed fields around the mounds. Trial holes did not find sherds deeper than ten inches, and the entire deposit seems to be superficial. Eighty-six sherds are classified from this site (Figure 1). Illustrations of the material are given in figure 43, and the pieces shown are described on the page opposite the plate. It will be noted that while sherds of the Marksville complex are in the majority, there are present types of the Deasonville, Coles Creek, and Natchez complexes. It is possible that the Natchez sherds were added while that tribe was in possession of the surrounding area, and are not part of the original deposition on the site.

Site No. 99, Fredricks place

E½S33, T11N, R6W

This village site is on Mr. Jesse Fredrick's place on the north side of Red River a short distance below Natchitoches, La. It was found by Miss Caroline Dormon who assisted in making a surface collection. The pottery was all of the Marksville complex. This was something of a surprise since it was not previously known that the Marksville complex had extended so far up the Red River.

The site consists of a rich midden deposit and a single conical mound seventy feet in diameter and twelve feet high, located on a fifteen-foot bluff bordering the eastern side of Clear Lake. Clear Lake is a narrow drowned stream channel that was formed into a lake as a result of the Red River raft. Since this is not far from the town of Natchitoches, Louisiana, which was placed at the foot of the raft in 1714, the small lake cannot be very old. It is easily possible that the site may have been established before the formation of the lake.

The ridge which the site occupies has been in cultivation for a number of years. The midden material consists of the usual black earth, mussel shells, fragments of animal bones, sherds, and a few chips of flint. Apparently the mound has not been plowed over. It has rather steep sides and its shape is definitely conical.

Excepting two sherds of Deasonville and one of Coles Creek, the decorated material may all be referred to the Marksville complex.

236

DESCRIPTION OF SHERDS IN FIGURE 44

Sherd	Type	Color of Paste	Finish (Good, Medium, Poor)	Temper	Hardness (Hard, Medium, Soft)	Thickness (inches)	Remarks
			PERIOD II—DEASONVILLE				
b	11;81;14	Dark blue	M	Vegetable	M	.2	....
			COLES CREEK				
a	61;24;6	Black	M	Grit	M	.2	....
n	....	Dark blue	M	Grit	M	.2	Corner of square bottom
			PERIOD I—MARKSVILLE				
c	$31;\dfrac{23}{101/102};\frac{1}{2}$	Black	M	Grit	M	.3	Thickened rim
d	$31;\dfrac{}{73};2$	Light blue	M	Grit	M	.2	....
e	Same as d	Black	M	Grit	M	.3	Rim
f	$31;\dfrac{23}{101/102};\frac{1}{2}$	Dark blue	M	Vegetable	M	.2	....
h	$31;\dfrac{23}{101/102};\frac{1}{2}$	Dark blue	M	Grit	M	.2	....
i	Same as h	Black	M	Grit	M	.2	Rim
j	Same type	Grey	M	Grit	M	.2	Rim
k	45;23;6	Dark blue	M	Grit	M	.1	....
l	51;23	Buff	M	Grit	M	.2	....
m	51;23	Grey	M	Grit	M	.2	....
			INDETERMINATE				
g	....	Tan	M	Grit	M	.2	....

Material from Churupa plantation (Site No. 102).

Sherd	Type	Color of Paste	Finish	Temper	Hardness	Thickness	Remarks
			PERIOD I—MARKSVILLE				
o	45;23;6	Black	M	Vegetable	M	.2	Wide mouthed pot
p	45;23;6	Grey	M	Grit	M	.2	....
q	45;23;6	Dark blue	M	Veg., Grit	M	.2	Notched rim
r	45;23;6	Grey	M	Vegetable	M	.2	....
s	45;23;6	Black	M	Grit	M	.2	....
t	$31;\dfrac{23}{101/102};\frac{1}{2}$	Grey	M	Vegetable	M	.3	....
u	$31;\dfrac{}{73};2$	Grey	M	Sand	M	.3	....
v	Same as u	Grey	M	Vegetable	M	.3	....
w	Part of clay platform pipe						
x	....	Grey	M	Grit	S	.3	Square bottom
y	....	Grey	M	Grit	M	.2	Small lug

Material from Fredericks plantation (Site No. 99).

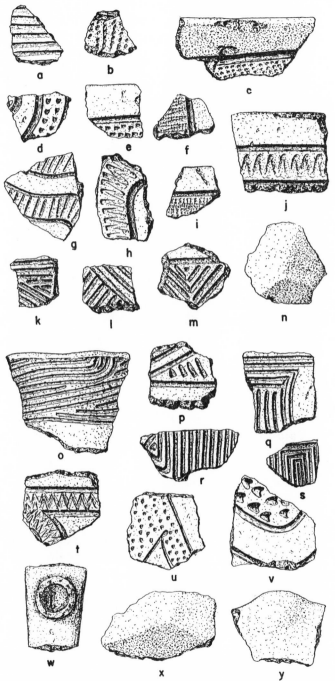

Figure 44. Selection of representative material from Churupa plantation (Sherds a-n) and Fredericks place (Sherds o-y).

237

Site No. 102, Churupa plantation

S½S29, T8N, R8E

This site is located in Concordia Parish, Louisiana, seven miles west of Ferriday and two miles north of Frogmore. It forms part of a very interesting geographical situation that has possibilities of demonstrating time relationships (Map, Figure 45). The site consists of a conical mound about ninety feet in diameter and ten feet high, located on the east side of the local road running north from Frogmore. Midden material is thinly scattered over the cultivated field south of the mound. Sherds from here are very small in size. This condition probably indicates long cultivation in recent times. Material other than pottery was very scarce.

As figure 45 shows, the site on Churupa plantation is one of a series of four mounds, spaced a mile or two apart, that are strung along the edge of a slightly elevated natural levee bordering an old meander of Mississippi River size. Fragments of natural levees and channel traces lie between this ridge and the present Tensas River two miles to the west. The Tensas occupies an old river bed which has meanders of Mississippi size. It appears that these sites were occupied at a time when either the Tensas or perhaps even the Mississippi ran through the now almost closed channel called at present Brushy Bayou. After that channel had filled up and the Tensas took its present course two miles to the west, the sites would probably have been abandoned.

Unfortunately surface material from the Frogmore, Elkhorn, and Cypress Grove plantation sites was very scanty. The only adequate collection is from the Churupa site. Chronological comparison can be made with the Dunbarton plantation site six miles north of Churupa. Here there is a small conical mound eighty feet in diameter and six feet high. A collection of sherds was made from the plowed fields around the mound. Another

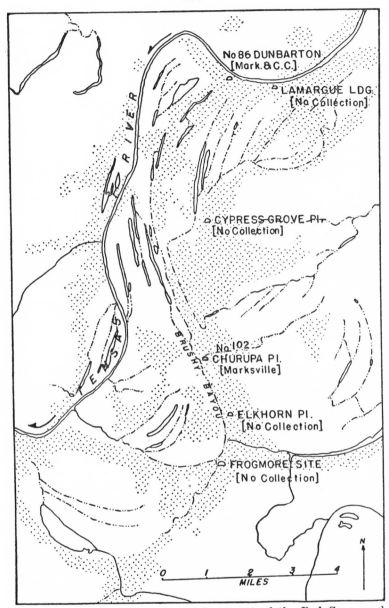

Figure 45. Map reproduced from part of the Red Gum quad-rangle, Mississippi River Commission, showing village sites scattered along an old course of the large stream whose channel is now occupied by the Tensas River. Dotted areas are natural levees.

mound, the shape of which has been destroyed by cultivation, is situated one-half mile to the east at Lamarque Landing, also on the Tensas. No material was found in the fields about this latter structure.

As is shown by the meander traces indicated in the map (Figure 45), the old natural levee, on which is situated the Churupa plantation site and the others of that series, was abandoned by the active stream. The river moved about two miles to the west. The Dunbarton plantation site is located near the present channel of the river, and is at the point where the stream pivoted in the western migration of this meander.

This condition indicates the possibility that if the channel of the river was shifting while the village sites were occupied, it was possible for the Dunbarton plantation site to have been inhabited longer than those strung along the old natural levee. These latter sites were left inland away from the river while conditions were unchanged for the Dunbarton site.

Comparison of the surface collections from Churupa (Site No. 102, Figure 1) and Dunbarton (Site No. 86, Figure 1) shows that the pottery from the site on the old abandoned levee is of the Marksville complex. The collection from Dunbarton plantation, at a point where conditions remained unchanged, has pottery of both the Marksville and the Coles Creek complexes.

Anderson Landing, Mississippi

Clarence B. Moore illustrates two vessels from a mound near Anderson Landing, Sharkey County, Mississippi, that show very definite Marksville features.[79] One is a four-lobed jar with a flat bottom. On the rim is a band of delicate crosshatching underlined with a row of hemi-conical punctates. The body is covered with bands of rouletting bordered by wide, rounded lines, and con-

---

[79]Moore, C. B. Certain Mounds of Arkansas and Mississippi, figs. 3-5.

trasted with undecorated bands of equal width. The other vessel has a similar rim treatment but the body is covered with three conventionalized bird figures made with the usual wide, rounded lines. No rouletting was employed. Neither of these vessels was shell tempered. What else Moore may have recovered from Anderson Landing is not detailed. The site has not been visited by the Mississippi survey party.

DESCRIPTION OF MARKSVILLE COMPLEX SITES

Site No.	Site Name	Burials: Cemetery	Burials: Mounds	Conical Low −10'	Conical Tall +10'	Pyramidal Low −10'	Pyramidal Tall +10'	Pyramidal Ramp	Enclosure	Midden Approximate Area	Midden Thin −10"	Midden Thick +10"	Collection Analysis	Minimum Date
97	*Yokena Site				2		1	x	x	4A	x		Natchez, Tunica, Coles Creek, Deasonville, Marksville	
98	Hill Pl.									4A	x		Marksville	
99	*Fredericks Pl.				1		1			2A		x	Marksville	
100	McIntosh Pl.			3			1			3A		x	Marksville	
101	Smithfield Pl.			1						4A	x		Marksville	
102	*Churupa Pl.				1		1			2A		x	Marksville	
103	*Marksville Site			1			1	2	x	20A		x	Marksville	

*Sites which are described in the text and from which material is illustrated.

Unrelated pottery types

The types and features of pottery decoration that are classed as "unrelated" are either those which do not appear often enough to identify themselves with any of the complexes, or those which appear frequently on sites of all the complexes. In other words, these are types which are not diagnostic; they are as likely to be connected with one complex as another.

Some of the unrelated types may occur promiscuously because their description is very indefinite and may actually include a great range of different decorations. Such a type is 01;71 (irregular arrangement of punctates made with a pointed instrument). These sherds may, and probably did, form part of any number of different decorations. Other types are probably indiscriminate because of their extreme simplicity. Sherds of type 11;41 (regularly brushed surfaces) were simple and very easy to execute. They may have been spread over a large area in a number of different complexes and may have existed practically unchanged for a long time.

Still other types appear to be typologically related to some one of the complexes, but do not occur frequently enough to prove their relationship. Type $\frac{61;24}{81;25}$; 8 is certainly such a case. Obviously it is a Coles Creek type, and is closely related to type $\frac{61;24}{81;25}$; 6. All of the features are Coles Creek, yet it does not occur frequently enough to be placed in the column of Coles Creek types.

Unrelated decorations

Type 01;71

01   Motif: Uncertain. The features of this type are usually irregularly spaced.

71   Elements: Punctates made with a pointed instrument. This designation is usually applied to very

small fragments which probably, in the majority of cases, are parts of some more complicated decoration of which the stippled surface was merely a part.

Several kinds of vessel paste bear this type. Generally the material is very similar to the rest of the collection in which the pieces occur.

Type 01;72

01   Motif: Uncertain. The features of this type are usually irregularly spaced.

72   Elements: Imprints of the blunt end of a small tubular tool, probably a cane.

This is another case where the pieces included in a type are probably small parts of different and more complicated decorations. The paste and temper of this type are similar to that of the collection in which it is found. It ranges all the way from the hard fine-texture ware of the Coles Creek complex to the porous shell tempered ware found in the historic complexes.

Type 11;41

11   Motif: Features irregularly arranged.

41   Elements: Surface brushed with a bundle of fibres. This type is generally very carelessly executed. The paste is usually fairly light, porous, grit and sand tempered, and varies from grey through brown to black in color.

Type 11;91

11   Motif: Features irregularly arranged.

91   Elements: Application of a paddle, carved to make a waffled surface. Usually referred to as check-stamp pottery.

Usual Accompanying Characteristics:

This decoration is generally applied to the entire exterior of the vessels on which it occurs.

The shape of the vessels so decorated is uncertain. They seem usually to have been small urns with rounded bottoms. The rims usually rise straight to the lip. In some cases the lips have been thickened by turning over a strap of clay one-half to one inch wide.

No appendages have been found.

The paste is fairly hard and is sandy. No other tempering material was used. The color of the ware is grey, buff, salmon, or black. No slips were used, but firing often left the exteriors a different color from the interiors.

The vessels were built by the coiling process as is shown by their tendency to break along the lines of juncture.

This pottery is recognized as belonging to the Louisiana Gulf Coast province. A number of collections that have been secured from the Louisiana area, as well as along the coast to western Florida, show this type.

Type 11;92

11 Motif: Irregular arrangement of features.

92 Elements: Application of a paddle carved with curvilinear designs. These designs are of various types, but as the material is so scanty, there has been no attempt to separate them.

Usual Accompanying Characteristics:

The shape of the vessels with this decoration is uncertain. The side walls extend straight to the rim lip. Sometimes the lip was thickened on the outside by bending over a strap of clay.

The paste is fairly hard. No tempering material other than sand was used. Paste colors range through shades of grey, buff, salmon, and black.

This decoration occurs very commonly in the states bordering the Atlantic seaboard.

Type 51;21

51 Motif: Chain of isosceles triangles. Alternate triangles are inverted and nested to form a solid band of decoration. The triangles are filled with straight lines parallel to one of the ascending sides. Every other triangle has its parallel lines parallel to the opposite ascending side.

21 Elements: Lines drawn with a pointed instrument.

The execution of this type is generally rather rough and careless.

Usual Accompanying Characteristics:

This decoration appears on different wares which are peculiar to the complex in which the type is found rather than to the type itself. Where it occurs in the Coles Creek complex, the vessels are likely to be square bottomed beakers of fine, hard, grit tempered paste. In the historic horizon it appears on globular pots with handles made of a rough, light, shell-tempered ware.

Type 51; $\frac{21}{71}$;11

51   Motif: Chain of triangular shaped areas around vessel. Alternate triangles are inverted and nested to form a solid band of decoration.

21   Elements: Lines incised with a pointed instrument. These are used to outline the triangular areas and are used as straight lines to fill in alternate triangles.

71   Element: Punctates made with a pointed instrument. These are irregularly arranged and are used as stippling to fill the areas enclosed in every other triangle.

11   Arrangement: Features are used alternately. One of the triangles is filled with the straight parallel lines, the next with punctates, etc. Very little care was used in executing the decoration or in finishing the ware. The usual accompanying vessel shape is uncertain. Where it has been found in the historic complexes, the shape was often the globular pot with handles, light porous paste, and shell tempering. In the Coles Creek the beaker is probably the usual shape.

Type 52;21;2

52   Motif: V-shaped flags arranged around the vessel.

21   Element: Lines incised with a pointed instrument. These outline the flags and are also used as straight, parallel lines to fill the enclosed areas. The lines are drawn parallel to one of the ascending limbs of the triangular figures.

2   Arrangement: The decoration is brought out in positive, and is shaded with the parallel lines while the background is plain.

The usual shape of the vessels with this decoration is not consistent. In at least one case in the historic horizon it is found on the globular, shell-tempered pot.

Type 60;21/27;13

60   Motif: Features are arranged parallel to one another.

Either 21   Element: Lines incised with a pointed instrument,

Or   27   Element: Lines scratched with a pointed instrument after the paste had become hard.

13   Arrangement: Decoration is found on the interiors of sherds.

Usually the execution is rather careless; lines are uneven. It is found on sherds which appear to be parts of the bottoms of vessels. Evidently these are shallow bowls. The paste and texture are similar to the types prevailing in the collection in which these pieces occur.

Type $\dfrac{61;24}{81;25};8$

61   Motif of body decoration: Features arranged parallel to one another and parallel to the vessel lip.

24   Elements: Overhanging lines.

8   Arrangement: Only one or two lines are used. These are spaced not more than one-half of an inch apart.

81   Motif of rim decoration: Features appear in the flat top of straight, square rim.

25   Elements: One or more incised lines with punctates spaced in them.

The execution of this type is generally rather neat.

Usual Accompanying Characteristics:

The body decoration forms a band about the upper part of the vessel walls. No border is left between the decoration and the rim. Rims are straight and usually nearly vertical.

Beakers and shallow bowls with straight, vertical sides appear to be the most common shapes. In a few cases the rim is thickened on the outside by a strap of clay that extends one-half to one inch below the lip. The incised lines are made in this thickened area. No appendages are found. The shape of the vessel bottoms is not known.

In texture this ware is smooth, fine grained, and hard. Although it does not have a polished finish the surface is smooth and slightly "soapy". The color varies through shades of gray, brown, and black. No slips are found.

This decoration is typologically related to the Coles Creek complex. Only on the basis of its scattered occurrence is it put in the column of Unrelated Types.

Type 62;21

62   Motif: Features parallel to one another and all drawn at a fifty-five degree angle to the vessel rim.

21   Elements: Lines incised with a pointed instrument.

This decoration occurs on the types of ware common to the collection in which it is found.

There is a very good probability that small sherds of this type are fragments of more complicated decorations involving parallel lines drawn at a forty-five degree angle to the rim.

Type 81;51

81   Motif: Features are placed in the top of vessel lip.

51   Elements: Deep notches pressed into the lip while the vessel paste was plastic.

The execution of this type is usually careless. Notches were unevenly spaced, and the displaced clay was not smoothed off. The rims are straight and in most cases were probably vertical. No other decoration is found on these sherds.

The paste of this type is similar to that of the collection in which the sherds occur.

Type $\dfrac{84;52}{11;41}$

84   Motif of rim decorations: Features placed on the outside edge of straight rims with squared lips.

52   Elements: Shallow notches impressed while the vessel paste was plastic.

11   Motif of body decoration: Irregular application of features.

41   Element: Brush marks made with a bundle of fibres. The type is generally carelessly executed, and the vessels are roughly finished. The paste is usually light and porous, sand and grit tempered, and is either grey, brown, or black in color.

The shape is uncertain.

CONCLUSIONS

The foregoing should give an idea as to the methods employed and the results obtained from the Louisiana and Mississippi surveys. It is hoped that the material is described in sufficient detail to be of service to future workers in the region, regardless of how factual the following theories may prove.

Although the avowed intention of the work was to attempt to establish some sort of chronological sequence for the region through studies of village-site collections, at its initiation there was no idea as to how this might be done. The standard method of vertical stratigraphic study was in mind, of course, to be applied where it might prove feasible, but most of the other reasonings presented here developed or were perceived as a result of the work.

The arguments pointing to a chronological relationship of the village sites that have been described are to a large degree based on the table of type percentages resulting from classification (Figure 1), and upon the map showing the geographical distribution of the sites (Figure 2).

Existence of complexes

Part of the conclusions has already been given as the outline of presentation. Division of the collection material into complexes is based on the marked tendency for certain groups of specific decorations to form the major part of the material from a substantial number of geographically separated village sites. This is clearly shown in the comparative table, (Figure 1). It is seen that the collections from four sites are predominantly of the Choctaw type; three of the Natchez types; thirteen of the Caddo; five of the Tunica; twenty-three of the Deasonville; fifteen of the Coles Creek; and seven of the Marksville. These different associations of types are repeated

249

often enough to demonstrate that they are not fortuitous but really are the products of distinct and definite complexes of ceramic art styles.

The number of different decoration types in the seven complexes ranges from only one in the Choctaw to as many as thirty-six in Coles Creek. However, a notable condition is apparent in the collections representing each complex. Certain types tend to form the dominant percentage and to occur most consistently at the different sites. These have already been discussed in the introduction, where they are given the name of "marker types". In the comparative table, figure 1, percentages of the marker types are identified by being brought out bolder than the other type percentages.

It is a very fortunate fact that nearly all the marker types are distinctive. There is little possibility of confusing them with the other decorations. For the most part they are so complex that the possibilities of an aboriginal artist making any one of them entirely by chance are practically nil.

For these reasons marker types are regarded as the most diagnostic decorations of each complex. They are especially useful where there is any question of trade or influence of one complex upon another. The chances are that, as they are numerically dominant in their own group, they will be the subjects rather than one of the less common types. As they are readily recognized, marker types serve as the best proofs of such occurrences.

Age differentiation of complexes

Old sites, the remains of which comprise a complex that is entirely uninfluenced by other complexes, are supposed to be the results of one of two kinds of isolation: either geographical segregation with all intercourse cut off, or a difference in the time periods of their existence. The point has been argued that two entirely distinct cultures might exist contemporaneously at different sites, intermingled in the same area, with no indication of inter-influence appearing. This seems rather improbable. If any other reasonable hypothesis can be developed to fit the situation, it is certainly preferable.

In this study the geographic factor is known. (See map, Figure 2). Sites of the Natchez complex (Nos. 5-7), certain of the Coles Creek sites (Nos. 61-75), and several Marksville sites (Nos. 98, 99, 101, 102, and 103) are situated in the same general region of southwestern Mississippi and the adjacent part of Louisiana. Referring to figure 1, it is seen that there is no indication of interinfluence or trade among these complexes. Northward an analogous condition is found in the lower Yazoo River valley in Mississippi, where the unrelated complexes are represented by the Tunica sites (Nos. 21-25), the Deason-ville sites (Nos. 26-48), and not far to the west, in Louisiana, is situated a Marksville site (Site No. 100). A possible Marksville site was excavated at Anderson Landing on Sunflower River, by C. B. Moore (page 240). Since Natchez, Coles Creek, and Marksville sites are found in the same geographical area and show no evidence of interinfluence, they evidently existed at different time periods. The same applies for the Tunica, Deasonville, and Marksville.

The sites of the Choctaw complex (Nos. 1, 2, 3) are found in eastern Mississippi. (This excepts Site No. 4 which resulted from a historical westward movement of the Choctaw about 1850). Although that section has not been as thoroughly surveyed as the central part of the area, there is enough evidence to show that at least part of the region was covered by the Deasonville (see Sites Nos. 26, 27, 38, 42, 48, 59).

Caddo sites (Nos. 8-20) are found in northwestern Louisiana around the Red River. This is another part of the area that has been somewhat neglected by the surveys, but it is known that at least one Marksville site is situated in the Caddo territory (Site No. 99).

The decoration complexes named after the tribes of the Choctaw, Natchez, Caddo, and Tunica form the historic horizon and are known to have been in existence as late as 1700. This argues that Coles Creek, Deasonville, and Marksville must then be prehistoric.

Evidence of interinfluence among complexes

As the converse of the above assumption that the consistent lack of interrelation indicates time difference, it is expected that complexes existing at the same time, not necessarily in the same area but even in neighboring areas, should show evidence of trade. The first place to look for this is, of course, in the historic complexes which are known to be contemporaneous. The evidence is not as abundant as might be expected. One sherd of a marker type of the Tunica was found on a Choctaw site (Site No. 1), but no material of the other historic complexes. The Natchez sites show small amounts of the Tunica marker types and less of the Caddo types. Only one sherd of Choctaw was found on one of the Natchez sites (Site No. 5). Caddo sites show small amounts of both Natchez and Tunica, but no marker types in either case. The best evidence of the relationship of certain types of the Natchez and Caddo lies in the occurrence of ware of both complexes in the historic burial site at Angola farm (see page 129). Tunica collections contain Natchez, Caddo, and one site (Site No. 24) shows two sherds of Choctaw.

Interinfluence is more obvious in the prehistoric complexes. This may be the result of larger and more numerous collections. From the table (Figure 1) it is apparent that Coles Creek (Sites Nos. 61-75) exerted a relatively small but consistent influence on the Deasonville sites (Nos. 26-48), and vice versa. The marker types of the two complexes generally furnish this evidence. A remarkable case of adoption of neighboring ideas is found at several Coles Creek sites. Cord marking—more neatly executed than at Deasonville sites—is applied to the lower parts of vessels which bear typical Coles Creek decorations on the upper part of their walls (Figure 35 n, p). This is interpreted as indicating that for a part of the time at least, Deasonville and Coles Creek were contemporaneous.

The seven village sites, collections of which consist almost entirely of the Marksville decoration types (Sites Nos. 97-103), are scattered rather widely over the central part of the area. A few scattered types of the Deasonville and Coles Creek complexes, and one sherd of a rather indeterminate Natchez type, are the only extraneous elements in the collections. (This excepts Site No. 97, which appears to be a special case, and which will be discussed later). The homogeneity of these sites is further demonstrated by the collections which were excavated from the type site at Marksville by Setzler.[80] Of 1,218 decorated sherds and vessels secured as the results of excavation, all except 4.68 per cent of miscellaneous material can be identified with the Marksville complex. This evidence appears to warrant the hypothesis that at one time the Marksville styles occupied at least the central part of the area without any of the other complexes in close proximity.

From the above it is seen that the seven decoration complexes existed in the area at three general time horizons. The latest or historic horizon (III) included the Choctaw, Natchez, Caddo, and Tunica complexes. One prehistoric horizon included the Deasonville and Coles Creek complexes; the other was occupied solely by the Marksville complex. Considering the distribution of the various sites ascribed to these complexes (Figure 2), the possibilities of this relationship are apparent. At each of the three periods, the area would have been rather evenly populated.

---

[80]Setzler, Marksville; A Louisiana Variant of the Hopewell Culture. Manuscript in preparation. Will be published by the U. S. National Museum.

Overlapping of complexes

In searching for connections between the historic and prehistoric horizons, it will be noted that the sites of the Tunica and Caddo have a conspicuous amount of types that are characteristic of the Coles Creek complex. Also several of the Coles Creek sites show small amounts of Caddo and Tunica marker types. As typical Coles Creek sites are not found in the region of either of the two historic complexes, it is easily possible that at one time Coles Creek may have existed in its geographical area alongside the Caddo and Tunica. The evidence of interinfluence points to this condition. Neither the Choctaw nor the Natchez complexes shows any relation to the Coles Creek or any other of the prehistoric complexes. Evidently the Tunica and Caddo were established in their regions before the Choctaw or the Natchez appeared in the area.

None of the historic complexes show any direct relation to Deasonville. Although at one time it was contemporaneous with Coles Creek, it seems to have disappeared before the advent of either of the two earlier historic complexes, Caddo and Tunica. Tunica took over part of the area that Deasonville had occupied.

If it is true that the Coles Creek-Deasonville time horizon interlocks in this way with the historic horizon, then the time horizon of Marksville complex must have been the earliest of all. This rests, of course, on the assumption that the collecting surveys have secured a sample of all the ceramic complexes in the area. Considering the intensiveness of the work in the Mississippi Valley region, this assumption seems fair for the central part of the area at least. This line of reasoning might be called "complex linking"—connecting time horizons by the overlapping of complexes occupying neighboring areas.

Complexes overlapped by village sites

The second kind of phenomena to be examined deals with the tendency for the period of occupation of specific villages to have extended through the time of two or more subsequent decoration complexes.

The probability that village sites were being settled at different times along the time scale has already been mentioned in the introductory paragraphs. There is certain evidence that the period of time through which the average village was occupied was short in comparison to the length of time covered by the whole time scale. Sites nos. 98 to 103 were settled and were abandoned while the Marksville complex of types was in vogue; sites nos. 61-75 were occupied only during the existence of the Coles Creek which followed the Marksville in the southern part of the area. How true this phenomenon is for most of the other sites may be seen by inspection of the comparative table (Figure 1).

Most village sites have an area of intensive midden deposit ranging from two to five acres in extent. After a site had once been abandoned and had grown up in woods, whether there were earthworks to mark the spot or not, it would be unlikely that a succeeding people should select the exact habitation spot for their use. If the old locality had been intentionally reoccupied, the odds are that the dumps of the succeeding group would be located near but not precisely on those of the original inhabitants. It might also be expected that an indiscriminate mixture of complexes that prove to be subsequent might be found. Such is not the case. Very few examples of apparent reoccupation of old abandoned sites have been found. Since primitive peoples usually have a superstitious fear of old occupation sites, these early inhabitants probably would not have returned to old sites knowingly.

It seems more reasonable to suppose that sites on which apparently subsequent complexes are mixed were either settled in the time of the older and were occupied on into the time of the following complex; or that the villages were inhabited during a period of transition from one complex to the other.

Evidence of this nature is provided by the villages which are found in the Coles Creek area, and whose collections are composed of different proportions of types of the Coles Creek and Marksville complexes (Sites Nos. 76-96). A parallel situation is found in the Deasonville area, where sites nos. 49-60 yield both Marksville and Deasonville. There is a substantial number of these sites in both regions. The condition is accepted as indicating that the villages were inhabited in the time of the Marksville complex, and existed into the later horizon with its two complexes. Whether there was a real transitional period or not is not indicated by this means. If the art styles changed without disturbance of the population, it is reasonable to expect that there should be such a period. There is other evidence that points to a short transitional time in the Coles Creek area at least.[81]

There are few cases that suggest that certain villages were settled in the middle horizon and inhabited on into the time of the historic complexes. Sites nos. 3 and 97 extend all the way through the column. Their collections contain types of all of the complexes that have occurred in their respective regions. There are two possibilities: either they were settled, abandoned, and then re-inhabited, or else they were inhabited continuously. In view of the lack of evidence of other villages having been inhabited continuously through horizons II and III, the former hypothesis seems more probable. Site No. 3, Nanih Waiya, figures in the creation myths of the Choctaw In-

---

[81]Ford, J. A., Ceramic Decoration Sequence at an Old Indian Village Site, near Sicily Island. Most of the deposit at the Peck village site appears to have been laid down during the transition from Marksville to Coles Creek. This is shown by the material from the various vertical midden sections which contain smoothly changing proportions of the two complexes.

dians. One version says that they found the mound there when the people moved into the country from the west. This appears probable (page 45).

There is a hint that possibly the Deasonville complex entered its region and replaced the Marksville complex before the Coles Creek did the same thing in the southern part of the area. This lies in the absence of evidence of Coles Creek influence on most of the sites which yield both the Marksville and Deasonville complexes (Sites Nos. 53-60). On the other hand there is abundant evidence of Deasonville influence on the sites that show the transition from Marksville to Coles Creek. This negative evidence is only suggestive. Beyond the fact that there are only eight collections from Marksville plus Deasonville sites is the fact that several of the sites are located at a distance from the Coles Creek area.

However, the stratigraphic study at the Peck village site (Site No. 95) seems to point to the same thing. As the cuts descended into the midden, there was a decided tendency for the proportion of the Coles Creek to decrease. The few Deasonville types were scattered but occurred from the top to the bottom, with no decided tendency either to become more or less numerous. After all, it would be a remarkable coincidence if both the Coles Creek and the Deasonville should have supplanted the Marksville complex in their respective areas at identically the same time. Further work should clear up this minor point. Excavation at a Marksville plus Deasonville site might yield pertinent information.

Direct evidence for parts of chronology

The chronological relationships of the complexes as indicated by the lines of argument just considered are diagrammed in figure 50. In several points this sequence is supported by more direct evidence.

The stratigraphic excavation at the Peck site (Site No. 95, which was published as Anthropological Study No.

1 of this series) shows that the Coles Creek complex followed Marksville in the valley region of central Louisiana. The writer examined the collection made by Winslow Walker from excavations of the large mound at Jonesville (surface collection given as Site No. 89). Walker found large quantities of both Marksville and Coles Creek material on the surface. From the interior of the mound and from the old surface at the base of the mound, he collected 75 decorated sherds. All were of the Marksville types. A detailed report of this work will be published by the United States National Museum. Additional evidence on this same point may lie in the geographical positions of the Churupa (Site No. 102) and Dunbarton (Site No. 86) villages. This possibility has already been discussed on page 238.

The comparative ages of the Deasonville complex and the sites that are referred to as the Big Black series (provisionally assigned to the Tunica complex) are found at the Gross plantation, page 121. This situation indicates that Deasonville pottery is older than the Tunica varieties found in the Big Black mounds.

The recent reports of Lemley[52] and Dickinson[53] on the excavation of the Crenshaw site on the Red River in Miller County, Arkansas, leave little doubt as to the relative chronological positions of the Coles Creek and Caddo ceramic complexes in that area. Both from illustrations of the material, and from Dickinson's descriptions and comparisons, it is possible to identify the older "Pre-Caddo" pottery with the material that in Louisiana is ascribed to the Coles Creek complex. It is probable that a potsherd collection from the Crenshaw site made by the methods used in this study would be directly comparable to the Caddo sites numbered 12-20 in figure 1; that is, it would show a proportion of both Caddo and Coles Creek types.

---

[52]Lemley, Harry J., Discoveries Indicating a Pre-Caddo Culture on Red River in Arkansas.

[53]Dickinson, S. D., The Ceramic Relationships of the Pre-Caddo Pottery from the Crenshaw Site.

Overlapping of decorations

Certain vessel features and a few decoration types tend to overlap several complexes, both horizontally and vertically. At the same time they mark a distinct difference between the two ends of the time scale. Notable are the features of shell tempering, handles, knobs, carinated bowls, bottles, and scratched lines used in decoration. These are common in horizon III. They are found more frequently in Caddo and Tunica complexes than in Choctaw and Natchez, but they occur in all. Handles and shell tempering are found at a few of the Deasonville (horizon II) sites but not in all. None of these features appear in either the Coles Creek (horizon II) or the Marksville (horizon I) complexes.

On the other hand, the features of square bottomed vessels and platform pipes are restricted almost entirely to the Coles Creek and the Marksville complex sites. Square bottoms are found on a few vessels from the Big Black River series of sites (horizon III). While the material from these sites refers to the Tunica complex for the most part, there is strong indication of Coles Creek (horizon II) influence (page 125).

Beaker-shaped vessels predominate in Marksville (I) and Coles Creek (II), but are scarce in the historic horizon (III). In the Natchez and Choctaw complexes they are not found at all.

Several decoration types are consistently found in more than one complex. For that reason they have been placed in the "Unrelated" group of types since they do not serve to differentiate the complexes. However, they do serve to tie them together.

Type 01;71 (punctates made with a pointed instrument) is found in all the complexes except the Choctaw. It cannot have much significance, however, as it is very poorly defined and certainly includes many small sherds that form parts of more complicated types.

Type 11;41 (brushed with bundle of fibers) is found in all the complexes except the Choctaw and Natchez. A typologically related decoration occurs in the Natchez (type 64;41). A different variation appears in the Caddo (type 60; $\frac{61/64}{41/21}$).

Type 51;21 (chain of isosceles triangles filled with lines parallel to one ascending leg of triangles. Alternate triangles are inverted and have their parallel lines parallel to the other ascending limb. Lines are made with a pointed instrument). This decoration occurs in all the complexes except the Choctaw. Variations of this are found in two complexes as will be explained below (page 263).

Type 81;51 (Straight rim with deep notches) is found scatteringly in all complexes except the Choctaw and Caddo.

Type 41;21;3 (Scroll formed of a number of incised lines) is found in the Coles Creek, Deasonville, Tunica, and Caddo complexes. A variation occurs in Natchez (type 41;21;5) and what may be another variation is found in Choctaw (type 40;31;4).

The horizontal overlapping of these features into contemporaneous complexes can be attributed either to interinfluence or to a common derivation. The cases of vertical overlapping may be significant from a chronological point of view.

In a primitive culture the life of any specific decoration style may usually be expected to be continuous and uninterrupted. After a type has once been discarded there is slight chance of its coming into vogue again with all of its original peculiarities. Such a phenomenon as the resurrection of the ancient Sikyatki ware by the Hopi woman, Nampeo, is extremely improbable under primitive conditions. Then, cases where a pottery type or feature covers part of a time scale may usually be accepted as indicative that the cultural units (complexes or cultures) including that feature are temporally adjacent to one another.

This reasoning has ignored the possibility that some unknown neighboring decoration complex may be responsible for the presence of the feature. This complex might be removed geographically for a time and then return and again exert its influence in an identical manner. Unless such an unusual circumstance is suggested by other evidence there is little reason to suspect that the simpler condition stated above is not actually the case.

Decoration type evolution

This section will treat certain decoration types which suggest that they are the results of an evolutionary trend

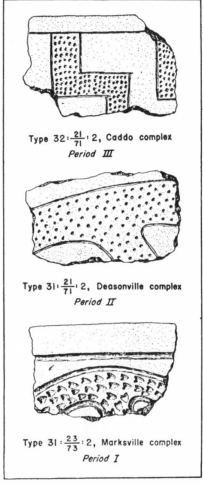

Type 32 : $\frac{21}{71}$: 2, Caddo complex
Period III

Type 31 : $\frac{21}{71}$: 2, Deasonville complex
Period II

Type 31 : $\frac{23}{73}$: 2, Marksville complex
Period I

Figure 46. Possible evolution of decorations from type 31; $\frac{23}{73}$;2.

which runs through two or more of the subsequent complexes. This does not imply that this evolutionary process occurred in the local geographical area. In most cases it is more likely that the evidence is a reflection of the process taking place in some nearby territory.

A simple case is that of type 51;21 mentioned above. In its least specialized form it is found in every complex except the Choctaw, but is most common in horizon III. In addition to this simple form it is found in the Marksville complex as a rim decoration made of wide, deep lines, type 51;23. In the Coles Creek it is usually formed by overhanging lines, type 51;24. The simple type extended all through the column, but also took on, in each complex, the features peculiar to that complex.

Type $31;\dfrac{23}{73};2$ (broad, deep lines enclosing curving bands of hemi-conical punctates, bands often branching) is a Marksville type (horizon I). From it may have developed a type found in the Deasonville complex (horizon II), type $31;\dfrac{21}{71};2$ (curving bands of punctates bordered by incised lines. Both punctates and lines made with a pointed instrument, bands often branch). A still later development of this may be a type found in horizon III, especially in the Caddo complex: type $32;\dfrac{21}{71};2$ (angular bands of punctates bordered by incised lines, both lines and punctates made with a pointed instrument). This possible line of development is illustrated in figure 46.

The Coles Creek (period II) type 63;101 (rouletted or rocker stamp zigzags running perpendicular to vessel rim and placed side by side to form a wide band of decoration about the vessel) appears to have developed from the unnotched rocker (or roulette) stamping confined between broad lines, type 31 ; $\dfrac{23}{101/102}$; 1/2, that is found

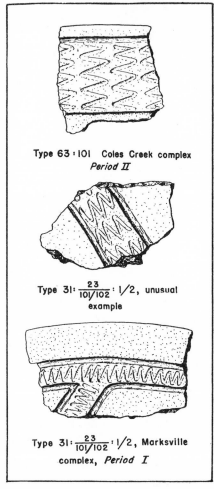

Type 63 ᐧ 101   Coles Creek complex
Period II

Type 31: $\dfrac{23}{101/102}$: 1/2, unusual
example

Type 31: $\dfrac{23}{101/102}$: 1/2, Marksville
complex, *Period I*

Figure 47. Possible evolution of decorations from type 31; $\dfrac{23}{101/102}$; ½.

in the Marksville complex (period I). As found at a few of the sites which yield both complexes, this latter type is effected with zigzagged stamping perpendicular to the axis of the line-enclosed band. This is illustrated by figure 47.

The most common type in the Coles Creek complex, type 61;24;6, is found at Caddo complex sites in northwestern Louisiana. Modifications are also found in which lines made with a pointed instrument are used, type 61;21;6. A few examples of a more localized and peculiar adaptation of the type is effected by the use of lines formed by fingernail markings. Another variant shows alternate incised lines and rows of fingernail imprints. The markings are placed closely together, are parallel to the lip, and extend up to the lip exactly as does the original Coles Creek type. Both the Coles Creek type and these two possible variants are shown in figure 48. The profiles of these sherds are all quite similar; they are straight side walls, probably from beaker-shaped vessels, and become thin as they approach the lip. This is a typical Coles Creek profile. Fingernail markings are used extensively on several other types in the Caddo complex. Possibly this is an example of modifications of a borrowed ceramic decoration.

Very interesting possibilities lie in the resemblances of the peculiar Caddo type $(34; \frac{26;27}{21/27}; 1)$ that has so often been found at Caddo burial sites and certain of the Coles Creek types. All of the Coles Creek types with motif 34 are variations of the simple idea of an undecorated, line-bordered band from one-half to one inch wide forming a meander design. In type $\dfrac{34;24;1}{61;24;6}$, the back-

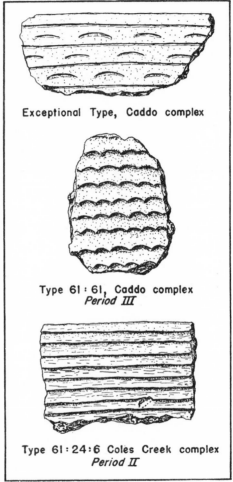

Exceptional Type, Caddo complex

Type 61 : 61, Caddo complex
Period III

Type 61 : 24 : 6 Coles Creek complex
Period II

Figure 48, Possible evolution of decorations from type 61;24;6.

ground outside the band is filled with close spaced over-

hanging lines. In $34;\dfrac{24}{74};10$, the background is undecorated and large punctates are used at the ends of lines.

In type 34; $\dfrac{24/104}{104}$;1, small punctates arranged in rows

are used as background. Type 34; $\dfrac{21}{111/28}$ utilizes either red slip or delicate crosshatching as background. In all of these decorations the motif is often outlined by incised lines with punctates spaced in the lines.

The resembling Caddo type is 34; $\dfrac{26,27}{21/28}$;1. (Meander outlined by a line enclosed band and brought out in negative by a background filled with plain ovals formed by delicate crosshatching in the angles. Lines are usually scratched. Spurred lines are frequently centered in the motif band.)

The significant point of resemblance is the highly specialized motif consisting of a line-bordered undecorated band forming a compressed meander which is accentuated by a decorated background. Delicate crosshatching is sometimes used for this purpose in both complexes. There may be some connection between punctated lines and spurred lines.

Despite this resemblance no types have been found that appear to be intermediate between the two decorations. However, the fact that the historic Caddo complex appears to have adopted other types from the Coles Creek complex, as explained above, lends some weight to the resemblance.

If the resemblance may be allowed, the question arises as to whether the influence is from the Coles Creek to the Caddo or vice versa. The "34" decorations are found at many Coles Creek sites, at which there are no indications of Caddo influence, and increase in number and complexity toward the southern part of the Coles Creek area. In view of this it seems that Caddo would be the recipient of the type.

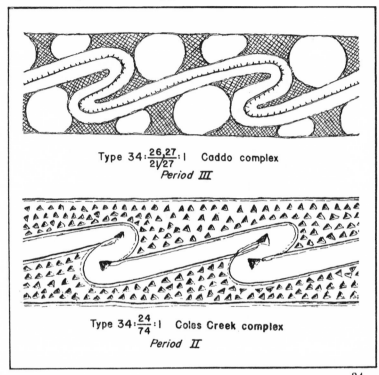

Type 34:$\frac{26,27}{21/27}$:I Caddo complex
Period III

Type 34:$\frac{24}{74}$:I Coles Creek complex
Period II

Figure 49. Possible evolution of decorations from type 34;$\frac{24}{74}$;1.

The report on the material found at the Crenshaw site[84] in Southwestern Arkansas, published since the foregoing was written, lends considerable weight to these comparisons of Coles Creek and Caddo types. In fact it now appears to be a safe guess that the Caddo decorations utilizing the negative meander owe their genesis directly to the "34" motif types found in the Coles Creek complex.

[84]Lemley, Harry J., Discoveries indicating a Pre-Caddo Culture on Red River in Arkansas.

Dickinson, S. D., The Ceramic Relationships of the Pre-Caddo Pottery from the Crenshaw Site.

Geographic relations of village sites of subsequent time periods

There appears to be a tendency for village sites of immediately subsequent time periods to be located in close proximity to one another. This is especially true of the complexes that appear to have replaced one another without serious disturbance of the population. In the southern part of the area, these are the Marksville and Coles Creek complexes; to the north the Marksville and Deasonville. For example, the tendency for Coles Creek sites to be located near Marksville plus Coles Creek (transitional) sites, and for some of these transitional sites to be near Marksville sites, is illustrated too often to have been entirely fortuitous.

A good illustration of this is found at the type site of Marksville (Site No. 103), which better than any other site illustrates the pure pottery complex of that name. Four-fifths of a mile northward is a group of mounds on the Greenhouse place (Site No. 91). Fowke considered this part of the Marksville group but Walker found both Marksville and Coles Creek pottery intermingled there.

The following list shows this and similar situations in tabular form.

SITE NO.	NAME	DISTANCE TO	SITE NO.	NAME
Marksville complex sites			**Marksville and Coles Creek sites**	
103	Marksville V. S.	4/5 miles to	91	Greenhouse Place
102	Churupa Place	6 miles to	86	Dunbarton Place
101	Smithfield Place	1 mile to	—	Smithfield No. 2*
*This site collection consisted of 20 sherds of Coles Creek types—not described.				
Marksville and Coles Creek sites			**Coles Creek sites**	
87	Gorum Mound	1½ miles to	75	Chevalier Mound
76	Picketts Island	1¼ miles to	70	Old Rhinehart
83	Alphenia Landing	2½ miles to	64	Hedgland Place
78	Barfield Place	1 mile to	74	White Oak Ldg.
82	Veasey Place	½ mile to	68	Morgan Place
Marksville and Deasonville sites			**Deasonville sites**	
54	L. M. Coody	5 miles to	44	Walker Place
56	Exum Place	3 miles to	43	Taylor Place
60	Phillipi Place	6 miles to	32	Gamewood Place
Deasonville, and Deasonville plus Marksville sites are so numerous in the middle Yazoo River valley that significant associations cannot be indicated.				

The tendency for an undisturbed people to abandon their old villages for various reasons and to settle new sites in the immediate neighborhood of the old has often been observed. The Southwest and the Eskimo territory of northern Alaska show numerous examples of this phenomenon. The above described situations in Louisiana and Mississippi might be interpreted in this way.

Summary

The tentative sequence of pottery decoration complexes resulting from the foregoing detailed analyses and comparisons is shown in figure 50. Near the top of this graph is a horizontal line representing the year 1700 A.D., the dawn of the historic period. Below this the blocks representing the decoration complexes are arranged according to their supposed temporal relationships.

The future steps in investigating the old cultures of this region follow logically. A program of excavation based on this information may be expected to check the chronology; to yield cultural elements and information illustrating the various stages; and to make clear any changes that may have occurred in the population.

Even with this modest beginning there is quite a temptation to see a story of ancient movements of people and cultural forces in the local region with ramifications spread over much of the eastern United States. A guess at this broad outline would be pleasant but premature. However, it is far from being as hopeless a task as it appeared a few years ago. Great strides have been made in Eastern archeology in the past ten years. Perhaps, after the elapse of another decade, the well directed work that is under way in many parts of the region will have answered so many of the questions, that timid theories will not be necessary.

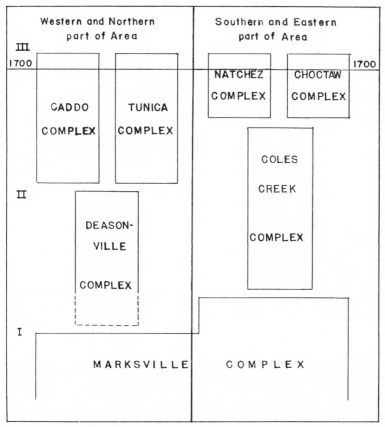

Figure 50. Graphic representation of time relations of pottery complexes. The horizontal line near the top represents the year 1700, the beginning of the historic period. The three periods are marked down the left side of the graph.

GLOSSARY

The terms listed here are those which are used in this article in what very often is probably an unusual or unfamiliar sense. There are also a few technical words peculiar to archeology that need to be defined for those who are not specialists in the field. The definitions given are not standard dictionary definitions. Rather they are attempts of the writer to explain just what he intends to express by these different words and phrases.

Appendages, of vessels
  Additions to a vessel for either practical or ornamental purposes: handles, knobs, effigy figures, ears, etc.

Bayou
  Americanized form of a Choctaw word, bayuk, meaning stream or river.

Beaker
  Vessel with straight, almost vertical walls and a flat bottom.

Beamer
  An instrument shaped something like a drawshave, generally made from the matapodal bone of a deer, used in tanning hides.

Bottle
  A vessel with a comparatively large body, small neck, and small mouth.

Carinated form of bowl
  Bowl with low, outward cambered sides, sharp angle between side walls and bottom, and a concave bottom. In shape the bowl is round.

Complex, of decorations
  A group of distinct decoration types, all of which were used by people living within a definite area at the same time.

Cord marked
  The imprints of twisted fiber impressed in the surface of the vessel before the paste had hardened. A number of marks are usually parallel, indicating possibly that the cord was wrapped around a flat paddle to form a type of stamp.

Culture
  All things which are originated or adapted by man. Usually the archeologist can deal directly only with material culture.

Decoration
  Any additions to or marks upon the surface of a vessel which are mainly ornamental in nature: incising, slips or washes, nodes, etc.

273

Design of a vessel

The entire plan of construction of a vessel. This includes shape, appendages, and decoration.

Dump (see midden)

Ear (see lug)

Element, of decoration

The features, incised lines, p nctates, etc., that are used in constructing a decoration.

Handle

A loop of clay attached to the vessel, usually near the rim, for the purpose of suspension. Two handles placed on opposite sides of the vessel are usual in the area considered.

Hemi-conical

Shaped like half a cone which is cut lengthwise. Usually applied to punctates, and in these cases means that the hole produced is thus shaped.

Horizon

Generally used to mean a sample of all cultural forms in existence at any one time.

Incised lines

Lines trailed in a clay vessel before the paste had hardened.

Knob

A projection from vessel wall usually near the rim apparently used to assist in handling the vessel. Two knobs placed on opposite sides of the vessel are usual in the area considered.

Levee (see natural levee)

Lip, of vessel

The extreme end or edge of the vessel wall.

Lug (ear)

A projection extending from the vessel rim. Lugs appear to have no functional value and to be purely ornamental. In the area considered they are generally triangular in shape and extend outward horizontally. Four were generally used on each vessel.

Midden (dump)

Deposit of refuse unintentionally accumulated near dwellings.

Motif, of decoration

Plan of decoration. The basic idea about which the decoration is constructed.

Mound

A structure built intentionally, which usually has or had some definite form. In the area considered mounds are always constructed of earth.

Natural levee

Low ridges formed on each side of a stream channel by silt deposited by flood waters as they leave the channel. Typically these ridges are highest near the banks of the stream and decrease in elevation away from the channel. Mississippi River levees are usually about one mile wide and reach an elevation of ten feet.

Negative decoration

A decoration in which the motif is made to appear by differentiating the background. This is done by means of punctates, rouletting, closely spaced lines, paint, etc.

Node

Small teat-like projection placed on the body of the vessel for ornamental purposes.

Overhanging lines

Lines trailed in soft vessel paste with a flat pointed instrument held at such an angle to the vessel wall that the top of the line is deeply incised while the bottom rises to the surface of the wall.

Paint (see slip)

Paste

The material of which a vessel is made, i.e., clay and tempering material.

Period (see horizon)

Pinched decoration

Decorations made by pinching the surface of the vessel with the tips of the fingers.

Place (Plantation)

The only difference in these terms is one of locality. Farms are usually referred to as "places" in the hill sections; in the valley they are called "plantations."

Plantation (see place)

Positive decoration

Decoration in which the motif is brought out by differentiating the area included within it from the unornamented background. The means used to effect this are generally punctates, rouletting, paint, etc.

Pot

Vessel with globular body and slightly constricted mouth. Rim is often outflaring. Bottom may be either concave or flat.

Potsherd

A fragment of a pottery vessel.

Punctate

An indentation made with a tool on the surface of a vessel before the paste had hardened.

Pyramidal

In reality no mounds in this area are true pyramids. A more descriptive term would be a truncated or cut-off pyramid.

Ramp

Approach or roadway up the side of mound which provides easier means of ascent (there is certain evidence to indicate that these are probably stairways).

Random collection
A collection from all parts of a site gathered without any discrimination as to the exact location of specimens.

Rim, of vessel
The part of the vessel wall around the mouth which is differentiated in any way from the body wall.

Rouletting
Impressions, possibly made with a wheel or a semicircular implement before paste had hardened.

School of Art
A group of art styles which exist in the same area at the same time. Synonymous with complex.

Scratched line
A line made on the surface of a vessel after the paste had hardened.

Slip (wash)
A coating of clay applied after the vessel was formed. Often the coating is different in color from the paste of the vessel.

Stamp decoration
Impressions of a carved or natural object, made before the paste had hardened.

Stratum, cultural
A layer of a deposit which represents a limited period of time. This layer may be differentiated from other layers either by significant differences in the deposit or by the material contained in it. The latter condition is probably more common.

Stratified cut
An excavation from which material is removed in thin layers. The artifacts from each layer are saved separately for purposes of comparison. The "strata" are made by the excavator in the process of lowering the cut.

Temper
Finely divided material worked into the clay before the vessel is formed. This material allows the clay to expand without cracking during the firing process. Sand, grit, charcoal, vegetable matter, or finely ground shell are the usual tempering materials.

Triangular punctates
Punctates which form a triangular shaped depression in the surface of the vessel. These are shaped as though made by the corners of a cube.

Type, cultural
A standard about which a cultural expression clusters.

Village site
All remaining indications of a permanent dwelling place inhabited by at least a small group of people. House remains, graves, earthworks, etc.

Wash (see slip)

BIBLIOGRAPHY

Beyer, George E., Report on the Mounds of Louisiana, Publications of the Louisiana Historical Society, Vol. I, part IV, New Orleans, 1895.

The Mounds of Louisiana, Publications of the Louisiana Historical Society, Vol. II, part I, New Orleans, 1897.

Investigation of Some Shell Heaps in Calcasieu Parish, Publications of the Louisiana Historical Society, Vol. II, part II, New Orleans, 1898.

Brown, Calvin S. Archeology of Mississippi, Mississippi Geological Survey, 1926.

Bushnell, David I., The Choctaw of Bayou Lacomb, St. Tammany Parish, Louisiana, Bureau of American Ethnology, bull. 48, 1909.

Calhoun, Robert Dabney, The Taënsa Indians, The Louisiana Historical Quarterly, Part I, Vol. 17, No. 3, July, 1934; Part II, Vol. 17, No. 4, October, 1934.

Charlevoix, Father, Histoire de la Nouvelle France, Vol. III, p. 413, Letter 30, Paris, 1744. Rollen Bros.

Chawner, W. D. The Geology of Catahoula and Concordia Parishes, Geol. bull No. 9, Louisiana Department of Conservation, New Orleans, Louisiana, 1936.

Collins, H. B. Jr., Archeological and Anthropometrical Work in Mississippi, Explorations and Field-Work of the Smithsonian Institution in 1925, Vol. 78, No. 1.

Potsherds from Choctaw Village Sites in Mississippi, Journal of the Washington Academy of Sciences, Vol. 17, No. 10, May 19, 1927.

Excavations at a Prehistoric Indian Village Site in Mississippi, Proceedings of the United States National Museum, Vol. 79, Art. 32, 1932.

Archeology of Mississippi, Conference on Southern Prehistory, National Research Council, pp. 37-42, Ann Arbor, Michigan, 1932.

Culin, Howard, The Dickson Collection of American Antiquities, U. of Penn. Publs., Philadelphia, 1900.

Ford, J. A., Outline of Louisiana and Mississippi Pottery Horizons, Louisiana Conservation Review, Vol. IV, No. 6, March, 1935, pp. 33-38.

Ceramic Decoration Sequence at an Old Indian Village Site Near Sicily Island, Louisiana. Anthro. Study No. 1, Louisiana Department of Conservation, Louisiana Geol. Survey, 1935.

Fowke, Gerard, Archeological Work in Louisiana, Smithsonian Miscellaneous Collections, Vol. 78, No. 7, 1927.

Explorations in the Red River Valley in Louisiana, 44th Annual Report, Bureau of American Ethnology, pp. 405-435, 1928.

French, B. F., Historical Collections of Louisiana and of Florida, (seven volumes) New Orleans, 1846.

277

Glover, W. B., A History of the Caddo Indians, Louisiana Historical Quarterly, Vol. 18, No. 4, October, 1935.

Green, John A., Governor Perier's Expedition Against the Natchez Indians, The Louisiana Historical Quarterly, Vol. 19, No. 3, July, 1936.

Halbert, H. S., The Small Indian Tribes of Mississippi, Publications of the Mississippi Historical Society, Vol. V.
Bernard Roman's Map of 1772, Publications of the Mississippi Historical Society, Vol. VI, pp. 415-439.

Howe, Henry V. and others, Submergence of Indian Mounds, pp. 64-68, Geology of Cameron and Vermillion Parishes, Geological Bulletin No. 6, Department of Conservation, New Orleans, Louisiana, November 1, 1935.

Jones, C. C., Antiquities of the Southern Indians, 1873.

Kniffen, Fred B., The Historic Indian Tribes of Louisiana, Louisiana Conservation Review, Vol. IV, No. 7, July, 1935, pp. 5-12.
A Preliminary Report of the Mounds and Middens of Plaquemines and St. Bernard Parishes, Lower Mississippi River Delta, Geological Bulletin No. 8, Louisiana Department of Conservation, New Orleans, Louisiana, 1936.

Lemley, Harry J., Discoveries indicating a Pre-Caddo Culture on Red River in Arkansas, and Dickinson, S. D., The Ceramic Relationships of the Pre-Caddo Pottery from the Crenshaw Site, Bulletin of the Texas Archeological and Paleontological Society, Vol. 8, September, 1936, pp. 25-69, pls. 3-11.

Moore, Clarence B., Certain Mounds of Arkansas and of Mississippi, Part II, Journal of the Academy of Natural Sciences, Philadelphia, second series, Vol. 13, Part IV. art. X, 1905-1908.
Certain Aboriginal Mounds of Florida Central West-Coast. Journal Academy Natural Sciences, Philadelphia, second series, Volume XII, 1903.
Some Aboriginal Sites on Red River, Journal of the Academy of Natural Sciences, Philadelphia, Vol. XIV, No. 4, 1912.
Antiquities of the Ouachita Valley, Journal of the Academy of Natural Sciences, Philadelphia, Vol. XIV, No. 1.
Some Aboriginal Sites on Mississippi River, Journal of the Academy of Natural Sciences, Philadelphia, Vol. XIV, Art. IV, 1911.
Some Aboriginal Sites in Louisiana and Arkansas, Journal of the Academy of Natural Sciences, Philadelphia, Vol. XVI, Part I, Art. 1, 1913.

National Research Council, Report on the Conference on Southern Pre-history, held at Birmingham. Alabama, December 18, 19, and 20, 1932 (mimeographed). Washington, 1932.

Russell, R. J., Larto Lake, An Old Mississippi River Channel, Louisiana Conservation Review, Vol. III, No. 3, July, 1933.

Setzler, F. M., Hopewell Type Pottery from Louisiana, Journal of the Washington Academy of Sciences, Vol. 23, No. 3, March 15, 1933.

Pottery of the Hopewell Type from Louisiana, Proceedings of the U. S. National Mus. No. 2963, Vol. 82, Art. 22, pp. 1-21, Washington, 1933.

A Phase of the Hopewell Mound Builders in Louisiana, Exploration and Field-Work of the Smithsonian Institution in 1933, publ. 13235, pp. 38-40, Washington, 1934.

Marksville: A Louisiana Variant of the Hopewell Culture (In Manuscript).

Swanton, John R., The Relation of the Southwest to General Culture Problems of American Pre-history. Conference on Southern Pre-history, National Research Council, Washington, 1932.

Indian Tribes of the Lower Mississippi and Adjacent Coast of the Gulf of Mexico, Bureau of American Ethonology, Bull. 43, 1911.

Source Material for the Social and Ceremonial Life of the Choctaw Indians, Bureau of American Ethnology, Bull, 103, 1931.

Early History of the Creek Indians and Their Neighbors, Bureau of American Ethnology, Bull. 73, 1922.

Notes on the Cultural Province of the Southeast, American Anthropologist, Vol. 37, No. 3, July-September, 1935, pp. 373-385.

Veatch, Arthur C., The Shreveport Area, in Harris and Veatch, A Preliminary Report on the Geology of Louisiana. State Experiment Station, Baton Rouge, 1899.

Notes on the Geology Along the Ouachita, Paper No. 4, The Geology of Louisiana, appendix notes on Indian mounds and village sites between Monroe and Harrisonburg, Louisiana State University and Agricultural and Mechanical College, Baton Rouge, 1902.

Walker, Winslow, Trailing the Mound Builders of the Mississippi Valley, Explorations and Field-Work of the Smithsonian Institution in 1932.

Pre-Historic Cultures of Louisiana, Conference on Southern Prehistory, Natural Research Council, pp. 42-48, Ann Arbor, Michigan, 1932.

A Caddo Burial Site at Natchitoches, Louisiana, Smithsonian Miscellaneous Collections, Vol. 94, No. 14.

A Reconnaissance of Northern Louisiana Mounds, Explorations and Field-Work of the Smithsonian Institution in 1931, pp. 169-174.

A Variety of Caddo Pottery from Louisiana, Journal of the Washington Academy of Sciences, Vol. 24, No. 2, Feb. 15, 1934, pp. 99-104.

The Troyville Mounds, Catahoula Parish, La. Bureau of American Ethnology, Bull. 113, 1936.

6

Archaeological Methods Applicable
to Louisiana

J. A. FORD

Louisiana State University

The task with which the archaeologist is primarily concerned in attempting to rediscover dead and forgotten cultures is that of determining a time scale, or chronology. In other words, he must develop a history of the people with whom he is concerned. Naturally, this must be in terms of the material culture; all else has usually been destroyed by the passage of centuries.

A complete chronology is yet to be established for the southeastern United States. Only the more durable portions of the material cultures of the ancient peoples remain, owing to the moist climatic conditions. Only such things as pottery, stonework, shell, bone, and a small amount of worked metal—principally copper—survive. Of course, numerous mounds and earthworks are scattered through the country.

Two principal lines of approach to the problem of untangling the story of the past have been attempted in this area. The usual method is hardly systematic. It consists of excavating various sites, keeping accurate records of the work, and finally attempting to correlate the sites and determine their relative ages.

The plan of approach which is at present being applied to the practically unknown prehistory of Louisiana does not involve excavation in its primary steps. It starts by recognizing that pottery is the most plastic remaining element of the old cultures and probably changed most with the passage of time. And further, that the material—broken potsherds, flint, chips, etc.—that was thrown away as garbage on the old village sites, and is now exposed by cultivation of many of the sites, represents a better cross section of that phase of the material life of the people than the artifacts which were selected to accompany the dead.

Thus collections of broken pieces of pottery gathered from the old sites constitute the best evidence from which an outline of the story may be pieced together. Actually, the stylistic periods of the ancient inhabitants of the state are reflected very well by these pottery fragments. The problem of determining the relative ages of these periods may be approached from several angles.

First, by identifying the sites of villages mentioned in the chronicles of the first explorers of the State. This connects these sites with a definite time period, and gives a starting point for the projection of the chronology back into the prehistoric. Work of this nature that affects the situation in this State has been done by Collins for the Choctaw;[1] by Chambers for the Natchez[2] by Chambers and Ford for the Tunica;[3] and, in a recently published report, Walker[4] describes material from a historic Caddo village.

Second, a chronology may be determined by means of a large number of site collections from a comprehensive, though restricted area. Comparison will demonstrate the different groups of art styles which have the same distribution yet show no inter-influence, as well as the neighboring areas with distinct art styles which did influence one another. If handled carefully, this will give an indication of the period characteristics. Then, by means of the phenomena of type, site, and area-overlap, the relative positions of the artistic periods may be determined. This is not a simple method, and must be handled with great care in order to give results that are at all helpful. The application of this approach to parts of Louisiana and Mississippi has been described in the April issue of the *Louisiana Conservation Review*[5] of last year.

Third, if evidences of two or more periods appear on any one village site, and the midden material or kitchen refuse on the site has collected to any appreciable depth, careful excavation may reveal that material representing one period is later or deposited after another. This is known as vertical stratigraphy. In this case, the evidence is direct. This method constitutes the best basis for the relating of time changes. Such evidence has been found at an old village site near Sicily Island,[6] and in the site at Jonesville,[7] both in Catahoula Parish.

Fourth, in unusual situations, sites may be related to changes in the natural features of the landscape in order to determine their relative ages. Of course, this dates the material they yield. It is probable

---

[1] Henry B. Collins, Jr., "Postherds from Choctaw Village Sites in Mississippi." *Jo. Wash. Acad. of Sciences,* Vol. 17, No. 10 (May 19, 1927).

[2] Material in Mississippi Department of Archives and History Museum at Jackson, Mississippi. Reports have not been published.

[3] *Ibid.*

[4] *Ibid.*

[5] Ford, J. A. (1935-I)

[6] J. A. Ford, "Ceramic Decoration Sequence at an Old Indian Village Site Near Sicily Island, Louisiana."

[7] Excavated by Winslow Walker of the Bu. Am. Eth. in 1932. Report in Preparation.

that when archaeological work is done along the Louisiana coast the depths to which various sites have sunken beneath sea level, due to the depressing effect of the delta deposits, will be an important and useful factor.

In the central and northeastern parts of the State some assistance may be expected from shifting of the stream meanders. One example is found on the east side of the Tensas River, six miles west of Ferriday. The Tensas has moved two miles to the westward, leaving four sites along an old natural levee. To the north of these are two other sites which have not been abandoned by the river. This makes it possible that the two later sites were inhabited for a longer period than the ones that were abandoned—a condition which is borne out by the material collected from the sites.

These are by no means all the methods or situations that will yield evidence of time differences and relations of culture periods. Almost every village site has something to offer, and, by careful and close observation, the peculiarities of each situation may be adapted to the problem in hand.

This is merely the initial step in the systematic study of Louisiana prehistory. After a chronology of the pottery, the "key fossils" of culture, have been determined, there will remain the task of excavating sites that will give evidence to test the time and relations, and will give all recoverable information. This is the problem for the not distant future, and one that cannot be approached lightly. Field archeologists trained in the highly technical job of excavating will have to labor longer and more carefully than the layman realizes to complete the records of the past.

The interested amateur can render valuable assistance by protecting the sites (records of the past, of which all too few remain); by making careful collections of surface material and notes giving location; and, by calling the attention of agencies working in the field to such collections and sites which possibly may not have been examined.

BIBLIOGRAPHY

H. B. Collins, Jr., "Postherds from Choctaw Village Sites in Mississippi." *Jo. Wash. Acad. Sciences,* Vol. 17, No. 10 (May 19, 1927).

"Exacavations at a Prehistoric Indian Village Site in Mississippi. *Proceed. U. S. Nat'l Museum,* No. 2898, Vol. 79, Art. 32, pp. 1-22 (Washington, 1932).

"Archaeology of Mississippi." Conference on Southern Prehistory, Nat'l Research Council, pp. 37-42 (1932).

J. A. Ford,. "An Introduction to Louisiana Archeology." *Louisiana Conservation Review*, Vol. IV, No. 5, pp. 8-11 (January, 1935).

"Outline of Louisiana and Mississippi Pottery Horizons." *Louisiana Conservation Review*, Vol. IV. No. 6, pp. 33-38.

"Ceramic Decoration Sequence at an Old Indian Village Site Near Sicily Island, Louisiana." Anthropological Study No. 1, Louisiana Geological Survey, Dept. of Conservation (Aug. 1, 1935).

G. Fowke, "Explorations in the Red River Valley in Louisiana." *44th Ann. Rept.*, Bu. Am. Eth., pp. 405-434 (1928).

"Archeological Work in Louisiana. *Smithsonian Misc. Cols.*, Vol. 78, No. 7, pp. 254-259 (1927).

F. B. Kniffen. "The Historic Indian Tribes of Louisiana." *Louisiana Conservation Review*, Vol. 4, No. 7, pp. 5-12 (July, 1935).

C. B. Moore, *Journal of Philadelphia Academy of Sciences*, Second Series, Vol. 14 (1909 to 1912): "Antiquities of the Ouachita Valley, Art. I, pp. 7-173; "Some Aboriginal Sites on Mississippi River." Art. IV. pp. 367-482; "Some Aboriginal Sites on Red River," Art. V, pp. 483-638.

F. M. Setzler, "Hopewell Type Pottery from Louisiana." *Jo. Wash. Acad. Sci.*, Vol. 23, No. 3 (March 15, 1933).

"Pottery of the Hopewell Type from Louisiana." *Proceed. U. S. Nat'l Museum*, No. 2963, Vol. 82, Art. 22, pp. 1-21 (1933).

"A Phase of Hopewell Mound Builders in Louisiana." *Explor. and Field Work of the S. I. in 1933*, Publ. No. 3225, pp. 38-40 (Washington, 1934).

W. M. Walker, "A Variety of Caddo Pottery from Louisiana. *Jo. Wash. Acad. of Sci.*, Vol. 24, No. 2, pp. 99-104 (Feb. 15, 1934).

"Prehistoric Cultures of Louisiana." *Conference on Southern Prehistory*, Nat'l Research Council, pp. 42-48 (1932).

7

THE INDIAN MOUNDS OF IBERVILLE PARISH

Fred B. Kniffen*

Introduction

This study of Indian mounds is the second such to be included with a Parish geological bulletin.[1] The study was undertaken both on its own merits as a contribution to the archaeology of Louisiana, and as an aid to the unravelling of the most recent geologic history of Iberville Parish. It was planned originally to cover both Iberville and Ascension Parishes, as is the case with the sections on geology, but with limited time available it seemed desirable to restrict the study to what appeared to be, with the objectives in mind, the more important of the two Parishes, Iberville. However, not only was every known Indian mound in Iberville Parish visited and examined, but field work was extended to a generous area of overlap into the neighboring Parishes.

The present survey of prehistoric remains is the second to be conducted for this part of Louisiana. Late in 1912 and during the early months of 1913, the area was visited by Clarence B. Moore [2] of the Academy of Natural Sciences of Philadelphia, as a part of his great archaeologic survey of the southeastern United States. Moore made no pretense of including every site, restricting his visits to points easily accessible by river steamer. He gives excellent and accurate descriptions of each mound or group of mounds visited, but he paid little attention to surface collections of potsherds and other artifacts, being mainly interested in skeletal remains and burial

---

* The writer gratefully acknowledges the very material field and laboratory assistance rendered by Mr. Walter Beecher.

[1] The first: A preliminary report on the Indian mounds and middens of Plaquemines and St. Bernard Parishes: Louisiana Dept. Cons. Geol. Bull. 8, pp. 407-422, 1936.

[2] Some aboriginal sites in Louisiana and in Arkansas: Acad. Nat. Sci. Philadelphia Jour., 2d ser., vol. 16. pt. 1, pp. 6-19, 1913.

furniture.[3] The present survey conducted no excavations, but rather stressed the making of surface collections. The difference in point-of-view and method of the two surveys is such that there is little duplication effort; rather, the two supplement each other.

Types of sites

The search for sites was largely limited to visits to mounds known to the inhabitants of the area studied. (See map, fig. 22.) A thorough questioning of local trappers, moss-gatherers, fishermen, and swampers yielded probably as complete a cataloging of the sites as can ever be compiled. In very few instances was constant vigilance along the line of travel rewarded with the discovery of a previously unreported site.

All the sites examined may be placed in one or two classes: mound or midden. The map includes another class of somewhat different category: reported sites, or those not visited by the survey, whose map location is only approximate.

The term "mound" is applied to those structures given definite and intentional form by their builders. In this area mounds are composed primarily of earth, occasionally with minor amounts of shell. They appear to have been used largely as *tumuli*, since nearly every one contains human remains. The mounds are quite uniform in shape, nearly all being referable to the class described as truncated pyramids. They vary greatly in size, from one that is some 25 feet square on top and four feet high, to one that is 200 feet square by 18 feet in height, and supports a group of farm buildings on its terrace-like surface.

Middens are irregular accumulations of shells and animal remains, the domestic refuse resulting from a period of residence by a primitive population. In this area middens frequently take the form of long, well-defined ridges, one reaching a length of 700 feet, a width

[3] Burial furniture: weapons, pottery, etc.. interred with bodies.

191

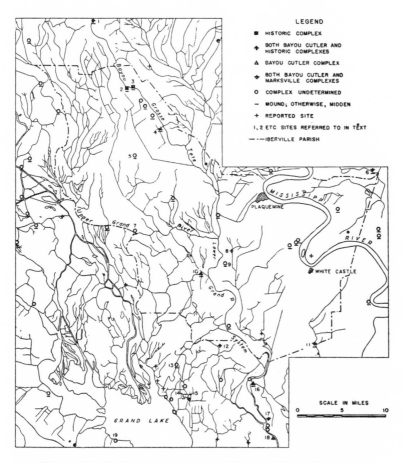

Figure 22. Indian mounds and middens of Iberville Parish and vicinity.

of 100 feet, and a maximum height of six feet. Intermingled with the primary constituents of the middens are slacked shells and other evidences of fire, potsherds, projectile points, and sundry additional suggestions of domestic activities. Midden heaps have frequently functioned as burial sites, so that as a whole they reveal much better cross sections of ancient Indian life than do mounds.

The term "village site" is employed as the name would suggest, to refer to the actual plot near the mounds formerly lived on by the Indian village population. Such sites are important because under favorable conditions they yield the best surface collections of potsherds and other artifacts representative of daily life. Collecting conditions are favorable when the old village site has been freshly cultivated; should it be mantled with vegetation it is difficult even to locate the site, and once located collecting is a slow and unremunerative task. Village sites also occur unassociated with mounds, but without such prominent markers can rarely be located. For the area under consideration very few village sites independent of mounds were discovered, and these few only by accident. No attempt was made to seek them out systematically, for the search would certainly be slow and unprofitable. For these several reasons village sites are not separately distinguished on the map.

Mounds in this area are probably somewhat more abundant than the average for Louisiana; several individual mounds and middens are impressive as to size and extent. But, there is nothing approaching the elaborate earthworks of Marksville and Jonesville, and even groups of two or more mounds are so few as to be the exception rather than the rule.

Distribution and location of sites

A glance at the map accompanying this report reveals that the sites show a remarkable affinity for waterways, and it will show that certain areas or streams have greater densities of sites than do others. At least for the thoroughly explored central area this distribution is not indicative of failure on the part of the investigator to visit certain sections, notably those interstream areas where travel is difficult.

As previously noted, for Iberville Parish the record of mounds and middens is probably as accurate and complete as it can ever be made; every site shown within the Parish has been visited. The same qualifications apply to the areas immediately adjacent to Iberville. Within the intensively studied area such impressions as are conveyed by the density and spacing of sites are probably correct. Farther outside the bounds of the Parish there are probably many mounds and middens not shown on the map; there the patterns of distribution may be misleading.

Certain sections within and outside of Iberville Parish may be mapped as devoid of sites for a reason other than failure to visit the areas. Notably is this true for the westernmost portion of the Parish and for the broad siteless strip extending northward from Grand Lake. It seems certain that for the sections specified the map represents an accurate picture of known sites. What appears to be a possibility is that recent sedimentation within the area may have completely covered a number of mounds and middens. Three feet of silt now cover the mound on Upper Grand River opposite Bayou Pigeon (no. 7 on map); less than 20 years ago this was a well-known landmark. The same fate is obscuring other sites lying within the area subject to flooding by the Atchafalaya River. Somewhat offsetting this explanation as applied to the siteless belt lying north of Grand Lake is the failure of the numerous dredges working in that area to report cutting through mounds or middens. However, such a possibility as the covering of sites by silting must be entertained in any theorizing regarding the region and its occupance by the mound builders.

Pertinent points with regard to the distribution of sites are: (1) their presence or absence along specific waterways; (2) the distribution of the two types: earth mounds and shell middens; and (3) the extent to which the sites lie in areas now possessing environments unfavorable to primitive occupance.

With regard to the first point, a notable fact is the presence of mounds associated with the levee slopes of the Mississippi. The first terrace level above the flood plain of the Mississippi barely touches the northeastern-most portion of the map (fig. 22). One of the sites included in the report, Kleinpeter (no. 6), lies on the terrace. This is but one of a series extending northward along the bluffs bounding the eastern side of the flood plain of the Mississippi. Paralleling the western bank of the river is another series, of necessity situated directly on the flood plain. South of the terrace and bluffs mentioned above, the two series of mounds continue to the southward through the area studied, apparently ending somewhere in the vicinity of New Orleans.

West of the Mississippi there are notable clusterings of sites along upper Bayou Grosse Tete and along Lower Grand River and its continuation in Goddel Bayou and Belle River. No sites are known for Bayou Maringouin, in spite of the fact that at present it appears to possess significance as a drainage feature equal to that of Bayou Grosse Tete. On the other hand, there are a number of individual sites associated with what appear to be relatively insignificant streams (e. g., nos. 9 and 5).

Another clustering of sites is associated with the Atchafalaya drainage system over an area extending from the northern boundary of the map to the parallel of 30° 15′. It is a significant fact that the mounds of this area are not associated with the present Atchafalaya channel, but rather with tributary and distributary streams.

From the above-mentioned parallel southward is the elongated, rectangular, apparently moundless area previously mentioned. Mounds or middens are found on both sides of Grand Lake, whose shores in effect mark the southward continuation of the bounds of the moundless area. With one possible exception, that of Charenton Beach (no. 19), the mounds and middens are associated with streams tributary to Grand Lake, rather than with the shores of the lake itself. Since the eastern shore of Grand Lake is now receding, there is always the possibility that the streams and associated mounds once extended farther westward.

Between the eastern shore of Grand Lake and the Lower Grand River system are a number of streams, in the main distributary from Grand River and tributary to Grand Lake. Associated with these streams are several known sites; there may possibly be others.

As for the second point in this discussion of distribution, the character of each individual site is indicated by appropriate symbols on the map (fig. 22). The major sites are distinguished as (earth) mounds or (shell) middens. What the map fails to make clear is the fact that many of the earth mounds contain an appreciable proportion of shells and that shells are found in some of the village sites associated with the earth mounds.

In general the most northerly sites are earth mounds, the most southerly, shell middens. Intermediate in position are found shell middens in close proximity to earth mounds. In our present knowledge of the area too much importance must not be attached to these distinctions insofar as they may reflect temporal or cultural differences. However, in the observed distribution of shells there are data of considerable utility in the recognition of past environmental conditions.

Probably 90 percent of the shells associated with earth mounds or composing shell middens are the familiar clam, *Rangia cuneata*. *Rangia* seems to demand rather precise brackish water conditions, quickly giving way before a change to saline or fresh water. The local inhabitants say that Grand Lake until recently has contained living Rangias, now rapidly disappearing before the flood of fresh water from the Atchafalaya. Lake Verret is reputed still to contain live Rangias. Current opinions differ with regard to the edibility of these clams; good or not, they were consumed by the aboriginal inhabitants in enormous quantities, as is impressively indicated by vast accumulations of shells in middens.

The other 10 percent of the shell content of mounds and middens are made up mainly of several species of *Unio*, a common freshwater clam. *Unio* apparently demands definitely freshwater conditions, so that it will not live in a habitat supporting Rangias. It should be pointed out, however, that the two may be found in close proximity in a deltaic region, where a freshwater stream may support Unios, while lakes or ponds on its levee flanks may be sufficiently brackish for Rangias.

Great midden accumulations of Rangias must indicate close proximity to a source of supply at the time the structures were built. It seems unlikely that a primitive people, however fond they might be of these clams, could or would afford to transport them more than a few miles in an amount sufficient to build middens measurable in terms of hundreds and thousands of cubic yards. If this reasoning is valid, one must postulate environmental conditions substantially different from the present for the time when many of the shell middens shown on the map were built.

A few Rangias are found associated with the earth mounds at the northern edge of the area (nos. 2 and 4), along Bayou Grosse Tete. True *Rangia* middens have been found just off the mapped area along the edge of the bluff north of Kleinpeter site (no. 6). The southernmost earth mounds (nos. 11, 14, 16) in general show an increasing percentage of Rangia, although one (no. 13) revealed absolutely no trace of shell of any description.

On two sites there was exposed a stratification of Unios and Rangias indicative of either change in environmental conditions or of remarkably complete change in food habits on the part of the middens' builders. The Miller site (no. 18) is one; the other is the Big Bayou Pigeon Canal site (no. 15).

The Miller site on Belle River was visited in mid-July, a time when the water stood at about mean level. Some 4½ feet of midden accumulation lay above water level at the landing. A foot in thickness and just above the water was a solid stratum of Unios. Next above was a two-foot accumulation of black earth. Above the latter was the uppermost stratum of 1½ feet of Rangias, seeming to grade upward from small to larger shells. Potsherds were found in place throughout the exposure, and, if the collections from the lower strata are adequate, show a distinct change in character from top to bottom. Such subaqueous exploration as the difficulties permitted suggested another soil layer and another shell stratum in that order below the Unios. Reference to the possible significance of the stratification will be made in the section dealing with the physiographic implications of the mounds.

A situation somewhat similar to the above apparently exists at the Big Bayou Pigeon Canal site (no. 15), where there appears to be a concentration of Unios overlain by Rangias. True relations of the various strata are obscured by a mantle of dredged material derived from the operations of some 20 years ago.

The third significant point is concerned with the extent to which these old Indian sites are now uninhabitable as measured by the standards which must have guided their primitive builders. Minimum requirements necessitate a natural elevation lying at least several feet above mean water level, a permanent supply of potable water, areas suitable for maize fields, and a nearby source of such animal food as may have formed a considerable part of the primitive diet. The loss of these essential conditions is a matter of natural rather than man-made changes. It is difficult to discount offhand the recent alterations effected by such agencies as levee building and artificial diversion of streams as they may have reduced the occupance quality of each individual site.

In general it appears that the sites in the northern portion of the region and reaching as far south as the Sorrel mound (no. 10) might still be habitable for a primitive people. With the exception of number 9, each site has the necessary prerequisites of high ground, a perennial stream of potable water, and the lesser qualities above stipulated.

South of the Sorrel mound a number of the sites lack one or more of the qualities necessary to give them acceptable habitat value. Goddel Ridge (no. 17) lies in a swamp, a good quarter mile from the nearest stream; the same lack of accessibility characterizes the earth mounds on Big and Little Pigeon Bayous (nos. 13 and 14). In the lower country there is constantly the impression of gradual submergence, of the steady encroachment of the swamp, leaving the mounds and middens as the last emergent remnants of a once higher land.

But the apparent change most difficult to explain is the disappearance of a ready source of Rangias. This deficiency becomes even more striking when one considers the distance to the shell middens found on the bluff near the Kleinpeter site. Recent flood waters may explain in part the disappearance of living Rangias from the region of the more southerly mounds; they cannot equally explain the isolation of the Kleinpeter middens.

Relative age of sites

The most reliable criterion of relative age yet developed for the prehistoric Indian sites of Louisiana is based on the study of the pottery associated with them. Both time and space differences are reflected in variations in form, composition, and nature and execution of decorative design of the pottery. Making particular use of the latter characteristic, Ford[4] has found it possible to group the sites of northern Louisiana and adjacent sections of Mississippi into a number of pottery complexes expressive of differences of either time or space or of both. Ford has come to the conclusion that relatively few sites are occupied for long periods of time. Few

---

[4] Ford, J. A., Analysis of Indian village site collections from Louisiana and Mississippi: Louisiana Dept. Cons. Anthropological Study 2, 1936.

sites are "pure," in the sense that they contain pottery all belonging to a single complex. Based on the percentage dominance of design types the sites are assigned to a single complex or to an intermediate position between two complexes differing in time or in place.

Figure 23 is an analysis of the 12 sites for which the pottery collections are considered sufficiently large to be representative. The sites are so arranged in the table that the youngest appear at the top, the oldest at the bottom. The analysis is based on Ford's criteria. Figure 23 is really a summary of the several analyses; instead of expressing the percentage representation of each design type, the individual site is summarized as to percentage of "marker" (M) and percentage of characteristic but "other than marker" (OT) types for each complex represented. The percentage representation of design types not peculiar to, or diagnostic of, any complex is shown in the column headed "unrelated."

Of the several complexes listed in the table, all but Bayou Cutler were distinguished by Ford for central and northern Louisiana. The Bayou Cutler complex was identified and named by the writer in the study of the prehistoric sites of Plaquemines and St. Bernard Parishes.[5] The Bayou Cutler complex appears to be roughly the age equivalent of the Coles Creek complex, with the strong possibility that it is more precisely contemporaneous with the upper and younger Coles Creek phase. The difference between the two complexes, then, is one of space rather than one of time.

On the basis of pottery characteristics, two adjacent sites, Rosedale and Peter Hill (nos. 2 and 3), have been classed as Historic. Neither strictly qualifies since neither has yet yielded that positive identification necessary to establish a site as historic: articles of European manufacture. However, the pottery found on the two sites is of similar nature to that found on known historic

[5] *Op. cit.*, p. 411.

SITES

POTTERY COMPLEXES

TIME

Map No.	Name	No. sherds	Natchez M	Natchez OT	Tunica M	Tunica OT	Caddo M	Caddo OT	Bayou Cutler M	Bayou Cutler OT†	Coles Creek M	Deasonville M	Deasonville OT	Marksville M	Marksville OT	Unrelated	Periods
3	Peter Hill	80	5	29	9	6	..	7	..	1	..	..	..	1(?)	..	46	HISTORIC
2	Rosedale	205	19	14	4	13	..	10	..	8	1	2	4	..	..	28	HISTORIC
1	Livonia	35	6	11	..	..	..	3	20	36	4	..	..	..	..	61	HISTORIC & BAYOU CUTLER
12	Big Bayou Pigeon		..	..	2	9	..	10	34	36	..	..	2	..	..	4	
15	Big Bayou Pigeon Canal	28	11	..	..	..	..	3	72	10	..	..	..	..	..	9	
4	Reed	114	1	..	1	..	..	1	82	5	..	..	..	..	..	12	BAYOU CUTLER
16	Little Goddel Bayou	428	..	..	..	..	..	..	84	11	3	..	..	..	..	..	
10	Bayou Sorrel	85	..	..	..	..	..	..	86	8	2	1	..	..	..	3	
18	Miller Pl.	124	..	..	..	..	..	..	86	8	2	..	..	..	..	5	
11	Grand Bayou	98	..	..	..	..	..	..	66	15	1	2	..	2	..	13	BAYOU CUTLER & MARKSVILLE
6	Kleinpeter	54	..	..	..	..	..	4	33	10	15	2	2	17	..	17	
17	Goddel Ridge	15	..	..	..	..	..	..	27	40	..	..	..	20	..	14	

M = "marker" design types.

OT = characteristic but "other than marker" design types.

Figures are percentages of total for each site.

†OT common to both Bayou Cutler and Coles Creek complexes.

Fig. 23. Pottery analyses of 12 sites.

sites in other sections of Louisiana. There can be no reasonable doubt as to the historic or proto-historic age of the Rosedale and Peter Hill collections.

The oldest site, Goddel Ridge (no. 17), yields an appreciable percentage, although by no means a dominance, of potsherds referable to the Marksville complex, the oldest identified for Louisiana. The pottery collection is dominated by Bayou Cutler types, but not in sufficient amount to class the site as Bayou Cutler. Rather, it belongs to a stage marked by the waning influence of Marksville types and the growing importance of Bayou Cutler types.

Louisiana archaeology has not yet reached the point where it can speak confidently in terms of spans of years and calendar dates, yet it is called upon constantly to do just that thing. With hesitancy and reservations it may be timidly suggested that the youngest or so-called Historic sites probably go back to some years before 1700, while the age of the oldest or Marksville-Bayou Cutler sites can be indicated only as measurable by a scale of magnitude expressed in terms of *hundreds* of years. Beyond this brief commitment the hard-pressed investigator will not go.

With a great deal of confidence in the correctness of the *relative* ages expressed for the 12 sites shown in the table, attention may be called to the age-area relationships revealed by the map. Fortunately the 12 sites for which pottery-age determinations have been made are sufficiently scattered that they are more meaningful than their number would seem to warrant. That is, based on experience in other sections of Louisiana, it seems justified to extend the age determinations of the 12 known sites to the undetermined sites lying around them, insofar as this is simply an attempt to see areas in terms of successive periods of human occupance.

Each of the three oldest or Marksville-Bayou Cutler sites has a distinctive geographic setting. The Kleinpeter site (no. 6) lies on the bluff bounding the eastern edge of the

Mississippi flood plain and is a member of the northward extending series previously referred to. The Grand Bayou mounds (no. 11) lie on the stream of the same name, but what is more important, they rest on the natural levee of an extinct stream (Bruly St. Martin crevasse) that once discharged westward from Bayou Lafourche. Goddel Ridge (no. 17) lies a difficult quarter mile from Goddel Bayou, a part of the Lower Grand River system, but it lies on the remnant natural levee of a larger stream ancestral to the present Lower Grand.

The second or Bayou Cutler age group embraces four sites showing a linear distribution and definite association with the Bayou Grosse Tete-Lower Grand River drainage way. Bayou Sorrel mound (no. 10) lies about half a mile off the main drainage line on the distributary stream of the same name. The Reed mounds (no. 4) lie far outside the area heretofore considered, on the lower course of Bayou Grosse Tete.

The third age group, Bayou Cutler-Historic, includes three sites and adds new areas of occupance. Two sites, Big Bayou Pigeon and Big Bayou Pigeon Canal (nos. 12 and 15), lie between Lower Grand River and Grand Lake on a bayou that is apparently distributary from the river to the lake. The Livonia mound group (no. 1) lies at the point where Bayou Fordoche and Bayou Grosse Tete unite under the name of the latter stream to flow southward into Bayou Plaquemine and Lower Grand River.

The fourth or Historic age group includes two identified sites (nos. 2 and 3), situated in close proximity to each other on upper Bayou Grosse Tete. Based solely on the evidence of the 12 pottery collections, the location of the two Historic sites would indicate continued occupance of upper Bayou Grosse Tete and the retreat of population from virtually the remainder of the area under consideration. While such movement seems possible, it must be remembered that further exploration of the sites whose relative ages are not yet established may yield contradictory evidence.

If such evidence as is submitted above be acceptable only to the extent of demonstrating population shifts, it must inevitably lead to speculation concerning the motivation for such movements. The indicated distribution for various time periods is not fortuitous; in part it must represent a choice of locale on the part of the inhabitants; in larger part it must be the result of restrictive guidance on the part of environment. In the rapid shifting and changing importance of stream courses in this area we can find ample explanation for changing human occupance. It follows then, that conversely we may work from effect to cause, outlining the gross physiographic changes from the population shifts that they effected. To this matter the next section is devoted.

Physiographic implications of mound distribution

If the facts of distribution and age differences of the Indian sites are to be used as evidence of physiographic change, it is necessary to accept certain basic assumptions, well substantiated by previous experience in Louisiana:

1. The mounds, middens, and other observable remains are indicative of the distribution of past Indian populations. As these sites vary areally or temporally they directly reflect past population differences.

2. If the area was favorable for settlement it was occupied. This statement implies that no considerable area providing the ground necessary for cultivation, fresh water, and abundant animal food was for long without its inhabitants. As an area became newly habitable it was occupied; with the loss of habitable qualities it was abandoned.

3. Sites whose importance is indicated by the presence of mounds and middens were inhabited only when they lay on the natural levees of significant, active, perennial, freshwater streams. This seemingly dogmatic assumption is ventured only after abundant confirmation from other sections of Louisiana. The last-mentioned relationship of occupance to natural conditions is specifically designated

for flood plains; it does not strictly apply to the Kleinpeter mounds (no. 6), the one site in the area that lies on a terrace.

With the above-mentioned points in mind and the map before us, we may, with some degree of confidenc trace in broad outline the development of the drainage pattern of Iberville Parish and adjacent territory:

During the oldest stage of occupance represented by the three Marksville-Bayou Cutler sites, the Mississippi apparently followed something like its present course: possibly it swung somewhat to the eastward against the terrace edge below the Kleinpeter site (no. 6). Lower Grand River existed as an important stream independent of either of its present headings in Upper Grand River and Bayou Grosse Tete. There is a strong suggestion that the ancestral Grand River left the Mississippi at a point near Plaquemine and flowed southward past the two sites (nos. 8 and 9) that are now isolated from any stream. Bayou Lafourche, at perhaps a slightly later period, was a stream of sufficient volume to have an important distributary. Bruly St. Martin crevasse, that flowed westward past the site of the Grand Bayou mounds (no. 11).

With the arrival of the Bayou Cutler stage, Bayou Grosse Tete had attained sufficient significance as a drainage feature to support the Reed mounds (no. 4) on its lower course. Continued favorable environmental conditions along the Lower Grand are indicated by the presence of the several Bayou Cutler sites along its course.

The appearance of the Livonia mound group (no. 1) during the Bayou Cutler-Historic stage suggests a growing importance for the site at the junction of the two bayous. and also it means a continued significance of Bayou Grosse Tete in the Grand River system. The presence of two sites (nos. 12 and 15) on the well-defined levees of Big Bayou Pigeon points to the increased importance of this and other westward-flowing distributaries of Lower Grand River. Sites of the same or slightly earlier age situated on the west side of Grand Lake may be interpreted to indicate eastward-flowing distributaries from Bayou Teche.

The location of the two identified Historic sites (nos. 2 and 3) on upper Bayou Grosse Tete means the continuing importance of this stream in the Grand River system. The absence of known Historic sites for the remainder of the area hardly condemns it as uninhabitable at the time. In the inadequate potsherd collections from several other sites there is the suggestion that at least Lower Grand River remained inhabited territory.

Nothing has been said of the sites situated within the Atchafalaya Basin proper, for the very good reason that they have yet to yield pottery collections sufficient for age identification. It can only be pointed out that there is no known site situated directly upon the Atchafalaya, the present main channel of the stream apparently being too young to have afforded attractive situations even during the most recent phase of mound building. The area extending northward from Grand Lake may be moundless for the same reason—too great youth. If this latter conjecture be true, Grand Lake was once considerably larger than it is at present, that is, in a north-south direction. If the presence of sites directly on its east and west shores is any criterion, Grand Lake has not narrowed recently. In fact, there is marked evidence of the recent recession of its eastern shore. The trend of the evidence suggests that at an earlier date the important discharges into Grand Lake were from distributaries of Grand River and Bayou Teche, while in more recent times the significant influx of water and sediment has been from the north.

The basis for speculation concerning a changing environment for the Lower Grand River area is furnished by the *Rangia-Unio* relationships referred to in a previous section. The oldest site, Goddel Ridge (no. 17), is composed entirely of Rangias. The lowest and oldest identified stratum of the Miller site (no. 18) is composed entirely of Unios, which in turn are overlain by a black-earth layer, and the latter capped with Rangias. If our explanations be confined to natural causes, one interpretation would see the initial Lower Grand as a vigorous Mississippi distributary, confined by its levees and flowing through a region still sufficiently brackish to support an abundant growth of Rangias in its ponds and lakes. A continued flow of fresh water with its accompanying alluviation caused a diminution in the supply of Rangias and led to the extensive use of Unios represented by the lower stratum of the Miller site. The final stage anticipated the present, coming about as the result of a decreasing importance of Grand River as a distributary stream, and permitting the return of brackish conditions to bodies of water like Lake Verret. This change is reflected in the uppermost layer of Rangias in the Miller midden.

All the nice reasoning of the preceding paragraphs is predicated upon the operation of natural causes only. To those conscious of the unpredictable vagaries of human choice it is unnecessary to point out that the explanation of the change from Unios to Rangias might easily lie in the exercising of some forgotten chief's prerogative.

The problems concerned with the distribution of clams and their use as food by the primitive inhabitants of Louisiana are bigger than Iberville Parish. Their solution must await further knowledge, both geologic and archaeologic, concerning coastal Louisiana.

Conclusion

This section on mounds is the second in a series, which, it is hoped, will eventually be extended to cover all of Louisiana's Parishes. At first there was simply the thought of taking advantage of an excellent opportunity to make artifact collections on hitherto unvisited sites. At the present stage there are three well-defined objectives that the field investigator has in mind:

First, the simple but systematic cataloging of sites remains a fundamental task that will not end until every observable mound in Louisiana is accurately described and located on a map. Surface collections of potsherds and other artifacts are made wherever they are available. From these surface collections it is possible to check, extend, and refine the pottery complex chronology already initiated for

Louisiana. Even surficial knowledge of the sites over a considerable area forms the basis of good judgment as to where excavations can be expected to be fruitful. For example, the study of Iberville Parish and adjacent areas points to the Miller midden as a site where the hard labor of digging might well be rewarded with significant scientific data.

Secondly, it is hoped that the joining of archaeology with geology in common undertakings may continue to be mutually profitable. Archaeology may initially point to areas and streams as older or younger; geology may eventually reduce the cultural chronology to a reasonable basis in time units.

Finally, the third field has to do with human geography, and it deals with gradually emerging concepts as to the relationships between a primitive people and the area they inhabited. It points out preference as to site and food; it gives an idea of minimum and optimum habitats. It is this last lead, more than any other, that lends a thread of continuity between the almost forgotten mound builders of the prehistoric past and the modern inhabitants of the same region.

8

Report of the Conference on Southeastern Pottery Typology[1]

Held at
The Ceramic Repository for the Eastern United States,
Museum of Anthropology, University of Michigan
Ann Arbor, Michigan
May 16–17, 1938

By James A. Ford and James B. Griffin

[11] The Conference on Southeastern Ceramic Typology was an informal meeting of archeologists directly concerned with the problems of analyzing the pottery recovered in the course of archeological investigation of aboriginal sites in the Southeastern United States.

The purpose of the meeting was to attempt to establish in the Southeast a unified system of pottery analysis. Methodologies that have been successfully applied in other areas were reviewed. Viewpoints and procedures listed in the following pages were selected as being most applicable to the Southeastern area.

---

1. *Editors' note*: No authorship is indicated on the original of this paper; however, James A. Ford and James B. Griffin wrote it (Williams 1960). The original unpaginated manuscript was issued in mimeographed form as *The Proceedings of The First Southeastern Archaeological Conference*. It was reprinted in 1960 in the *Newsletter of the Southeastern Archaeological Conference* 7(1):10–22 (Williams 1960). Page numbers are assigned here on the basis of that reprint and are indicated in [brackets]. Typographical errors have been corrected, and several modifications in the spacing of lines and paragraphs have been made in the interest of saving space. Footnotes have been added to clarify several points.

Additional copies of this report may be secured from J. A. Ford, School of Geology, Louisiana State University, University, Louisiana.

[12] Purposes of Pottery Study

1. For the purposes of discovering culture history, pottery must be viewed primarily as a reflector of cultural influence. Its immediate value to the field and laboratory archeologist lies in its use as a tool for demonstrating temporal and areal differences and similarities. Interpretations of technological processes are of value in making comparisons of the similarities of the material. However, at this time, when there is still so much disagreement among the specialists in that field, the more subtle technological distinctions cannot be depended upon to provide a basis for classification. It is possible to make useful divisions in material which was manufactured by processes that are not yet completely understood.

2. The inadequacy of the procedure of dividing pottery into "types" merely for purposes of describing the material is recognized. This is merely a means of presenting raw data. Types should be classes of material which promise to be useful as tools of interpreting culture history.

Identification of Types

3. There is no predetermined system for arriving at useful type divisions. Types must be selected after careful study of the material and of the problems which they are designed to solve. A type is nothing more than a tool, and is set up for a definite purpose in the unfolding of culture history. If divisions in an established type will serve that purpose more accurately, they should be made; otherwise there is little purpose in crowding the literature with types.

4. A type must be defined as the combination of all the discoverable vessel features: paste, temper, method of manufacture, firing, hardness, thickness, size, shape, surface finish, decoration, and appendages. The range of all of these features, which is to be considered representative of the type, must be described. By this criteria two sets of material which are similar in nearly all features, but which are divided by peculiar forms of one feature (shell contrasted with grit tempering, for example), may be separated into two types if there promises

to be some historical justification for the procedure. Otherwise they should be described as variants of one type.

5. A type should be so clearly definable that an example can be recognized entirely apart from its associated materials. Recognition must be possible by others who will use the material, as well as by the individual proposing the type.

Systemization of Type Recognition

6. As it is possible for certain features of pottery, such as shape or decoration, to be distributed apart from the specific features with which they may formerly have been associated, it is necessary to select a set of mutually exclusive features to serve as a primary framework for the classifications. This is to prevent the possibility of defining one type mainly on the basis of a paste feature, and still another on the basis of decoration. This procedure would eventually lead to a condition in which almost every vessel would be of two or more "types."

[13] 7. As in practice the classification will usually be applied to sherds, it was decided to utilize the features of surface finish and decoration as the bases for the primary divisions of the material. There is also the possibility of difficulty if one type is selected on the basis of a rim decoration and another has its reference to body decoration. Crossing of types would again occur as the results of a defect of the system. It was decided that body finish and decoration should define the type.

List of Constants

8. The term constant is applied to each of the list of apparent techniques selected by the conference as the primary divisions of Southeastern surface finishes and decorations. The constants selected, with some modifying adjectives, are as follows:

	Constant	Modifiers	Definition
1.	Plain		No marked alteration of vessel surface.
		smoothed	Hand smoothed, no reflective surfaces.
		polished	Marks of polishing tool show—some reflective surfaces.
2.	Filmed		Material added to surface of vessel

		after initial scraping of surface.
	red	Red slip or wash applied all over vessel exterior.
	red and white	Red and white pigment applied in separate areas to contrast with one another.
	zoned red	Red pigment applied on uncolored vessel surface in areas.
3. Incised		Lines drawn in paste while plastic.
	narrow	Made with pointed tool.
	bold	Lines both wide and deep.
	broad	Wide lines.
	punctate	Punctates spaced in incised lines.
4. Engraved		Lines made by a pointed tool after paste had hardened. This may have been done either before or after firing.
5. Roughened		Surface scarified or made irregular in a number of ways. Some of the techniques that will be included in this constant are not fully understood.
	brush	Surface apparently stroked while plastic with a bundle of fibres.
	stipple	Shallow indentations apparently made by patting the plastic surface with a brush.
[14] 6. Combed		Lines similar to incised lines but made with an instrument having several teeth so that width between lines is mechanically constant. (Choctaw is only known example).
7. Stamped		Impressions made in vessel surface with tool having designs carved on it.
	simple	Impressions apparently made with a paddle having parallel grooves cut in it. In some cases these impressions may have been made with a thong-wrapped paddle.

	complicated	Die in which were carved complex designs used to make impressions on vessel surface.
	check	Die in which incisions were arranged in crosshatched fashion. Result of use of stamp is a "waffle" surface.
	dentate or linear	Single or double row of square impressions evidently made with a narrow stamp.
8. Punctated		Indentations made one at a time with the point of a tool
	finger	Indentations apparently made with the tip of the finger or finger nail.
	triangle	Punctates triangular shaped, as though made with the corner of a cube.
	reed	Punctated circles made with a hollow cylinder, apparently a piece of cane, reed, or bone.
	zoned	Punctations arranged in areas which contrast with unpunctated areas of the vessel surface.
9. Pinched		Tips of two fingers used to raise small areas of the vessel surface by pinching.
	ridge	Raised areas form ridges.
10. Applique		Clay added to vessel surface to form raised areas.
	effigy	Applied clay indicates parts of some zoomorphic form (frog bowls, etc.)
	ridge	Applied strips of clay form ridges.
	node	Applied clay forms small protuberances.
[15] 11. Cord marked		(Pragmatically cord marking might be considered as a stamped. However its distinctiveness, wide areal range, and usual name warrant the use of this separate constant.) Vessel surface

	roughened by application of a cord wrapped paddle. Twist of cords usually discernible.
12. Fabric marked	Surface marked by application of fabric to plastic clay. This constant will include the so-called "coiled basket" (plain plaited) imprints. Also applied to fabric impressions found on salt pans.

9. It is recognized that there is no assurance that each of these constants includes techniques which can be considered as genetically related. They do attempt to describe all that can be determined regarding the technique of decoration. However, in some cases the techniques are in dispute and there is no certainty that this arbitrary placement is correct.

Type Nomenclature

10. In order to facilitate reference to a pottery type, each type will be given a name, which will normally consist of three parts.

11. *The Geographical Name*

The first part of the name will be taken from a geographical locality. It may be the name of a site at which the type is well represented, or the name of an area in which a number of sites bearing the type are found. If possible, the names of sites from which the type has already been described in the literature should be selected. It is advantageous that the name be both distinctive and associated with the material in the minds of the workers in the area. Numerically common types should not be given the same geographical name. In practice, the type will usually be referred to by its geographical name only. Confusion will result if more than one common type can be designated this way. Illustrations of some good geographical names are: Lamar, Lenoir, Marksville, Moundsville, Tallapoosa, Tuscaloosa, etc.

12. *The Descriptive Name*

The second part of the name will sometimes consist of a descriptive adjective which modifies the constant. In certain cases the "modifier" is practically demanded by peculiarities of the constant. Some of these modifiers were determined by the Conference and are contained in the foregoing list of constants (paragraph 8). Examples are: check (stamped), complicated (stamped), red and white (filmed). In other cases the modifier may be a term which serves [16] to suggest the peculiarities of the constant. Examples: bold, fine, narrow, etc. However, it should be stressed that to be useful, a name must be as short as possible. Unless the middle term is particularly helpful in calling the type to mind and fits naturally into the type name, it should be omitted.

13. *The Constant Name*

The last part of the name will consist of one of the listed constants given in paragraph 8. The material should be examined carefully to determine to which of these categories it appears to belong. If it does not belong to any of them, a new constant may be proposed.

Examples of Type Names

14. Examples of some names which are already in use and which promise to become standard are:

Georgia - Lamar Complicated Stamped, Swift Creek Complicated Stamped, Vining Simple Stamped, Deptford Linear Stamped.

Louisiana - Marksville Zoned Stamped, Coles Creek Incised, Fatherland Incised, Deasonville Red and White Filmed.

Which Types Should be Named?

15. Only the materials which appear to have been manufactured at a site should receive type names based upon materials from the site. Extensive aboriginal trade in pottery seems to have occurred. Trade material had best remain unnamed until it can be examined in a region where it seems to have been manufactured and consequently is more abundant.

Plain Body Sherds from Decorated Vessels

16. Most Southeastern site collections will include a number of plain sherds which come from the lower parts of vessels that were decorated about the shoulder. These sherds should not be set up as types but should be described, with some indication as to the pottery types with which they may have been associated. In cases where there is little doubt as to the derivation of the plain pieces, they may be listed under the type name but should be distinguished from the sherds showing more fully the requisite type features.

Distribution of Type Samples

17. The Conference decided that in order to permit consistent use of Southeastern Ceramic types it was necessary to provide each of the institutions working in the area with sets of specimens representing the recognized types. Each set should illustrate the range of material to be [17] included in the type. Accompanying the specimens should be outline drawings of the vessel shapes.

For the present these collections are to be distributed to the following:

Mr. William G. Haag
Museum of Anthropology and Archeology
University of Kentucky
Lexington, Kentucky

Mr. David DeJarnette
Alabama Museum of Natural History
University of Alabama
University, Alabama

Mr. T. M. N. Lewis
Department of Archeology
University of Tennessee
Knoxville, Tennessee

Dr. James B. Griffin
Ceramic Repository for the Eastern United States
Museums Building
Ann Arbor, Michigan

Mr. Joffre Coe
Archeological Society of North Carolina
University of North Carolina
Chapel Hill, North Carolina

Dr. A. R. Kelly
Ocmulgee National Monument
Macon, Georgia

Mr. J. A. Ford
School of Geology
Louisiana State University
University, Louisiana

Board of Review for Proposed Types

18. The Conference recognized the need for a Board of Review to control and unify the processes of type selection, naming, and description. The board selected to serve until the time of the next meeting is composed of James B. Griffin, Gordon Willey, and J. A. Ford (addresses in paragraph 26).

Handbook of Recognized Type Descriptions

19. Descriptions of recognized types are to be issued in the form of a loose-leaf handbook. This form is adopted to permit additions and replacements [18] from time to time as necessary. For the present the handbook will consist of mimeographed sheets, to be issued by J. A. Ford.

Procedure for Proposing a Type

20. The procedure for proposing a new type will be as follows: the investigator proposing the type will send a representative collection of sherd specimens to all the corresponding institutions (paragraph 17). With the type specimens will be a tentative description (paragraph 24).

All comments on the proposed type should be sent both to the investigator proposing the type and to the Board of Review. If the type appears to be a valid and necessary one, the Board of Review will approve it, and the type description will be issued as pages of the handbook. To avoid confusion type names should not be used in publications without this recognition.

Definition of Some Descriptive Terms

21. In order to make possible a more uniform description of pottery, the Conference recognized the desirability of a defined nomenclature.

This problem required too much discussion to be fully considered at this time. It was only because of the immediate demands of type description that the following terms were discussed and agreed upon.

The following parts of vessels were not to be considered as accurately definable and measurable sections of the vessels, but rather as areas of the exterior surface. As these areas are formed by peculiarities of vessel shape, and there is a wide variation of shapes, all the defined areas are not present on every vessel.

Lip area–The area marking the termination of the vessel wall. More specifically, the lip lies between the outside and inside surfaces of the vessel. It is thus possible to speak of a squared lip, a rounded lip, a pointed lip, notched lip, etc.

Rim area–The area on the outside of the vessel wall below the lip which may be set off from the vessel wall by decoration or other special treatment. (thickened rim, smoothed rim, decorated rim, wide rim area, etc.)

Neck area–The neck area is found only on vessels which show a marked constriction between body and rim. In general, it is an area of constriction below the rim.

Shoulder area–Shoulder area appears only on certain forms. It is marked by inward curving walls. The area is considered to lie between the point of maximum diameter and the area of constriction that marks the neck.

Body–The body is the portion of the vessel which gives it form. This means that necks and rims are not considered to form part of the body.

[19] *Base or basal area*–The base is the area upon which a vessel normally rests. In the case of vessels with legs the base is the area of the body to which the supports are attached.

Appendages–Appendages are additions to the vessel which may have either functional or decorative utility. This term will refer to handles, lugs, feet, effigy heads, spouts, etc.

Strap handle–A handle which is attached to the vessel wall at two points and which in cross section is definitely flattened and strap like.

Loop handle–A handle which is attached to the vessel wall at two points and which in cross section is rounded and rod like.

Complex of types–A complex is considered to be all the types that were in use at any one village at the same period of time. The association of the different types found on any village site must be proven—it cannot be assumed that every village site presents only one complex of types. Many sites show two or more recognizable complexes.

22. *Measurements*

Gross measurements–In presenting measurements of vessels and of their parts, the members of the Conference have agreed to use the Metric System.

Hardness measurements–Hardness is to be measured on the exterior surface of the vessel wall by means of the Mohs scale of graded minerals. The procedure is described in March: *Standards of Pottery Descriptions* pp. 17-22.[2]

Color–Surface coloring, paste interior coloring, and color penetration are to be described by the terms already in use. (White, grey, brown, buff, fawn, black, red, yellow, etc.)

23. *Shapes*

Present descriptive terms will continue to be used for shapes. Mr. Charles Wilder, who has already done some work on the classification and nomenclature of Mississippi Valley pottery shapes, has consented to prepare a simplified classification and nomenclature of shapes to be presented for consideration at the next meeting. Members of the conference are requested to send to Wilder outline drawings of all vessel forms found in their areas (address in paragraph 26).

24. **Outline for Description of Types**

Illustrations of specimens of type should be placed here. Both body and rim sherds should be shown. Photographs or outline drawings may be used to show the range of shapes.

SUGGESTED TYPE NAME - - -

[20] PASTE:

Method of manufacture–coiled, moulded, etc.

Tempering–material, size, proportion.

Texture–consolidated, laminated, fine, coarse, etc.

---

2. The full reference is given below.

Hardness–use geological scale on exterior surface.

Color–surface mottling, penetration of, paste core.

SURFACE FINISH:

Modifications–smoothing, paddling, brushing, scraping.

Filming–slip, wash, smudging. (In cases where there is any doubt as to whether the surface treatment should be classed as either finish or decoration, the terms may be combined into Surface Finish and Decoration. Discussion of both may be included under this heading.)

DECORATION:

Technique–the method by which the decoration was executed; engraving, incising, punctating, etc.

Design–describe the plan of decoration, scroll, negative meanders, etc.

Distribution–portion of vessel surface occupied by the decoration.

FORM:

Rim–treatment of rim area, i.e., thickened rim (tell how thickened) out-curving rim, cambered rim, etc.

Lip–features of, or modifications of, i.e. squared lip, pointed lip, notched lip, etc.

Body–general form of vessels.

Base–shape of, peculiar treatments of, additions to.

Thickness–of the different parts of the vessel wall.

Appendages–handles, lugs, legs, etc.

USUAL RANGE OF TYPE: Geographical position of sites at which type is found in sufficient abundance to be considered native.

[21] CHRONOLOGICAL POSITION OF TYPE IN RANGE: Time position in relation to other types and complexes. Be certain to state reliability of evidence supporting this conclusion.

BIBLIOGRAPHY OF TYPE: References to publications where material representative of type has been illustrated and described.

It will be noted that in general this outline follows the form given in Guthe's introductory section to Standards of Pottery Description, by Benjamin March (Occasional Contributions from the Museum of Anthropology of the University of Michigan, No. 3.) Any details which are not considered in the foregoing will conform to the suggestions set forth in this volume.

25. **Wording of Descriptions**

Make the descriptions of material as concise as practical. Complete sentences are not always necessary. First give in detail the usual conditions of each feature; then the range of variation allowed for the type.

26. **List of Members**

The following archaeologists attended the Ann Arbor Conference:

M. John L. Buckner (University of Kentucky, Museum, Lexington, Kentucky)
307 West 2nd St.
Paris, Kentucky

Mr. Joffre Coe
University of North Carolina
Chapel Hill, North Carolina

Mr. David I. DeJarnette
Alabama Museum of Natural History
University, Alabama

Mr. Charles H. Fairbanks (University of Tennessee, Archaeology, Knoxville, Tennessee)
Charleston, Tennessee

Dr. Vladim[i]r J. Fewkes
Irene Mound Excavations
Savannah, Georgia

Mr. J. Joe Finkelstein (University of Oklahoma, Norman, Oklahoma)
Department of Anthropology
University of Chicago
Chicago, Illinois

[22] Mr. J. A. Ford
School of Geology
Louisiana State University
University, Louisiana

Dr. James B. Griffin
Ceramic Repository for the Eastern United States
Museums Building
Ann Arbor, Michigan

Mr. William G. Haag
Museum of Anthropology and Archaeology
University of Kentucky
Lexington, Kentucky

Mr. Claude Johnston (Museum, University of Kentucky, Lexington,
Kentucky)
335 West 2nd. St.
Paris, Kentucky

Dr. Arthur R. Kelly
Ocmulgee National Monument
Macon, Georgia

Mr. T. M. N. Lewis
Department of Archaeology, University of Tennessee
Knoxville, Tennessee

Mr. Frederick R. Matson
Museum of Anthropology
Ann Arbor, Michigan

Mr. St[u]art Neitzel (Department of Archaeology, University of
Tennessee, Knoxville, Tennessee)
Box 81
Charleston, Tennessee

Mr. Charles G. Wilder (Museum of Alabama, University, Alabama)
Box 233
Scottsboro, Alabama

Archaeologists who were not able to attend the meeting, but who should be considered members of the Conference because of their interest in its purpose and their valuable assistance in developing the ideas presented are:

Mr. Preston Holder
326 W. 107th St.
New York, N.Y.

Mr. Gordon Willey
Ocmulgee National Monument
Macon, Georgia

9

CORRESPONDENCE

A Chronological Method Applicable to the Southeast

Any archaeologist who considers that his science is pledged to the task of rediscovering unrecorded and lost history, rather than to the collection of "curios," is hardly in a position to deny the paramount importance of chronology. Lacking a scale which demonstrates the relative ages of the various activities of an ancient people, we are at best merely the collectors of disconnected fragments of history, and can never hope to fit these fragments together to form a complete and logical story of the past.

Before the work of Nelson and Kidder in the Southwest, the archaeology of that area was in about the same condition as that which exists today in the Southeastern states. However, the work of these pioneer scientists and the well directed researches of those who have followed them have succeeded in giving a clear picture of the course of prehistoric Southwestern cultures that in some ways is better and more complete than would have been the story of the Indians themselves, had they left written records of their history.

Although the Southeastern states seem to be as wealthy in evidences of prehistoric occupation as the Southwest, unfortunately the same conditions of thick refuse deposits are not usually present, and the same reliable methods of vertical stratigraphy cannot be applied as frequently as in the Southwest. It seems that in this area archaeologists will have to adopt existing standard methods or develop new ones to determine relative age. The largely accidental discovery of superposition in occasional village sites, and similar evidence given by later intrusions into old burial mounds, provide valuable evidence, but such cases have so far been too infrequent to give anything like a complete chronology for even one small area. If we must trust to similar accidental discoveries to complete the entire picture, we must reconcile ourselves to a long wait.

However, there is the possibility that direct and constructive work may be done on southern chronology along lines that have been somewhat neglected. It is commonly accepted, apparently with good reason, that the pottery found so abundantly at the old sites must bear the main burden of comparative dating. Considerable attention has been given this cultural feature by a number of investigators working in this region, but the major part of their material has been burial furniture found accompanying the dead in mounds or cemeteries. Usually they seem to have overlooked the apparent fact that the potsherds found in the village refuse may be expected to give a better example of the full range of the people's ceramic styles than the pieces that were chosen to accompany the dead; moreover, the refuse material is usually much more abundant. Logically it appears that the approach to chronological problems lies in the study of the changes that have occurred with time in ceramic decorations as revealed by potsherds. This is not a new idea. Kidder's chronology at Pecos was based essentially upon the same thing.

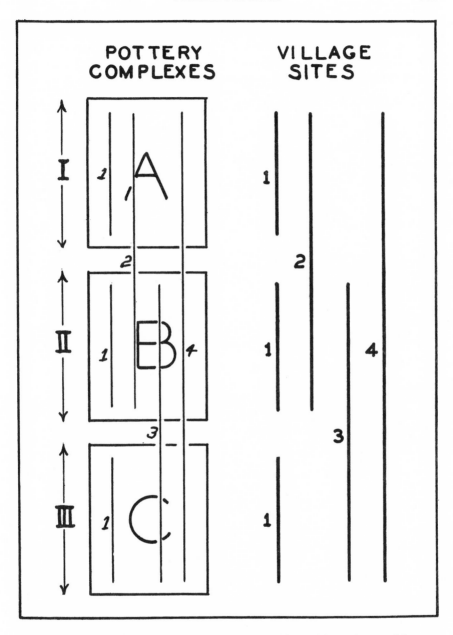

POTTERY COMPLEXES

VILLAGE SITES

FIG. 18—Theoretical diagram of a chronological history illustrating possible actions of complexes (A, B, and C), pottery types (*1, 2, 3,* and *4*), and village sites (1, 2, 3, and 4).

In order to fully apply the methods of analysis outlined in the following pages, it is necessary that a collecting survey be made and representative samples of refuse material be secured from as many sites as possible in some area of comprehensive size—say one hundred miles square. The survey must be thorough enough for the investigator to be reasonably certain that he has secured at least a sample of every variety of material found in the area. The village sites of the Southeast are now very often cultivated fields, and the field-worker engaged in this type of survey will find little use for his spade.

The next step is that of classifying the material. The classification should be detailed. Repeated occurrence of a certain decoration at separate sites will determine for the investigator whether or not the decoration represents a real and significant type or is merely a local variation. It will probably develop that not only one but several distinct decorations will be found associated at a number of different sites. These associated decorations will be a group of styles that occur together, and form what has been termed a "decoration complex." A decoration complex covering a restricted area such as that under consideration probably represents a distinct time horizon. The stylistic time horizons that have existed in the area may now be logically separated.

However, there are numerous possibilities of becoming confused in this attempt. A review of conditions present in chronological histories that have been thoroughly developed will probably explain some of the peculiar conditions that are found. A generalized representation of a chronology is given in Figure 18. In this diagram the time periods I, II, and III are represented by the stylistic groups (or complexes) A, B, and C. These are shown by blocks placed one above another as they occurred in time. Within these blocks are lines representing the actions of definite style types. Such types as those marked *1* serve to differentiate the complexes. However, some types, such as those marked *2* and *3*, may have extended through two of the time periods but not the other. Others (*4*) may have extended through the entire time scale.

The length of tenure of a village site may act in a similar manner. This is indicated in the diagram by heavy black lines. Some sites, such as those marked 1, may have been inhabited only during the time when one complex of styles was in vogue. Others (2 and 3) may yield samples of two of the time periods but not of the third. Still others (4) may have existed all through the time scale.

Application of these phenomena of cultural chronology will not only serve to explain some of the conditions that are met with in attempting to determine complexes; they will also assist in arranging the complexes in their temporal relations. A linkage may be provided both by the overlapping of specific decoration types and varying lengths of tenure of village sites. Additional evidence may lie in the evolution of decoration types from one complex to another. This is not necessarily true. The area chosen for investigation may be distant from the region in which the actual evolution took place, and one complex may be replaced by another with no indication as to how the later types came into existence.

Another kind of overlapping may be present if, in the region adjoining that in which there were two subsequent complexes, an entirely different one existed through the time when one of the complexes was being replaced by the other. Trade material from this overlapping complex may then be expected on sites representing both of the subsequent complexes.

Of course the possibilities of readoption of abandoned decoration styles and reoccupation of old village sites would complicate this ideal scheme, but neither of these phenomena may be expected as a usual occurrence.

Preponderance of evidence must be accepted in determining types, in separating them into complexes, and in discovering relationships. Therefore, the reliability of these processes is in direct proportion to the size and number of site collections

Collections should be made from as many historic and protohistoric villages as can be located. The material from these sites will show which complex was the most recent and will determine which end of the chain of complexes constructed by overlapping is the latest. Without this tie-up it would be as logical for one end of the chronology to be recent as for the other. In some cases it may be more expedient to begin by determining the historic complex. Working back from this, the other complexes can be arranged in their true order.

A sequence of stylistic periods determined in this manner cannot be accepted as more than tentative. There are many possibilities of error in this method. Most of the work of classifying and comparing is highly subjective, and the worker is called upon to make many close decisions where he may be influenced by his preconceived ideas and desires. Then too there is the possibility that some unforeseen complication may be present to upset the apple cart.

However, such a tentative chronology is far better than no beginning at all. It is now possible deliberately to select sites at which superposition of materials may be expected. Stratigraphic study of these sites will provide a reliable check on the relative ages of the parts of the time scale that are involved.

After the chronology is established, the archaeologist will find himself in a position that, for the Southeast at least, will be novel. No longer must he excavate sites because they "look good." Instead, by paying attention to surface material, it will be possible to develop all the recoverable features of the various time levels in the area. New finds will appear in their true relation to one another instead of being a source of wonder and vague hypotheses.

However, it cannot be accepted that these ceramic complexes will represent different cultures or culture phases. It is entirely possible that two cultures may have used the same pottery, or at different times a culture may have changed its pottery types. What the method attempts to do is to use ceramic decoration, probably the most flexible of the remaining cultural features, as "type fossils" to distinguish the passage of time.

I do not insist that the foregoing is the only, or even the best method by which Southeastern chronology can be determined, but it is impossible to see, without chronology, how we can ever hope to rediscover the cultural history of the Indians of the Southeast.

Bibliography

FORD, J. A. Analysis of Indian Village Site collections from Louisiana and Mississippi, Anthro. Study No. 2, La, Geol. Survey, Dept. Conservation, New Orleans, La.

KIDDER, M. A. and A. V., Notes on the Pottery of Pecos, Amer. Anthro., N. S., Vol. 19, No. 2, July–Sept., 1917, pp. 325–360.

KROEBER, A. L., On the Principle of Order in Civilization as Exemplified by Changes of Fashion, Amer. Anthro., N. S., Vol. 21, No. 3, July–Sept., 1919, pp. 235–263.

NELSON, N. C., Chronology of the Tano Ruins, New Mexico, Amer. Anthro., N. S., Vol. 18, pp. 159–180, 1916.

SPIER, LESLIE, Stratigraphic Technique in the Reconstruction of Prehistoric Sequences in Southwestern America, Methods in Social Science, Steward Rice, editor, University of Chicago Press, 1931.

J. A. FORD
School of Geology
Louisiana State University
Baton Rouge, Louisiana

10

STATE OF LOUISIANA
DEPARTMENT OF CONSERVATION

B. A. HARDEY
Commissioner

ANTHROPOLOGICAL STUDY No. 3

Crooks Site, A Marksville Period Burial Mound in La Salle Parish, Louisiana

by
J. A. FORD AND GORDON WILLEY

Partially Based on Field Reports
by
WILLIAM T. MULLOY AND ARDEN KING

Published by
DEPARTMENT OF CONSERVATION
LOUISIANA GEOLOGICAL SURVEY
New Orleans, La.
June 1, 1940

I

FOREWORD

The excavation of the Crooks site in La Salle Parish, La., was begun October 2, 1938, and was completed April 20, 1939. This investigation was undertaken as part of the program of the state-wide Archeological Project of the Louisiana Works Progress Administration. The project was sponsored by Louisiana State University and was under the direction of J. A. Ford, Research Associate in Archeology, of that institution.

Two units of the project, a field unit and a laboratory, were directly concerned with the exploration of the Crooks site. The field unit, which did the actual work of excavation, was under the direction of William T. Mulloy and Arden King. Their technical staff usually consisted of three clerks who attended to many of the details of recording the provenience of the materials, exposing burials and other delicate discoveries, and packing finds for shipment to the laboratory. The administrative staff of the field unit consisted of two foremen and a timekeeper. An average of 35 laborers was used during the course of this work.

Discoveries and notes from the site were sent to the laboratory located in New Orleans. This unit of the project was under the immediate direction of Gordon R. Willey, who was also supervisor for the entire project. The laboratory served both the Crooks site and the Greenhouse site which were the two field explorations undertaken during the winter of 1938-1939.

In the laboratory the material was run through the various divisions as rapidly as it came in from the field. It was successively washed, cataloged, restored, and classified, and type specimens were photographed or drawn. The results of the studies were analysed and compiled in graphic form in preparation for the final report. Large scale drawings were made of each five-foot mound profile, and tracing paper shells were prepared which were fitted over these profiles. Finds and burials were marked in their proper locations on the shells so that the burials and burial furniture might be studied in relation to the building stages of the mounds.

Outstanding among the 25 or more clerical workers and technicians who contributed to the success of the laboratory studies are Mr. C. H. Hopkins, who classified the Crooks site pottery, and Mr. B. B. Levy, who made the analyses. Mr. John Anglim prepared two-thirds of the drawings for this report. Approximately one-third of them were made by Mr. Alvin Doria. The successful operation of the entire project must in large measure be credited to the administrative work of Mr. Paul J. Fourchy, Administrative Assistant.

The work has been greatly facilitated by the co-operation of Mrs. Leo G. Spofford, former State Director of the Professional and Service Division of the Louisiana Works Progress Administration, and Miss Alma S. Hammond, the present director. Miss Birdie C. Busey and Miss Willie Lurry, Supervisor and Assistant Supervisor, respectively, of the Alexandria District, took a constant interest in the work and assisted in all of the many ways which lay within their power.

The "Exploration," "Burials," and "Physical Stratigraphy" sections of this report were originally written by William T. Mulloy and Arden King, the field Supervisors. These sections have been extensively altered and revised by J. A. Ford and Gordon R. Willey, who have collaborated in preparing the remaining sections. Walter W. Beecher has assisted in preparing the manuscript for printing. The criticisms and corrections of Dr. Fred B. Kniffen have been most helpful.

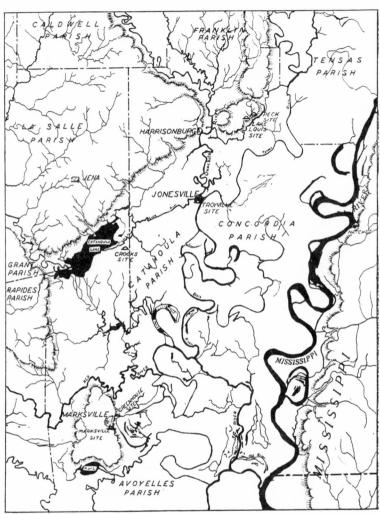

Figure 1. Map of east-central Louisiana showing location of Crooks
site, near Catahoula Lake, Peck site, Marksville site, and
Greenhouse site.

EXPLORATION

Location of the Crooks site and the related topography

The Crooks site was situated in La Salle Parish,[1] La., about four miles south of the little settlement of Archie. The nearest town of any size is Jena, 12 miles to the northwest (fig. 1). The site was on the property of Mr. N. D. Crooks, who very kindly gave Louisiana State University permission to undertake explorations, and who, with his family, assisted the work with many kindnesses.

A large conical mound, 85 feet in diameter and 18 feet high, was the outstanding feature of the site. This will be referred to as Mound A. One hundred and ten feet to the south of Mound A was a smaller structure, about 50 feet in diameter and two feet high, which was designated as Mound B. Cultural material, such as potsherds and flint chips, was very scarce on the eroded slopes of Mound A. No artifacts of any kind could be found on Mound B or in the nearby fields.

The mounds were located in the south side of a plowed field, in the edge of the hardwood swamp that stretches for 25 miles to the southwest between Catahoula Lake and Black River. Neither of the structures had ever been subject to cultivation. Around the site in all directions the almost level flood plain of the Mississippi River stretches for miles. River courses, both active and abandoned, are the dominant topographic features. Slight elevations are provided by the natural levees that border all the streams. The prehistoric native peoples inhabiting this area commonly took advantage of these elevations for their settlements, just as the white farmers do today.

The Crooks mounds were situated about 400 yards southeast of French Fork Bayou, and about 150 yards southwest

---

[1] In the archeological survey of the State this site has been assigned the symbol, La-3. Its exact location was NW¼ SE¼ sec. 1, T. 6 N., R. 4 E.

5

of its small distributary, Cypress Bayou. The soil upon
which the mounds stood, and of which they were constructed,
was deposited as the back slope of the natural levee which
borders the Cypress Bayou distributary channel.

Physiographically French Fork Bayou has had a very
interesting history. There is evidence that at one time it
formed part of the Arkansas River. (See Huner, 1939, pp.
23-28, fig. 1.) The Arkansas left its present channel near
the town of Pine Bluff, Ark., and at different times flowed
down the channels of the present Ouachita River and Bayou
Bartholomew, an eastern tributary of the Ouachita. As is
demonstrated by the characteristic meander pattern and the
pinkish sediment laid down by the waters of the Arkansas,
this stream flowed southward to the location of the town
of Jonesville, La. Here it turned to the southwest and followed the channel which is now called Little River in its
upper part and French Fork lower down (fig. 1). French
Fork can be traced part of the way along the southeastern
side of Catahoula Lake, but about half way it disappears
beneath sediments deposited after this channel had been
abandoned. In part the natural levees of the French Fork
channel help form the dam which impounds Catahoula Lake
against the Prairie Terrace escarpment to the west.

Fisk (1938, pp. 18-26) treats part of the history of the
Ouachita-Little River-French Fork channel in detail in
his "Geology of Grant and La Salle Parishes." At the
time the Ouachita-Little River-French Fork channel was
active, the Mississippi River was occupying a course a short
distance to the eastward now marked by Tensas River and
Black River. The waters coming down the French Fork
channel probably emptied into the Black River course southeast of Catahoula Lake. The channels in this region have
been obscured by later sediments and cannot be traced with
much confidence.

The abandonment of the Little River-French Fork part
of the old Arkansas River course was caused by the westward progression of a large meander of the Tensas-Black
channel of the Mississippi, which cut into a bend of the

smaller stream at the site of the present town of Jonesville, La. The old Mississippi course received the full force of the current of the smaller stream by this means, and, as a consequence of the steepening of the stream gradient, the Ouachita was straightened just above Jonesville leaving several ox-bow lakes on both sides of the active river course.

Subsequent to this event the Mississippi has changed to its present channel along the eastern side of its flood plain. Here it has since built up the flood plain by levee deposition until its present natural levees are about five feet higher than those of the abandoned channels to the west. As a consequence, when the Mississippi overflows its banks, the lower lands along the old courses are flooded to a depth of from five to ten feet or more by the impounded waters of the tributary streams. This appears to have been the condition of affairs as far back as 1542 when DeSoto's party probably wintered in the Mississippi valley near the present town of Jonesville (Walker, 1936, pp. 55-62).

The excavation of the Crooks site has demonstrated that both the mounds are placed upon a surface which is of the same character and level as the surrounding ground. Active deposition on this surface had ceased by the time the site was constructed, and it appears probable that the Jonesville cut-off of the Ouachita had already occurred. The high backwater to which the site has been subjected every spring seemingly has not deposited materials of any appreciable thickness. Such deposits would be easily recognizable as they should be fine clays, contrasting markedly with the coarser clays and silts of an active stream levee.

Although the Arkansas occupation of the Ouachita-Little River-French Fork channel appears to antedate the early part of the Marksville period as represented by the Crooks site (fig. 2), it is by no means certain that the Mississippi was in its present channel at that time. Conditions found by Walker in his excavations of the base of the large mound at Jonesville might be interpreted as indicating that, late in the Marksville period, the Mississippi was still in its old Tensas-Black channel. The cultural material which Walker

(1936, p. 40) found at the base of the Great Mound was all characteristic of the Marksville period. From an examination of this material, which is now deposited in the U. S. National Museum, the writers think that the pottery shows features which are indicative of the latter part of the Marksville period.[2] It is more similar to the material from the Marksville site and from the Greenhouse site near Marksville than it is to the finds from the Crooks mounds. This basal deposit of the Great Mound at Jonesville lay about 4.5 feet below the present ground surface (Walker, 1936, p. 21). This 4.5 feet of deposit, added to the surface of the levee on which the site is located, may represent deposit of the Mississippi. On the other hand, it may have been added by the streams which now occupy this channel, the Tensas and the Ouachita.

Artificial levees along the Mississippi River now protect most of the alluvial valley from spring floods. However, the low-lying swamp area to the south of the Crooks site, between the Mississippi and the Red, is utilized as a reservoir for flood water, and in average years the waters back up around the site to a depth of five or six feet. In exceptional years, and particularly when the levees along the Mississippi River give way as in 1927, the territory around the site is covered to a depth of 15 or 16 feet.

Previous history of site

The Crooks site was examined by Clarence B. Moore in 1909, and was discussed briefly by him as, "Mound near Chevalier Landing, Catahoula Parish" (Moore, 1909, p. 103).

The text of his remarks is as follows:

> "About half a mile in a southeasterly direction from the landing, on the Chevalier Place, which is the property of Mr. D. D. Chevalier, living nearby, in sight from the landing, is a mound, much of which has been washed away by rain, leaving sections that

---

[2] This material is illustrated by Walker, 1936, p. 10.

expose raw-looking clay, but no bones or artifacts. The height of the mound is 21 feet.

"Digging into what remained of the summit-plateau brought no return, and trial holes in the adjacent woods and fields yielded no sign of a place of burial."

Cultural problems of the site

The excavation of the Crooks site was undertaken because its superficial aspects indicated an occupation during the Marksville period. The only intensive excavation of a site wholly of this period prior to the Crooks site operations were those of Fowke (1928, pp. 405-434) and Setzler (1934) at Marksville, La. Any additional information that could be obtained about the Marksville time period would be an extremely valuable addition to the knowledge of the early period of occupation of the Lower Mississippi Valley.

In order to appreciate the position which the Crooks site occupies in Lower Mississippi Valley pre-history, and to follow the discussion of relationships, it will be necessary to review briefly the chronological framework of this area. Recent stratigraphic studies at the Greenhouse and Marksville sites [3] and comparisons with other sites make it possible to present the accompanying outline, figure 2. This chart presents the cultural stages that are found in Louisiana in the region of the Mississippi, Red, and Ouachita River valleys. All of the relationships have been demonstrated stratigraphically in detail. From Marksville through to historic Caddoan, a developmental sequence can be seen in most artifact forms. There is some suggestion of development of forms from the Tchefuncte period to Marksville, but this connection is not yet so clear as it is for the later periods.

---

[3] Report in preparation.

10

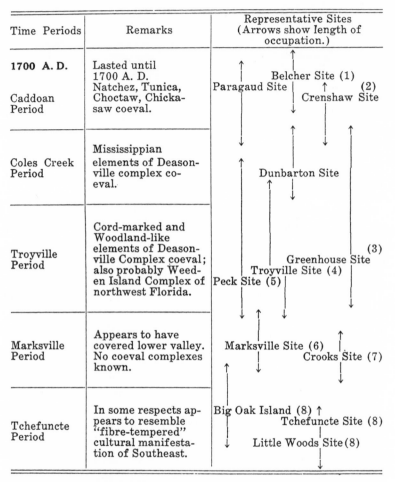

Time Periods	Remarks	Representative Sites (Arrows show length of occupation.)
1700 A. D. Caddoan Period	Lasted until 1700 A. D. Natchez, Tunica, Choctaw, Chickasaw coeval.	Belcher Site (1) Paragaud Site (2) Crenshaw Site
Coles Creek Period	Mississippian elements of Deasonville complex coeval.	Dunbarton Site
Troyville Period	Cord-marked and Woodland-like elements of Deasonville Complex coeval; also probably Weeden Island Complex of northwest Florida.	(3) Greenhouse Site Troyville Site (4) Peck Site (5)
Marksville Period	Appears to have covered lower valley. No coeval complexes known.	Marksville Site (6) Crooks Site (7)
Tchefuncte Period	In some respects appears to resemble "fibre-tempered" cultural manifestation of Southeast.	Big Oak Island (8) Tchefuncte Site (8) Little Woods Site (8)

Figure 2. Table showing the time periods of Lower Mississippi Valley pre-history, remarks on coeval manifestations of the area, and a listing of some of the sites which have been examined with the time span of each indicated.

1. Dr. Clarence Webb, report in preparation.
2. Lemley and Dickinson (1936).
3. Report in preparation.
4. Walker (1936).
5. Ford (1935).
6. Setzler (1934).
7. Present paper.
8. Report in preparation.

Method of excavation

Construction details of mounds of the Marksville period suggested the possibility that Mound A of the Crooks site might contain a large central vault in which most of the burials were placed (Setzler, 1934). The possibility of secondary and tertiary mantles heaped over a central burial was also indicated. A stripping technique would appear to be the most effective means of handling such a compound structure, but at the initiation of the work there was no certainty that it would be possible to discover the lines of demarcation between the possible mantles. It was decided that the method of vertical slicing would be the safest to employ. When old surfaces were discovered, as they were later, they could be peeled in five-foot sections across the mound. The excavators were prepared to change to a stripping technique at any time should a complicated central vault or similar structure be found. However, it proved feasible to follow the plan of slicing in five-foot sections through the mounds without changing the excavation technique.

In addition to the above technical considerations, a purely practical point was involved. The mounds had long served their owners as a refuge for stock during the annual inundation, a fact which was largely responsible for the eroded condition of the larger mound. Excavation was permitted with the understanding that the removed earth would again be piled up above high-water level so that it could still be used for this purpose. Necessarily the techniques of excavation had to be adapted to the necessity for keeping the dump dirt from becoming too widely dispersed and making the cost of restoration prohibitive.

Engineering grid

Base lines running north-south and east-west were laid off to the north and east of the large mound, about 15 feet from the toe of the structure. The intersection of these two lines was marked as a permanent point of reference for both horizontal and vertical measurements. The southwestern quadrant of the coordinate field thus established enclosed both mounds. This quadrant was gridded with stakes set at five-foot intervals, over an area 140 feet east to west, and 200 feet north to south. Each stake was marked with its distance from each of the base lines and its elevation above the datum point. The datum point was assigned an arbitrary elevation of 100 feet and, as there was no bench mark convenient, its actual elevation above sea level was not determined. From the contour lines shown on the Jena Quadrangle[4] which covers the area, the datum point was about 50 feet above sea level.

All burials and artifacts which appeared to have been intentionally placed during the construction of the mounds were located both vertically and horizontally. Scattered material found in the soil was collected in bags and labeled as coming from ten-foot sections of the five-foot slices. These bags were differentiated vertically according to the mantles apparent in the mound profiles. Profile drawings were made of the structure lines revealed by each five-foot slice.

[4] Quadrangle of the Mississippi River Commission survey of the Mississippi River flood plain.

Figure 3. View of the Crooks site excavations from the northeast. Mound B in the process of excavation can be seen to the left; Mound A in the center; and the large borrow pit to the north of mound A is shown to the right, filled with water.

Excavation of Mound A

The large conical mound, Mound A, measured 86 feet along its north-south axis and 83 feet east and west. According to the grid system, it extended from S-014 to S-100, and W-023 to W-106. The sides of the structure were rather steep and there was a small area, about five feet in diameter, on the top, which was nearly level. The highest point was 17.3 feet above the datum point. This certainly was not the original height as the top parts had been badly eroded in recent times. Moore's (1909, p. 103) estimate of a height of 21 feet in 1909 was probably very nearly correct. Erosion had been particularly bad on the south and west sides where the wash material on the flanks formed slopes that were much more gentle than those of the other sides. Fragments of human bones and a few potsherds were exposed near the top.

The mound had several trees that had to be removed. Three or four were over 18 inches in diameter and one large oak on the north slope measured over three feet. Vines and small undergrowth covered the structure. About half way down the slopes, an encircling wire fence had been erected to form a corral.

Excavation was begun by cutting a trench 10 feet wide and 140 feet long, north of the east-west base line. This was carried well into the undisturbed subsoil which was found at a depth of 4.5 feet. Along the central part of this base line, the original ground surface was covered with a stratum of recent wash from the mound. Excavation was continued by cutting adjacent five-foot slices southward into the mound (fig. 4).

Fifteen feet to the south of the east-west base line, the edge of the undisturbed mound began to appear. This surface, as well as the original ground, was easily discernible. Both were capped with a zone of soil which had been bleached by weather action to a light gray. This contrasted markedly with both the mottled, dark, reddish brown clay of the subsoil, and the similar but slightly

Figure 4. Excavation of Mound A showing method. Part of the top of the primary mound has been peeled.

Figure 5. Detailed view of Mound A profile. Part of the top of the primary mound has been exposed. The stratum of lightcolored soil at the base of the primary mound is the top of the burial platform.

lighter soil of the mound mantle. The mound surface and the base were peeled in each five-foot slice.

Ten feet farther to the south, it became apparent that the mound was composed of at least two superimposed layers. Because of a later discovery, the upper strata will be referred to as the "secondary mantle," and the lower will be termed the "burial platform."

Ten feet farther to the south, and 35 feet from the base line, a third mound mantle was discovered (fig. 9b). This lay on the burial platform and was capped with the secondary mantle. This will be called the "primary mound." Its surface was also well marked by a bleached stratum.

Considerable difficulty was caused in the central portion of the mound by the large number of burials encountered. It proved feasible to excavate the east and west flanks much more rapidly than the center. After the flanks had been dug well past the center, work was begun on the south side of the central portion. The usual techniques were followed except that it was necessary to reverse the profile drawings.

Excavation of Mound B

The small mound designated as Mound B lay approximately 110 feet southwest of Mound A. Its outline appeared to be oval, but a large pit dug into the center by local treasure seekers had completely masked its original shape, giving it the appearance of a small low crater (fig. 6). The top of Mound B was only two feet above datum point and about the same height above the surrounding ground. Its apparent diameter along its long axis was 58 feet. A few small trees stood on the south side of Mound B, and it was fairly clear of undergrowth.

The grid system applied to Mound A was extended southward to cover Mound B. The excavation technique was a simplified duplication of that used on the larger mound. Mound B proved to be homogeneous structure erected as a single unit. The few burials were in exceptionally poor condition and could not be saved.

Figure 6. Mound B before excavation. Treasure hunters have dug a large hole into the center of this mound.

Figure 7. Mound b in the process of excavation.

Borrow pits

Slight depressions in the surface of the ground around Mound A could be seen before excavations were begun. A large depression to the north was particularly well marked. It was about 55 feet in diameter and two feet deep. Stratigraphic tests were made of this area in the hope that it might be a large borrow pit which had been filled during the period through which the site was in use. Material was saved in 2.5 foot squares and at 0.5 foot levels. Profile drawings were made at each 2.5 foot interval.

Test trenches

Two test trenches were excavated in the fields near Mound A. Each of these trenches was five feet wide. One, an extension of the first north-south trench that was run across the north borrow pit, ran 100 feet to the north of the east-west base line of the grid. Beyond the limits of the borrow pit, it cut through a normal surface soil development, and below that showed nothing but the raw clay which forms the subsoil of this region. No cultural evidence was found.

The second test trench was an extension to the west of the trench that was first run along the east-west base line of the grid. This trench extended 300 feet to the west from the bench mark. Beyond the limits of the wash from Mound A, this excavation shows a normal soil development, and no cultural material or other evidence of occupation was found.

Further testing of the areas about the mounds was halted by the annual inundation which covered the fields with several feet of water and confined excavation to the higher parts of the structures.

ARTIFACTS

Pottery

The most common varieties of pottery found at the Crooks site are described in the following paragraphs. Types of material which are sufficiently well represented at this site have been named and are described according to the plan presented by the Southeastern Archeological Conference Reports.[5] Types which are less numerically important at this site are described more briefly, and references are made to more adequate descriptions elsewhere.

The classification and analysis of the Crooks site pottery were made as the material was received from the field. Most of the work of classification was done by one individual, Mr. C. H. Hopkins. It is hoped that in this way the identifications have been more consistent than they would be had there been several engaged in this work.

Analysis of the material appears to demonstrate that there were two distinct periods of aboriginal occupation of the Crooks site. It seems that both the mounds were completely constructed during the Marksville period, and that nothing but materials characteristic of this early period should be considered as inclusive in these structures. After a period of desertion the structures were once more utilized by Indians, apparently at some time very close to 1700 A. D. This latter occupation seems to have been a brief one, and is indicated by potsherds of late Caddoan, Natchez, and Tunican types mixed in the wash soil on the slopes of Mound A. These late types have been identified at the early eighteenth century sites of the aforementioned tribes by previous work in the Lower Mississippi Valley (Ford, 1936. In the list of the types found at Crooks, the late types will be described first and will be followed by a section describing the Marksville types found in these structures.

---

[5] Edited by William G. Haag, Department of Anthropology, University of Kentucky, Lexington. Mimeographed.

47

Haynes Bluff Plain
(fig. 14)

Paste:

>   *Method of manufacture*: Coiled. *Tempering*: Clay, grit, and sand. *Texture*: Coarse, medium granular. Occasionally contorted. Fairly compact. *Hardness*: Average 2.5. *Color*: Exterior, gray and buff. Core is black.

Surface finish:

>   *Modifications*: Moderate interior and exterior smoothing. Occasional tooling marks are evident on both surfaces. Erosion causes some but not excessive surface pitting.

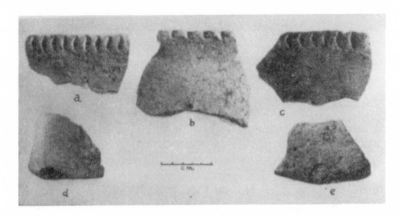

Figure 14. ˋSherds of type *Haynes Bluff Plain* from the wash on the slopes of the secondary mantle, Mound A.

Form:

>   *Rim*: Outslanting unmodified rim. Outslanting rim with everted lip. An incised line is placed just below the lip on vessel interior. Notching is usually on exterior edge of lip. *Lip*: Pointed-ovate, usually notched. *Body*: Carinated bowls are the only shape found at Crooks site. This is the usual form of *Haynes Bluff Plain*, but pot-shaped vessels have been found on other sites. Bowls have outcurving side walls, sharp angle between walls and bottom, convex bottoms, and small flattened bases. *Size*: Diameter 16-25 cm. Height 6-10 cm. *Base*: Small, circular, flattened. *Thickness*: Range 4.5-8 mm. Upper walls and rim thicker than lower walls and base.

Usual range of type:

> Found sparsely on late sites through central eastern Louisiana.
> It is a characteristic type of historic Tunica sites in the Yazoo
> River Valley of Mississippi.[6]

Chronological position of type in range:

> Appears to have developed late in Lower Valley pre-history and
> to have existed up to 1700 A. D.

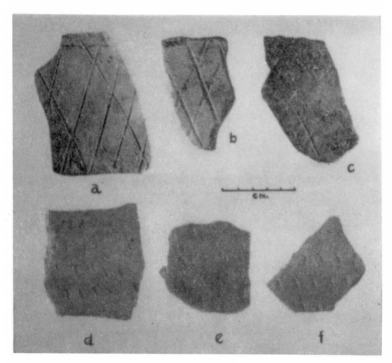

Figure 15. Late sherds from the Crooks site: a-c, *Harrison Bayou
Incised;* d-f, *Wilkinson Punctated.*

Probable relationships of type:

> The peculiar treatment given the rim and lip of *Haynes Bluff
> Plain* does not appear to have been duplicated in any other type
> of the Lower Valley. However, the vessel shape generally found
> is a very usual one in the Caddoan and Tunican complexes
> (Moore, 1909, pl. 5 and figs. 31-53; Harrington, 1920, pls. 33-38
> and pl. 39, fig. a). This shape does not occur in earlier horizons.

---

[6] Ford, 1936, pp. 105-107 (types 82;20, 82;52, and 82;52/20),
figs. 12g, 19a-g, 20a-h,j, 21a-d, 22k-n, and 26a-b.

Harrison Bayou Incised
(figs. 15a-c, 20f)

Coiled; clay and fine grit tempered; texture fairly fine; paste interior black, surfaces dark gray; fairly well smoothed. Decoration: large crosshatching confined to a band about the upper part of the vessel walls. Incising done crudely with a pointed instrument. Vessels apparently breakers about 15 mm. in diameter with slightly outslanting walls and slightly outflared rims. Lips direct.[7]

Wilkinson Punctated
(fig. 15d-f)

Paste:
> *Method of manufacture:* Coiled. *Tempering:* Clay and medium amount of sand. *Texture:* Coarse granular to lumpy and slightly contorted. *Hardness:* Average 2.5. Range 2-3. *Color:* Buff, gray, and black. Core, black with buff firing differential in most instances.

Surface finish:
> *Modifications:* Smoothed on interior and exterior. Occasionally smoothing marks show on interior. Soot staining on exterior quite common.

Decoration:
> *Technique:* Finger nail punctations evenly spaced, or sometimes the surface has been lightly pinched in vertical rows. The long axis of the punctation is usually oriented vertically. *Design:* Placed at random or in rows. Both individual punctations and rows are about 0.5 to 1 cm. apart. *Distribution:* Apparently on most of exterior surface of vessel.

Form:
> *Rim:* Unmodified rim slightly out-flared. *Lip:* Rounded or flattened ovate. *Body:* Probably large cauldron shape, similar to *Catahoula Incised. Base:* Probably circular and flat. Thickness: 4.5-9 mm. Average 6-7 mm. *Appendages:* None.

Usual range of type:
> Central and northwestern Louisiana.

Chronological position of type in range:
> Was in use until 1700 A. D. This type is most common on sites of the Caddoan stage in Louisiana. Small percentages are found on sites representing the late part of the Coles Creek period where it is always accompanied by other Caddoan types.[8]

---

[7] Ford, 1936, pp. 187, 188 (type 71;21), figs. 16l, 18j, 20k.
[8] Ford, 1936, p. 78 (type 11/21;61), figs. 16d, 18k.

Probable relationships of type:

Pocahontas Pinched, a shell-tempered type of Middle Mississippi affinities found on late sites in the Yazoo River Valley of Mississippi; resembles *Wilkinson Punctated* in that both are treated with the tips of the fingers. However, *Pocahontas* decoration is slightly more specialized. Pinching and finger nail punctating are decorative techniques which are widely spread in the Middle Mississippian cultures to the northeast.

Catahoula Incised
(figs. 16, 17)

Paste:

Method of manufacture: Coiled. *Tempering:* Clay with some sand and grit. *Texture:* Coarse, granular, and sometimes lumpy. *Hardness:* Average 2.5. Range 2-3. *Color:* Surfaces black, dark brown, buff, or gray. Paste core usually black and darker than exterior. Many of the sherds have thick layers of soot on the exterior.

Surface finish:

Modifications: Generally rough finish. Smoothing marks sometimes show very faintly on interiors. Surfaces often badly eroded and show pitting due to loss of temper particles.

Decoration:

Technique: Incising roughly applied. Lines vary from shallow grooves U-shaped in cross section to fine lines almost indistinguishable from brushing. The lines are generally bolder and deeper at the beginning of each stroke, and tend to become finer toward the end. *Design:* The very simple designs are always formed by closely spaced lines. A common arrangement is a band of four or more lines running parallel to the rim in a band just below it. Below this band incised lines or deep brush marks are arranged vertically or diagonally. *Distribution:* Most of the exterior surface. The vertical or diagonal lines which cover the middle and lower portions of the vessel wall usually stop just short of the base. The lines around the upper wall are usually separated from the lip by an undecorated plain zone of approximately one centimeter in width.

Form:

Rim: Straight and out-turned rims. *Lip:* Usually rounded, rarely rounded-point. *Body:* Deep cauldrons; or pots with straight sides having a very slight shoulder, slight neck constriction, and out-turned rim. *Base:* Doubtful in most cases but best evidence is for circular, flat type. *Size:* Often rather large, about 30 cm. in diameter and 40 cm. high. A few examples are smaller. *Thickness:* Averages about 6 mm. Base is slightly thicker than vessel walls.

Figure 16. Sherds of the type *Catahoula Incised*.

Figure 17. Parts of vessels reconstructed from large sherds of the type
Catahoula Incised. These are from the wash on the secondary
mantle of Mound A.

Usual range of type:

>Has been found in La Salle and Avoyelles Parishes, La. Probably widespread throughout central and south Louisiana and parts of southern Arkansas.

Figure 18. Late sherds from Crooks site: a-d, are of the type *La Salle Punctated;* e-h, are of the type *Sanson Incised.*

Chronological position of type in range:

>Probably a Coles Creek-Caddo transition type. Its appearance late in Greenhouse site[9] deposits indicates this, and the type seems to be intrusive in Crooks Mound A.

Probable relationships of type:

>Closely resembles *Anna Brush Roughened,* an early Caddoan period type. Principal difference is in paste composition. Is very similar in shape, size, and decoraton to several varieties of brushed ware found on Caddoan period sites in southern Arkansas and northwestern Louisiana (Ford, 1936, figs. 16i,k,n, 26th; Moore, 1912, fig. 57).

Sanson Incised
(fig. 18e-h)

Paste:

>*Method of manufacture:* Coiled. *Tempering:* Clay, sand, and grit. *Texture:* Coarse granular in cross section, but fairly com-

---

[9] Ford, Willey, and Neitzel, report in preparation.

pact. *Hardness:* 2.5. Range 2-3. *Color:* Black and brown. Core black. Exterior often soot covered.

Surface finish:

Modifications: Moderate interior and exterior smoothing. Some cases of interior smudging.

Decoration:

Technique: Deep wide incised lines which are either U-shaped or rectangular in cross section. *Design:* Herringbone pattern running around vessel parallel to rim. Usually effected by close-spaced lines. Quite often an undecorated rim border of 1 to 2 cm. separates decoration from lip. Occasionally, roughly executed angular or hemi-conical punctates are placed along the junctions of the straight lines forming the herringbone pattern. *Distribution:* Always on vessel exterior; upper portion of vessel and shoulder. May extend a half to three-quarters of the way down vessel walls.

Form:

Rim: Slightly out-flared. *Lip:* Pointed-ovate. Everted. *Body:* Cauldron shape with out-flared rim and slightly constricted neck. *Size:* Diameter 10-16 cm. Height 13-18 cm. *Base:* Probably circular flat. *Thickness:* Averages about 5-6 mm. *Appendages:* None.

Usual range of type:

Sanson Incised appears to have an unusually small geographical range. It has been found only on sites in the vicinity of Catahoula Lake in east-central Louisiana. Most of the known specimens have come from the Sanson site on the southwestern side of this lake.[10] Moore found vessels of this type in the Mayes Mound on Larto Lake (Moore, 1913, figs. 9-12).

Chronological position of type in range:

Sanson Incised is usually associated with features and artifacts typical of the latter part of the Cole Creek stage and early Caddoan. It has not been found on any historic sites.

Probable relationships of type:

In vessel shape and plan of decoration arrangement, this type shows similarity to *Catahoula Incised* and several other crudely incised and brushed types which are widely distributed throughout the Caddoan area in southwestern Arkansas, northwestern

---

[10] This site was a burial mound which was excavated by local residents. A report has not been published. Some of the material is in the Louisiana State University collections.

Louisiana, and eastern Texas. Angular arrangements of straight lines forming a panel around the vessel below the rim, and usually, a body decoration of straight lines or brushing is common to all these types.

Coles Creek Plain

Coiled; clay-tempered with small carbonized spots scattered through paste; paste texture fine and sightly contorted; core gray in color, surfaces gray or gray-brown; paste is hard. Surfaces are fairly well smoothed and show tooling marks. Very little erosion.

No decoration. There is occasionally a single line incised at the "overhanging" angle encircling the vessels near the rim. Few small exterior rim folds. Vessel shapes uncertain.

Figure 19. Sherds from Crooks site: a-d, unidentified sherds with punctated decoration; e, *Anna Interior Engraved*.

Anna Interior Engraved

(fig. 19e)

Coiled; grit tempered, fine-textured paste; paste black; surfaces fairly well smoothed, moderately eroded. Decorations are rectilinear and curvilinear arrangements of lines engraved with a pointed tool after the paste had hardened. Lines are arranged parallel to one another and are fairly close together. Vessels appear to be shallow bowls; in one case a carinated bowl. Decoration is on interior in bottom of bowl (Ford, 1936, figs. 21n, 22d,j, 26e).

Fatherland Incised
(fig. 20e)

Coiled; clay and grit tempering; dark paste interior, light gray exterior; fairly well smoothed. Curvilinear band of three lines incised with pointed instrument forms decoration.

Type is found in central-eastern Louisiana. Is found on several sites occupied by Natchez Indians in historic times. Was made up to 1700.[11]

Miscellaneous types of the late horizon

Some of the sherds collected from Mound A can be identified as belonging to the late horizon, but are not well enough represented at Crooks to justify full type descriptions. Most of the specimens belong to types of the Caddoan complex. Some have been given names in the laboratory which will probably continue to be used. Others have not yet been named although they are well recognized. Full type descriptions will have to await the publication of a Caddoan complex site report, planned for the near future.

Figure 20b is a rim sherd of a beaker-shaped vessel with a diameter of approximately 14 cm. The rim is direct. The sherd is thin (4 mm.) and hard; well fired. Core is blue-gray; cortex buff. Surface is badly eroded. The paste is tempered with clay and small organic stained areas. The decoration is zigzagged stamping in parallel vertical rows placed closely together to form a band encircling the upper part of the vessel wall. This is a typical example of *Chevalier Stamped*.[12] This type, which was most popular in the Coles Creek stage of Lower Valley pre-history, persisted in a steadily decreasing quantity to the end of that period and on into the early part of the Caddoan.

Two almost identical bottle necks were found (fig. 20a). They have a medium hard paste with black core and brown cortex. The paste is tempered with small clay particles. The necks indicate rather large bottles. Their rims are

[11] Ford, 1936, pp. 54, 55 (types 41;21;5 and 43;21;5), figs. 8. 12a-e, 13a,c,n, 9a,c-e,g,l.
[12] Setzler, 1933B, pl. 6, right panel, top row, center; Ford, 1936. p. 187 (type 63;101), figs. 34m,o, 36h,u, 38b, 39e, 40g.

Figure 20. Sherds from Crooks Mound A: a-g, are sherds representing
the late occupation of the mound; h-m, are unusual sherds
of the marksville period occupation.

everted and rounded. The necks are relatively short, and on one sherd there is a line at the base of the neck. This plain ware has not yet been named although it is readily recognizable on the basis of paste features and shape. Bottle forms do not appear in any of the Lower Mississippi Valley horizons earlier than Caddoan.

One small sherd shows a fragment of a curvilinear decoration with a delicately crosshatched background (fig. 20c). The sherd is 5 mm. thick with a dark core, brown surfaces, and small clay particles used as tempering. Its features are very commonly found in Caddoan pottery.[13]

There are two examples of the type *Maddox Finger Brushed* (fig. 20g). They have a fairly soft black paste, tempered with small particles of grit or fine clay. The surfaces are rough and soot coated. The decoration appears to have been effected by allowing the vessel to dry, and then applying a thick wash, through which the fingers, held side by side, were trailed from the rim to the base. The shape accompanying this decoration is practically always the same: a deep cauldron with flattened bottom; slightly bulging sides; and slightly constricted at the mouth. The rim is turned outward sharply. The larger of the sherds has shallow notching on the lip.[14]

The sherd shown in figure 20d is part of a small bowl with incurving walls. The ware is 4 mm. thick. Paste is light gray, with large particles of clay used as tempering. The exterior is covered with a red slip. This is not the slip of the *Larto Red Filmed* type of the Troyville period, but is the brighter and less firmly attached slip found on a number of vessels from Caddoan sites.

---

[13] Only a few examples will be cited: Moore, 1909, figs, 16, 17, 53-54.
[14] Ford, 1936, pp. 84-85 (types 63;42), figs. 16j, 18i.

Marksville period types
Marksville Plain
(figs. 21-27)

Paste:

Method of manufacture: Coiled. *Tempering:* Clay, with grit and small amount of sand. Some pieces show considerable carbonized vegetal material. *Texture:* Coarse, contorted. Occasionally very coarse and granular. *Hardness:* Poorly fired. Soft when wet, when dry, average 2. Range 2-3. *Color:* Buff, light brown, and brown. Cross section buff and reddish buff; sometimes black with buff firing differential.

Surface finish:

Modifications: Has smoothing on both interior and exterior. Tooling marks occasionally visible on exterior. Coarse temper particles which have leached out of the pastes give a pitted surface appearance in many cases. Temper particles often protrude on both surfaces. Some pieces take a low polish although the surface is uneven.

Form:

Rim: Usually direct. Occasionally thickened to the outside or inside, or both. Some notched. In most cases straight. A few are slightly out-curved or in-curved. A few thin and cambered.

Figure 21. A vessel of the type *Marksville Plain* from Mound A.

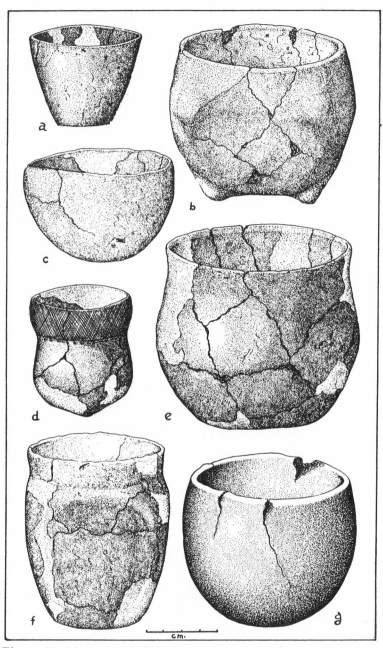

Figure 22. *Marksville Plain* type vessels.

61

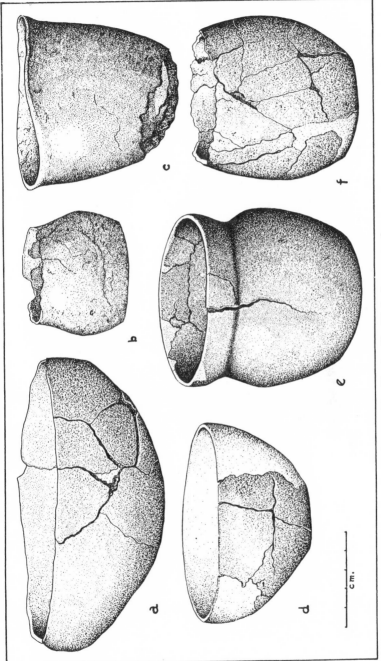

Figure 23. *Marksville Plain* type vessels.

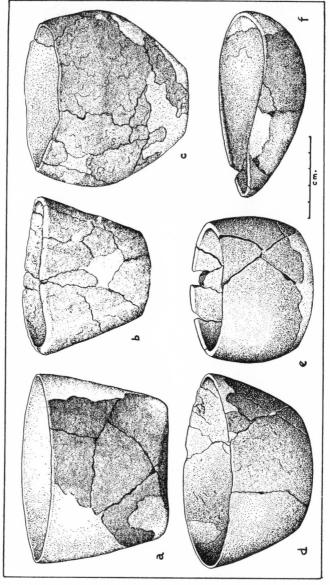

Figure 24. *Marksville Plain* type vessels.

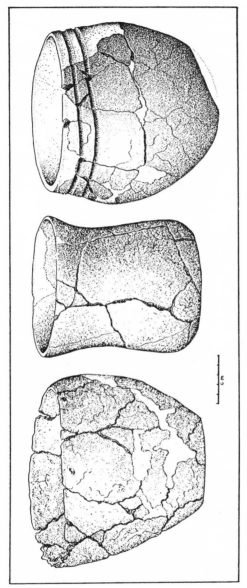

Figure 25. *Marksville Plain* type vessels.

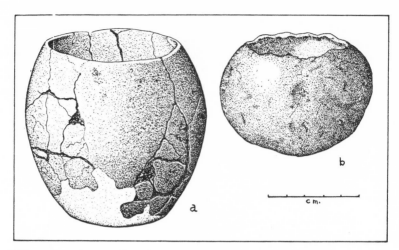

Figure 26. *Marksville Plain* type vessels.

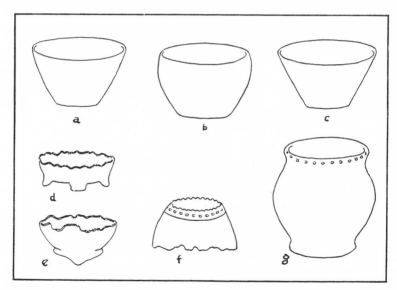

Figure 27. Outline drawings of unusual *Marksville Plain* type vessels as reconstructed from large sherds. Sketches d-g show relationship to Tchefuncte period pottery.

Body: Flat-bottomed, medium shallow bowls; beakers with in-curved walls; flat-bottomed pots with slight neck constriction and out-turned rim. *Base:* Flat; circular, and square. Basal flanges rare. A few show four legs. These legs are small rounded knobs. *Thickness:* Ranges from 6 to 10 mm. Bottoms are thicker than walls.

Usual range of type:

Found throughout the Lower Mississippi Valley in Louisiana and southwestern Mississippi.

Chronological position of type in range:

Marksville period.

Probable relationships of type:

Undoubtedly the prototype of the later *Troyville Plain. Marksville Plain* is sandier and coarser in texture than *Troyville* and usually thinner. Differences in rim and body shape also noted between these two.

Remarks:

The category of *Marksville Plain* has been too loosely applied to the Crooks site sherd material. In it has been included nearly all the plain ware from the site. Many of these sherds undoubtedly belong to the later occupation. However, the badly eroded condition of the pottery has made it impossible to distinguish the late plain ware in most cases.

The description of the type has been based on material from the interior mound structures which can be identified as *Marksville Plain* with very little doubt.

Marksville Stamped
(figs. 28-34)

Paste:

Method of manufacture: Coiled. *Tempering:* Predominantly clay with small amounts of sand and grit. *Texture:* Fine. Tempering material gives a lumpy or granular appearance to paste. *Hardness:* Average 2. Poorly fired. Very soft when wet. *Color:* Buff, dark brown, or dull black. Core is dark. Some exterior fire clouding.

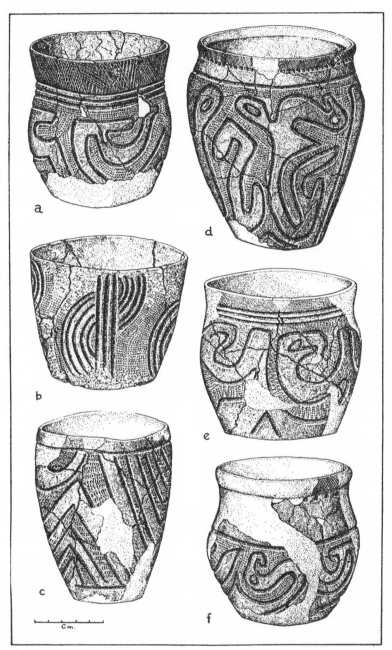

Figure 28. *Marksville Stamped* type vessels from Crooks site.

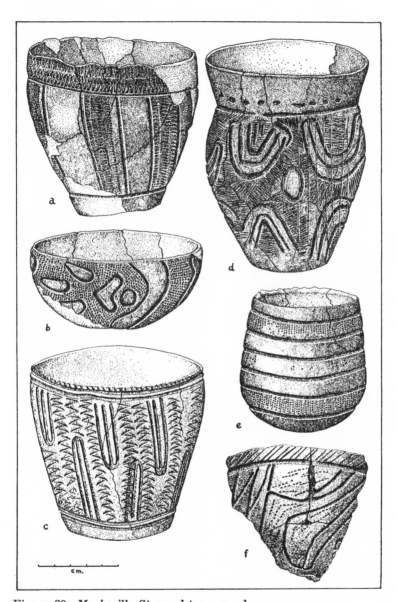

Figure 29. *Marksville Stamped* type vessels.

68

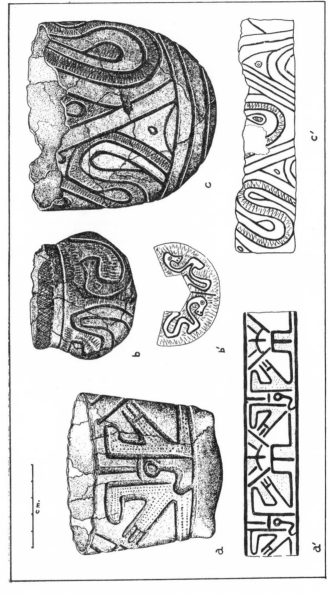

Figure 30. *Marksville Stamped* type vessels.

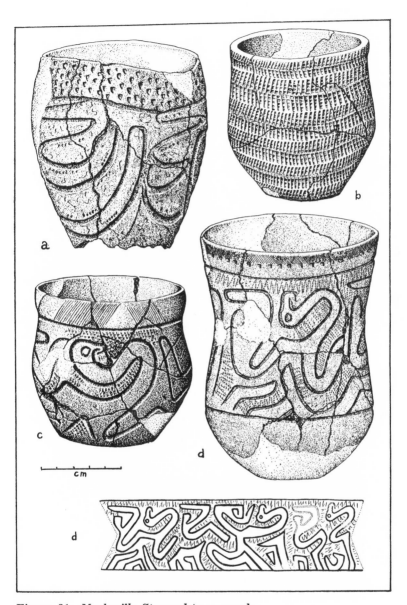

Figure 31. *Marksville Stamped* type vessels.

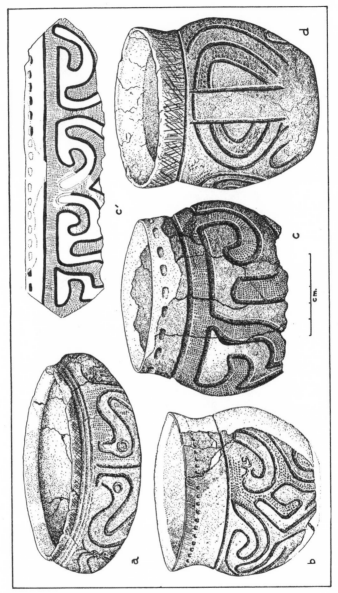

Figure 32. *Marksville Stamped* type vessels.

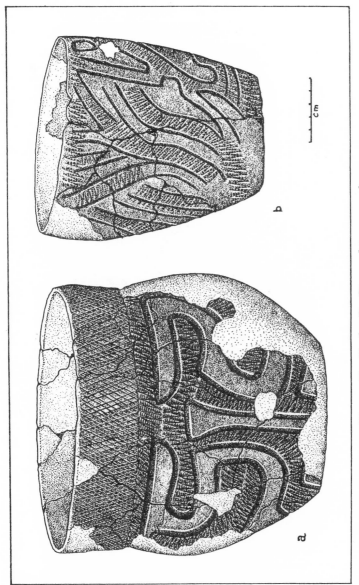

Figure 33. *Marksville Stamped* type vessels.

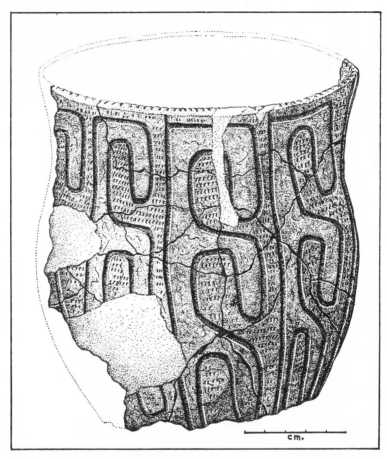

Figure 34. Variant of the type *Marksville Stamped*. The background is roughened by impressions of a small cord-wrapped stick.

Surface finish:

Exterior smoothing superior to that on the inside. Exterior will sometimes take a high gloss from brushing. Interior surface is inclined to be bumpy and coarse temper particles protrude on both surfaces. A few pieces have smudged interiors.

Decoration:

Technique and design: Deep wide lines, U-shaped in cross section, are used to outline the designs. Figures are always depicted by smoothed bands, and the backgrounds are roughened by rocking a fine dentated stamp as it is moved sideways. The designs are so arranged that smoothed and roughened bands alternate. The most common decoration motif features the bird figure characteristic of the ceramics of the period. The head can usually be identified, and behind the head is an appendage which looks like a conventionalized wing (figs. 28d-f, 30a-b, 31c-d, 32a). The exact arrangement of the decorations varies. No two are identical and the details frequently change on different sides of the same vessel.

On other vessels the alternate smoothed and roughened bands form large concentric circles. There is usually a vertical smoothed band cutting through the center of each circle (fig. 32d).

A fairly common arrangement of the decoration exhibits alternate smoothed and roughened bands running either vertically from the lip to the base or horizontally around the vessels (figs. 28b, 29a,c,e, 31b). On one vessel from Crooks the exterior is covered by encircling rocker stamping (fig. 31b).

On nearly all vessels with undifferentiated rim forms, the decoration covers the entire exterior from the lip to the base. A separate decorative treatment is commonly given to vertical, outslanting, cambered, or thickened rims. Many of them are smoothed but most common is the application of fine straight lines in several characteristic patterns as is described later (page 75).

Form:

Pot forms are most common. Usually they have high rounded shoulders and below that curve slightly to a fairly small flattened base. Some bodies are four lobed, in which cases the bottoms are generally square. Otherwise they are round and flat. Above the shoulders most of the vessels have well-defined rims or collars which are either vertical or slightly outslanting. These may be unthickened, thickened, by the addition of a smoothly rounded strap to the exterior, or cambered with a well-pronounced interior channel (figs. 41a′,b′). Height range 7-16 cm. Diameter 5-10 cm. Small bowls with rounded bottoms and slightly incurving upper walls are rare. Small ovate-shaped bowls are also rare. *Base:* Usually flattened, square or round. Rarely rounded. Tetrapodal supports are not common. *Thickness:* Average 5-7 mm. Range 4-9 mm. Bases are generally thicker than vessel walls. Cambered rim collars are usually thinner than walls.

Usual range of type:

Known from east-central Louisiana (Setzler, 1933B, pls. 1, 2; pl. 3, figs. a-b; pl. 4, fig. c; and figs. 2-5: 1934, figs. 44, 45, 46 right) and western Mississippi (Moore, 1908, p. 587, fig. 3).

Chronological position of type in range:

> Marksville period. Everywhere the type is found it is accompanied by cultural traits and other pottery types characteristic of this period.

Probable relationship of type:

> Is very similar to the common type of so-called ceremonial ware found in the Hopewell culture sites of Ohio (Shetrone and Greenman, 1931, pp. 430-438, figs. 51c, 52h̄,j), and the Hopewellian cultural manifestations of Michigan, Illinois, Missouri (Wedel 1938, pls. 3, 5-8), and Wisconsin (McKern, 1931, pl. 45, figs. 1, 2; pls. 46, 47). In some instances the similarity amounts almost to identity. The distinction between the specimens lies mainly in paste features. Similarities noted are: the use of delicately crosshatched rims, either cambered or slightly thickened, with a single row of hemiconical punctates below the rim decoration; body decorations formed of smooth bands bordered by wide round-bottomed incised lines, and a background roughening made by rocking a notched stamp; similar bird figured described by the decorations; and occasional use of a vertical smoothed panel cutting through a design of concentric circles of curvilinear designs.[15] An infrequent decoration arrangement consists of zigzagged stamping running either vertically or horizontally and completely covering the vessel body. In such cases the body decoration is not divided into bands by incised lines.[16]

> The size, certain shapes,[17] and proportions of the vessels are also quite similar over this entire range. Globular bodies with flattened or rounded bottoms (rarely four legs), with four distinct lobes, moderately high rounded shoulders, short vertical rims which show either a slight cambering or a thickening to the outside, and flattened lips which may slant slightly inward and are infrequently notched, are the vessel forms on which this decoration type is most commonly found. The surface is often smoothed so that it has a low polish.

> In Louisiana, *Marksville Stamped* is ancestral to *Troyville Stamped*, a type of the Troyville period.

---

[15] Compare figs. 28-34 with McKern, 1931, pl. 45, fig. 1; pls. 46, 47.

[16] Compare fig. 33b with Wedel, 1938, pl. 7, fig. b, and pl. 8, fig. a: McKern, 1931, pl. 47, lower right: Shetrone and Greenman, 1931, fig. 51c.

[17] This applies particularly to such shapes as figs. 28a,c-f, 29d, 30b, 31a,c, 32b-d, 33a.

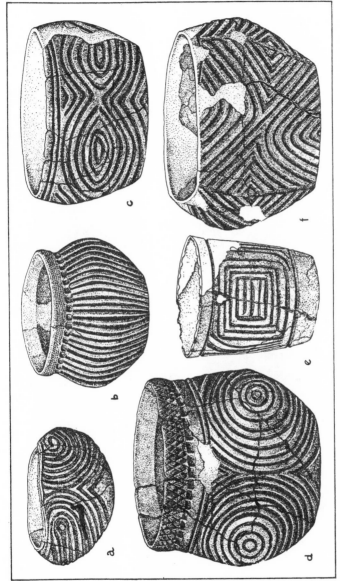

Figure 35. Vessels of the type *Marksville Incised*. These decorations illustrate the close-spaced line variation. Vessel c, is oval in shape; d, has four well pronounced lobes in the body.

Figure 36. *Marksville Incised* type. These vessels illustrate the wide-spaced line variety of incised decoration.

Figure 37. Sherds from Mound A: a-f, are sherds of the type
      Marksville Incised; sherds g-j, are similar to a type of
      the Troyville period, *Churupa Punctuated*, except for the
      paste characteristics which are typically Marksville.

Marksville Incised

(figs. 35, 36, 37a-f)

Paste:

Method of manufacture: Coiled. *Tempering:* Clay, sand and grit. *Texture:* Coarse granular, lumpy, slightly contorted. *Hardness:* Poorly fired. Very soft when damp. When dry average 2-2.5. *Color:* Buff, brown, and grayish black. Paste core dark brown, with buff coating caused by differential firing. Exterior surface mottled because of firing.

Surface finish:

Modifications: Moderate interior and exterior smoothing. Smoothing striations usually not evident. Interior surface is quite often bumpy.

Decoration:

Technique: Deep U-shaped incised lines. *Design:* May be either widely or closely spaced. The lines may form either curvilinear or rectilinear patterns of concentric loops, circles, and squares. Conventionalized bird figures are fairly common. Terminal punctations or punctations within lines are rare. *Distribution:* Vessel exterior. Decoration extends from below rim area down to the base. In instances where there is no separate rim treatment, these incised line decorations continue from base to lip. Rims are sometimes crosshatched, similar to *Marksville Stamped.*

Form:

Rim: Direct, out-slanted, and in-curved rims all occur. There is a slight tendency toward cambering in some. Most rims are perceptibly thinner than body wall. Rim surface treatment is usually differentiated from body surface. Rims may be plain or decorated. *Lip:* Ovate and flattened-ovate most common. Some pointed-ovate. *Body:* A variety of shapes is found. Small, squat, bulging pots with cambered, direct, or outslanting rims. Beakers with slightly out-slanted sides. Elongated or ovoid vessels. Exotic forms (fig. 36a). Diameters range 6-16 cm. *Base:* Flat or convex. The flat bases are usually circular. *Thickness:* Averages 5-6 mm. Range 4-9 mm. Upper body wall usually thinner than lower wall and base.

Usual range of type:

East-central Louisiana (Setzler, 1933B, pl. 3, figs. c, d, pl. 4, figs. a, b, d; 1934, figs. 44, 45, and 46, vessel to left and half of center vessel: Moore, 1912, figs. 6, 9) and west-central Mississippi (Moore, 1908, p. 587, fig. 4).

Material which appears to be similar, in decoration at least, is illustrated from Seip Mound in Ohio (Shetrone and Greenman,

1931, fig. 52c,m.). On the whole, this decorative type appears to be rare in Hopewellian culture sites.

Two sherds illustrated by Cole and Deuel (1937, pl. 2, figs. 14, 15) from Illinois do not appear to resemble *Marksville Incised* as closely as they do *Troyville Incised*, the descendant type of the Troyville period.

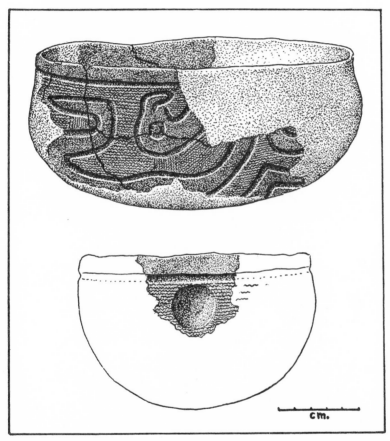

Figure 38. Side and end view of a vessel of the type *Crooks Stamped*. This bowl is oval in shape. A small round depression in the wall is shown in the end view.

80

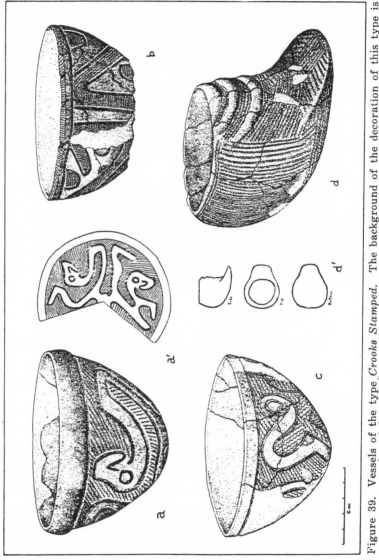

Figure 39. Vessels of the type *Crooks Stamped*. The background of the decoration of this type is roughened by stamping with the edge of a variety of pecten shell.

Crooks Stamped

(figs. 38, 39)

Paste:

Method of manufacture: Coiled. *Tempering:* Predominantly clay, some sand and grit. *Texture:* Medium coarse and lumpy to medium granular. Compactness varies. Temper particles easily distinguishable in cross section. *Hardness:* Poorly fired. Soft when wet. When dry, averages 2.5. Range 2-3. *Color:* Dark brown to light brown usual, rarely buff on both interior and exterior. Core usually light brown.

Surface finish:

Modifications: Smoothed to a low polish on both interior and exterior. Surface often lumpy. Interior sometimes crackled.

Decoration:

Technique: Zigzagged stamping, produced apparently by application of the edge of small scallop shell. Incising done with the end of a cylindrical instrument. The instrument was held at an angle so that the lines are round-bottomed and 4-6 mm. wide. *Design:* Bold, incised lines, U-shaped in cross section, form curvilinear and rectilinear bands. The background of these bands is filled with close-spaced shell stamping. The design, brought out in negative, usually involves the bird motif typical of the Marksville period. Occasionally decoration is carried out in the form of simple lines of shell stamping, closely spaced, and covering the entire vessel. *Distribution:* Exterior vessel surface, usually the entire surface including the base. May or may not have small undecorated rim area set off from decoration by an encircling incised line.

Form:

Rim: Straight, slightly out-slanted, or slightly in-curved. Usually direct and unmodified, although exterior folds, large and ovate in cross section, are sometimes noted. *Lip:* Flattened-ovate, and pointed-ovate. Flattened lips with shell stamping on top are rare. *Body:* Small vessels averaging 8 to 15 cm. in maximum diameter, which is usually at orifice. Hemispherical bowls or bowls with pointed-convex bases. Elongated oval or boat shapes. Exotic cornucopian shapes. One boat-shaped vessel has two depressions just below the rim at either end. These are undecorated, and show a corresponding interior bulge. Depressions are about 2 cm. in diameter. *Size:* Diameter 7-14 cm. Height 5-14 cm. *Base:* Convex. *Thickness:* Average 5 mm. Range 4-6 mm. Very little variation in rim, wall, and base.

Usual range of type:

> Southern and central Louisiana. Setzler illustrates this type from the Marksville site (Setzler, 1934, fig. 44, last three sherds to right in center row).

Chronological position of type in range:

> *Crooks Stamped* appears to be the earliest of the Marksville period types. This is indicated by stratigraphic position at the Marksville site (fig. 59) and by the fact that it is the first Marksville period type to appear on top of Tchefuncte period material at the Big Oak Island site, now being excavated. The same type has also been found at two other Tchefuncte period sites, but there its stratigraphic position was not determined.

Probable relationships of type:

> Decoration and design arrangement closely parallel *Marksville Stamped.* The technique of shell stamping differentiates this type. The usual lack of the incised rim treatment which is characteristic of *Marksville Stamped* is another point of distinction.

Marksville Red Filmed

(fig. 40)

Paste:

> *Method of manufacture:* Coiled. *Tempering:* Clay, with sand and grit used in small to medium amounts. *Texture:* Core lumpy and contorted. Tempering particles easily distinguished in paste. *Hardness:* Poorly fired. Soft when wet; when dry, average 2.5. Ranges from 2 to 3. *Color:* Core gray with buff firing differential occasionally seen. Interior and exterior dark brown or black. Some fire mottling on vessel exterior.

Surface finish:

> *Modification:* Exterior smoothed to polished. Interior smoothed. Temper particles protrude on interior.

Decoration:

> *Technique:* Deep U-shaped incised lines and dark red paint or filming. *Design:* Curvilinear decorations formed by incised lines. Zones formed by incised lines are covered with red paint which has been applied before firing. There is no paint within the incised lines themselves. *Distribution:* Vessel exterior covered. A rim band of 2 cm. which is undecorated and set off from the decoration by an encircling incised line.

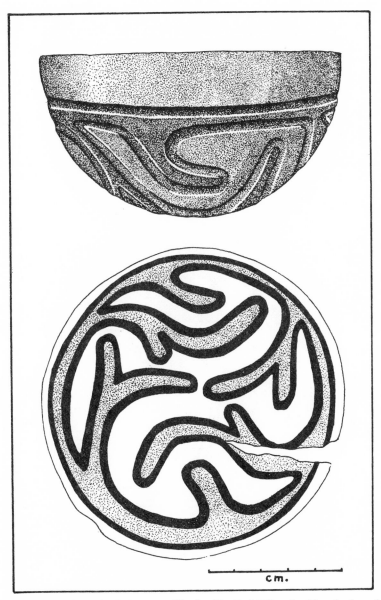

Figure 40. Vessel of the type *Marksville Red Filmed*. The darkened zones are covered with red slip. In the other areas the vessel surface is the normal color, dark gray.

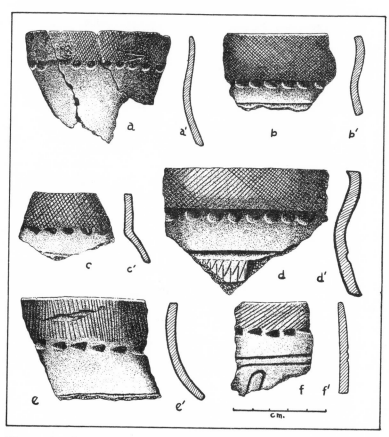

Figure 41. Crosshatched rim sherds from the Crooks site.

Form:

> *Rim:* Direct and slightly thinned. Rim evidence very limited.
> *Lip:* Pointed-ovate. *Body:* Small hemispherical bowl, 10.5 cm.
> in maximum diameter at orifice. Only one entire vessel found.
> *Base:* Convex. *Thickness:* Ranges from 2 to 7 cm. with rims
> thinner than lower walls or bases.

Usual range of type:

> East-central Louisiana.

Chronological position of type:

> *Range:* The Marksville period.

Probable relationship of type:

> May be prototype of an incised and red painted type in the Troy-
> ville norizon, *Woodville Red Filmed.* Is the earliest known ap-
> pearance of painted pottery in the Lower Mississippi Valley.

The Marksville period rim

The decorated cambered rims characteristic of many vessels of the Marksville period are fairly common in the sherd collections (fig. 41). Sherds showing only this peculiar rim will not be assigned to a formal type, as they doubtless were broken from vessels which were decorated on the body with one of the body decorations used at the same time. However, as these rims are so readily recognizable and are so diagnostic of the period, they are listed in the table showing the provenience of types from the Crooks site.

The paste of the rim sherds is similar in all respects to that of the other types of the Marksville period. The sherds are usually somewhat thinner than the body sherds bearing decorations; this is a characteristic feature. Typically the rim is slightly cambered and the lips are flattened and slope slightly inward. In some cases the interior walls of the rims are straight, and the exterior walls bulge. The work is too neatly done to determine whether or not the thickening was effected by folding the rim.

A smoothed band between the body decoration and the lower part of the rim decoration is found in a few instances. The lowest part of the rim decoration is nearly always a single row of large punctations made with a tubular instrument held at an angle to the wall of the vessel. From these punctations to the lip, the rim is generally covered with an arrangement of fine incised lines. Most often these lines are crosshatched. In other cases they are placed parallel and vertical, slanting, or in line-filled nested triangles. In rare cases arrangements of punctations or parallel vertical rows of zigzagged stamping fill the space (figs. 29a, 31a, 35b, 38e).

It should be noted that these crosshatched rims are not so large as those from the Marksville site and seem to be less common. However, they are decorated with similar patterns.[18]

Identical variations of this rim are found at several Hopewekian sites to the northward. The typical delicately crosshatched rim occurs in Illinois (Cole and Deuel, 1937, pl. 2, figs. 5, 6), Missouri (Wedel, 1938, pl. 3, figs. a, b, d; pl. 5, figs. a, h; pl. 7, figs. a, b; pl. 8, fig. a), Wisconsin (McKern, 1931, p. 225, pl. 45, fig. 1; pl. 47), Michigan,[19] and Ohio (Shetrone and Greenman, 1931, p. 432, figs. 51c, 52a, h, j).

Rocker-stamped rims with the usual single row of punctates are found in Illinois (Cole and Deuel, 1937, pl. 2, fig. 12) and Missouri (Wedel, 1938, pl. 3, fig. c; pl. 6, fig. b).

La Salle Punctated
(fig. 18a-d)

Paste:
> *Method of manufacture:* Coiled. *Tempering:* Clay, grit, and sand. *Texture:* Coarse granular to lumpy and contorted. *Hardness:* Average 2.5. Range 2-3. *Color:* Buff, gray, black. Gray to black core.

Surface finish:
> *Modifications:* Moderate smoothing on interior and exterior. Occasional tooling marks on interior. Slightly pitted surface due to leaching.

---

[18] Comparisons based on village site collections from Marksville.
[19] Material examined at the museum of the University of Michigan.

Decoration:

Technique: Small triangular punctates. Punctations may be long and deep, averaging about 2 or 3 mm. in length, or they may be shallow equilateral triangles about 2 to 4 mm. long. Design: Deep narrow punctations are arranged in horizontal rows around vessel, with individual punctations about 3 or 4 mm. apart. Broad, flat punctations usually form lines as though the punctating instrument had been dragged and repeatedly indented over the surface. Distribution: Sherds show design distribution to be around upper exterior walls. Seem to be arranged in horizontal rows parallel to the rim.

Form:

Rim: Straight rims with marginal thickening both to inside and outside. Rims with very slight incurve, unmodified margins. Rims with everted lip. Lip: Flattened-ovate, pointed-ovate, and frequently notched. Body: Unknown. Base: Unknown. Appendage: None.

Usual range of type:

Has been recorded only from Crooks mounds in La Salle Parish, La.

Chronological position of type in range:

Probably Tchefuncte period.

Miscellaneous types

Eight sherds from the burial platform, one from the primary mound, and 20 fragments of one vessel from the secondary mantle show interesting features. They are similar in all respects to material of the type *Marksville Stamped* except that the background of the decoration is roughened with closely spaced hemi-conical punctates instead of stamping. Although the patterns incline to be more angular, the decorations are quite similar to those of a type of the Troyville period, *Churupa Punctated.*[20] However, there is a marked difference in paste, surface finish, and vessel shapes (figs. 37g-j).

Sherds of several other types which appear to have been coeval with the typical material of the Marksville period were found scattered through the soil of Mound A. None

---

[20] Ford, 1936, pp. 220-222 (type 31;23/73;2), figs. 38a, 40t, 42m, 43h-i, 44d,e,v: 1935, pl. 11, type 14d.

of these types was represented by enough material to justify full descriptions based on the Crooks site collections. From the scarcity of material, these sherds might be considered to represent trade items from other areas or vestigial remnants of earlier periods in the Lower Valley.

Five sherds are of the type *Tchefuncte Incised,* found on sites of the Tchefuncte complex located near Lake Pontchartrain in southern Louisiana (fig. 20h-i). (See Czajkowski, 1934, fig. 6, extreme right, second row from top of plate). Two of the specimens came from the fill of the burial platform and three from the primary mound. The simple vessel shape, rim profile, rim notches, simple decoration, surface crackling on the interior, and hardness and paste composition identify these sherds. *Tchefuncte Incised* will be described in detail in a future publication.

Six sherds, apparently parts of the same vessel, came from the fill of the burial platform (fig. 20j-k). The sherds are from a small vessel about 12 cm. in diameter with straight, slightly outslanting sides. The rim is direct and the lip rounded. The entire exterior of the vessel is covered with impressions made with a small stick wrapped with cords. A close examination reveals the twist of the cords. The stick was applied horizontally and the impressions are very close together.

Three sherds, one from the fill of the burial platform and two from the primary mantle, show impressions which appear to have been made by the tip of a reed which had been split in half (fig. 21l-m). The paste is quite similar to that of *Crooks Plain*. The shape of the largest of the sherds suggests that the vessel of which it was a part had a squared base. The decorations are suggestive of material found in Hopewellian sites in Illinois (Cole and Deuel, 1937, figs. 9, 10, 19, 20; pl. 2, fig. 3).

Provenience of pottery

In the accompanying table (fig. 42) is shown the distribution of the types of vessels and sherds from Crooks site. A total of 14,402 vessels and sherds was found and classi-

LATE PERIOD TYPES

	MOUND A					Mound B	North borrow pit	Recovered from dump	Totals
	Original surface	Burial platform	Primary mound	Secondary mantle	Wash on secondary				
Fatherland Incised	0	0	0	0	1 *.0003*	0	0	0	1
Haynes Bluff Plain	0	0	0	2 *.0003*	10 *.0029*	0	0	0	12
Anna Interior Engraved	0	0	0	2 *.0003*	2 *.0006*	0	0	0	4
Harrison Bayou Incised	0	0	0	16 *.0025*	5 *.0014*	0	0	0	21
Sanson Incised	2 *.011*	0	0	8 *.0013*	39 *.0012*	0	0	0	49
Wilkinson Punctated	0	0	0	6 *.0009*	41 *.0118*	0	0	3 *.009*	50
Catahoula Incised	2 *.011*	10 *.007*	0	359 *.056*	791 *.228*	15 *.071*	5 *.005*	49 *.14*	1232
Coles Creek Plain	1 *.005*	2 *.001*	0	47 *.0074*	38 *.011*	3 *.014*	6 *.007*	0	97

MARKSVILLE PERIOD TYPES

Marksville Plain	157 *.853*	1243 *.88*	1209 *.807*	5263 *.828*	2394 *.689*	177 *.834*	906 *.983*	271 *.774*	11,620
Marksville Period Rim	3 *.016*	11 *.008*	15 *.01*	55 *.0086*	0	0	0	0	84
Marksville Incised	3 *.016*	45 *.032*	33 *.022*	139 *.022*	34 *.0098*	8 *.038*	0	9 *.027*	271
Marksville Stamped	15 *.082*	90 *.064*	210 *.14*	424 *.067*	56 *.0161*	6 *.028*	0	16 *.046*	817
Crooks Stamped	0	3 *.002*	7 *.005*	2 *.0003*	1 *.0003*	1 *.005*	0	0	14
Marksville Red Filmed	0	0	8 *.005*	0	0	0	0	0	8
Tchefuncte Incised	0	2 *.001*	3 *.001*	0	0	0	0	0	5
La Salle Punctated	0	0	2 *.001*	14 *.0022*	40 *.0115*	0	5 *.005*	1 *.003*	62

UNIDENTIFIED

Unidentified Sherds	1 *.005*	8 *.007*	8 *.006*	19 *.003*	17 *.0049*	2 *.009*	0	1 *.003*	55
TOTALS	184	1,414	1,495	6,356	3,469	212	922	350	14,402

Fig. 42. Table showing provenience of the types of pottery found at Crooks site. Figures in italics are percentages.

fied. It will be noted that all except 17 of the sherds assigned to late period types come from either the secondary mantle or from the wash on the flanks of this mantle. The presence of these sherds in the lower strata of the structure (mound base, 5; burial platform, 12) is rather hard to explain. The classification of these particular sherds has been reviewed and their identification appears to be correct. It is possible that the materials were either mixed or mislabeled in the field.

A total of 454 sherds of late types is recorded as coming from the fill of the secondary mantle. This is another point which detracts from the clearness of the record, but in this case the explanation is apparent. The excavators were more than half way through the structure before it was recognized that a stratum on the east flank was not a part of the secondary mantle as was supposed, but was slump or wash material which had been deposited without apparent water sorting. The sherds came from this stratum. With the error of identification corrected, the fill of the secondary mantle ceased to show appreciable amounts of the late types.

Eighteen sherds of late types are recorded from Mound B. No vertical differentiation was made of the material from this structure so that it is impossible to determine whether the sherds came from the surface or not.

All the decorated sherds from the large borrow pit to the north of Mound A were of late types. Only 10 sherds were decorated, and the two types which they represented are none too diagnostic. None of the pottery recovered from the pit was found more than two feet below the present ground surface.

The facts seem to be that the occupation (indicated by the pottery listed as belonging to recent types) was entirely superficial. This most recent occupation did not affect the interior structures of the mounds, but was confined entirely to their surfaces. It is possible that the mounds may have served the proto-historic peoples of the area as refuges in time of high water just as they have served the white farmers of the vicinity in recent years.

The relative proportions of types of the Marksville period in the different structures of Mound A do not appear to indicate significant trends. There seem to be no evidences of stylistic changes occurring during the time which elapsed between the deposition of the earliest material on the site, and the construction of the last mantle.

A total of 12,732 sherds of Marksville period types was found scattered through the soil which comprised the mantles of the two mounds. The appearance of the surrounding borrow pits seems to indicate that the soil for the structures was scraped up from nearby. However, the two test trenches run out from the Mound A excavations did not discover a single potsherd. Neither did a careful examination of the plowed fields in the vicinity. Only a few chips of flint were found. Under these circumstances it is a little difficult to account for the numerous small sherds scattered through the mounds. Possibly the exposure of the poorly fired Marksville period sherds on the surface of the ground has resulted in their complete disintegration due to weathering. There does not seem to be any other very logical explanation.

Pottery accompanying burials

Eighty-four vessels were discovered which could be partially or entirely restored. About half could be associated with burials. In nearly all cases only one vessel was associated with a skeleton. One burial had two pots placed with it and one had three. There were no instances of a number of vessels accompanying a single skeleton. Burials were crowded so closely in certain parts of the structure that, in many cases, it was difficult to determine which of several skeletons a vessel was intended to accompany. Presumably most of these almost complete vessels were deposited as mortuary offerings. Their distribution is shown in the accompanying table (fig. 43).

So far as could be determined, there was no evidence of any of the vessels having contained anything when buried.

This does not mean, of course, that these vessels were not buried as food containers. The extreme acidity of the soil may have destroyed bone fragments and similar evidence.

	Original surface under mound A	Burial platform	Primary mound	Secondary mantle	Wash on secondary	Mound B	Barrow pit	Total
Late Types:								
Catahoula Incised	0	0	0	0	2	0	1	3
Marksville Types:								
Marksville Plain	0	0	14	17	0	2	0	33
Marksville Stamped	1	3	7	17	0	1	0	29
Marksville Incised	1	1	4	7	0	0	0	13
Crooks Stamped	0	0	5	0	0	0	0	5
Marksville Red Filmed	0	0	1	0	0	0	0	1
TOTAL VESSELS	2	4	31	41	2	3	1	84

Fig. 43. Table giving location and classification of reconstructable vessels in Mound A.

All except one of the 84 restorable vessels were badly broken at the time of discovery. Almost all had been crushed flat by the weight of the soil. There does not appear to be any very clear evidence of intentional breakage prior to interment except in one case, a vessel of *Marksville Plain*, which had the bottom broken out before it was buried.

The three large fragments of vessels of the late type *Catahoula Incised*, recovered from the wash on the secondary mantle of Mound A and from the fill of the large borrow pit to the north, did not accompany burials. A feature of the interments of the late Caddoan and Natchez groups is grave burial with a relatively large number of pottery vessels accompanying each skeleton. The fact that none of the burials exhibited this characteristic appears to corroborate the conclusion that in no case are they to be associated with the late occupation of the site.

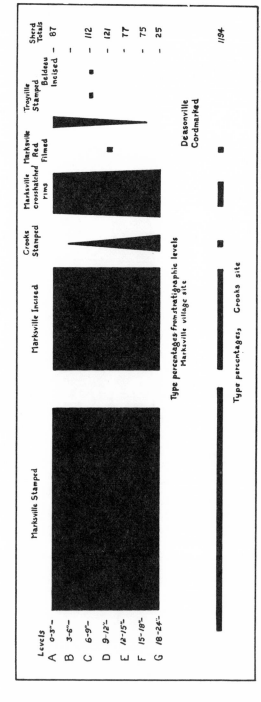

Figure 59. Diagram comparing the proportions of pottery types and their trends, discovered in stratigraphic tests of the village deposit at the Marksville site, with the pottery of the Marksville period from Crooks site.

Comparisons

When work was begun on the report for this site it was intended that extensive comparisons should be made with Hopewellian-like manifestations found scattered through much of the Mississippi Valley. However, it has not proved feasible to do this at the present time. Several reports which will render such an analysis much more comprehensive are now in preparation for different parts of the area, and, as a superficial tabulation is bound to be misleading, it has been thought best to delay such a comparative study until it can be undertaken in a thorough fashion. Throughout the preceding text, points of Marksville-Hopewellian resemblance have been dismissed after a brief presentation. These resemblances will be summed up very briefly here.

The complete report of Setzler's work at the Marksville site is not yet available. The ways in which certain aspects of that site resemble and differ from Crooks have been touched upon briefly. A suggestion that in time of occupation Crooks site may be coeval with the early part of the Marksville site occupation is found in comparing the Crooks site pottery with stratigraphic collections recently made from the Marksville village site (fig. 59). The pottery types, *Marksville Stamped* and *Marksville Incised*, occur in about the same proportions at each site. *Crooks Stamped* increases toward the bottom of the Marksville village deposits and is also found at Crooks in a small percentage. The types *Deasonville Cordmarked*, *Troyville Stamped*, and *Chevalier Stamped*, are found in very small percentages near the top of the Marksville village deposits but do not occur in the Crooks mounds. The latter three types reach the peak of their popularity in the Troyville period. Their absence at Crooks is negative evidence, and can only be considered as suggestive that that site was not occupied so long as the type site at Marksville.

Certain features of the Crooks site suggest typological relation to the sites of the Tchefuncte period, which from recent evidences appears immediately to precede the culture of the Marksville stage in southern Louisiana.[22] Five sherds of the Tchefuncte type *Tchefuncte Incised* were found in the fill of the burial platform and in the primary mantle of Mound A. Also some of the material listed as *Marksville Plain* shows very close typological relationship to *Tchefuncte Plain*. This is seen particularly in the fragments with tetrapodal supports, flanged bases, and notched rims shown as figure 27d-g. The tendency for the Marksville type *Crooks Stamped* to increase in popularity early in Marksville time, as indicated by stratigraphic studies (fig. 59), is also of significance in light of the fact that where Marksville period types have been found in Tchefuncte sites, this type is relatively abundant.

Other items of Marksville-Tchefuncte similarity are as follows: conical burial mounds containing predominantly flexed burials; small amount of grave goods; no evidences of occupation in vicinity of burial mounds (Crooks site); stone projectile points of hafted types—*Simple Haft 1C, Simple Haft 3A,* and *Barbed Haft 3B;* simple turtle-back scrapers, type 1; long chipped-flint drills; grooved and ungrooved boatstones; plummets of hematite; worked stone slabs, apparently used for grinding; water-worn pebbles collected and deposited in sites; ulna awls with wedge-shaped point; small tubular pipes of untempered clay (usual Tchefuncte type); biconical objects of fired clay; quartz crystals; red ochre; lumps of asphaltum; conch shell drinking cups; and use of conch shell columella.

In most of these features the Crooks site appears to show a closer relationship to Tchefuncte than does Marksville site Mound 4 excavated by Fowke and Setzler. This gives more weight to the tentative conclusion that Crooks represents a slightly earlier date than does Mound 4.

Superficial comparison of Marksville traits from the two sites which have been thoroughly examined shows that nearly all features found in the complex occur in most of the Hopewellian manifestations of the northern part of the Mississippi Valley. Further, it appears that in some in-

[22] A report on sites which represent the Tchefuncte occupation is now in preparation.

stances these traits have rather simple forms in the Lower Valley and are complicated in various ways in the different northern areas.

The list of comparable traits include earth-wall enclosures; conical mounds built solely for burial purposes, constructed in two or more stages; burial platforms on floors of mounds; log-covered vaults containing burials included in mounds; evidence of secondary burial; articulated burials usually flexed, extended but rarely; possibly cremation; small amount of grave goods usual; some evidence of cranial deformation; small pottery vessels, often with four lobes, short vertical cambered rims decorated with incised crosshatching, and body decorations of smoothed bands often depicting bird figures, with background roughened by notched rocker stamping; platform pipes with curved base, rarely animal effigies sitting on platform; stone pummets, usually of limonite; boatstones; conch shell drinking cups; pearl beads; ground stone celts with pointed polls, rather thick and oval in section; cymbal-shaped ear spools of solid sheet copper; copper beads rolled from a small sheet; nugget beads of copper; copper bracelets; galena beads; stemmed projectile points with wide ovate blades and small base; stemmed projectile points with relatively narrow thick blades; small objects made of carboniferous shale (or cannel coal); quartz crystals deposited with burials; and small masses of red ochre deposited with burials.

It is noteworthy that traits which are found in the Marksville site in a highly specialized form, such as log-covered tombs, copper ear spools, effigy platform pipes, and the complicated pottery, are also found in the Hopewellian sites of the Upper Valley. On the other hand, there are highly specialized traits in the Wisconsin, Illinois, and particularly in the Ohio area which have no counterparts in the south.

The pottery which is commonly referred to as the Hopewellian ceremonial ware is very similar to the utility ware found at Marksville period village sites in Louisiana. The predominating pottery of Hopewellian sites in the various northern centers is a grit-tempered cord-marked ware, commonly referred to as Woodland. So far not a single cord-marked sherd has been found in a Marksville period burial mound, and only a few have been discovered in the top levels of the Marksville village site. However, a cord-marked type, *Deasonville Cordmarked,* is very common in the Troyville horizon, which immediately succeeds the Marksville in Louisiana.

Trade sherds found in the Hopewell sites of Ohio are often limestone tempered. The limestone-tempered types, *Pickwick Complicated Stamped* and *Wright Check Stamped,*[23] appear in several sites. These types are native to the Pickwick Basin area of the Tennessee River valley in northern Alabama. By some of the investigators in that region the limestone-tempered types are thought to be the pottery which accompanied the Copena culture recently described by Webb (1939, pp. 188-201).

There is some evidence that the limestone-tempered types of northern Alabama are coeval with the Troyville period of Louisiana. This is shown by the presence in these sites of pottery types, such as *Mulberry Creek Plain* and *Wright Check Stamped,* which are comparable with Louisiana types of the Troyville and Coles Creek periods. Even more directly comparable are the slightly later clay-tempered Alabama types, *McKelvy Plain* and *Wheeler Check Stamped.* Direct evidence of trade has been provided by the identification of typical *Troyville Stamped* sherds from limestone-tempered sites.

Other evidence of an indirect nature is provided through the Weeden Island cultural stage of the northwest coast of Florida. Detailed comparisons have shown that Weeden Island was derived from the Lower Mississippi Valley area at the beginning of the Troyville stage and flourished at the same time as Troyville. In a recent article Greenman (1938, pp. 327-333) has pointed out the close resemblances between artifacts from some of the sites of this Florida

---

[23] These types are described in News Letter of the Southeastern Archeological Conference, vol. 1, no. 1, Feb. 1939. Mimeographed.

culture and the Hopewell of Ohio. Some of the similarities which he cites are also found in Marksville, and their appearance in Florida and Ohio may be the result of derivation from a common source. Other traits, such as copper breastplates, geometrical designs cut out of copper or mica, the bear-paw design cut out of copper, imitation projectile points of mica, copper-covered deer antlers made of wood, copper spindles, and conjoined copper tubes, have not been found in Marksville. These appear to be specilizations which have developed at a later time. The high degree of resemblance between these objects in Ohio and in Florida argues for some sort of direct contact between the two areas.

The very fact that a Hopewellian complex of features is firmly planted in such widely separated areas as Louisiana, Illinois, Ohio, New York, Michigan, Wisconsin, Iowa, and Missouri, indicates that all of these occupations are not of the same age. The basic resemblances of the culture are so great that it must have been distributed from a common center which consequently would be older.

Among investigators in the Upper Mississippi Valley region the idea that Hopewellian was a ceremonial or burial complex has received a great deal of attention. There is some evidence to support this theory, and indeed a tendency toward the ceremonial survival of old traits is to be expected in the peripheral areas of a culture distribution. However, in the Lower Valley the Marksville complex appears to form the entire body of the culture. For example, pottery comparable to that which in certain Upper Valley areas is found only as burial furniture is a common type of Marksville-period village sites in Louisiana.

The preponderance of the evidence accumulated to date suggests that the cultural influence which all the Hopewellian manifestations had in common, appeared first in the lower Mississippi Valley. The Crooks site and Marksville Mound 4 both appear to represent this early undifferentiated period. The principal movements of this influence were toward the north, up the valley of the Mississippi and up the larger tributaries. Somewhere in the comparatively unexplored region between Louisiana and southern Illinois, this stream of cultural influence became thoroughly mixed with Woodlandlike culture, a fact demonstrated principally by the addition of cord-marked pottery. Cord-marked pottery seems to have been spreading down the Mississippi Valley, and to have reached Louisiana in the Troyville period which succeeds the Marksville.

At least two major centers of Hopewellian specialization developed in the Upper Valley. One seems to have centered in Illinois and was the source of secondary distributions to western Michigan, Wisconsin, Iowa, and probably Missouri. The other is the classical Hopewell area of southern Ohio, from which the Hopewellian of western New York seems to have been derived.

The scanty physical evidence at hand suggests that the Marksville period saw the introduction into the Lower Valley of a broadheaded people who practiced cranial deformation. The population of the preceding Tchefuncte period was cranially undeformed and dolichocephalic. At least a portion of the people carrying the Hopewellian culture in the northern centers: Ohio, Illinois, Michigan, and Wisconsin, is known to have been brachycephalic and to have practiced cranial flattening. In several of these Upper Valley areas, the period of Hopewellian culture saw the introduction of brachycephals into regions formerly held by longheaded peoples.

Thus it is indicated that the northward drift of Hopewellian was not merely a movement of culture up the valley of the Mississippi; it rather was an actual movement of people. These people seem to have carried with them what were at least the germs of intensive agriculture, making a sedentary life possible.

It is easy to see how the rich alluvial valley of the Mississippi, thinly settled by a population with a hunting and gathering economy, could serve as routes for the rapid distribution of people practicing agriculture. Increase in population would be expected. Some mixing of peoples through absorption of the weaker groups may have taken place, and this may be what is indicated by the addition to the cultural complex of Woodland traits. However, since the simple hunting peoples who were being displaced probably had little to offer in the way of complex ceramic art, metal ornaments, smoking pipes, burial practices, or mound construction, it is not surprising that there is as much similarity in certain artifact forms as exists between the widespread manifestations. Most of the changes with time and the areal specializations had to come from within this cultural base.

It can now be demonstrated that in the Lower Mississippi Valley the later cultural stages, Troyville, Coles Creek, Caddoan, and the west coast of Florida developments, Weeden Island, and Safety Harbor, derived mainly from the cultural base provided by the Marksville stage. Intensive investigations in the central part of the Mississippi Valley will very probably show that the widespread Middle Mississippi cultures were developing at the same time, principally from Hopewellian. One result to be expected from this postulated phenomenon is that traits directly comparable with those of Hopewellian will appear sporadically in peripheral Mississippian cultures and in the adjacent Woodland cultures at dates very near the beginning of the historic period.

The accumulated data on eastern archeology is beginning to yield to synthesis and to outline a story of the distribution of cultures over a large part of the Mississippi Basin. The plot of this story is gradually emerging, and after a few more years of the intensive research now under way in many areas, it should be possible to narrate in detail how primitive agriculturalists built a complex and thriving culture in the Eastern United States centuries before Europeans appeared on the scene.

BIBLIOGRAPHY

Cole, Fay-Cooper
  1937   (with Deuel, Thorne) Rediscovering Illinois, University of
         Chicago Press.

Czajkowski, J. R.
  1934   Preliminary report of archaeological excavations in Orleans
         Parish: Louisiana Cons. Rev., vol. 4, no. 3, New Orleans.

Fisk, H. N.
  1938   Geology of Grant and La Salle Parishes: Louisiana Dept.
         Cons. Geol. Bull. 10, New Orleans.

Ford, J. A.
  1935   Ceramic decoration sequence at an old Indian village site
         near Sicily Island, Louisiana: Louisiana Dept. Cons.
         Anthropological Study 1, New Orleans.

  1936   Analysis of Indian village site collections from Louisiana
         and Mississippi: Louisiana Dept. Cons. Anthropological
         Study 2, New Orleans.

Fowke, Gerard
  1928   Exploration in the Red River Valley in Louisiana: Bureau
         of American Ethnology, 44th Ann. Rept., Washington.

Greenman, E. F.
  1938   Hopewellian traits in Florida: American Antiquity, Society
         for American Archaeology, vol. 3, no. 4, April.

Harrington, M. R.
  1920   Certain Caddoan sites in Arkansas, Indian notes and mono-
         graphs, Museum of the American Indian, Heye Foundation,
         New York.

Huner, John, Jr.
  1939   Geology of Caldwell and Winn Parishes: Louisiana Dept.
         Cons. Geol. Bull. 15, New Orleans.

Lemley, H. J.
  1936   (and Dickinson, S. D.) Discoveries indicating a pre-Caddo
         culture on Red River in Arkansas, and The Ceramic rela-
         tionships of the pre-Caddo pottery from the Crenshaw site:
         Texas Archeological and Paleontological Society Bull., vol.
         8, pp. 25-69, pls. 3-11.

Miner, Horace
  1936   The importance of textiles in the archeology of the eastern
         United States: American Antiquity, vol. 1, no. 3, January.

145

Moore, C. B.
 1908 Certain mounds of Arkansas and Mississippi: Acad. Nat.
      Sci. Philadelphia Jour., vol. 13, pt. 4.

 1909 Antiquities of the Ouachita Valley: Acad. Nat. Sci. Phila-
      delphia Jour., vol. 14, no. 1.

 1912 Some aboriginal sites on Red River: Acad. Nat. Sci. Phila-
      delphia Jour., vol. 14, no. 4.

 1913 Some aboriginal sites in Louisiana and Arkansas: Acad.
      Nat. Sci. Philadelphia, vol. 16, pt. 1, art. 1.

 1915 Aboriginal sites on Tennessee River: Acad. Nat. Sci.
      Philadelphia Jour., vol. 16, pt. 2.

McKern, W. C.
 1931 A Wisconsin variant of the Hopewell culture: Bulletin of
      the Public Museum of the City of Milwaukee, vol. 10, no.
      2, pp. 185-328, Milwaukee.

Setzler, F. M.
 1933A Hopewell type pottery from Louisiana: Washington Acad.
      Sci. Jour., vol. 23, no. 3, March 15.

 1933B Pottery of the Hopewell type from Louisiana: U. S. Nat.
      Mus. Proc., vol. 82, no. 2963, art. 22, pp. 1-21.

 1939 Marksville: a Louisiana variant of the Hopewell culture
      (in preparation).

Shetrone, H. C.
 1930 The mound builders, New York, D. Appleton & Co.

 1931 (and Greenman, E. F.) Explorations of the Seip group of
      prehistoric earthworks: Ohio Archaeological and Histori-
      cal Quart., vol. 40, no. 3, pp. 343-509, July.

Southeastern Archeological Conference
      Reports (mimeographed) edited by W. G. Haag, Museum
      of Anthropology, University of Kentucky, Lexington.

Walker, Winslow
 1936 The Troyville mounds, Catahoula Parish, Louisiana: Bu-
      reau of American Ethnology, Bull. 113, Washington.

Webb, W. S.
 1939 An archaeological survey of Wheeler Basin on the Ten-
      nessee River in northern Alabama: Bureau of American
      Ethnology, Bull. 122, Washington.

Wedel, W. R.
 1938 Hopewellian remains near Kansas City, Missouri: U. S.
      Nat. Mus. Proc., vol. 86, no. 3045, pp. 99-106.

11

American Anthropologist

NEW SERIES

| Vol. 43 | JULY-SEPTEMBER | No. 3, Part 1 |

AN INTERPRETATION OF THE PREHISTORY OF THE EASTERN UNITED STATES

By J. A. FORD *and* GORDON R. WILLEY

INTRODUCTION

THERE has been a remarkably rapid increase in information concerning the prehistory of the eastern part of the United States in the last ten years. This has been the direct result of archeological researches undertaken by several federal agencies and by universities or other institutions in nearly every one of the states. Undoubtedly the large amount of apparently disconnected data now in print, or yet unpublished but serving as common topics for discussion among specialists in this field, must be confusing to those who wish to make a survey of the prehistory of this area. There have been some very thorough syntheses of parts of the East, but unfortunately for the elucidation of the larger problem, these have dealt mainly with regions which appear to be peripheral (61, 62).[1][*]

The emergence of a comprehensive outline for eastern archeology has undoubtedly been seriously hampered by the unavoidable delays necessary for the preparation and publication of reports on the large research projects of recent years, many of which are still under way. However, as a result of this work, an outline of the story is beginning to take shape in the minds of some of the investigators working in this region. There is by no means a general agreement as yet on the details of this outline, but we feel that preliminary statements of opinions will be beneficial at this time.

For the deductions presented in this paper, we have drawn heavily upon both the published and unpublished work of our colleagues. We are particularly indebted to the archeologists who have participated in the several informal meetings of the Southeastern Archeological Conference where the problems of the cultural inter-relationships of the prehistoric Southeast have been thoroughly discussed.[2]

---

[1] See also F. M. Setzler, *Archeological Perspective in the Northern Mississippi Valley* (Smithsonian Miscelaneous Colls., Vol. 100, Washington, 1940).

[*] Numbers in parentheses refer to sites listed in the numbered bibliography and given in the various charts enclosed in circles.

[2] See News Letters of the Southeastern Archeological Conference, Wm. G. Haag, University of Kentucky, Editor (mimeographed).

THE PHYSIOGRAPHIC AREA

In a recent paper Kroeber has pointed out the correlation of the physiography and the historic culture of the Eastern Maize Area.[3] Archeologically this definition of an eastern cultural area appears to be fully as valid. There is no logical demarcation between the various parts of the East. All the vast region south of the Maritime Provinces and the southern portion of Canada near the Great Lakes and east of the Plains from the Dakotas to central Texas must eventually be treated as the theater of eastern prehistory. The Mississippi River and its tributaries form a great dendritic system of rich agricultural land through the central part of this region, providing an ideal artery for the dissemination of cultures based on an agricultural economy. This dominant feature of the physiography seems to have had a profound effect upon the history of native culture. The eastern cultural area is bordered on the west by the High Plains and the Staked Plains—effective barriers to the westward movement of sedentary primitive agriculturalists. To the north both climatic factors and dilution of cultural complexes delimit the area. The Atlantic seaboard forms the eastern boundary of the area but the Appalachian Mountains protected much of the coastal area from the full effects of the later and more advanced cultural distributions.

The heart of the eastern cultural area is the immediate valley of the Mississippi River and the lower portions of the valleys of its larger tributaries. Here are found the evidences of the largest population concentrations, and from these regions appear to have come the cultural complexes and movements of peoples which profoundly affected the course of aboriginal history in the entire area. It is rather unfortunate that the excellent work which has been done in certain peripheral areas and the remarkable finds which are occasionally made should have resulted in focusing attention on other parts of the East to the exclusion of the Mississippi Valley.

METHOD OF PRESENTATION

The present paper will pay particular attention to the prehistory of the southern and central parts of the eastern area. Even with this limitation it is not practical to discuss the cultural features of the various subareas and time periods in any detaill. Some of this detail may be gathered from the archeological reports of the various institutions which have been working in the East, a few of which are cited in the accompanying bibliography. Unfortunately much of the key information has not yet appeared in print.

[3] A. L. Kroeber, *Cultural and Natural Areas of Native North America* (University of California Publications in American Archeology and Ethnology, Vol. 38. University of California Press. 1939), pp. 60–61.

In the accompanying figures (2–6) are shown chronological profiles, analogous to geological profiles, which in a general way follow the principal drainage systems of the Mississippi Valley (map, fig. 1).

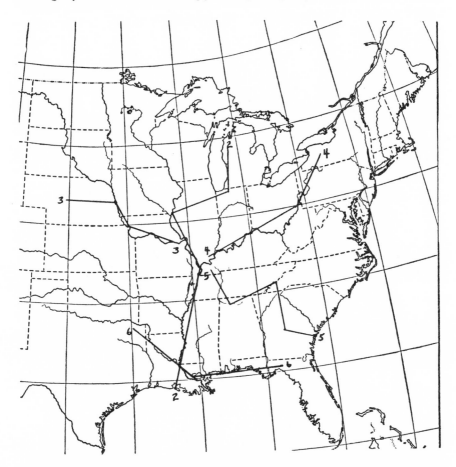

Fig. 1. Map of the Eastern Archeological Area. The heavy lines indicate the courses of the chronological profiles shown as figures 2–6. Numerals at the ends of each profile line are the figure numbers of the illustration in which the profile is given.

The first profile (fig. 2) runs from the Gulf of Mexico up the Mississippi River to the mouth of the Illinois, through the state of Illinois along the river of the same name, around the southern end of Lake Michigan into the western part of the state of Michigan.

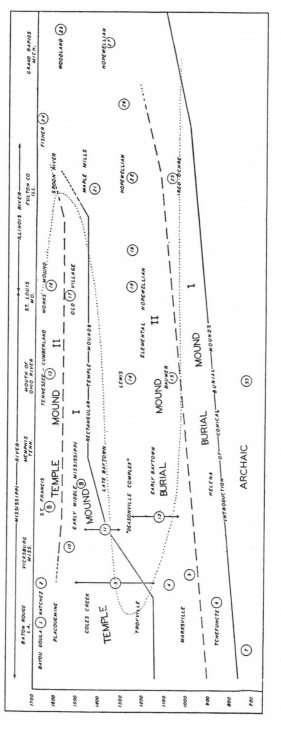

Fig. 2.

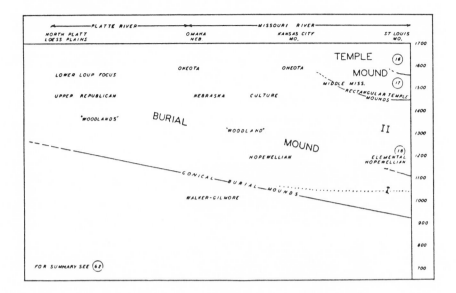

FIG. 3.

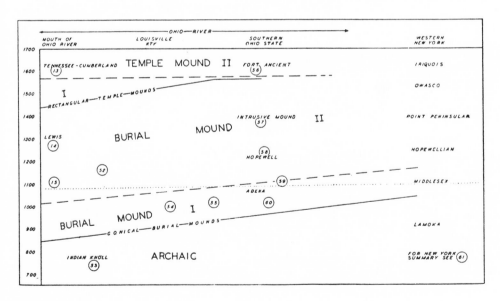

FIG. 4.

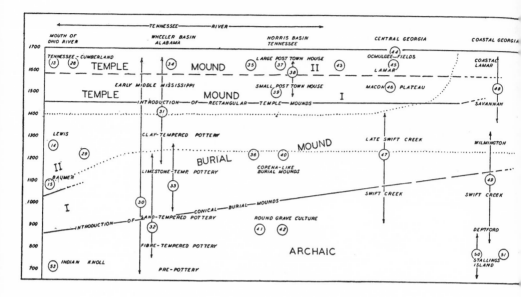

FIG. 5.

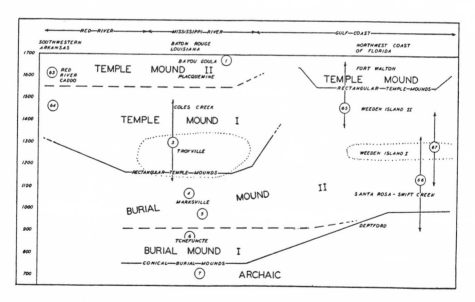

FIG. 6.

The second profile (fig. 3) extends from the mouth of the Missouri River to the mouth of the Platt and up that river into central Nebraska.

The third profile (fig. 4) extends from the mouth of the Ohio River into western New York.

The fourth profile (fig. 5) starts at the mouth of the Tennessee River and follows back up that river to eastern Tennessee into the Norris Basin area. From here it extends into central Georgia and down to the Georgia coast at Savannah.

The fifth profile (fig. 6) begins in southwestern Arkansas, follows the Red River down to its junction with the Mississippi, and extends along the coast of the Gulf of Mexico to about the vicinity of Tallahassee, Florida.

The localities indicated at the tops of these profiles are separated proportionately by the approximate geographical distances between them. Dates are given down the sides of each diagram, but these should not be taken too seriously. They are frankly guesses, the main purpose of which is to synchronize the details of this widespread story. These dates are occasionally used in the text for the same purpose.

Cultural names in common use have been placed in the diagrams in proper geographical position, and are arranged vertically in what is thought to be their relative temporal positions. The arrangements presented are based upon the best evidence available and are not contradictory.

Numbers in small circles in the diagrams indicate the areal and chronological positions of sites listed in the numbered bibliography. Where any appreciable length of time is indicated for a site occupation, arrows attached to the numbered circles indicate the approximate time span. It is hoped that by means of this device the reader may not only gain a more detailed knowledge of this rather involved history, but will be assisted in forming his own opinions as to the outline of eastern prehistory.

The chronological position of cordmarked surface treatment for pottery vessels is shown by means of a dotted line.

PLEISTOCENE MAN IN THE EAST

Indisputable evidence of the association of human remains or cultural evidences with extinct Pleistocene fauna has not been found in the eastern area. This by no means denies the possibility that such finds will be made, or that new evidence will bring general acceptance of some of the questionable associations already discovered. Folsomoid projectile points have come from almost every state in the area, and so far they have not been found to be related to any of the known archeological cultures. The great age of the similar type in the western states promises some very interesting discoveries for the East. However, in view of the present lack of evidence, a discussion of these early cultures in the East is impossible.

THE EASTERN ARCHAIC STAGE

It appears to be justifiable to apply the name "archaic" to the earliest known cultural horizon in the East. The cultures of this period were "archaic" in the true sense; horticulture was lacking, pottery is either absent or makes its appearance late in the stage, and the abundance, variety and quality of artifacts do not compare with the more complex later developments. On the other hand the archaic cultures established a complex containing many elements which lasted on into later periods. This stage appears to provide a sort of foundation cultural pattern for the East into which new traits and complexes were intruded to form the later cultural stages.

Sites which may be assigned to the eastern archaic are those of the Lamoka Focus of western New York (61), several sites scattered along Green River in western Kentucky (53), the lower levels of some of the large shell mounds on the Tennessee River in northern Alabama (30 and 32), sites along the Savannah River in eastern Georgia (50 and 51), the lower levels of sites in eastern Florida,[4] and the lower levels of several of the six sites which have been assigned to the Tchefuncte period in southern Louisiana (7). Materials indicative of occupation at this period have appeared at other sites in the south but few of those have been adequately investigated.

A common feature of nearly all these sites is the fact that they are located at points where an abundant supply of shell fish was available and the occupation areas are marked by large accumulations of discarded shells. The economic value of these stations appears to have been so obvious that many of them continued to be occupied throughout the cultural stages which succeeded the archaic.

A simple hunting and gathering economy seems to have prevailed during the archaic. The entire region of the East was probably thinly populated by nomadic hunters and the sites which have been examined merely mark spots where population stability and concentration was possible.

Nothing is known of dwellings at this time. Burials were made in shallow pits in the middens and the bodies were usually buried in the flesh, tightly flexed, and accompanied by small amounts of grave goods. Frequently the bodies were covered with red ochre. Human bones are also commonly found scattered through the refuse of the middens.

---

[4] W. H. Holmes, *Earthenware of Florida* (Moore Collection, Journal Academy Natural Sciences, Second Series, Vol. X, Part I).

Widespread common artifacts are socketed projectile points of either bone or antler; several varieties of crudely chipped stemmed flint points, including long and narrow but thick points with small shoulders and rather wide stems, broad ovate-triangular bladed points, and stemmed medium sized points with blade in the shape of an equilateral triangle; awls made from deer ulnae; canine teeth perforated for suspension; animal jaws placed with burials and probably used as ornaments; large tubular shell beads; worked sections of turtle shell; mussel shell spoons; antler drifts which may be tapping tools; small flat grinding stones; numerous fire-cracked stones or clay balls which may indicate the practice of stone boiling; and notched pebbles which possibly served as net sinkers.

In addition to these rather simple and uniformly distributed traits are a number of items which are localized in various parts of the East at this time. This localization and specialization would seem to indicate that the archaic stage had a long history in the East. In the Lamoka focus in New York, the bevelled adze, choppers, mortars, and bone whistles are found in this early complex. Peculiar to the early sites in Kentucky, northern Alabama, and Georgia are the expanded base flint drill; stemless and leaf-shaped flint knives; long, carved bone pins with expanded heads which are sometimes decorated with engraved designs; bannerstones; and the full-grooved axe. Adding Louisiana to the list of southern localities, the following traits are observed in all four areas: bone atlatl hooks; bar atlatl weights (also crude boatstones in Georgia and Louisiana); conch shell containers; drumfish teeth with burials; and bone fish hooks carved in one piece. In Louisiana, Kentucky, and Alabama asphaltum is used for fastening socketed tools. The penis bone of the raccoon, sharpened or perforated for suspension, is found in both Louisiana and Kentucky. Eyed needles of bone are peculiar to Kentucky; small triangular chisels cut from the lip of the conch shell and plummets are found only in Louisiana and Florida. The technique of cutting bone by sawing with thin pieces of sandstone has been noted on unfinished tools in both Louisiana and Georgia. Bone work from Alabama and Kentucky suggests the use of this method of cutting, but the evidence is not clear. Skeletons of small dogs are recorded from the burials and middens of both Louisiana and Kentucky. It is not known whether all the archaic cultures had this animal or not, but in later time levels the dog was widespread in the East.

The Eastern Archaic cannot be well characterized by any group of artifacts that are peculiar to this stage. Most of the traits found in it continue on in more or less altered form into the later cultural horizons. This is to be expected. The essential simplicity of the cultural congeries and the consistent absence of such advanced traits as metal working, polished stone celts, pottery, and mounds are undoubtedly of great significance.

Neither the New York nor the Kentucky sites have pottery and this trait is also missing from the lower levels of the sites in northern Alabama, Georgia, and what appears to be the oldest site in Louisiana. In the eastern part of the South, the earliest pottery is crudely moulded into simple bowl forms with rounded bases and is poorly fired. It is tempered with vegetable fibers which have burned out leaving the paste porous and it is undecorated (51). Somewhat later, this ware is decorated with simple straight-line arrangements of dragged punctations or fingernail indentations (50). Another variety of ware heavily tempered with sand accompanies the fiber-tempered. The decorations and shapes of this ware are similar to those of the fiber-tempered in Georgia, but in northern Alabama there are additional shapes and designs which are more complex. In the Lower Mississippi Valley an initial period of undecorated pottery is also suggested, but the evidence is not yet adequate. The pottery complex best known in this area appears to date right at the end of the Archaic, and while it is similar to the fiber-tempered wares to the eastward, it differs in certain important respects (6, 7). It also is crudely made and underfired but was manufactured by coiling. In addition to bowl forms there are straight-sided jars, and small pots with short collars, high rounded shoulders, and straight lower walls slanting in to a small base. The bases are occasionally flattened, but most common are four short legs. The earlier form of these legs is wedge-shaped, a flattened oval in cross section. These are gradually replaced by four legs which are round in section. If this pottery was tempered at all, it was by the addition of lumps of hard clay. The few fiber-tempered sherds that are found in association are apparently intrusives from the eastward. A few types in the Tchefuncte pottery complex were tempered with sand and bore decorations similar to those of the sand-tempered types of northern Alabama, mainly simple arrangements of straight incised lines. The decoration of crude rocker stamping on clay-tempered vessels is peculiar to the Louisiana area at this time. Approximately ninety per cent of this early pottery was undecorated.

BURIAL MOUND I STAGE

In addition to the peculiar ceramic features just noted, there are other traits that seem to belong to the latter part of the Tchefuncte period which mark the appearance in the Mississippi Valley of a strange complex of cultural ideas centering around the custom of burial in mounds. At present it is impossible to point to any extraneous culture from which these ideas may have been derived, but present evidence indicates that at a guess date of about 900 A.D. they began moving up the valley of the Mississippi from south to north.

The most notable trait of this complex is the use of cone-shaped mounds for burial purposes. These mounds are always placed some distance from dwelling sites, and are characteristically on the crests of ridges, or along the brow of bluffs. In them are found the remains of numerous individuals, most of which were partially or entirely stripped of flesh before burial. A few were buried in the flesh, closely flexed, or extended. The idea of partial cremation was also common as shown by a slight charring of many of the secondary burials. Important central burials are found in the center of the structures on the mound floor or in a subfloor pit or tomb. Grave goods are scanty and pottery was not used for burial offerings. The trait of intentionally breaking, or "killing" the objects intended for the use of the dead was common.

The evidence of tubular clay pipes implies the introduction of smoking. Circular gorgets of shell and quartz crystals placed with the dead are probably part of the new complex; the polished stone celt is undoubtedly new. Traits such as boatstones, plummets of hematite and galena, conch shell containers, pierced canine teeth, stemmed projectile points, and the use of ochre with burials continued on, in conjunction with the new elements, as carry-overs from the Lower Valley Archaic.

Whether or not new increments were added to the long-headed population of the earlier stage at this time cannot be determined from the scanty and badly decomposed remains recovered from the Louisiana sites. As a small element of broad-headed people who practiced cranial flattening (Centralids) formed a part of the population which had these early traits in the northern part of the East, it appears probable that a minor proportion of Centralid skeletons will be found in these early burial mounds of the Lower Mississippi Valley.

Finally, it is probable that horticulture was introduced with these earliest mounds. This is suggested by the location of the early mound sites in areas suitable for agriculture rather than on the coast or near streams where shell fish were particularly abundant.

These new traits and the germ, at least, of an agricultural economy must have spread rapidly northward up the valley of the Mississippi. Sites which probably represent this stage are known in the central part of the valley but have not yet been excavated. In Indiana (54), southern Ohio (60), and northern Kentucky (59), the Burial Mound I complex provided the basis for the well-known Adena culture. In picturing this cultural spread and those which follow in this paper, we do not wish to give the impression that these features were moving in a cultural vacuum—quite the contrary. This first distribution of burial mound building and accompanying features was passing through regions in which cultures of the Archaic varieties had doubtless been established for a long time. Considerable merging and interaction was inevitable. However, as very often happens, the simple indigenous cultures were not prepared to make any profound changes in the exotic elements or ideas that were introduced.

From the indigenous cultures of the Ohio Valley, Adena appears to have acquired the bannerstone type of atlatl weight, the two-holed, expanded-center bar gorget, the large leaf-shaped chipped stone knife, animal jaw ornaments, now cut, and the carved bone pins with expanded heads. Metal working seems to have been known in the Great Lakes area prior to the introduction of Burial Mound I traits. Copper ornaments and tools also appear in the Laurentian culture of New York which is thought to be partially coeval with the Archaic of that area and to immediately precede the Middlesex focus. The latter period is equated with Adena (61). From these sources the materials and techniques for making solid copper celts, C-shaped bracelets, finger rings, and bi-cymbal earspools may have come into Adena.

Specializations in the Adena culture of the Ohio Valley consist of such items as engraved stone tablets, thin stone gorgets of a number of shapes, the presence of a fire-hardened floor at the base of some burial mounds, and occasionally evidence of the burning of a mortuary structure before construction of the mound was begun. Log tombs containing important central burials are widely used, and in northern Kentucky where burial mounds of very large size were constructed, a number of such tombs are found in each mound. In western Kentucky and southern Indiana the mounds are small and the central tombs are more frequently formed with stone slabs. Burials in these sites tend to be extended on the back more frequently than is the case in burial mound sites of other regions. Along with the central stone tombs there begin to appear individual stone boxes in which one or two skeletons are extended on the back.

Pottery was not commonly used as a mortuary offering, but its appearance as sherd material in the burial mounds shows that it was known. Generally this ware is tempered with crushed limestone and is undecorated, although some incised designs have been found. In the feature of the rim cross section there is a marked resemblance to plain ware of the Tchefuncte culture of Louisiana.

Tubular pipes are characteristic of Adena sites but in those sites near the mouth of the Ohio are also found elbow pipes of both clay and stone which were used with separate stems. The possibility should be noted that sites showing such features as elbow pipes, extended burials in single stone-lined graves, etc. may have been later than the other Adena sites lacking these features. The scarcity or absence of ceramic material from most of the sites which have been assigned to the Adena culture makes an estimate as to their exact period of occupation rather difficult.

The Copena culture described in northern Alabama by Webb (33) seems to have ascended the Tennessee River from the Adena center near the mouth of the Ohio. Specialized traits such as large limestone spades, reel-shaped artifacts of copper, large stone effigy pipes, and an abundance of galena mark this culture, although basically it conforms to the general pattern of the Burial Mound I stage. Attenuated Copena-like sites are found as far up the Tennessee River as Norris Basin in eastern Tennessee (40).

Pottery was not used as burial furniture in the Copena burial mounds, but sherds in the fill of some of the mounds reveal that most of the pottery of this period was tempered with crushed limestone, either plain or showing plain plaited fabric impressions. Some sand-tempered wares were also found.

These wares are well known from the large shell mounds which are found on the Tennessee River in the vicinity of these burial mounds. They have a chronological position just later than the fibre-tempered pottery described above as the earliest in the northern Alabama region. There is some suggestion that the Copena culture lasted longer in the Tennessee Valley than did most of the Adena sites in the Ohio region. During its later stages Copena was probably contemporaneous with the Hopewell culture of Ohio, a culture which has been assigned to the Burial Mound II stage.

At about the time of this dispersion of Burial Mound I traits into the valley of the Tennessee River, a similar distribution was occurring up the Mississippi River and the valley of the Illinois River to the north central part of the state of Illinois where it has been described as the Red Ochre focus (23).

A similar movement can be followed out the valley of the Missouri River as far as Kansas City, Missouri[5] (62). This latter manifestation is characterized by small burial mounds arranged along the tops of ridges, central stone vaults with doorways, containing burials which may be charred, disarticulated, flexed, or a few extended. Mullers, celts, flint knives, marginella beads, hematite paint, cylindrical shell beads made from conch columella, elbow or projecting stem pipes of clay or stone, and a small amount of pottery are some of the features of the scanty grave goods found in these sites. Some of the pottery is limestone tempered and is either undecorated or bears simple incised designs. One piece was fabric marked. However, the ma-

[5] Gerard Fowke, *Antiquities of Central and Southeastern Missouri* (Bureau of American Ethnology, Bulletin 37. Smithsonian Institution, Washington, 1910).

jority is of small "cocoanut" or "amphora" forms covered with impressions of a cordwrapped paddle. The presence of cordmarking suggests that although these sites are characteristically Burial Mound I, they were used somewhat later than the Adena sites of the Ohio Valley and were coeval with the Burial Mound II stage of that area. A pre-cordmarked occupation, apparently lacking mounds, is known for the Missouri River valley at the Walker-Gilmore site (62).

BURIAL MOUND II STAGE

While the adena-like culture was spreading through the upper Mississippi drainage and developing areal peculiarities, changes were going on in the Lower Mississippi Valley transforming the Tchefuncte to the next recognized culture period, the Marksville (4, 5). Some of these changes are attributable to locally developed features of the earlier complex; other traits like copper and galena probably spread down from the north; still others, such as a sophisticated ceramic tradition, are presumably additions from the hypothetical outside source which furnished the previous crystallizing elements of burial mounds, a crude pottery, and rudimentary agriculture to Tchefuncte.

Significant in the Marksville period is the heightened emphasis on the treatment of the dead as seen in increased secondary burial, cremation, elaboration of log tombs, and the burial of decapitated skulls, possibly as trophies. Whether this trend is the result of hypothetical southern influence or "backwash" from the advanced Adena peoples of the north cannot be estimated from present synchronization data for the Upper and Lower Mississippi regions. The building of the burial mounds in two or more stages and the erection of large, functional earth enclosures around mound groups are two traits which are probably earlier in the south. Platform pipes of clay, human figurines showing flattened heads, and rectangular semi-subterranean houses also suggest a new influx of cultural ideas into the Mississippi Valley.

Most distinctive of all of the new traits of the Marksville period is the pottery. It is of better construction and firing than that of the Tchefuncte period. A number of basic pot forms are retained, however. Cambered collars, body divided into four lobes, flat square bottoms instead of tetrapodal supports, are diagnostic changes in form. Decoration is unique. Although rocker stamping and incising were employed in Tchefuncte, the well-known negative bird design is not seen in the Lower Mississippi Valley until Marksville times. Close-spaced, wide-bottomed incised lines forming curvilinear and angular patterns and occasional instances of red painted areas bordered by similar incised lines are also unlike anything found earlier. The cambered collar with delicately incised straight-line arrangements underlined by a row of hemi-conical punctation is another important marker for Burial Mound II ceramics.

Evidence for agriculture, which is still indirect, is considerably greater than in Tchefuncte. Sites are nearly all inland and are much larger than before. The population itself, from the scant physical anthropological data, shows some brachycephals with fronto-occipital flattening, mixed in with the long heads.

At the same time the Burial Mound II complex of traits was moving northward up the Valley of the Mississippi, certain characteristic pottery types were appearing independently and spreading over parts of the East. A plain plaited, fabric-impressed pottery has a distribution from southern Illinois (15) up the valley of the Tennessee (32, 41, and 42) and around the southern end of the Appalachians. The suggested direction of this spread is from east to west. From Georgia to northern Alabama this type appears on sand-tempered vessels with vase-like shapes, conoidal bases, and four legs. It is associated with a culture essentially Archaic. From northwestern Alabama to southern Illinois this ware is limestone or clay tempered, has heavy square flattened bases, and is associated with Burial Mound I.

Accompanying pottery types spread across Alabama and Georgia at this time were the simple stamped and simple dentate stamped decoration (49 and 30, 32) or surface finishing styles. The latter style also occasionally appears on fibre-tempered ware, a dying temper mode in northern Alabama.

From South Carolina along the coast to north Florida, linear check, bold check, and simple stamped decorations on sand-tempered ware appeared in the late Archaic, contemporaneously or slightly before this time. The vase form was associated with these surface decoration styles, and occasionally tetrapodal supports occur. These styles mark what is known as the Deptford period (49). There is a possibility that the linear check stamping may have developed from the old linear punctating of the Archaic fibre-tempered pottery of this same region. The tetrapods probably derived from the Tchefuncte pottery of the Lower Mississippi Valley via the Gulf Coast. In this connection it should be mentioned that the Deptford complex occurs stratigraphically early on the Florida Gulf as well as the Atlantic coast (66).

A peculiar pottery decoration consisting of complicated designs, both curvilinear and rectilinear, carefully stamped on vessels appeared at the end of the Deptford period and replaced the Deptford decoration styles in the southeastern states. This type, or group of types, is considered to mark the Swift Creek horizon (47) and its inception was probably about 1000 A.D., essentially coeval with that of the beginning of Burial Mound II, or Marksville, in Louisiana. This decoration complex spread inland to a greater extent than the Deptford, covering most of Georgia, north Florida, northern Alabama, and parts of Tennessee. Along the Tennessee River, like most of its accompanying types, it was limestone tempered.

Going back to the Mississippi Valley, it was probably about 1000 A.D. that the new features listed in the Marksville culture of the south began to move up the river in the wake of the spread of the earlier burial mound building stage. This later wave of cultural influences may have entailed some movements of an already mixed long and round headed population from the south. Of this we cannot be certain. However, this infiltration of Burial Mound II traits is clearly marked by notable increases in population in the two specialized areas of Illinois (22) and Ohio (58), and by a much wider dissemination of features than had occurred in the earlier Adena period. From Illinois appear to have originated the distributions to western Michigan (27), to Wisconsin,[6] and up the Missouri River (62). The influences of the particularly vigorous Ohio Hopewell area reached to western New York state (61).

Cordmarked Pottery

Whether this second wave entailed a movement of population or not, there is very good evidence that it moved through and was being assimilated by indigenous peoples who had already acquired a great deal of cultural virility, possibly as a result of absorbing the essentials of an agricultural economy from the preceding Adena stage. In the region to the south of the Arkansas River, a utility pottery finished with impressions of cordwrapped paddling is the dominant type of the late burial mound period of the region (12). In the northern Hopewellian areas the Marksville style of decoration with negative bird figures and rocker stamping is retained mainly as a mortuary ware, with cordmarked pottery making up the bulk of the ceramics.

Cordmarked pottery appears all across the south during the climax of the Burial Mound II stage in the north. From the Mississippi Valley to the coast of Georgia it was moving in from the north southward. Evidently it was not in the valley of the Ohio River or the Illinois region in Adena times when the wave of Burial Mound I culture arrived. McKern's recent suggestion that it came from Asia offers a possible explanation for its presence.[7]

---

[6] W. C. McKern, *A Wisconsin Variant of the Hopewell Culture* (Bulletin of the Public Museum of Milwaukee, Vol. 10, No. 2), pp. 185–328.

[7] W. C. McKern, *An Hypothesis for the Asiatic Origin of the Woodland Culture Pattern* (American Antiquity, 1937, Vol. III, No. 2), p. 138 ff.

However, cordmarking is but one variety of the stamping applied with paddles which appears in many parts of the East in fairly early times. Others which have been noted are plain plaited fabric impressions, simple stamping, linear check stamping, and complicated stamping. It may be that these various facings for the surface malleating paddles were developed out of old, somewhat dormant, paddling techniques associated with modelling rather than coiling. The earliest fibre-tempered ware of the Archaic is a modelled pottery. The subsequent introduction of coiling techniques from the west and south, along with horticulture, would have given an impetus to pottery making which may have continued, in part, along old channels of habit, especially in the matter of surface treatment. This theory by no means denies the possibility that these types may originally have crossed from Asia.

Cordmarking as a pottery surface treatment arrived in the Lower Mississippi Valley at the close of the Marksville period and achieved the peak of its popularity in the succeeding Troyville period. In the Tennessee Valley it appeared after the limestone-tempered wares which in their earlier forms accompanied the Copena burial mound complex. Clay-tempered aplastic, as in Louisiana and Mississippi, is in common association with the cordmarkings of the vessel surface. Georgia felt the southward shove of the cordmarked pottery toward the latter part of the Swift Creek, or complicated stamped pottery, period. On the Georgia coast, where this northern influence was particularly heavy, it almost entirely submerges the complicated stamped tradition at many sites and is considered as marking a separate period, the Wilmington (49). Circa 1200 A.D. appears to be a good "guess date" for this wholesale movement of the cordmarking idea into the southern part of the East. This specific mode of finishing vessel surfaces became adapted to local paste and shape standards in the various parts of the south; rose to a peak of popularity more or less great, dependent mainly on the distance of the particular area from the northern cordmarking hearths; and then gradually disappeared.

About the western and northern peripheries of the Mississippi Valley as far south as the Ohio Valley, and east of the Appalachian Mountains, cordmarking continued until historic times. In this distribution it seems to be caught up with a general "lag" of other old ceramic traits. Hence, it occurs along with small percentages of simple stamped, plain plaited fabric impressed, and cordwrapped stick impressed techniques.

It seems pertinent at this point to bring up the question of the Woodland Cultural Pattern. As the term is generally applied it would seem to be a designation for a combination of a number of traits derived from some of the influences discussed above. Local variants of the Eastern Archaic appear to serve as a base. Into these have been infused features persisting from the burial mound building stages of the Mississippi drainage such as: conical burial mounds; exposure of the dead and cleaning of skeletons before burial (the burial complex tends to break down into secondary burial in large pits or ossuaries); tubular, platform, and "projecting stem" pipes; use of incised rim decorations on pottery vessels; celts, and earspools. Plummets, boat-stones, bannerstones, and the several other varieties of carved stone objects are either old local Archaic forms or distributed from the Adena and Hope-well stages of the burial mound influence in the Ohio Valley. Projectile points and chipped stone tools tend to retain Archaic forms. Cordmarked pottery, the possible origins of which have been discussed, was probably a later addition to this mixture. This strange mixture of old Eastern cultural ideas lasted until historic times about the peripheries of the Mississippi Valley, beyond the distribution of the later cultural features. Thus, although there is considerable local variation in detail, some essentially similar traits are found in the Plains, Great Lakes region, and down the Atlantic seaboard as far as South Carolina in 1700.

The Gulf Coast of Florida

On the northwest coast of Florida some of the shell middens have small amounts of fiber-tempered pottery in their lower levels suggesting that this was the earliest ware in the region. However, pure sites have not been found. The succeeding period, the Deptford, is well represented and, as in Georgia, is essentially Archaic in cultural content (66).

The next period is marked by the Swift Creek pottery types, already mentioned as having a similar chronological position in Georgia. These are considered to mark the Santa Rosa period (66). At this time pottery of the Marksville type is found in western Florida, and it is probable that the burial mound complex is being introduced from the Lower Mississippi Valley along with this pottery. The characteristic Burial Mound II burial traits are well established in this area in the next period, the Weeden Island (66, 67).

Following the Santa Rosa period the principal part of the cultural history appears to be related to the Mississippi Valley rather than to the Atlantic coastal area. Developments of pottery in Weeden Island were partly from Marksville types and cross-fertilization with Troyville is also under-rated. Weeden Island retained much of the old freedom in arrangement and execution of the incised and punctated designs that grew out of the negative decorations of Marksville pottery and escaped the formalization that affected the developments in Louisiana during the Troyville period. Red slipped ware and red painted areas bordered by incised lines are a small though persistent part of the ceramic complex.

A similar tendency appears in both Louisiana and Florida at this time— that of confining the decorated area, which previously had covered the vessel exterior, to a band about the upper part of the body. This also applies to the Swift Creek stamped ware which at the same time develops larger and simpler design elements. During the Weeden Island period a very small amount of cordmarked ware filtered into Florida from the northward.

Although the Weeden Island period flourished after 1100 A.D. and was roughly coeval with the time of the introduction of rectangular temple mounds into the Lower Mississippi Valley, that is during the Troyville period, it retained and modified the burial complex of the old burial mound stage. Many of the less essential details were dropped. Skeletons were stripped of flesh; were closely flexed; or a few were cremated. Remains were piled up and covered with ochre, shell, and sand. Large offerings of pottery vessels which were "killed," or specially made for burial purposes, were also placed on the ground, usually on the eastern side of the burials. A small low sand mound of conical shape was heaped over the lot. These burial mounds are always some distance from the middens which mark the dwellings of the period.

Weeden Island in Florida, the latter part of the Swift Creek period in Georgia, the latter part of the limestone-tempered and early clay-tempered periods of the Tennessee River Valley in northern Alabama, and the high development of the Hopewell culture in southern Ohio were approximately coeval and probably existed circa 1100–1300 A.D. Similarities between Ohio and Florida at this time have been pointed out by E. F. Greenman.[8]

In the foregoing we have attempted to show how a set of strikingly unique cultural ideas, centering around a mortuary complex and cult of the dead, spread throughout the Eastern United States by way of the Mississippi Valley. Two recognizable stages have been considered as Burial Mound I, the Tchefuncte-Adena cultures, and Burial Mound II, the Marksville-Hopewell cultures. It seems likely that the real driving factor behind the spread of these new ideas was a basic horticulture. There are strong suggestions that these horticultural, mound building, coiled pottery cultural traits were introduced and promulgated by a new physical type, brachycephals who also practiced cranial deformation. This new population increment, and the new cultural complex, merged with the peoples and cultures

---

[8] E. F. Greenman, *Hopewellian Traits in Florida* (American Antiquity, Vol. III, No. 4, 1938), p. 327 ff.

of what has been referred to as the Archaic stage. By the time of the first arrival of the burial mound builders, the Archaic people were already developing various regional specializations in their culture. These specializations, environmental differences, and the complexities of trait diffusion account for some of the local differences in both of the burial mound stages. After the advent of Burial Mound II in the north, the fusion of the Archaic with the new resulted in such an elaborate and well integrated culture as the Ohio Valley Hopewell.

It is not the purpose of this present article to go into the details of the high developments of Adena, or of the Hopewellian as it culminated in Ohio, Illinois, and other centers. These have been ably pictured by various writers to whom we have referred. The history of these influences in both the eastern (61) and western (62) peripheries has been ably described.

TEMPLE MOUND I STAGE
The Lower Mississippi Valley

At the time of the close of the Marksville period and at the beginning of Weeden Island and Hopewellian efflorescences, new cultural influences, which were to profoundly change established burial mound patterns in the East, appeared in the Lower Mississippi Valley. A corresponding increase in proportion of deformed brachycephals over undeformed dolichocephals may indicate that these new traits were carried by an invading people from the south. However, an infiltration into, rather than a replacement of, indigenous population is suggested.

The most marked feature of this new complex was the construction of rectangular flat-topped mounds about a court or plaza (3). These mounds are usually almost square in shape, and the two principal mounds of a group are generally at opposite ends of the plaza. Round temples made by planting wooden poles in the ground stood on the mound tops and within the temples were circular firebasins lined with clay. Stairways with a more gentle slant than the sides of the mound led from the tops down into the plaza. At intervals the temples were destroyed, an additional mantle of soil added to the mound, and a new temple constructed. As many as ten or twelve stages of construction are not uncommon.

Methods of disposing of the dead also underwent alteration at this time. Some evidence indicates that many were cremated in large bath-tub shaped pits in the plaza area. A few were stripped of their flesh and buried together in large shallow pits with few or no grave offerings. It seems obvious that this period marks the introduction of a new cult which emphasized new religious ideas connected with the plaza, and temples situated upon mounds, rather than rites dealing simply with the dead. However, the use of conical burial mounds was not entirely given up.

In the Troyville period and for a long time in the cultural periods which inherited this cult, the mound groups do not appear to mark the sites of actual villages. Most of the refuse found in such sites has been swept down from the structures on the mound surfaces. Probably these mound groups each represent religious centers for scattered agricultural communities.

Other cultural features found at this time include rectangular houses, elbow pipes of clay, small and very thin stemmed projectile points, pottery, trowels, small solid clay figurines, and short cylindrical ear spools of clay. Features retained from the Marksville and earlier periods include such items as celts, boatstones, quartz crystals, awls made from deer ulua, bone atlatl hooks, and several types of large stemmed projectile points. The remarkable scarcity of burials and the lack of any objects buried with the few that have been found undoubtedly shortens this list.

The pottery of this period, like that of the preceding periods, is about eighty-five percent undecorated. The decorated types can mostly be traced as developments from the decorations on the bodies of the vessels of the preceding period. They consisted mainly of curving negative areas outlined by incised lines with backgrounds roughened in several different ways. Closely spaced incised line designs, red slip ware, and painted designs bordered by incised lines, are fairly common. As previously mentioned, cordmarking appears at this time. In the main the vessel forms appear to have been derived from those of the Marksville period, but there is a much greater variety and the vessels tend to be larger. Paste is clay tempered and well fired.

In decoration and shapes this ware is similar to that of the Weeden Island period of Florida, which appears to be coeval. It differs principally in showing a strong trend toward stylization of both decoration and vessel forms.

Tendencies toward the development of folded rims and the confining of the area of vessel decoration to the neck or shoulder can be seen in both the Lower Valley and Florida. These traits also begin to appear in the pottery of the Swift Creek horizon of central Georgia (47).

The Troyville period in the Lower Valley gradually develops into that designated as Coles Creek (3). This latter period is differentiated mainly by changes in ceramic features. The ware tends to become thinner and better fired. Some of it has well polished surfaces. Beakers, bowls and related forms take precedence over the large jars so popular in the preceding period, and decorations show even more tendency to be confined to the neck or shoulder area. Predominating are combinations of straight lines which can be traced from the rim decorations of the Marksville Period pottery. By this time cord-marked pottery has disappeared from Louisiana and a new decoration is arriving in small quantities from the eastward. This is the small check stamp which is so characteristic of the latter part of the Weeden Island period in northwest Florida. The Coles Creek period in Louisiana probably lasted until the middle of the sixteenth century, and developed into the cultures of the historic groups of that region, the Natchez (2), Bayougoula (1), and Choctaw.

The dissemination of Burial Mound II influences from the Marksville culture into western Florida has already been described. During the Temple Mound I stage, or the Troyville, there appears to have been a movement up the valley of the Red River toward northeastern Texas (64). The historic culture of the southern Caddoan speaking peoples can be traced from these influences (63). It is very apparent, however, that the peak of the population in this region was not achieved until after the end of the Coles Creek period, that is after 1550.

The closely connected development which can be traced connecting the Caddoan area in northeastern Texas, southwestern Arkansas, and northwestern Louisiana; the Lower Mississippi Valley; and the west coast of Florida, forms a distinct branch of the cultural history of the East.

The Central Mississippi Valley

In outlining the sequence of events in the Lower Mississippi we have gone ahead of the chronology of the story. In the Mississippi Valley area of eastern Arkansas and western Mississippi, north of the mouth of the Arkansas River, the wave of cordmarked pottery which arrived from the north about 1200 was much stronger than in Louisiana. It formed about fifty percent of the ware of the culture of the Early (12) and Late Baytown (11) periods.

Early Baytown, like all the other early stages of this region, is known only from surface evidence gathered in the course of recent surveys. It appears to belong to a typical Burial Mound II stage, and the sites generally have a number of small conical burial mounds arranged in lines along the tops of low ridges. Stemmed projectile points have been found and fragments of celts. Besides the prominence of cordmarking already mentioned the ceramic complex is characterized by the following features: clay tempering, thick square bases, plain ware, red slip ware, four small ears on vessel rims, rocker stamped designs, and trade sherds from Louisiana sites of Troyville period types. Although Early Baytown retained the diagnostic features of the Burial Mound stages, it is evident that either ceramic influences from

Louisiana were being felt, or developments were occurring in this area parallel to those taking place farther down the river.[9]

The population of the entire Mississippi floodplain region appears to have increased rapidly and the sites which may be assigned to the Early and Late Baytown time periods are extremely plentiful in both Arkansas and Mississippi.

The Late Baytown period correlates with the Coles Creek period of Louisiana. During this period cordmarked finish of vessel surfacing disappeared and a plain clay-tempered ware formed fully ninety percent of the ceramic complex. Flattened square bases were largely replaced by flat round and rounded bases and a wide-mouthed bottle form developed. Red slipped ware and the use of ears on the rims of bowls continued. A notable feature was the introduction of polished ware from the Lower Valley. Trade sherds found on the sites of this period came from the Coles Creek period sites of Louisiana and some of the straight line decorations were adopted and simplified. In addition there is a small amount of check stamped ware which appears to be derived from the Tennessee River Valley area. A small percentage of the pottery is decorated by red painted areas separated from the unpainted background by narrow incised lines, a descendant of an old Marksville period type previously described.

Toward the close of Late Baytown rectangular temple mounds arranged about a central court are found on many sites. Apparently this feature is coming from the south, lagging behind the spread of certain ceramic traits. In a few instances conical burial mounds were retained and used along with the rectangular structures, but these are rare. Most of the sherds found on these sites are near the temple mounds, and even this fragmentary material is often scarce. Burials with accompanying artifacts are almost unknown for this period.

Indications of the trends of developments during the Late Baytown-Coles Creek periods can be seen at a few burial sites located near the boundary between the two areas and somewhat back from the Mississippi River (10). These usually consist of one or two burial mounds, although in a few cases temple mounds were also constructed. Numerous primary and secondary burials were placed at various points in the mounds and were accompanied by fairly large quantities of grave goods including celts, discoidal stones, copper covered ear spools of stone, elbow pipes of pottery, pottery

---

[9] Some of the sites described as belonging to the Deasonville Complex in the Yazoo River area in western Mississippi may be assigned to this same time horizon. See J. A. Ford, *Analysis of Indian Village Site Collections from Louisiana and Mississippi* (Anthropological Study No. 2, Louisiana Department of Conservation, Sites 49 to 60).

vessels, etc. The pottery is predominantly clay-tempered but shell was used in some instances. Vessel forms and decorations show clearly the transition which was occurring from the typical Coles Creek and Late Baytown forms to those of the succeeding period of eastern Arkansas and western Mississippi, the Early Middle Mississippi.

Middle Mississippi is a term first used by W. H. Holmes[10] to characterize the typical shell-tempered pottery found in such great quantities accompanying burials in the central part of the Mississippi Valley.

This division of eastern ceramics has come to be accepted as a term applying to the entire cultural complex which usually accompanies this characteristic pottery, and Deuel[11] has attempted to define a Middle Mississippian cultural unit. This paper is not using the term exactly as defined by Deuel. While essentially similar, the Middle Mississippi manifestations vary from area to area and two recognizably distinct periods can be discovered.

An early Middle Mississippian period succeeds the Late Baytown in eastern Arkansas and western Mississippi (9). It should be emphasized that the changes do not suggest a complete replacement of cultural features, but rather a development and an intrusion of some new ideas. Shell tempering and the use of handles on pottery vessels are the most marked changes in ceramics. Clay-tempered polished vessels are gradually replaced by vessels of similar shapes tempered with finely ground shell. Red slipped bowls, ears on bowl rims, types of incised decorations, wide-mouthed bottle forms, round bottomed bowls, flat bottomed bowls with flaring sides, beakers, and many other ceramic features change but little. Rectangular mounds in plaza arrangement, small thin projectile points, elbow pipes, and pottery trowels all come from the Late Baytown of the same region.

There is a peculiar difference which can be noted in the shape of the rectangular mounds built in this period; a difference from the temple mounds of earlier periods which also appears at some of the Coles Creek period sites in Louisiana. Instead of being nearly always square in plan, the mounds at many sites are now elongated rectangles. One of the long sides of the rectangle faces the plaza and the stairway leads down the center of this side.

A few of the mounds and mound groups of this period are of great size, indicating possibly that political unification was being effected and that

---

[10] W. H. Holmes, *Pottery of the Eastern United States* (20th Annual Report of the Bureau of American Ethnology, Smithsonian Institution, 1903).

[11] Thorne Deuel, *The Application of a Classification Method to Mississippi Valley Archaeology* in *Rediscovering Illinois* by Fay-Cooper Cole and Thorne Deuel (Chicago, University of Chicago Press, 1937), Appendix I, pp. 207–223.

these were the ceremonial centers of large communities. If so, these populations must have been scattered over large areas. Midden material is generally rather scanty on these sites, and there is little indication of any dwellings in their immediate vicinity.

The actual temple structures of the earlier periods had a round ground plan, but at the beginning of the early Middle Mississippi period a square form of structure came into general use. Earlier structures appear to have been intentionally destroyed, but now evidence of the practice of burning the temples can be found at every site.

Very little is known of the details of the prehistory of the Mississippi Valley between Memphis, Tennessee, and the mouth of the Ohio River. However, good suggestions of the probable course of development are given by recent work in the valley of the Tennessee River a short distance to the eastward and in western Kentucky. It appears probable that a parallel but slightly different development from that just described was also leading toward the culture known as Middle Mississippi.

In some respects the developments of this area appear to have taken place more directly out of the old Hopewellian base. Near the mouth of the Ohio River the typical small Hopewellian pot of the Burial Mound II stage frequently develops a globular body. Small limestone tempered pots with globular bodies, short vertical rims, and two loop handles placed on opposite sides of the vessel have been noted in the Tennessee Valley area and in western Kentucky (29). Apparently they date from the Burial Mound II stage. These are very likely indications of the evolution of the typical Middle Mississippi pot form.

Other significant traits noted in Burial Mound II stage sites near the mouth of the Ohio are clay elbow pipes, large triangular projectile points, pottery trowels, and discoidal stones (29). Besides the secondary burials in central stone vaults, some of the mounds have extended burials in individual boxes. At other sites, burials of this period were not placed in mounds. They were all extended on the back in individual stone-lined graves arranged in groups of two or three, each group separated from the others. The arrangement suggests burial beneath the floors of houses (52).

There is a very strong suggestion that such early features of the Upper Valley as these were spreading to the southward when the Middle Mississippi culture was developing and became welded into it. However, the principal movement of culture, and very likely of people, during the development of Middle Mississippi appears to have been to the northward. A notable Upper Valley addition to this complex which did not reach the Arkansas area was the salt pan marked with netting impressions. Early

Middle Mississippi occupations have been described from the lower levels of the Cahokia site (17) and from the Aztlan site[12] in central Wisconsin.

THE TENNESSEE RIVER AND GEORGIA

At a period which we will guess to be about 1400, very widespread and rapid movements of this early Mississippian culture out of the immediate Mississippi Valley region took place. The stretch from Memphis to Cairo seems a likely center for this diffusion of peoples and culture. The largest and certainly the most far-reaching line of dissemination moved to the southeast along the Tennessee River. The remains of this stage are found in the top levels of many shell middens in northern Alabama (31, 34), although here they have blended somewhat with the later Mississippian influences. Sites more purely typical of this earlier stage are found on the fringes of its distribution in eastern Tennessee (39).

Moundville, in central Alabama, may have been settled at this time, but it is clear that this important center did not reach the peak of its popularity until later. The Ft. Walton period (65), a post-Weeden Island survival on the northwest coast of Florida, exhibits strong Mississippian influence, some of which may be attributed to this early spread. This last marks the southernmost outpost of this diffusion.

Mississippian peoples moved down into Georgia from the drainage of the Tennessee and established the well-known large mound center at Macon[13] (46). In brief, this early Middle Mississippian complex in Georgia comprises rectangular mounds supporting temple structures which were destroyed by fire, rectangular houses with wall posts set in trenches, pottery trowels, celts, triangular projectile points, plated copper ear spools of stone or wood, "chunky" stones, pottery discs cut from sherds, pin-shaped ear ornaments of shell, and clay figurines. A few burials were made in pits in the temple mounds. While most of these were primary burials, some of the skeletons had been stripped of flesh and were in log tombs. The two largest sites were surrounded by earth wall fortifications. The pottery complex consists of a majority of plain ware in bowl, beaker and wide-mouth bottle forms. Pot shapes usually have two handles with nodes or small effigy heads projecting above them. Some of the ware is polished. Thick shell-tempered salt pans plain or marked with fabric imprints are also common.

In addition to the above traits, which appear to characterize the entire

---

[12] S. A. Barrett, *Ancient Aztalan* (Bulletin, Public Museum, Vol. 13, Milwaukee, 1933).

[13] The high degree of resemblance of the pottery and other artifacts between this site and such distant examples of this distribution as the Old Village at Cahokia appear to bear out this conclusion as to the rapid spread of this culture.

spread of this early Middle Mississippi complex and probably originated in the Mississippi Valley center from which this cultural wave came, this eastern periphery had developed a peculiar type of earth-covered ceremonial chamber which was not placed upon a mound (46). There is a possibility that this is an early form of the earth-covered rotunda used by the southeastern Muskhogeans.

It is very tempting to see in this southeastward spread of Middle Mississippian culture the original migration of Muskhogean-speaking peoples into the southeast. The Creek and related peoples found in this region in 1700 had the remnants of this Middle Mississippi culture, and the geographical spread of this linguistic stock corresponds roughly to the part of the southeast in which Mississippian cultural remains are found.

As the early influx of Middle Mississippi culture established itself in central Georgia, the people of the indigenous culture remained intact to the north, along the coast, on the Savannah River, and to the south. Their pottery styles at the time of the Mississippian invasion were in a late Swift Creek and transitional complicated stamped stage. The Savannah style, localized about the mouth of the Savannah River, is one form of this complicated stamping which had evolved from the Swift Creek. Farther south on the coast and in the lower Flint River drainage there is evidence that late forms of the classic type Swift Creek complicated stamped existed coevally with the transitional types. The local culture, although since early Swift Creek times carried by a numerically increasing population, had little or no immediate effect on the intruding Mississippians. Just what changes were brought about in the native Georgia cultures is not fully known as this transitional interval has not been clearly revealed by excavation. However, sites in south and coastal Georgia which are, ceramically, late Swift Creek show the rectangular temple mounds so characteristic of Middle Mississippian cultural influence.[14]

The gradual absorption of these introduced Middle Mississippi influences by the indigenous culture, the gradual breakdown of the local stamped pottery tradition into simpler patterns of decoration more carelessly applied, and the addition of many new features characteristic of the later Middle Mississippi stage, to be described, led to the formation of what is recognized as the Lamar period (45, 48). This was probably well formed and had taken over the southeastern area, submerging the earlier Middle Mississippi culture, by 1600.

---

[14] *Evelyn Plantation Site*, near Brunswick, Georgia (excavated by Preston Holder); *Kolomoki*, near Blakely, Georgia (not yet excavated).

DeSOTO AND THE 1540 DATE LINE

DeSoto's party of exploration passed across the Southeast in the years 1540–1542. This gives us the first basis for serious chronological estimates. The question of the cultural groups through which he passed, and the exact sites which he visited is too detailed to be examined here. It will be sufficient to say that the people with whom he came into contact in Georgia, Tennessee, and Alabama appear to be those bearing this early stage of Middle Mississippi culture. The careful tracing of his route by Dr. John R. Swanton and his collaborators reveals some very interesting and significant data.[15] Although they passed near, DeSoto's party did not visit the large sites of Etowah or Moundville. As this party seems to have been travelling through the most densely settled regions they could find and searching out the largest towns, this suggests that either these sites had already been abandoned, or had not yet reached their later prominent positions. Correlations with other parts of the southeast, and comparisons of the material from these sites with that of sites dating around 1700 shows that the latter is by far the more likely hypothesis.

Farther to the westward after crossing the Mississippi, DeSoto crossed the St. Francis River only about forty miles south of the numerous large sites in the vicinity of Parkin, Arkansas (8). These sites too show the later Middle Mississippi features, and very likely had not been settled when these explorers passed.

After travelling through Arkansas, the Spaniards followed the Ouachita River down to a point near its mouth in Louisiana where they spent the winter of 1541–1542. Here they found what is referrred to as the largest population encountered since leaving the Appalache country. Apparently they had arrived in Louisiana before the end of the Coles Creek period when this area sustained a most impressive population. At the close of the Coles Creek period, the Mississippi Valley area of Louisiana was almost entirely abandoned and remained unpopulated until 1700.

Winslow Walker's identification of the Troyville and Coles Creek period site near Jonesville, Louisiana as the former town of Anilco visited by DeSoto's party may be correct (3). Whether or not this is the identical town, the time of its desertion marks the latest period at which a large population was to be found in the vicinity of the mouth of the Ouachita River, where DeSoto is thought to have died.

---

[15] John R. Swanton (chairman), *Final Report of the United States DeSoto Expedition Commission* (1939, 76 Congress, First session, House Document No. 71).

TEMPLE MOUND II STAGE

The Temple Mound II stage is the best known of the prehistoric Eastern cultural stages. This is due principally to the large cemeteries which accompany the village sites and the enormous amounts of burial goods which have been found in the graves. Holmes' well-known classification of Eastern pottery is based primarily on the material of this stage, and the relatively short time period that this stage covers explains the success of this study in classifying Eastern ceramics into areal groups.[16]

Southern Caddo

Although a small population was already in the southern Caddoan area of northwestern Louisiana, eastern Texas, and southwestern Arkansas (64), the crystallization of the well-known southern Caddo culture and the marked increase in population in that region, appears to have occurred after 1540 (63). As previously stated, this culture was derived mainly from the Lower Mississippi Valley development, the Marksville, Troyville, and Coles Creek periods. To a degree features developed from the earlier Marksville and Troyville periods can be seen in the Caddoan culture farther up the valleys of the Red and Ouachita Rivers than those coming from the later Coles Creek period.

Elaborate pottery decorated with negative designs, red slip ware, polished ware, incising, punctating, rocker stamping, and many other features are characteristic. A few burial mounds were used in Arkansas and Texas and numerous temple mounds are also found. However, the trait of mound building appears to have been on the decline. Other traits were derived from Middle Mississippi or were the result of parallel development from common influence. Some of these were primary burial extended in graves, very copious deposits of grave goods in which pottery figured prominently, shell ear pins knobbed at one end, copper plated ear spools, discoidal stones, and small sharp celts.

The Central Mississippi Valley

The late stage of the central Mississippi Valley derived mainly from the earlier. However, there are some new features which have a very wide distribution over the South and may have intruded from the upper valley where they also figure prominently in such late cultures as Fort Ancient. Briefly this stage shows the concentration of population into large compact villages; utilization of temple mounds as adjuncts to the village in contrast

---

[16] W. H. Holmes, *op. cit.*

to the earlier practice of not placing houses in their vicinity; burial of the dead beneath the floors of the houses in extended position; surrounding villages with wooden stockades, generally without earth walls; accompanying the dead with large amounts of grave goods, mainly pottery; marked increase in the size of pottery vessels; use of large flakes of shell tempering; development of thin outflaring lips on the pot form; common use of strap handles, often more than two; development of bottles with small necks; red slip ware; red and white painted ware without incising used to outline the contrasting areas; negative painting; row of nodes on the rim exterior or the use of an exterior luted rim strap; effigy vessels; and the use of small celts with very sharp blades in addition to the larger blunt celts of earlier stages.

In Eastern Arkansas the late Middle Mississippi period is well known from the large towns scattered along the St. Francis River and along the Mississippi opposite Memphis, Tennessee. Some of these have been described by C. B. Moore. Along the St. Francis, such sites as the one at Parkin (8) are marked by large rectangular midden areas surrounded by ditches and orientated with the cardinal directions. The principal temple mound stands on the western side of the village. The unbelievable number of vessels which have been looted from the graves which were placed beneath the floors of the houses arranged around the border of the towns have made these sites famous among collectors.

TENNESSEE-CUMBERLAND

The Tennessee-Cumberland culture which is distributed across western Kentucky and down into central Tennessee belongs to the Temple Mound II stage and also seems to have reached its peak after 1540. In addition to most of the traits cited above for this stage, single stone-lined graves for extended skeletons are a common feature of this culture. This type of grave is also found at this time in eastern Missouri and in northern Kentucky. In the latter region it is a feature of the coeval Fort Ancient culture.

Tennessee-Cumberland is characterized by its ceramic features; predominance of shell-tempered plain ware, pot forms with strap handles and arched decorations on shoulders, straight-line decorations, incised guilloche and scroll decoration, frequent multiplicity of handles, luted rim strips, hooded water bottles, and large thick salt pans bearing netting impressions. The sites have rectangular mounds showing several building levels and the temples were square and had been destroyed by fire. Flint hoes and large chipped flint blades are suggestive of similar forms found with burials in the Burial Mound sites of this region.

Eastern Tennessee

Sites in the Norris Basin area of eastern Tennessee which Webb has assigned to a "Large Post Townhouse" complex show the features of this stage (35, 37). These sites are rather similar to Tennessee-Cumberland but show enough difference not to be included in that culture. In this region historic Cherokee sites have been identified and have essentially the same cultural features. An interesting fact is that the old decorations of complicated stamping, cordmarking, and check stamping have lagged considerably and appear on the large shell tempered vessels characteristic of this latter culture.

The Southeastern States

In parts of North Carolina, South Carolina, and Georgia the Temple Mound II traits appear in the Lamar period. This period is an interesting mixture of cultural influences. Sand tempering, vessel forms, and complicated stamped designs have been modified from the indigenous cultures. To this were added rectangular temple mounds, the burning of temples, rectangular houses, small triangular projectile points, pottery trowels, discoidal stones, pottery discs cut from sherds. Later came the features of wide curvilinear incising in scroll or guilloche patterns applied to the necks and shoulders of vessels, strap handles, occasional use of effigy vessels and rare painted vessels. Shell tempering showed a gradual increase in the western part of the area. Burials were extended and accompanied by grave goods at the Etowah site and near Columbus, Georgia. Near Macon the bodies were buried in the flesh but were flexed and had little grave goods. On the Georgia coast where this period lasted until historic times, bodies were cremated or were exposed and stripped of the flesh. The bones were buried in large common ossuaries or sometimes in small conical mounds.

This trait of secondary burial is well known from historic records along the Atlantic seaboard and a drawing of one of the houses of the dead or Quiogozons was made in the early 17th century by White.[17] This doubtless is a peripheral survival of Burial Mound practices. As already mentioned above many of the old ceramic traits, such as fabric impressed and cordmarked surface finishes, lasted until the historic period in North Carolina.

Through Georgia and South Carolina there are sporadic examples in Lamar period sites of burial in large urns. This practice appears to have been concentrated in southeastern Alabama where it is known from the work of

---

[17] D. I. Bushnell, Jr. *Native Cemeteries and Forms of Burial East of the Mississippi* (Bureau of American Ethnology, Bulletin 71. Smithsonian Institution, Washington, D. C.), p. 133 ff.

Peter A. Brannon and his associates.[18] Although the familiar stamped pottery is infrequently found in this region, the incised decorations, vessel shapes, and many of the other features of material culture are similar to those of the Lamar stage. This occupation lasted until the historic period and probably was the culture of some of the Lower Creek groups.

The large site at Moundville in west central Alabama is well known from the publications of C. B. Moore.[19] It was occupied during the Temple Mound II stage but was abandoned some time before 1700. In spite of the large size of this site, it seems to have been occupied only a short time. The cultural content suggests that its builders moved into central Alabama from the northward. The material is more closely related to Tennessee-Cumberland than to the Lamar culture to the eastward. It appears probable that Moundville is prehistoric western Creek.

The culture of the Choctaw in southeastern Mississippi developed principally from the Lower Mississippi. They did not build temple mounds, and their burial practices of stripping the skeletons of flesh and occasionally burying the bones in small conical mounds indicate a certain amount of lag in this respect. This is compatible with their geographical position on the periphery of the principal center of Temple Mound trait distribution, the Middle Mississippi area.

Historic Chickasaw culture, in north Mississippi state, is a blend of Middle and Lower Mississippi Valley developments. They were not building temple mounds when first described about 1700. However, they were burying beneath the floors of their rectangular houses, lived in palisaded villages and made shell-tempered pottery which in decoration and shape features revealed the admixture of Tennessee-Cumberland and Lower Valley traits.

UPPER MISSISSIPPI GROUPS

Brief as have been the discussions of the various Temple Mound II cultures of the southeast, the treatment of the so-called Upper Mississippi culture must be even shorter. It will suffice to suggest that such cultures as that of the Iroquois, in New York (61); Fort Ancient along the Ohio River (56); Oneonta in Wisconsin, Iowa and Nebraska (62); were formed as a result of first Burial, and later Temple Mound influences. These tended to become merged along the northern periphery of their distribution and were firmly welded to the Archaic traits of the various localities. Most of the puzzling

---

[18] P. A. Brannon, *Urn Burial in Central Alabama* (American Antiquity, Vol. III, No. 3), p. 228 ff.

[19] C. B. Moore, *Moundville Revisisted* (Philadelphia, Journal Academy of Natural Sciences, Vol. XIII, 1907).

similarities between Upper Mississippian cultures had best be examined from the viewpoint of these features having derived from a common source. The "woodland" cultures found even farther away from the Mississippi Valley centers tend to show an even greater retention of the older trait complexes.

The various Upper Mississippian cultures probably began to be formed before 1500 but they all reached their peaks after that date and all lasted until historic times.

The Population Decline and the Southern Cult

The period of the late Middle Mississippi or Temple Mound II stage seems to have been an uneasy one in the South. The valleys of the large streams, which had served as the principal routes of cultural dissemination, and had held the largest concentrations of population, tended to be deserted. People began to move back into the hill country and settle along small streams. It was just those regions which previously were most thickly settled that now were abandoned. This tendency can be seen by the locations of the sites in the Tennessee-Cumberland, Lamar, Choctaw, Chickasaw, Caddoan, and St. Francis cultures.

Not only did the population of this period tend to cluster into compact towns, as previously pointed out, but nearly every village was surrounded by a stockade. Fortified towns had been known since the Burial Mound II stage, but never before were they so numerous. The stockade of the Temple Mound II stage differed from the earlier examples in that the posts were generally set directly into the ground without the use of an earth wall.

Toward the end of this stage it can be seen that a marked decrease in population is occurring. In areas where sites of the early and late Middle Mississippian cultures must have numbered in the thousands, not an Indian was to be found in the latter part of the seventeenth century when the French and English explorers entered the region. This is particularly true for the Mississippi and Ohio valleys and for much of the country covered by the Tennessee-Cumberland and Lamar cultures.

During the Temple Mound II stage there appears to have arisen a curious cult which shows little relationship to anything which has previously transpired, and which spread rapidly over the entire Mississippi Valley area, although most common in the south. The paraphernalia from which the presence of this cult is deduced show a high degree of similarity all over the area. Included are such items as conch shell masks marked with the winged or "weeping" eye symbol; copper and shell pendants with circles and crosses engraved, repousse, or with background cut out; engraved conch shells or thin copper plates on which are depicted dancing figures wearing eagle masks, carrying a human head in one hand and a peculiar shaped baton in the other; shell gorgets showing fighting turkey cocks or rattlesnakes; monolithic stone axes; large stone batons; the horned and winged rattlesnake engraved on circular paint palettes or on pottery; and fairly large stone figures with negroid faces and characteristic arrangement of hair in two rolls on the top of the head.[20]

Some items of this paraphernalia have been found at nearly every site of this period which has been thoroughly investigated. However, some of the larger centers have become well known for the quantity of these materials which they have yielded. Outstanding are the Kincaid and Angell sites near the mouth of the Ohio River, the Etowah site in north Georgia, Moundville in central Alabama, and Spiro in eastern Oklahoma. Although the cult which spread these objects probably flourished about 1600, there are some finds showing that certain features, at least, lasted until after 1700.

The suggestion of Mexican influence in these objects has been recognized.[21] Aside from that, there is a great temptation to interpret these objects as evidence of some sort of religious revival quite similar in purpose to the well known Ghost Dance cult of the Plains. This, also, may be the evidence of a reaction to a rapid decimation of the population of a formerly vigorous and thriving culture.

Early contacts with Europeans may have brought among the native peoples highly contagious and, to them, very fatal new diseases such as measles, smallpox, cholera, etc. DeSoto's party of exploration across the south, 1539–1543; the early settlements of the Virginia coast, 1607; Spanish Missions and settlements in Florida and Georgia following 1520, may all have served as foci of contagion. The early disappearance of the native peoples from Florida and the vicinity of the Atlantic coastal settlements is well attested by the historical sources.[22]

The same cause, the impact of highly destructive epidemics, may account for the change of population centers noted above. In the thickly settled valleys of the larger rivers the epidemcs would have been most destructive. The surviving remnants abandoned the old villages and gathered

---

[20] A. J. Waring, Jr. and Preston Holder, (MS, to be published in The American Anthropologist).

[21] P. Phillips, *Middle American Influence on the Archeology of the Southeastern United States*, in *The Maya and Their Neighbors* (D. Appleton-Century Co., New York, 1940), pp. 349 ff.

[22] J. R. Swanton, *Notes on the Cultural Province of the Southeast* (American Anthropologist, Vol. 37, 1935), pp. 373–385.

in new settlements back in the hills. Perhaps the unrest of the period is reflected in the compact settlements and extensive use of stockades.

Much of the widespread scattering of peoples, notably the Yuchi, may have occurred at this time. These same factors may also account for some of the curious mixed villages described about 1700 such as the Yazoo, Tunica, Coroa, and Ofogoula, gathered into a village on the Yazoo River in Mississippi. It is suggested that the native peoples and culture, as described about 1700, were, for the most part, already a broken people with a declining culture.

COLUMBIA UNIVERSITY
NEW YORK, N. Y.

SELECTED BIBLIOGRAPHY

(The numbers in parentheses correspond to the numbered
references in the text and the numbers enclosed in
circles in the various figures, 2 to 6)

(1) Quimby, G. I., *The Bayougoula Site*
    (Report in preparation, Louisiana State University, Baton Rouge, La.)
(2) Ford, J. A., *Fatherland Site*
    "Analysis of Indian Village Site Collections from Louisiana and Mississippi,"
    Anthro. Study no. 2, La. Dept. Conservation, New Orleans, 1936, p. 59 ff.
(3) Walker, Winslow M., *The Troyville Site*
    "The Troyville Mounds, Catahoula Parish, Louisiana," Bu. Amer. Eth.,
    Bull. 113, Washington, 1936.
    Ford, J. A., *The Peck Site*
    "Ceramic Decoration Sequence at an Old Indian Village Site near Sicily Island, Louisiana," Anthro. Study no. 1, La. Dept. Conservation, New Orleans, 1935.
(4) Setzler, F. M., *Marksville Site*
    "Pottery of the Hopewell Type from Louisiana," Proceed. of the U. S. National Museum, vol. 82, No. 2963, Art. 22, Washington, pp. 1–21, 1933.
(5) Ford, J. A., and Willey, Gordon R., *Crooks Site*
    "Crooks Site, A Marksville Period Burial Mound in La Salle Parish, Louisiana," Anthro. Study, no. 3, La. Dept. Conservation, New Orleans, 1940.
(6) *Lafayette Site*, Report in preparation, Louisiana State University.
(7) *Tchefuncte Site*, Report in preparation, Louisiana State University.
(8) Moore, C. B., *Rose Mound*
    "Antiquities of the St. Francis, White, and Black Rivers," Jour. Acad. Nat. Sci., Philadelphia, vol. XIV, pp. 276–303. 1910.
(9) Moore, C. B., *The Blum Site*
    "Certain Mounds of Arkansas and Mississippi," Jour. Acad. Nat. Sci., Philadelphia, vol. XIII, pp. 594–600, 1908.

(10) Lemley, Harry J., and Dickinson, S. D., *Hog Lake Site*
     (Later culture) "Archaeological Investigations on Bayou Macon in Arkan-
     sas," Bull. of the Texas Archaeological and Paleontological Soc., vol. 9, p.
     19 ff.
     and
     Ford, J. A., *Big Black Valley Sites*
     "Analysis of Indian Village Site Collections from Louisiana and Mississippi"
     Anthro. Study no. 2, La. Dept. Conservation. pp. 115–128, New Orleans,
     1936.
(11) Collins, H. B., Jr., *The Deasonville Site*
     "Excavations at a Prehistoric Indian Village Site in Mississippi," Proceed.
     U. S. National Museum, vol. 79, art. 32, pp. 1–22, Washington, 1932.
(12) Lemley, Harry J., and Dickinson, S. D., *Alma Brown Site*
     "Archaeological Investigations on Bayou Macon in Arkansas" Bull. of the
     Texas Archaeological and Paleontological Society, vol. 9, p. 37 ff.
(13) *Kincaid Site* (Work now under way by the University of Chicago)
(14) *Lewis Site* (Work now under way by the University of Chicago)
(15) *Baumer Site* (Work now under way by the University of Chicago)
(16) Moorehead, W. K., *Cahokia—"Bean Pot Culture"*
     "The Cahokia Mounds" Part 1, University of Illinois Bull., vol. XXVI, no.
     4, 1929.
(17) Kelley, A. R., and Cole, F-C., *Cahokia—"Old Village Culture"*
     "Rediscovering Illinois" Illinois State Bluebook, 1931–1932, pp. 318–341.
(18) Titterington, P. F., *Bluff Mounds*
     "Certain Bluff Mounds of Western Jersey County, Illinois," American An-
     tiquity, vol. 1, no. 1, pp. 6–46, 1935.
(19) Moorehead, W. K., *Neteler Farm Site*
     "The Cahokia Mounds" Part I, U. of Illinois Bull., vol. XXVI, no. 4, 1929.
(20) Cole, F-C., and Deuel, Thorne, *Dickson Cemetery*
     "Rediscovering Illinois," U. of Chicago Press, Chicago, pp. 120–126, 1937.
(21) Ibid., *Robert Gooden Site*, pp. 195–198.
(22) Ibid., *Ogden-Fetti Site*, pp. 171–181.
(23) Ibid., *Mound F⁰ 11*, pp. 58–69.
(24) Langford, George, *The Fisher Site*
     "The Fisher Mound Group, Successive Aboriginal Occupations near the
     Mouth [?] of the Illinois River," American Anthropologist, vol. 29, pp. 153–
     205, 1927.
(25) Greenman, E. F., *The Younge Site*
     "The Younge Site," Occ. Contri. from the Museum of Anthropology, Uni-
     versity of Michigan, Ann Arbor, 1937.
(26) Quimby, G. I., and Black, Glenn, (Report on Hopewellian Sites on the St.
     Josephs River in Michigan and Indiana in preparation).
(27) Quimby G. I., Hopewellian Pottery Types in Michigan. Papers of the Michigan
     Academy of Science, Vol. XXVI, 1941.

(28) Webb, W. S., and Funkhouser, W. D., *The Williams Site*
"The Williams Site in Christian County, Kentucky" U. of Kentucky Publs. in Archaeology, vol. I, no. 1, Lexington, 1929.

(29) Ibid., *The Page Site*
"The Page Site in Logan County, Kentucky" (above series) vol. I, no. 3, 1930.

(30) Webb, W. S., *Sites Lu⁰ 86 and Ctᵛ 17*
"An Archeological Survey of Wheeler Basin on the Tennessee River in Northern Alabama," Bureau of Amer. Eth. bull. 122, pp. 21–33; 34–43; 157. Washington, 1939.

(31) Ibid., *Sites Liᵛ36 and Maᵒ4*, pp. 71–81; 88–90; 157.

(32) Ibid., *Site Mgᵛ2*, pp. 80–83; 157.

(33) Ibid., *Sites Laᵒ37 and Laᵒ14*, pp. 44–53; 53–61. Also see discussion of "Copena Complex," pp. 188–201.

(34) Ibid., *Sites Laᵒ13, Maᵒ1, and Maᵒ3*, pp. 61–67; 85–86; 87.

(35) Harrington, M. R., *Hiwassee Island*
"Cherokee and Earlier Remains on the Upper Tennessee River," Muse. of the Amer. Indian, Heye Foundation, Indian Notes and Monographs, No. 24, pp. 93–142, New York, 1922.

(36) Ibid., *Mounds near Lenoir City and near Rhea Springs*, pp. 34–46; 83–92.

(37) Webb, W. S., *Sites 10, 11, and 19*
"An Archeological Survey of Norris Basin in Eastern Tennessee," Bureau of Amer. Eth., bull. 118, pp. 83–115; 115–126; 161–179. Washington, 1938.

(38) Ibid., *Sites 5 and 17*, pp. 38–60; 140–159.

(39) Ibid., *Sites 2, 4, 6, and 9*, pp. 10–25; 32–38; 60–63; 69–83.

(40) Ibid., *Sites 16, 18, 21, and 22*, pp. 133–140; 159–161; 180–185; 186–189.

(41) Harrington, M. R., *Lenoir or Bussell's Island Site*
[See reference (35)], pp. 63; 80; 147; 167.

(42) Webb, W. S., *Sites 3, 12, and 13*
[See reference (37)], pp. 25–32; 126–128; 128–130.

(43) Moorehead, W. K., *The Etowah Site*
"Etowah Papers," Phillips Academy, Andover, Mass., Yale University Press, New Haven, 1932.

(44) Kelly, A. R., *Trading Post Site*
"A Preliminary Report on Archeological Explorations at Macon, Georgia," Bureau of Amer. Eth., bull. 119, pp. 51–57. Washington, 1938.

(45) Ibid., *The Lamar Site*, pp. 46–50.

(46) Ibid., *The Macon Plateau Site*, pp. 14–22.

(47) Ibid., *The Swift Creek Site*, pp. 25–45.

(48) Caldwell, J. B. and Associates, *The Irene Site*
(Report in Preparation.)

(49) Waring, A. J., Jr., *The Deptford Site*
(Report in Preparation.)

(50) Claflin, W. H., *Stallings Island (Lower Levels)*
"The Stallings Island Mound, Columbia County, Georgia," Papers of the Peabody Muse. of Amer. Ethnology and Archaeology, Harvard U., vol. XIV, no. 1, Cambridge, 1931.

(51) Waring, A. J., Jr., *Bilbo Site*
(Report in Preparation.)

(52) Webb, W. S., and Funkhouser, W. D., *The Chilton Site*
"The Chilton Site in Henry County, Kentucky," U. of Ky. Publs. in Archaeology, vol. IV, no. 1. Lexington, 1940.

(53) Webb, W. S., and Haag, W. G., *Chiggerville Site*
"The Chiggerville Site," U. of Ky. Publs. in Archaeology, vol. III, no. 6, Lexington, 1939.

(54) Black, Glenn S., *Nowlin Mound*
"Excavation of the Nowlin Mound," Indiana Historical Bulletin, vol. 13, no. 7, 1936.

(55) Setzler, F. M., *Mound Camp, Stoops Mound, and Whitehead Mound*
"The Archaeology of the Whitewater Valley," Indiana Historical Bulletin, vol. 7, no. 12, 1930.

(56) Willoughby, C. C., and Hooten, E. A., *Madisonville Site*
"Indian Village Site and Cemetery near Madisonville, Ohio," Papers of the Peabody Muse. of Amer. Eth. and Arch., Harvard U., vol. VIII, no. 1, Cambridge, 1920.
also
Griffin, J. B., *Fort Ancient Culture* (An analysis of this culture in press)

(57) Mills, W. C., *Intrusive Mound Culture*
"Exploration of the Mound City Group," Ohio Archaeological and Historical Soc. Bull., vol. XXXI, p. 563 ff., Columbus, 1922.

(58) Shetrone, H. C., *The Hopewell Culture*
"The Mound Builders," pp. 185–222, D. Appleton and Co., New York, 1930.
also
Shetrone, H. C., "Exploration of the Hopewell Group of Prehistoric Earthworks," Ohio Archaeological and Historical Society, Bull. vol. XXXV, pp. 144–172, Columbus, 1920.

(59) Webb, W. S., and Funkhouser, W. D., *Ricketts Site*
"Ricketts Site Revisited," U. of Kty. Publs. in Arch., vol. III, no. 6, Lexington, 1940.
also
Webb, W. S., *Wright Mounds*
"The Wright Mounds, Sites 6 and 7, Montgomery County, Kentucky," U. of Kty. Publs. in Arch., vol. V, no. 1, Lexington, 1940.

(60) Greenman, E. F., *Adena Culture*
"Excavation of the Coon Mound and an Analysis of the Adena Culture,"[11] Ohio Arch. and Hist. Soc., Bull. vol. XLI (List of traits for the Adena Site, see page 420).

(61) Ritchie, W. A., *Summaries of New York Archaeology*
    "Cultural Influences from Ohio in New York Archaeology," American
    Antiquity, vol. II, no. 3, pp. 182–194, 1937.
    "A perspective of Northeastern Archaeology," American Antiquity, vol. IV,
    no. 2, pp. 94–112, 1938.

(62) Strong, W. D., *Summaries of Plains Prehistory*
    "An Introduction to Nebraska Archaeology," Smithsonian Misc. Colls.,
    vol. 93, no. 10, Washington, 1935.
    also
    Wedel, W. R., "Cultural Sequence in the Central Great Plains," Smithsonian
    Misc. Colls., vol. 100 (Swanton Anniversary Volume), pp. 291–352. Wash-
    ington, 1940.

(63) Harrington, M. R., *Southern Caddoan Culture* (as defined)
    "Certain Caddo Sites in Arkansas," Muse. of the Amer. Ind., Heye Found.,
    Indian Notes and Monographs, New York, 1920.

(64) Lemley, Harry J., and Dickinson, S. D., *"Pre-Caddo"*
    "Discoveries Indicating a Pre-Caddo Culture on Red River in Arkansas,
    etc.," Texas Archaeological and Paleontological Society, Bulletin, vol. 8,
    pp. 25–69. 1936.

(65) Willey, Gordon R., and Woodbury, R. B., *The Sowell Site*
    "A Chronological Outline for the Northwest Florida Coast," MSS. in press.

(66) Ibid., *The Carrabelle Site*

(67) Ibid., *The Mound Field Site*

Index

Arkansas River, 66, 546
Ascension Parish (La.), 21, 415
Attakapa, 166, 169
Attribute states, 18
Avoyel, 168, 169, 264
Avoyelles Parish (La.), xi, 7, 36, 168, 233, 351, 358
Aztalan site (Wisc.), 556

Bannerstones, 219, 542, 548
Baton Rouge (La.), ix, x, xi, 25, 42, 43
Battle Place site (Lafayette County, Ark.), 207
Bayou Cutler complex, 20, 21, 23, 425, 427, 428, 430
Bayou Cutler period, 22, 23
Bayou Cutler–Historic period, 428, 430
Bayou Cutler–Marksville period, 22, 23, 24
Bayou Cutler sherds, 21
Bayou Goula site (Iberville Parish, La.), 37, 45, 48
Bayou Petre complex, 20, 21
Bayou Petre sherds, 21
Bayougoula, 552
Baytown period: Early, 552, 553; Late, 552, 553, 554
Beall, Homer, 59, 60
Big Black River, 247, 252, 254, 256, 257, 290, 298, 391
Big Oak Island site (Orleans Parish, La.), 36, 39, 44
Biggs site (Madison Parish, La.), 305
Binomial system of pottery types, x, 23, 27, 28, 29–30, 32
Birmingham Conference, 18
Boatstones, 219, 539, 548
Bolivar County (Mississippi), 65
Brand, Donald, 32
Brown, Calvin S., 177, 234, 242
Brown, Ian, 28, 33
Bureau of American Ethnology, xvi, 58, 79, 137n, 138, 166, 177, 351, 412n
Burial Mound I stage, 43, 44, 540, 541, 542, 543, 544, 545, 546, 549, 560,

561, 562
Burial Mound II stage, 43, 543, 544, 545, 546, 548, 549, 550, 552, 555, 560, 561, 563

Caddo, 8, 9, 16, 79, 137, 166, 169, 204, 205, 206, 207, 209, 210, 225, 323, 384, 412, 518, 552, 559; history of, 204–6
Caddo complex, 10, 16, 48, 50, 86, 87, 160, 171, 217, 219, 225, 228, 239, 282, 381, 385, 390, 391, 392, 395, 463, 484, 527, 563; pottery, 8, 23, 80, 206, 212, 218, 225, 234, 272, 316, 319, 384, 386, 399, 400, 482; sites, 383, 384, 386, 397, 473
Caddo Parish (La.), 228
Cadohadacho, 169, 204, 205
Cahokia site (Ill.), 556
Catahoula Incised, 477, 480, 518
Catahoula Parish (La.), 7, 11, 37, 95, 200, 338, 412
Catawba ware, 234
Ceramic complex. See Decoration complexes
Ceramic periods, 35
Chaco Canyon (N. Mex.), ix, 25, 27, 32
Chambers, Moreau B., 1, 2, 4, 5, 7, 15, 50, 59, 65, 66, 80, 137, 177, 191, 193, 196, 247, 250, 273, 275, 285, 286, 290, 299, 331, 412
Chapman Plantation site (Hinds County, Miss.), 247, 254, 257
Charenton Beach site (St. Mary Parish, La.), 420
Cherokee, 185, 234, 561
Chevalier site (LaSalle Parish, La.), 305, 334, 462, 521
Chevalier Stamped, 482
Chickachae site (Clarke County, Miss.), 174, 176
Chickasaw, 168, 172, 232, 263, 284, 562, 563
Childe, V. Gordon, xiv
Chocchuma, 168, 284, 285
Choctaw, 8, 9, 67, 161, 166, 168, 169, 174, 176, 185, 233, 247, 284, 384,

braided-stream model, 18, 44, 50

Culture history, 8, 25, 30, 31, 33, 46, 49, 50, 79, 436

Cultures, 34, 39, 43, 44, 393, 411, 450, 453, 538, 542

Cummings, Byron, 27

Deasonville (Miss.), 97n, 273

Deasonville complex, 9, 10, 12, 14, 15, 16, 38, 86, 87, 97, 104, 116, 160, 171, 177, 253, 273, 281, 282, 285, 291, 324, 330, 339, 344, 351, 381, 384, 385, 386, 388, 389, 390, 391, 392, 401; pottery, 16, 17, 106, 117, 123, 124, 170, 225, 228, 257, 287, 290, 295, 298, 299, 302, 305, 323, 325, 331, 334, 367, 385; sites, 170, 281, 283, 286, 291, 302, 313, 383, 384, 553n

Deasonville Cordmarked, 40, 521, 524

Deasonville period, 49

Deasonville Red and White Filmed, 441

Deasonville site (Yazoo County, Miss.), 4, 5, 6, 7, 10, 12, 273, 274, 304; description, 59; pottery, 60, 62–64, 65, 66, 67, 275, 276, 302

Decoration, 11, 22, 104, 121, 123, 150, 151, 175, 323, 324, 484, 544, 551, 552; list of, 437–40; used for chronology, 10; used for pottery-type construction, 13, 14, 16, 31, 35, 101, 102, 152, 437, 452

Decoration complexes, 9, 10, 11, 12, 13, 14, 17, 19, 20, 22, 24, 35, 44, 47, 88, 95, 96, 115, 162, 302, 374, 381, 382, 383, 387, 388, 393, 394, 400, 402, 424, 425, 452, 453, 541, 544; as temporal units, 35; definition of, 86, 160, 444; geographical segregation versus difference in time periods, 382–84; mixing of, 17, 18, 391

Decoration types, 18, 35, 104, 148, 161, 170, 185, 210, 217, 286, 345, 357, 382, 385, 391; evolution, 394–400, 452

DeJarnette, David, 442

Dendrochronology, 27, 82

Deptford Linear Stamped, 441

Deptford period, 545, 546, 548

Design complex, 49

De Soto expedition, 166, 204, 461, 558, 564

De Vaca, Cabeza, 205

Diffusion, xiii, 17, 18, 39, 40, 41, 42, 43, 50, 144

Direct Historical Approach, 4

Discontinuity, 48

Division of Mound Exploration, xvi

Douglass, A. E., 27

Dunbarton Plantation site (Concordia Parish, La.), 372, 390

Dupree Plantation site (Hinds County, Miss.), 247, 250, 257

Earthen Mound period, 20

Earthlodge, viii

Earthworks, xiii, 75, 76, 80, 544, 556

Eastern Archaic Stage, 538, 539, 540, 541, 542, 545, 547, 548, 550

Eastern Maize Area, 532

Effigies, 64, 196, 219, 255, 256, 331, 523, 560

Etowah site (Ga.), 558, 561, 564

European artifacts, 6, 7, 66, 67, 80, 176, 181, 192, 193, 197, 200, 206, 207, 209, 225, 268, 269, 425

Evolution, 33, 41, 43, 47, 50, 104, 118, 162. See also Cultural evolution; Decoration types, evolution

Fatherland Incised, 441, 482

Fatherland Plantation site (Adams County, Miss.), 10, 191, 192, 200, 201, 203, 234, 304; Mound C, 192, 193, 202; village, 196

Fayette (Miss.), 97n

Federal relief archaeology, viii, xviii. See also Civil Works Administration; Works Progress Administration

Ferguson Mounds site. See Truly Place site

Figgins, Jesse, xv, xvix
Fish Hatchery site (Natchitoches Parish, La.), 79, 206
Florida, xiii, 38, 67, 125, 376, 524, 525, 527, 537, 538, 545, 546, 548, 549, 551, 552, 556, 564
Florida Gulf Coast, xii, xiii, 545
Folsom (N. Mex.), xv
Folsomoid points, 537
Ford, Ethel, ix, xi, 50, 138
Ford, James A., vii, viii, ix, x, xi, xii, xiii, xiv, xv, xvi, 1, 4, 5, 20, 25, 30, 33, 44, 46, 50, 51, 59, 65, 66, 196, 247, 250, 273, 275, 290, 299, 331, 339, 345, 359, 412, 424, 425, 435, 436, 443, 457; analytical formula plan, 16, 24, 31; bionomial system of pottery types, 24, 27, 28, 32; chronology of Mississippi Valley, 2, 12, 37, 43, 45, 47, 49; decoration types, 18; education, 7, 19, 20, 25, 26, 32, 34; index system of pottery types, 13, 15, 31, 41; on complexes, 9, 11, 12, 13, 17, 22; on diffusion, 40–41, 42, 43; on Hopewell, 40–41; on long-term continuous occupation, 18; on pottery types, xviii, 10, 13, 14, 25, 29, 31, 39; thought processes, xix, 19, 50; use of marker types, 15, 17, 23; view of time, xvii, 49; Works Progress Administration projects, ix, xviii, 25, 36, 37, 38, 456
Fort Ancient (Ohio), 26, 31, 559, 560, 562
Fort Rosalie (Adams County, Miss.), 184, 192
Fort St. Peter (Warren County, Miss.), 231, 232, 233
Ft. Walton period, 556
Fortifications, 75
Foster Place site (Lafayette County, Ark.), 207
Foster site (Adams County, Miss.), 197
Fowke, Gerard, 351, 354, 359, 363, 401, 463, 522
Fredricks Place site (Natchitoches Parish, La.), 367

Galena, 80
Gamewood Plantation site (Holmes County, Miss.), 286
Gayton, Anna, 19
Georgia, vii, ix, xiii, 25, 27, 166, 441, 537, 538, 539, 540, 545, 546, 547, 548, 549, 551, 556, 557, 558, 561, 564
Ghost Dance cult, 564
Gibson, Jon, 13, 15, 16, 23, 24, 45
Gila Polychrome, ix
Gila Pueblo Conference, 27
Glass site (Warren County, Miss.), 201, 203, 366
Glendora Plantation site (Ouachita Parish, La.), 207, 209
Glover, William B., 204, 205
Gorgets, 219
Gorum site (LaSalle Parish, La.), 305, 334, 344, 348
Grand Bayou Mounds (Iberville Parish, La.), 428, 430
Grand Lake, 419, 420, 421, 431
Greenhouse site (Avoyelles Parish, La.), xi, xii, 36, 37, 38, 45, 363, 401, 456, 462, 463
Griffin, James B., ix, x, 2, 24, 25, 30, 32, 435, 442, 443; pottery classification, 26, 27, 28, 29, 31, 33, 42, 46, 51
Grigra, 230
Gross site (Madison County, Miss.), 247, 252, 253, 257, 390
Gulf of Mexico, 80, 169, 533, 537
Guthe, Carl, 31, 32

Haag, William, 20, 36, 50, 442
Halbert, Henry S., 65, 174, 284
Haley Place (Miller County, Ark.), 207
"Handbook of Northern Arizona Pottery Wares," 33
Hargrave, Lyndon, 33
Harrison Bayou Incised, 476
Harrison Bayou site (Harrison County, Tex.), 228

Middlesex focus, 542

Midwest, 44

Midwestern Taxonomic Method, x, xiii, 143

Migration, 18, 43, 50

Mississippi, x, xvi, xviii, 1, 2, 3, 4, 8, 19, 84, 95, 97, 102, 143, 166, 173, 180, 230, 254, 255, 273, 281, 283, 286, 290, 295, 312, 323, 325, 351, 381, 383, 402, 412, 547, 553, 554, 562; pottery from, 32, 67, 175; sites in, xix, 9, 13, 22, 65, 66, 81, 124, 137, 298, 299, 304, 337, 372, 424

Mississippi County (Ark.), 66

Mississippi Department of Archives and History, xv, 1, 50, 58, 60, 65, 80, 137, 176, 191, 201, 247, 275, 285; museum, 412n

Mississippi period, 527, 554, 555, 556, 557, 558, 559, 560, 563

Mississippi River, xiii, 20, 42, 43, 65, 66, 75, 80, 99, 121, 164, 168, 182, 185, 200, 201, 232, 243, 261, 264, 265, 268, 325, 358, 366, 370, 419, 420, 430, 459, 461, 462, 463, 532, 533, 537, 543, 553, 558, 560

Mississippi River Commission, 171, 192, 265, 466n

Mississippi State College, 138

Mississippi Valley, vii, xii, xiii, xiv, xvii, xviii, xix, 1, 3, 7, 10, 14, 16, 37, 40, 41, 43, 46, 48, 50, 80, 84, 86, 95, 97, 115, 137, 144, 145, 173, 180, 218, 305, 330, 357, 386, 445, 461, 463, 473, 484, 521, 522, 524, 525, 526, 527, 532, 533, 540, 541, 544, 545, 546, 547, 548, 549, 551, 552, 554, 555, 557, 558, 559, 563; middens, 164, 165

Missouri, 40, 512, 525, 526, 543, 560

Moore, Clarence B., xvi, 65, 66, 122, 125, 145, 201, 202, 207, 215, 234, 242, 243, 334, 339, 345, 372, 373, 383, 415, 462, 560, 562

Motif-and-element classification system, 155–59

Motley Plantation site (West Carroll Parish, La.), 345

Mounds, 8, 20, 38, 39, 45, 58, 59, 78, 85, 99, 164, 172, 177, 180, 181, 197, 203, 224, 242, 252, 284, 286, 295, 305, 334, 338, 389, 462, 527, 550, 557, 561, 562; burial, xi, xiii, 81, 176, 193, 247, 250, 253, 254, 255, 256, 411, 450, 470, 518, 540, 541, 542, 543, 544, 546, 548, 549, 550, 551, 553, 554, 555, 556, 559; groups of, 165, 192, 193, 196, 243, 272, 273, 287, 290, 299, 325, 330, 331, 338, 344, 345, 359, 366, 370, 390, 459, 460, 465, 473, 516, 544, 551, 554; in Iberville Parish survey, 415, 416, 418, 419, 421, 422, 423, 424, 428, 429

Moundville (Ala.), 286, 556, 558, 562, 564

Mulberry Creek Plain, 524

Mulloy, William T., xi, 456, 457

Muskhogee, 166, 168, 172, 284, 557

Nanih Waiya mound (Winston County, Miss.), 137, 172, 176, 177, 388

Natchez, 8, 9, 67, 137, 168, 169, 191, 192, 193, 217, 233, 263, 304, 384, 412, 518, 552; history of, 182–85

Natchez (Miss.), 8, 16, 80, 97n, 137, 168, 182, 197, 330

Natchez complex, 9, 10, 86, 87, 160, 171, 200, 202, 234, 239, 367, 381, 385, 386, 391, 392; pottery, 8, 23, 66, 80, 186, 201, 272, 384, 385; sites, 5, 16, 65, 66, 191, 383, 384, 473

Natchez Fort site (Catahoula Parish, La.), 138, 160, 185, 197, 200; "Grand Village," 183, 192

Natchez period, 45, 46

Natchez Trace, 247

Natchez wars, 184, 265

Natchitoches, 169, 204, 205, 206, 207; burial ware, 208

Natchitoches (La.), 169, 204, 205, 206, 209, 225, 367

Natchitoches Parish (La.), 209, 224

National Park Service, viii
National Research Council, 7, 50, 137,
    304n
Neal Place site (West Carroll Parish,
    La.), 305, 339, 345, 363
Nebraska, 537, 562
Neild, Edward F., 137
Neitzel, Robert S., xi
Nelson, Nels, xv, 35, 450
Neshoba County (Miss.), 173
New Mexico, ix, xv, 25
New Orleans, x, xi, xii, 19, 456
New York, xiii, 40, 525, 526, 537, 538,
    539, 540, 542, 546, 562
*Newsletter of the Southeastern
    Archaeological Conference*, 51, 435
Nick Plantation site (Avoyelles Parish,
    La.), 173, 175, 180
Norris Basin (Tenn.), 26, 29, 537, 543,
    561
North Carolina, 561
Numerical coding of pottery, ix

Ocmulgee Incised, ix
Ocmulgee National Monument
    (Georgia), viii, 442
Ofo, 168, 230, 231, 232, 233
Ofogoula, 565
Ohio, xiii, 40, 66, 80, 97n, 124, 512,
    523, 524, 525, 526, 541, 546, 549
Ohio River, xiii, 537, 543, 555, 562,
    564
Ohio Valley, 26, 542, 544, 547, 548,
    550, 563
Oktibbeha County (Miss.), 283
Old Hoover Place site (Holmes County,
    Miss.), 298
Oneonta, 562
Orleans Parish (La.), 36, 37
Ouachita Parish (La.), 208

Parkin site (Ark.), 560
Paste, 31, 101, 123
Pawnee, 204
Pearl River, 8
Peck, William, 95, 99
Peck Village (Catahoula Parish, La.),

7, 9, 10, 12, 13, 14, 15, 16, 37, 41,
    43, 45, 47, 49, 95, 96, 97, 98, 104,
    115, 124, 125, 137, 337, 388n, 389;
    excavation of, 100, 117; location,
    99, 116; pottery, 101, 104, 112, 119,
    120
Pecos Conference, 27, 32
Pecos Pueblo (N. Mex.), 450
Pepper, Claude H., 59
Percentage stratigraphy, 34
Periods, 44, 45, 452
Peru, 19
Pete Clark Place site (Adams County,
    Miss.), 295
Peter Hill site (Iberville Parish, La.),
    425, 427
Petrie, Flinders, xiv
Phillipi Plantation site (Holmes
    County, Miss.), 274, 275, 299
Phillips County (Ark.), 65
Phillips, Philip, xvii, 46, 47, 48
Pickwick Basin, 524
Pickwick Complicated Stamped, 524
Pipes, 81
Plains, xiii, 548, 564
Plaquemine period, 45, 47, 48
Plaquemines Parish, 19, 425
Pleistocene, 537
Pocahontas Mounds site (Hinds
    County, Miss.), 239, 243, 247, 253,
    255, 256, 257
Pocahontas Pinched, 477
Ponta site. See Coosa site
Portage of the Cross, 264, 265
Pottery analysis, 435
Pottery complexes. *See* Decoration
    complexes
Pottery types, ix, xviii, 13, 15, 16, 22,
    26, 30, 39, 452; based on decora-
    tion, 35, 101, 102; classifying, 151–
    52, 453; creation of, 31, 33;
    definition of, 436–39; naming, 440–
    41; proposal of, 443; use in chronol-
    ogy, 43, 79; use in writing culture
    history, 31; use of variation in
    classification, 29
Poverty Point site (West Carroll

Parish, La.), 345
Prichard's Landing site (Catahoula Parish, La.), 348
Projectile points, 219, 417, 523, 537, 539, 541, 551, 552, 554, 555, 561

Quafalorma Plantation site (Holmes County, Miss.), 287
Quapaw, 168
Quimby, George, xii, 37

Rangia cuneata, 421, 422, 423, 424, 431, 432
Rapides Parish (La.), 173
Red Ochre focus, 543
Red River, 66, 164, 169, 182, 185, 204, 205, 206, 219, 224, 232, 234, 261, 264, 265, 358, 367, 383, 390, 462, 463, 552, 559
Reed mounds (Iberville Parish, La.), 428, 430
Reoccupation of sites, 17, 18, 387
Rim shape, ix
Ring Cemetery (Warren County, Miss.), 201, 366
Rosedale site (Iberville Parish, La.), 425, 427
Rowland, Dunbar, 58, 59
Russell, Richard, 19, 20

Safety Harbor complex, 527
St. Bernard Parish (La.), 19, 425
St. Francis culture, 563
St. Louis, xiii
St. Martin Parish (La.), 37
St. Tammany Parish (La.), xii, 37
Sanson Incised, 479–81
Santa Rosa period, 548
Savannah style, 557
Sauer, Carl, 19
School of ceramic art, 17
Seriation, xvii, 16, 17, 34; frequency, 19; phyletic, 19
Setzler, Frank M., 7, 18, 25, 38, 40, 50, 80, 97n, 138, 351, 354, 359, 363, 385, 463, 521, 522
Sharkey County (Miss.), 66–67, 372

Shell middens, 20, 416, 417, 418, 419, 421, 422, 429, 548
Shell ridges, 166, 298
Sicily Island (La.), 95, 99, 197, 200, 412
Sioux, 166, 168, 230
Smith Creek site (Wilkinson County, Miss.), 325, 330
Smith Plantation site (Madison County, Miss.), 247, 253, 257
Smithsonian Institution, x, 2, 137n
Sorrel Mound site (Iberville Parish, La.), 423, 424, 428
South America, xvii
South Carolina, 545, 561
Southeast, x, xv, xvi, xvii, 2, 24, 30, 32, 58, 435, 452, 453, 454, 531, 558
Southeastern Archaeological Conference, 30, 31, 32, 531
Southeastern Archaeological Conference reports, 473
Southeastern archaeology, xi, 31, 58, 64
Southeastern pottery, 7, 67
Southwest, ix, xv, xvi, 4, 23, 24, 25, 26, 27, 29, 31, 32, 35, 44, 49, 64, 450
Southwestern archaeology, ix, 450
Spier, Leslie, xi, xv, 34, 35
Spiro site (Okla.), 564
Stirling, Matthew, 18
Stratigraphy, 11, 17, 453
Strong, William Duncan, 19
Style, 28
Superposition, xvii, 17, 19, 450
Surface collection, 9, 15, 19, 137, 139, 412; analysis, 148; and buried stratum, 145–46; methods, 147–48; representativeness of, 149–50, 452; sample size, 170
Surface decoration, ix, 31
Swanton, John, xvi, 138, 166, 172, 177, 182, 206, 230, 232, 264, 558
Swift Creek Complicated Stamped, ix, 441, 549
Swift Creek horizon, 545, 547, 548, 551
Swift Creek period, 549, 557